D0513723

Promise, Trust, and Evolution

Managing the Commons of South Asia

Edited by

Rucha Ghate, Narpat S. Jodha, and
Pranab Mukhopadhyay

UNIVERSITY PRESS

OXFORD

UNIVERSITY PRESS

Great Clarendon Street, Oxford OX2 6DP

Oxford University Press is a department of the University of Oxford.
It furthers the University's objective of excellence in research, scholarship,
and education by publishing worldwide in

Oxford New York

Auckland Cape Town Dar es Salaam Hong Kong Karachi
Kuala Lumpur Madrid Melbourne Mexico City Nairobi
New Delhi Shanghai Taipei Toronto

With offices in

Argentina Austria Brazil Chile Czech Republic France Greece
Guatemala Hungary Italy Japan Poland Portugal Singapore
South Korea Switzerland Thailand Turkey Ukraine Vietnam

Oxford is a registered trade mark of Oxford University Press
in the UK and in certain other countries

Published in the United States
by Oxford University Press Inc., New York

British Library Cataloguing in Publication Data

Data available

Library of Congress Cataloging in Publication Data

Data available

Typeset by SPI Publisher Services, Pondicherry, India
Printed in Great Britain
on acid-free paper by
MPG Books Ltd, Bodmin, Cornwall

ISBN 978–0–19–921383–2

10 9 8 7 6 5 4 3 2

Preface

This volume brings together research on common property resources (CPR) and the institutions that manage them, by grantees, advisors, and associates of the South Asian Network for Environmental and Development Economics (SANDEE). The focus of SANDEE since its inception in 1999 has been to build capacity by providing training and research grants in order to address the environmental issues associated with problems of poverty and development in South Asia. A major share of the early grants made by SANDEE was in the area of CPR research and the first set of working papers started trickling in around 2003. Though there is a routine process of dissemination of research findings by the secretariat as well as the researchers it was but a natural next step to put together a volume for wider and consolidated dissemination.

It was meant to be an easy task in the beginning since all SANDEE Working Papers are peer reviewed before publication, so the editorial effort for this volume seemed negligible to start with. However, we soon realized that while there were numerous papers on CPRs from India, Nepal, and Sri Lanka, there were gaps in other countries. There were no ready studies available from the grantees in other parts of South Asia (like Bangladesh, Bhutan, and Pakistan) on the commons. We decided at this point that we should invite SANDEE's associates and resource people to also contribute to this volume.

Carmen Wickramagamage helped us with the language editing of the papers despite her own time constraints as she moved house from Sri Lanka to the USA. Deepshikha Mehra at SHODH was marvellous with her format editing and made sure that all t's were crossed and i's dotted. Jennifer Wilkinson, Carol Bestley, and Sarah Baker at OUP were very supportive through the whole production process.

Karl Goran Maler and Monica Eberle hosted us at the Abdus Salam International Centre for Theoretical Physics, Trieste for the paper-writers' workshop and Rosa Del Rio did a great job coordinating this workshop. This was a follow-up of earlier meetings held at the Institute of Social and Economic Change (Bangalore), Institute of Economic Growth (New Delhi) and the International Centre (Goa) facilitated by SANDEE. E. Somanathan and Ingella Tergstrom helped us iron out many of the glitches that came up. We are grateful to them for their time and effort.

It is a marvel of technology and SANDEE's unwavering support that has allowed three geographically far-flung editors to bring together this volume. Anuradha Kafle and Kavita Shrestha took our demands on their time in their stride. Manik Duggar with his infectious smile and endless energy left midway through this book project. We missed his absence as a friend, colleague, and contributor. Priya Shyamsundar not only contributed a paper but also lent a shoulder to lean on whenever the need arose. SHODH had the lead responsibility of coordinating the book effort and it seemlessly moved between the academic and the executive needs of the book.

Rucha Ghate, Narpat S. Jodha,
and Pranab Mukhopadhyay

March 2007, Nagpur–Kathmandu–Goa

Contents

Contents

List of Figures

List of Tables

List of Contributors

Bhim Adhikari, University of Michigan, USA

R. Balasubramanian, Tamil Nadu Agricultural University, India

Partha Dasgupta, Cambridge University, U.K.

Lam Dorji, Royal Society for Protection of Nature (RSPN), Bhutan

Rucha Ghate, SHODH: The Institute for Research and Development, India

Asha Gunawardena, Institute of Policy Studies, Sri Lanka

A. K. Enamul Haque, East West University, Bangladesh

Gamini Herath, Deakin University, Australia

Narpat S. Jodha, International Centre for Integrated Mountain Development, Nepal

Keshav Raj Kanel, Forest Department, Nepal

Kalpa Karunanayake, Department of Inland Revenue, Sri Lanka

Shaheen Rafi Khan, Sustainable Development Policy Institute, Pakistan

Arun Khatri-Chhetri, West Virginia University, USA

Arabinda Mishra, TERI University, India

Pranab Mukhopadhyay, Goa University, India and South Asian Network for Environmental Economics, Nepal

Athula Senaratne, National Aquaculture Development Authority, Sri Lanka

Priya Shyamsundar, South Asian Network for Development and Environmental Economics, Nepal

Paul Steele, United Nations Development Programme, Sri Lanka

Edward L. Webb, Asian Institute of Technology, Thailand

Introduction[1]

South Asia as a region has experienced increasing rates of growth in the last decade and a half—its growth rate jumped from 5.2 per cent in 1991–5 to 6.4 per cent in 2001–5. It is expected that the region will continue to grow in the near future at comparable rates (ADB 2006). Is this growth sustainable in the long run? It has very often been asked whether economies can continue to grow indefinitely or whether there are limits to growth. Can the environment sustain the demands that the economy makes of it both for inputs of production as well as a waste absorption system?

The dynamism on the economic front if not tempered by judicious use of the natural resource base could have detrimental effects in the long term no matter how gleaming the present might look. Economic growth, as we know, has an ambiguous effect on the environment and in the short run could well lead to environmental deterioration (*à la* Environmental Kuznet's curve). In fact, genuine (or green) savings and growth in 'genuine wealth' in South Asian countries is much lower than the traditional macroeconomic measures. This raises serious questions about the sustainability of the current growth strategy in South Asia (Arrow *et al.* 2004; Dasgupta 2001; Hamilton and Clemens 1999).[2]

South Asia has its share of environment–economy conflicts and is continuously having to make choices on land use between industrialization, agriculture, forestry, and so on. Much of this conflict has to do with land and resources in the public sphere. In this context it is important to understand that the trade-off between higher economic growth and environmental quality can have non-uniform distributions—some sections of the population may bear the brunt of environmental degradation. This is critical given the scale of poverty in South Asia and is further complicated by the prevalence of ambiguous and poorly enforced property rights. This is true not only for

---

[1] We are grateful to Partha Dasgupta and Priya Shyamsundar for their comments on an earlier draft.
[2] In fact, for Sub-Saharan Africa and West Asia, the level of genuine savings (investment) has been negative for the period (roughly) between mid-seventies to 2001 (Arrow *et al.* 2004).

property that is in the private domain but also that which is in the state or community's control. Developed countries, over extended periods, have managed to establish well-defined property rights over many resources, for example, the enclosure movement for privatizing land in England. There are numerous situations where people enjoy non-exclusionary rights over privately owned resources, for example, the right to camp overnight on private fields in Sweden.

In developing countries, however, the share of community property is fairly large and right over these lands is shared by multiple beneficiaries.[3] The challenges of a globalizing world also has forced nation states to respond in ways which are intertwined with the dynamics of a larger world market. This has led to the coexistence of both community ownership of resources as well as evolving (and often incomplete) private property rights. Since the lion's share of the world's population lives in developing countries and since community resources support the livelihoods of large numbers of rural peoples, it is important to understand three related phenomena—recent changes in the status of common property resources (CPRs); the role of transforming agents such as state, society, and markets; and the sustainability of resources and institutions. These issues are particularly relevant for South Asia, where property rights over many different natural resources are either *de facto* or *de jure* held communally.

The presence of common property and its significance for rural livelihoods has led to many kinds of queries in developing countries. Some of these attempt to tease out the rationale for collective action. When community property exists, does it indicate rational behaviour on the part of the individuals who form that collectivity? In what kind of circumstances do people come together? Other queries focus on the circumstances that lead to better collective action to maintain CPRs. What impact does initial distribution of assets have on the outcome of resource use, rules of extraction of the resource, etc.? What is the effect of group size on the performance of institutional arrangement? What are the roles of different mechanisms for dispute settlements?

As CPRs become commercially valuable, they are often privatized and this is justified by efficiency-enhancing arguments. Does privatization help conservation of resources and how does privatization affect the poor? However, not all CPRs are sustainably managed. The question arises, whether there are other options for improving the management. With increasing degradation, the state is often motivated to strengthen or create community user groups to manage resources. Do these user groups reproduce traditional hierarchical social structures? Are they more susceptible to elite capture relative to a centralized authority? What role can the state play as a supra institution

---

[3] Resources that are owned by a group who have control over its access, use, and extraction are normally termed as Common Property Resources. Common property falls between the two well-understood types of ownership—state and private.

in either maintaining an existing common property resource (CPR) or in creating one with well-defined property rights in a situation where there has been degradation? As governments in South Asia increasingly move towards more decentralized systems of local governance, what types of institutional structure are most conducive to CPR management? Are there viable examples of nested institutions that can manage ecosystems at different scales? How do multiple levels of management interact and affect performance? Is institutional change imposed or is it chosen by the people?

These are not new questions but recurring ones that have failed to bring consensus amongst researchers on CPRs. They confront us in South Asia too, which not only has a shared history but also vast linked trans-boundary resources. This book intends to be a story of transforming commons in a rapidly changing South Asia.

South Asia is experiencing rapid changes with increasing integration into the world economy, a rapidly growing population, increasing per capita income, but with large numbers still living in absolute poverty. These changes are felt not only at the macro level but even micro situations. Given that a large number of people still depend on CPRs, the concern for their sustainable use is obvious since nation states are in the process of altering historically evolved norms and property-rights regimes. This part of the world has a coexistence of community ownership as well as evolving (and therefore incomplete) private property rights over natural resources. There have also been experiments at expanding community control over their resources. Large-scale changes in property rights have been witnessed across South Asia—in India and Nepal, experiments at handing over forests to communities have had varied degrees of success. In Sri Lanka, similar changes have been seen in the irrigation sector with co-management of irrigation systems. However, the jury is still out on the impact of these policy changes on CPR management. Therefore, there is an urgent need to understand which property-rights regimes work and which don't in a situation where newer forms of institutions are being evolved and there is a change in the relative valuation of resources.

Papers in this volume have attempted to understand three related issues— (a) the status of Common Property Resources, (b) role of transforming agents such as state, society, and markets,[4] and (c) sustainability of resources and institutions.

---

[4] There are a number of agencies that are involved in the creation, use, and management of CPRs in South Asia. The key agencies include the state (with its diverse motives and mechanisms); market forces accentuated by spread of economic globalization (inducing indifference or disregard towards community's collective stakes and action involving CPRs); the rural society (with rising socio-economic differentiation causing disintegration of collective stakes in local commons); NGOs, donors, and enlightened citizens including sections of gradually empowered rural communities. These agents have been also involved in new initiatives to form new institutions promoting community participation, group action (e.g. JFM India; UGF in Nepal).

This book is intended to be a story of transforming commons in a rapidly changing South Asia. Contributions from different parts of South Asia—Bangladesh, Bhutan, India, Nepal, Pakistan, and Sri Lanka—attempt to link people with the resources, deal with issues of equity in distribution, efficiency, productivity and sustainability of the resource as well as institutions.

In order to study change rigorously, there is need for comparable time-series data. Unfortunately, the measures of natural resource stocks and flows are not as well mapped out as are other economic variables: for example, the GDP, interest rate, trade flows. This limits the researcher's ability to comment authoritatively on trends, or make reliable predictions on natural resources at the macro level. Even though satellite imagery helps in the process, the use of it has been rather limited and selective.[5] This lack of national-level natural resource data is a constraint on macro-level discussions.[6] Most studies therefore have to resort to micro- or subnational-level studies relying primarily on their own field surveys or narrower national data sets. The problem that these studies face is one of scalability—they are indicative of a larger canvas but cannot substitute for a macro exercise. Despite this shortcoming, in-depth micro studies can be extremely useful for region- or resource-specific policy-making as well as informing academic opinion. The current volume is no exception to this trend.

0.1. Environment and economics—common property resources

Natural resource management interests economists because of its direct and indirect linkages with livelihoods, especially in rural areas. Since the bulk of the population in South Asia still lives in rural areas, the study of natural resource management is particularly important. The extent of livelihood dependence in South Asia by various estimates ranges from 15–29 per cent whereas in parts of Africa it has been found to be 35–51 per cent (Cavendish 2000; Chopra, Kadekodi, and Murty 1990; Jodha 1986, 2001; Kerapeletswe and Lovett 2001).

Earlier studies suggest that both the rich and the poor (relatively more) depend on natural resources for their livelihood, especially on CPRs. CPRs have been found to act not only as buffers during periods of crisis when normal sources of income fail, but also act as a source of income during

[5] The only large-scale country-wide survey of CPRs in South Asia has been undertaken in India (to the best of our knowledge)—the National Sample Survey Organization (NSSO) survey of CPRs in the 54th round in 1998 (Chopra and Dasgupta 2002; Menon and Vadivelu 2006).

[6] There have been attempts at generating estimates of Green GDP in India but these await their formal integration into the National Accounts statistics (Parikh and Parikh 1998; Atkinson and Gundimeda 2006).

normal times. In the case of forestry the dependence is largely on non-timber forest products (NTFP) since timber (extraction is state-regulated). In the case of coastal zones, fisheries are mainly undertaken in non-privately owned areas.

CPRs have been in existence for as long as private- and state-owned property—some argue even longer. Rules of access, extraction, and use are critical in the sustenance and efficient use of natural resources. Resource management involves a two-pronged strategy involving provision (stock of resources) and appropriation (flow of resources) and maintaining a critical balance between stock and flow of resources. The literature points to the use of two definitions of sustainability—one is the efficient measure of maximizing the net present value of intertemporal consumption and the other seeks to ensure that future levels of consumption do not fall below present ones. The second definition does not take recourse to any efficiency criteria and could lead to multiple sustainable paths (Arrow *et al.* 2004).

When a resource is not individually or state-owned it requires a collective of people to organize and protect the resource in order to avert open-access plunder.[7] CPRs represent the successful incentivization of a group of self-interested agents who come together and cooperate to maximize their welfare, which would be lower under non-cooperation given other things (like current institutional structure, technology, etc.). The CPR puzzle then (in Ostrom's words) is about 'solving' how individuals independently act when their action is interdependent on how others act (1990).[8] As Ostrom (1990) suggests, there are four things that a theory of collective action must address: (*a*) free-riding, (*b*) commitment problems, (*c*) supply of new institutions,[9] and (*d*) monitoring.

The theory of CPRs and collective action however is not new (Dasgupta and Heal 1979). The received literature suggests that collective action is sustained only if there is a significant gain for all the agents involved. This need not necessarily always be true. Dasgupta (this volume) presents an explicit model

---

[7] We have come a long way from Hardin's (1968) mistaken notion that CPRs are the residual property that was not owned by anyone, leading to the 'tragedy of the commons'. The literature now recognizes that this is a case of 'open access' and not necessarily a CPR. Open-access resources are bound to be unsustainable because all agents have an incentive to overextract the resource and even a renewable resource may be depleted beyond a critical point and face extinction.

[8] Economics is not new to the problem of seemingly uncoordinated action by individuals acting independently who arrive at optimal solutions albeit under restrictive conditions. The equilibrating mechanism (for the 'invisible hand') in such situations is the market clearing price which all agents accept. In the case of natural resources, however, we run into various ticklish issues—like some environmental goods and services do not have market prices because they are not traded goods, some goods do not have well-defined property rights, etc.

[9] 'Institutions include the legal structure, formal and informal markets, various agencies of government, interpersonal networks, and the rules and norms that guide their behavior' (Arrow, Dasgupta, and Mäler 2003).

which anticipates that lower welfare may result for certain groups even as a cooperative outcome and thereby allowing others in the group to take advantage of them. This could be a possible explanation why many groups accept seemingly disadvantageous outcomes under a cooperative framework an outcome referred to as the 'dark side' of CPRs (Dasgupta, this volume).

A large part of the action in CPR studies here however is in the empirical literature which complements the theory of successful collective action in natural resource management. This is what we turn to in Section 0.4.

0.2. Institutions and CPRs in South Asia

The sustenance of CPRs requires a set of rules that govern their extraction and use without which the resource would deplete to unsustainable levels. A large section of the CPR literature relates to these 'rules' or institutions—the process of rule-making, the agents involved in rule-making, and the mechanisms that ensure compliance, etc. Alternatively, one could ask what kind of institutions are suited to govern CPRs; how did they emerge, survive, and evolve in order to successfully manage these CPRs? In an attempt to answer these questions, the literature has borrowed from other domains of knowledge like anthropology and law to trace the evolution of norms and traditional practices which have sometimes translated and been integrated into modern legal systems.

The emergence and evolution of particular norms and practices have differed according to relative scarcity or abundance of the resource and the criticality of the need for collective action to use and sustain the resource. Many such traditional customs and practices eroded over the last few centuries as the state (in many developing countries) through its statutory authority declared ownership over natural resources and reduced the role of customary arrangements and the local autonomy. Consequently, except in some isolated tribal communities, CPRs in South Asia remain community resources mainly in a *de facto* sense, subject to any change as the state decides.

The tenurial authority and arrangements of state over natural resources (with *de facto* usage rights and control of the community) have several variations in South Asia in terms of type and degree of controls exercised by a range of feudal or tribal chiefs and local landlords. Many contributors in this volume discuss the emergence and evolution of institutions managing CPRs in their historical and socio-cultural contexts. This is crucial in order to understand the present status of CPRs and undertake policy measures that affect the governance of CPRs in the subcontinent. The nature of interaction between agents, the conflict and cooperation between state and communities, also need to be taken into account while undertaking institutional change.

This volume presents a set of micro studies dealing with CPRs and the institutions that manage them in the different countries in South Asia—Bangladesh (Enamul Haque), Bhutan (Edward Webb and Lam Dorji), India (Arabinda Mishra, R. Balasubramanian, Rucha Ghate, Narpat Jodha, and Pranab Mukhopadhyay), Nepal (Bhim Adhikari, Arun Khatri-Chhetri, and Keshav Kanel), Pakistan (Shaheen R. Khan) and Sri Lanka (Asha Gunawardena and Paul Steele, Gamini Herath, and Athula Senaratne and Kalpa Karunanayake).

The case studies cover a wide range of resource and institutional settings—forestry, water, land management and some overlapping ones. They cover institutional arrangements like the *Haors* (in deltaic Bangladesh), the sokshings (in Bhutan), Community Forestry (Nepal, Maharashtra and Orissa, India), the Jirga (in Pakistan), village tanks (in Sri Lanka and Tamil Nadu, India), *communidades* (in Goa, India), Water Users Association and fishery groups (in Bangladesh and Sri Lanka). Two themes that bind these papers are related to poverty-conservation, and state-markets, -communities.

0.3. CPRs are dead . . . long live the CPRs

As has been pointed out by various authors, there was a reluctance both in academic and policy circles to recognize that CPRs had economic value to local villages. Lands classified as 'wastelands' were useful to persons involved in animal husbandry, etc., and often formed a critical village CPR.

It has been more than two decades since CPR studies in South Asia came into prominence (dating from Jodha's seminal article in the *Economic and Political Weekly* (Jodha 1986) on semi-arid regions of India). In the intervening period, the dynamics of the state and market have altered not only most CPR resources but also the way people manage them—either by state policy intervention or market scarcities. A number of CPRs have been degraded or privatized. As Jodha (this volume) records, there has been a 40–50 per cent decline in CPR area in his study area and 25–85 per cent reported degradation. Part of the explanation probably lies in the decline of traditional management institutions and rules reported from 88–97 per cent of the villages studied.

The community as well as the state have acted in response to this degradation. The state in this period has become more sensitive to the role of the community in conserving natural resources and has responded under citizen pressures to enact laws that give sanctity to community institutions. The critical role that the state plays in providing an overarching framework is discussed in Section 0.3.3 below.

Simultaneously, however, demands on resources for the present generation's use has led both the state and the market to extract resources sometimes bypassing or overriding community demands, as evidenced in Pakistan's

Dir Kohistan region (Khan, this volume). In some cases, these resources have been privatized, and where the community has not been able to act quickly open-access conditions have emerged. In some other cases communities have innovated to protect resources in newer ways like in Sri Lanka's Negambu Lagoon (Gunawardena and Steele, this volume). One significant observation about this transition is that communities instead of protecting the aggregate CPR, seem to concentrate only on specific units of these CPRs (Jodha, this volume). This has implications both for policy and future research in CPR studies.

Forestry studies, not surprisingly, dominate this volume, probably reflecting the importance of forests to people's livelihood in this region. In India, the government's efforts to establish joint forestry institutions to manage degraded forests so that the community would have some control over the maintenance and also benefit from a flow of NTFP for their use have yielded mixed responses. However, the choice of institutions to manage these resources at the local level has often been a bone of contention. Should the local panchayat manage the resource, should a third party like a non-governmental organization (NGO) manage it, or should it be a village resource group? In Maharashtra (India), the state, NGO, and community interaction is found to have best results where JFM institutions emerge as a community initiative while the ones that have low community participation (even though they are state-initiated) do not yield desired results (Ghate, this volume).

In Orissa (India), communities empowered by national and state-level devolution enactments, have come together to form parallel management institutions with self-initiative. These new community associations are now strong enough to challenge the state's monopoly in marketing of forest products. The organization has achieved a state-wide network with district and village-level organizations forming a well-knit forest users group. The driving incentive for individual agents in this community has been the capture of rent that earlier flowed to the state even though the villagers rather than the state played a decisive role in protecting the forest resources from illegal timber traders. The forest user groups have evolved a system of mutual monitoring that has effectively checked forest encroachment (Mishra, this volume).[10]

The nature of the resource often determines the appropriateness of institutions. In forestry, for example, the resource (trees and NTFP) is not mobile. This is not valid for some other resources like fisheries, which are not static in one place, and move to different locations during specific periods of their lifetime, sometimes travelling across the jurisdiction of various countries and international boundaries adding to the problem of CPR management (for

---

[10] This is in line with received knowledge that mutual (inexpensive) monitoring is the first step towards successful CPR management, as commitments that cooperating agents make become credible and this results in supply of new institutions (Ostrom 1990).

example, the Whaling Convention of 1946). Expectedly, the fisheries sector is most likely to suffer from open-access problems and likely to experience the 'tragedy of the commons'. Can communities respond to such complicated problems? In the Negambu Lagoon of Sri Lanka, fishing communities who use stake-nets for shrimp-farming have been able to devise fairly complex management rules that have helped them to sustain fisheries for over 250 years (Gunawardena and Steele, this volume).

0.3.1. *Transaction costs*

We now turn our attention to another issue we have referred to earlier—the evolution of institutions and the costs associated with maintaining them. Community institutions take time, effort and involve costs to evolve. Traditionally managed CPRs have relied on social norms that have taken generations to fine-tune while many new ones are state-engineered. There is a rich literature on the various factors that influence group formation and supply of new institutions. Among other things, transaction costs play an important role in the supply of new institutions (Williamson 1981). If transaction costs (either initial or recurring) are high, they could threaten the initiation and sustainability of the CPR and the institution that manages it.

In Sri Lanka, an experiment at institutional innovation was attempted by the government, which involved handing over village tanks for aquaculture to increase income and nutritional intake. The government encouraged farmer groups to undertake multiple use of village tanks but this often did not lead to encouraging results as the transaction costs of collective action were high in many cases (Senaratne and Karunanayake, this volume). When revenue flows were not sufficient to cover these transaction costs, the institution became unsustainable. This is in line with received theory. There were three main kinds of institutional forms that were observed—where all farmers in the organization were involved, the monitoring costs were low but the relative individual benefits were also low. Incentives were insufficient to all members of a village to sustain the resource. Alternatively, when the management was handed over to a smaller group of farmers from within the village, the returns were relatively higher than when the whole village was involved or when a third party was contracted to manage the village tank. This has important policy implications as the success of such programmes will necessitate higher individual shares and incentive to an effective subgroup of participants.

This throws up one of the most intriguing questions in CPR studies—what incentivizes groups of people to come together and protect a resource by collective action? One explanation emanates from the consequences of asset and benefit distribution.

0.3.2. *Heterogeneity and sustainability*

An influential strand of the literature suggests that higher levels of heterogeneity would lead to better cooperation (Olson 1965). Microeconomic theory informs us that if there was monopoly ownership of the resource, there would be underextraction or inefficient utilization of the resource. It would, however, in a trivial sense minimize the transaction cost of negotiation since the monopolist has only himself to negotiate with regarding the use of the resource.

At the other end of the spectrum lies the argument that there is a direct relationship between equality and cooperation—the more homogenous a community, the easier it would be for consensus building. It may not be a coincidence that the high level of collective action achieved by the Negambu Lagoon's fishery association discussed earlier may be due to the greater homogeneity among participating fishers (Gunawardena and Steele, this volume). Homogeneity and equity, however, are not sufficient to ensure collective action, as demonstrated by the tenancy reforms in Goa where agrarian institutional change reduced heterogeneity but also lowered the cooperative effort of the community to maintain soil-conservation measures (Mukhopadhyay, this volume). Securitization of tenure in the post-land-reforms period did not lead to cooperation for soil conservation.

In between the two ends of the spectrum lies an intermediate position which suggests that heterogeneity and resource sustainability could take the shape of an inverted U, like the Environmental Kuznet's Curve (Dayton-Johnson and Bardhan 2002). At very high and low levels of inequality there would be lower levels of cooperation and sustainability.

0.3.3. *Institutions and distributional outcomes*

The heterogeneity debate arguably is directly linked to the cost of consensus-building—one of the components of total transaction cost of collective action discussed earlier. The received literature, however, has not provided much evidence on the relationship between heterogeneity and transaction costs. In the community forestry in Nepal, the state expects to stop the degradation of forests by handing over management to village communities and forest user groups (FUGs). Studies here find that there is a direct relationship between land inequality and transaction costs. Similarly, FUGs that have more heterogeneous agents seem to have higher transaction costs of group formation and lower levels of collective action (Adhikari, this volume).

The community forestry experiment in Nepal has met with considerable success in regenerating local forests as communities have the freedom to frame rules of access and extraction. While this has fulfilled one of the concerns of the Nepalese state (that is, forest degradation), it has been suggested that policy makers focus on distributional issues since long-term sustainability would depend on agents achieving satisfactory distribution of benefits (Kanel, this volume).

Issues in distribution also need to be looked at in the context of intertemporal choices. The forestry experiment has attracted attention not only in the context of forest regeneration but also in its ability to address rural poverty. While the poor have higher rates of discount and are less likely to be interested in benefits accruing too far into the future, those with alternative sources of income may be willing to have a longer waiting period.

In the context of poverty, when a local forest moves from an informal community management to a formal one, it is an expression of collective intertemporal preference for conservation as compared to current consumption. This implies restricting access to the forest in the short run and imposing a cost on those who have a higher discount rate. The consequences would be worse still if they have non-substitutable incomes from forests. The costs of conservation then are borne by the poor who were more dependent on the forests for their immediate livelihood needs. The rich who might have alternative sources of income can afford to wait for the higher returns from the forests in the long run (Khatri-Chhetri, this volume). This leaves room for the state to further innovate with such institutions while attempting to address issues of distribution and conservation.

0.3.4. *Role of the state: tradition and innovation*

We now turn to another factor that plays a critical role in ensuring success (or failure) of CPR institutions—the external institutional frameworks (Agrawal 2001; Ostrom 1990; Bromley 1990). The manner in which use and access rights are exercised is often influenced by the state's overarching policies within which micro institutions operate. The state plays a role in institutional change by either altering existing institutions, or creating new ones. Their success is dependent on a number of factors—cost of maintaining resources, community's preparedness, history of prior collective action, degree of state support, overlap of new institutions with traditional ones. The papers in this collection raise numerous issues in the context of the state and local institutions from all the countries in the region, some of which we have already talked about earlier. We now take up some cases of non-fulfilment of desired outcomes in the event of state intervention even though well-intentioned: (*a*) conflict with traditional norms that it supplanted; (*b*) withering away of old institutions and the new ones being unable to replace the old one holistically; (*c*) incomplete intervention leading to unsustainable outcomes.

The international experience suggests that states often undertake devolution either to reduce their own fiscal burden or accede to community demands for greater control of their local resources (Shyamsundar, this volume).

Communities seem to be able to provide for operational expenses of maintaining a CPR, but the cost of restoration of the natural resource base is often too large for them to bear. If the state financially assists restoration then the rejuvenation of the natural resource base is possible. However, crucial for this success is an enabling framework that the state has to provide for these community institutions to operate. The Orissa and Maharashtra forestry studies in India and the community forestry studies in Nepal clearly indicate that the success of forest user groups depended on the state's own policies being conducive to such group formations (Mishra, Ghate, and Kanel, all this volume).

It would be naïve to anticipate though that any institution that the state creates would sustain itself automatically. When these institutions are created without an endogenous demand for them, the chances of success are rather slim as compared to initiatives that come up from the grassroots. The study of irrigation user groups in Sri Lanka demonstrates that in the process of empowering water user groups there are mixed results. Those groups that have a prior history of collective action seem to add to their productivity while others don't (Herath, this volume).

Sometimes, the state intervention may take the form of new rules and institutions that do not supplant the old completely and come into conflict with traditional norms and practices. This is dealt with in two of the studies included in this volume. In Bhutan, the institution of sokshings evolved as a tax minimization response to the traditional tax system which was based on area cultivated rather than total output.[11] The farmers in order to maximize net post-tax returns undertook silvicultural practices in local forests. The biomass produce from the forests was used to enhance agricultural output without increasing the land area cultivated. This led villages to protect forest patches as sokshings by imposing social sanctions. However, the traditional norms that guided the sustainable management of forests protected as sokshings have been disturbed by the state's efforts to take over these forest blocks leading to concerns about the future sustainability of forests in Bhutan (Webb and Dorji, this volume).

Similar issues have been raised about forest management in Dir-Kohistan, Pakistan's North West Frontier Province. The forests in this region of Pakistan were managed by local norms and in case of any disputes, the traditional *jirga* would adjudicate. The social legitimacy of the traditional *jirga* is now being put to test by Pakistan's new forest policy. Further, there seems to be a non-conformity between statutory law and customary law (*garzinda wesh*)

---

[11] Any agency with either limited information gathering networks or the need for secure revenues would opt for a land tax which is area-based rather than production-based. This would cut down the cost of information gathering otherwise each year tax collectors would have to track levels of production in order to determine tax. Tax revenues would become variable—an undesirable situation on the part of the tax authority when productivity of land is fairly constant.

putting to test the conservation impact of either set of rules (Khan, this volume).

A study of traditional agrarian institutions called the *communidades* in Goa suggests that a state-induced change in institutional structures could see the withering away of the old but not provide incentive for the new ones to replace them, thereby affecting the ecological balance (Mukhopadhyay, this volume). *Communidades* which were responsible for embankment maintenance were replaced by new institutions which either did not have the fiscal capability to finance public works (the Tenants Associations) or did not have any direct incentive to undertake land management (the *panchayat*). This has led to long-term suboptimal outcomes.

Outcomes of state intervention become even more complicated when there are multiple resource uses involved from the same geographical area. This is portrayed in a study of the *haors* of Bangladesh's deltaic zone where there are three kinds of land use: water bodies that provide livelihood to fishers, wetlands (marshes) which provide flood protection and spawning area for fish, and flatlands which are used for cultivation. Farmers have been reclaiming the wetlands, thereby affecting ecological sustainability of the *haors*. This land-use conflict has forced the government to undertake protective activity—in this case rehabilitation of the wetlands by afforestation. However, the afforestation alone would lead to unsustainable outcomes. Simulations of a bio-economic model show that a well-intentioned policy of conservation (afforestation of wetlands alone) seems to reduce total future benefits. The state action, though well-intentioned, is ill-conceived in this case due to incomplete evaluation of options by policy makers (Haque, this volume). The best option which ensures both sustainability and efficiency seems to be one where afforestation is combined with other land-management practices.

Was this afforestation programme driven by a 'romantic' vision of CPRs among policy makers which has fallen prey to 'metaphors' to rejuvenate CPRs and consequently led to suboptimal policy prescriptions? Very often this happens because the analysis of institutions is not grounded firmly in a theoretical framework that allows objective assessment. Once one places the discussion of CPRs in a coherent framework as the contributions here attempt to do, one gets to see what Dasgupta (this volume) terms as 'the Good, the Bad' (and the Ugly) side of CPRs. The contributors to this volume both confirm and challenge the received knowledge on CPRs and therefore inform future studies in this area.

0.4. Discussion

It is evident from these studies that despite many transformations in CPRs and the institutions that manage them, CPRs survived and continue to play an important role. However, institutions are playing a new role—they focus on the conservation and use of specific disaggregated resources rather than the entire commons. Institutions that have evolved endogenously as a community response, have shown greater endurance. When the state's operative external framework has been conducive the institutions have survived; where modern and traditional laws have been in conflict, sustainability of the resource has been put to test.

Within the CPR management structure, those institutions that have devised ways of effective but inexpensive mutual monitoring have lowered the transaction cost of operation and been beneficial for institutional stability. Communities have also responded effectively whenever the resource at stake has a high market value by protecting it as a CPR in the face of attempts to privatize or illegally extract the resource.

Communities with greater levels of homogeneity exhibit greater cohesion and lower transaction costs. However, when homogeneity is achieved by state sanction which simultaneously imposes new institutions to replace traditional ones, the outcome seems to be detrimental. In general, when modern legal systems are not in tandem with traditional institutions there is a tendency towards unsustainablity. New institutions seem to evolve more easily among communities that have had a prior history of cooperation and mutual interaction.

0.5. Why 'Promise, Trust, and Evolution'

The term 'promise' conjures up two meanings. Firstly, it could mean opportunities, gains, and incentives that induce communities to promote, protect, and effectively manage CPRs. It could also mean an 'oath'—to undertake or fulfil a contract. If we promise to undertake a certain action (for example, not overextract from the forest, or bring too many cattle onto the grazing field) then we will keep our word. This is one of the pillars on which successful cooperative action stands.

For this promise to be effective or credible, there must be an element of trust involved. If we know someone is unreliable, then his/her promise is not worth taking note of. Contrariwise, if this person has a past record of keeping his or her word, then we can assume that the promise would be honoured. The supply of institutions (evolution) therefore is crucially dependent on promise being coterminus with trust so that the rules that govern allocation of resources are commonly held and followed by all agents in the group.

'Trust' lies at the core of institutional supply and manifests itself in community resources, community mobilization, and group action involving CPRs. Other arrangements and practices rooted in 'trust' are distribution of benefits and sacrifices, participatory decisions, and collaborative arrangements involving the community, the state, NGOs, and market agencies.

'Evolution' captures the dynamics of resource and institutional change that govern CPR management. It encapsulates the changes that occur in the resource (base and flows from it) as well as the changes in the rules that govern access and use. There is sometimes a positive bias to the use of the word 'evolution' just as there is a negative bias to the term 'degradation'. In the presence of promise and trust, the likelihood of evolution rather than degradation is very high.

The commons in South Asia therefore are alive and kicking. This is despite expectation from many quarters that they would dwindle and disappear in the face of increased market access to remote areas or due to the demands of an emerging modern state. Evidently, the institutions that manage the CPRs have evolved and in some cases new ones have emerged. CPRs are economically robust under certain conditions and therefore any institution that fulfils the necessary conditions would be able to undertake successful collective action.

The question that remains is—how do some communities effectively cooperate where others are unable? While we seem to have narrowed down the 'necessary' conditions for cooperation and collective action to emerge, the 'sufficient conditions' continue to elude us. This book is a humble attempt to capture these dilemmas and outcomes in South Asia.

References

ADB (Asian Development Bank) (2006). *South Asia Economic Report*. Report. Philippines: Asian Development Bank. Web access: <http://www.adb.org/Documents/Reports/South-Asia-Economic-Report/default.asp>. Last accessed on 15 January 2007.

Agrawal, A. (2001). 'Commons Property Institutions and Sustainable Governance of Resources'. *World Development*, 29/10: 1649–72.

Arrow, K. J., Dasgupta, P., and Mäler, K.-G. (2003). 'The Genuine Savings Criterion and the Value of Population'. *Economic Theory*, 21/2: 217–25.

—— —— Goulder, L., Daily, G., Ehrlich, P., Heal, G. M., Levin, S., Mäler, K.-G., Schneider, S., Starrett, D., and Walker, B. (2004). 'Are We Consuming Too Much?' *Journal of Economic Perspectives*, 18/3: 147–72.

Atkinson, G., and Gundimeda, H. (2006). 'Accounting for India's Forest Wealth'. *Ecological Economics*, 59/4: 462–76.

Bromley, D. W. (1990). *Environment and Economy: Property Rights and Public Policy*. Oxford: Basil Blackwell.

Cavendish, W. (2000). 'Empirical Evidence in the Poverty-Environment Relationship of Rural Households: Evidence from Zimbabwe'. *World Development*, 28/11: 1979–2003.

Chopra, K., and Dasgupta, P. (2002). 'Common Pool Resources and the Development Process: Evidence from India'. Paper submitted for the Ninth Biennial Conference of the International Association for the Study of Common Property (IASCP)—'The Commons in an Age of Globalisation', Victoria Falls, Zimbabwe, 17–21 June.

Web-access: <http://dlc.dlib.indiana.edu/archive/00000806/00/choprak270302.pdf>. Last accessed in November 2006.

——, Kadekodi, G. K., and Murty, M. N. (1990). *Participatory Development: People and Common Property Resources*. New Delhi: Sage Publications.

Dasgupta, P. (2001). *Human Well-Being and the Natural Environment*. Oxford: Oxford University Press.

—— and Heal, G. (1979). *Economic Theory and Exhaustible Resources*. Cambridge: Cambridge University Press.

Dayton-Johnson, J., and Bardhan, P. K. (2002). 'Inequality and Conservation on the Local Commons: A Theoretical Exercise'. *Economic Journal*, 112/481: 577–602.

Hamilton, K., and Clemens, M. (1999). 'Genuine Savings Rates in Developing Countries'. *World Bank Economic Review*, 13: 333–56.

Hardin, G. (1968). 'The Tragedy of the Commons'. *Science*, 162: 1243–8.

Jodha, N. S. (1986). 'Common Property Resources and the Rural Poor'. *Economic and Political Weekly*, 21: 1169–81.

—— (2001). *Life on the Edge: Sustaining Agriculture and Community Resources in Fragile Environments*. Delhi, India: Oxford University Press.

Kerapeletswe, C. K., and Lovett, J. C. (2001). 'The Role of Common Pool Resources in Economic Welfare of Rural Households', University of York, Digital Library of the Commons, <http://dlc.dlib.indiana.edu/archive>.

Menon, A., and Vadivelu, G. Ananda (2006). 'Common Property Resources in Different Agro-Climatic Landscapes in India'. *Conservation and Society*, 4/1: 132–54.

Olson, M. (1965). *The Logic of Collective Action*. Cambridge, MA: Harvard University Press.

Ostrom, E. (1990). *Governing the Commons: The Evolution of Institutions for Collective Action*. Cambridge: Cambridge University Press.

Parikh, J. K., and Parikh, K. S. (1998). *Accounting and Valuation of Environment: Vol. II, Case Studies from the ESCAP Region*. Report. New York: Economic and Social Commission for Asia and the Pacific Region, United Nations.

Williamson, O. (1981). 'The Economics of Organization: The Transaction Cost Approach'. *American Journal of Sociology*, 87/3: 548–77.

Part I

Issues and Challenges

1

Common Property Resources: Economic Analytics

Partha Dasgupta

1.1. Natural capital and economic development

Twentieth-century economics has in large measure been detached from the environmental sciences. Judging by the profession's writings, we economists see nature, when we see it at all, at best as a backdrop from which resources can be drawn in isolation. Macroeconomic forecasts routinely exclude natural resources. Accounting for natural capital, if it comes into the calculus at all, is an afterthought to the real business of 'doing economics'.

Official development economics has mirrored the rest of economics in its neglect of the role natural capital plays in economic activity. This should be a puzzle. Development economists, more than anyone else, would have been expected to know that 65 to 75 per cent of people in the world's poorest regions live in rural areas. Moreover, they needed only to think of agricultural land, threshing grounds, grazing fields, tanks and ponds, woodlands and forests, rivers and streams, coastal fisheries, mangroves, and coral reefs to recognize the importance of the local natural-resource base in the lives of the rural poor. Nevertheless, apart from agricultural land, natural capital has been absent from the formal models mainstream development economists have used to arrive at policy recommendations. Leading surveys and texts on the economics of development (Stern 1989; Dreze and Sen 1990, 1995; Ray 1998) ignore the local natural-resource base and the wide variety of institutions that have evolved for managing them.

Despite that lack of interest, an extensive applied literature has emerged in India on the economics of natural capital. Scholars contributing to that literature have noted that, excepting for agricultural land, the local natural-resource base is often communally owned. They have noted too that access is restricted to people who have historical rights; which, for most intents and purposes are villagers in the locality. There are anomalies and I shall return to a few later in this chapter, but the thrust of the literature has been that although the local natural-resource base consists of capital assets that are common property, the assets are not open-access. Among Indian scholars those assets are now called common property resources, or CPRs.

1.2. Open-access resources vs CPRs

The economic theory of open-access resources has been familiar to economists since Gordon (1954), who noted that an asset that is everyone's property is in fact no one's property. Gordon showed that resources to which access is open are overused, in that it is in the common interest to restrict their use. His reasoning was simple: given that resources are finite in size, they have positive social worth. But an open-access resource is free to all who use it. Moreover, the cost a user incurs isn't merely less than what it ought ideally to be; entry drives the resource rents to zero. The biologist Garrett Hardin later called that overuse 'the tragedy of the commons', insisting that 'freedom in the commons brings ruin to all' (Hardin 1968). Hardin must have had in mind the atmosphere and the open seas, where the tragedy he talked of is certainly unfolding today; but he chose a most unfortunate example to illustrate his point—grazing land.

Social scientists haven't been kind to Hardin. Dasgupta (1982) showed in the context of a fully dynamic model that an open-access renewable resource would not be ruined if the cost of extraction was large relative to the value of the resource itself. The motivations behind the finding were that the tropical rainforests had been safe until the chainsaw made its appearance and the fisheries of the open seas were not threatened until the emergence of sophisticated fishing equipments for tracking schools and trawling the sea bottom.

Anthropologists and political scientists took Hardin to task severely. They criticized him for his failure to recognize that geographically localized commons are most often CPRs, not open-access, and that local institutions have evolved to forestall the tragedy of the commons. Today one cannot but detect an air of academic triumphalism in those writings.[1] Certainly, it has not been uncommon for articles on CPRs to begin by denigrating Hardin's metaphor and then showing him to have been wrong by means of a case study. Applied economists in India also joined the fray. I have in mind the many articles published in the *Economic and Political Weekly* since the late 1980s.

---

[1] See, for example, Feeny *et al.* (1990).

In studying CPRs, we are in the realm not only of natural capital, but also of institutions. Economists have traditionally studied markets, while political scientists have studied the state. As CPRs have an academically unfamiliar ring to them, their study has an obvious appeal for social scientists. CPRs are not public nor private property, but are communal property. Unlike the global commons though, they are geographically confined and, as noted above, access is not open to all. Moreover, an emerging parallel literature on social capital hinted that it had something to say about the character of those communitarian institutions that have been built around CPRs. All this was a heady academic cocktail. The literature on CPRs is now enormous, not only in India.[2]

Oddly, economic theory has been missing from almost all of that literature. But without theory as guide, it isn't possible to understand either the institutions that govern CPRs or the policies that would be required if those institutions were found to be wanting. Casual empiricism suggests that communitarian institutions are fragile in the presence of growing markets elsewhere; but without theory one wouldn't know whether the evidence was real. By the same token, one may ask whether communitarian institutions were ever as good as they are made out to be by scholars who believe they are attractive alternatives to impersonal markets and coercive states. But without the disciplinary pressure of economic theory, we wouldn't know whether there is something in that belief or whether it is a mere romantic posture. After all, one can argue that communitarian institutions retard the emergence of more efficient institutions; but is that argument correct?

In fact, the basic economic theory of CPRs had been created some time ago, in Dasgupta and Heal (1979). At the time I drafted the chapter that presents the theory, I (and probably Heal also) had no idea of the prevalence of CPRs in the contemporary world. I developed the formal model (Section 1.5.1 below) so as to understand the externalities that are present when an asset is an unmanaged CPR. Once the model was constructed, it was but natural to study alternative ways a community could manage the CPR (Sections 1.5.2 and 1.5.3 below). However, had I been asked in 1979 whether CPRs form an important class of assets, I wouldn't have been able to answer. In this I was not alone. Judging by the prevailing literature, no one in the development field then knew much about CPRs in the contemporary world. Village commons in modern England are familiar enough, but

---

[2] See, for example, National Research Council 1986, 2002; Agarwal and Narain 1989; Chopra, Kadekodi, and Murty 1989; Ostrom 1990; Stevenson 1991; Bromley *et al.* 1992; Singh 1994; Baland and Platteau 1996; and Marothia 2002. Priya Shyamsundar's contribution to this volume is a remarkable synthesis of the findings in over 175 articles on the efficacy of a transfer of rights and responsibilities from the state to the users of natural resources. She concludes that the balance of evidence from literally hundreds of studies is that devolution leads to better resource management, other things being the same. She, of course, offers a discussion of what those other things are.

they are recreational grounds; they are not essential for survival. Economic historians knew of the past importance of CPRs, though, which is why the only illustrations we were able to offer in the book were from early-modern England.[3]

1.3. Why CPRs?

The trail-blazing empirical study on contemporary CPRs was Jodha (1986), who reported evidence from a number of dry rural districts in India that the proportion of income among poor families based directly on CPRs is in the range 15 to 25 per cent. Cavendish (2000) has arrived at even larger estimates from a study of villages in Zimbabwe: the proportion of income based directly on CPRs is 35 per cent, the figure for the poorest quintile being 40 per cent. Such evidence as Jodha and Cavendish unearthed does not, of course, prove that CPRs in their samples were well managed, but it does show that rural households would have strong incentives to devise arrangements whereby they would be managed.[4]

The economic importance of CPRs, as a proportion of total assets, ranges widely across ecological zones. In India they are most prominent in arid regions, mountain regions, and unirrigated areas; they are least prominent in humid regions and river valleys (Agarwal and Narain 1989). There is a rationale behind this, based on the mutual desire to pool risks. Woodlands, for example, are spatially non-homogeneous ecosystems. In some year one group of plants bear fruit in one part of a woodland, in another year some other group does in some other part. Relative to mean output, fluctuations could be presumed to be larger in arid regions, mountain regions, and unirrigated areas. If a woodland were to be divided into private parcels, each household would face a greater risk than it would under communal ownership. The reduction in individual household risks owing to communal ownership may be small; but as average incomes are very low in Indian villages, household benefits from communal ownership are large if woodlands are communally owned.

CPRs are prominent also because ecosystem constituents are mobile. Birds and insects fly, fish swim, inorganic materials defuse in space, and even earthworms are known to travel. Their mobility integrates an ecosystem's various components. Ecosystem dynamics are generally speaking non-linear, involving positive feedback in a wide range of states, meaning that the system

[3] My friend and colleague Paul David told me what to read on the commons and the enclosure movement. I learnt subsequently that there was an empirical literature on CPRs in Alpine Switzerland (Netting 1976), but I didn't know of the literature's existence then.

[4] The earliest study I have so far been able to locate of communitarian institutions governing CPRs in the poor world is Netting (1985).

as a whole is greater than the sum of its spatial parts. Ecosystems therefore have an element of indivisibility to them. If you slice off a significant portion for some other purpose, the productivity (for example, biomass production) per unit area of what remains is reduced.[5] But even if it were decreed that no portion could be converted for another use, parcelling ecosystems into private bits would be inefficient because of the externalities created by the mobile components. Admittedly, private monopoly would avoid the externalities, but it would grant far too much power to one person in the community.

CPRs are sometimes the only assets to which the otherwise disenfranchised have access. This is a virtuous by-product of the institutions governing CPRs. Economic theory says that even the casual wage rate of unskilled labourers would be higher in villages with more abundant CPRs (Dasgupta 1993; Barbier 2004; Pattanaik and Butry 2004). That said, I am not implying that assetless people featured prominently in community decisions to create the institutions governing CPRs. I am merely drawing attention to a good feature of CPRs.

The local resource base of rural communities consists of extractive, self-renewing capital assets (Dasgupta 1982). Woodlands, village ponds, and coastal fisheries are prominent examples. Even wetlands, noted for recycling organic pollutants, fit into that category: they provide continuing services at no extraction cost. No doubt investment in those assets can increase their productivity, but what sets them apart from manufactured capital is that they are self-renewing natural assets (see Webb and Dorji, this volume).

Agricultural land, especially in densely populated areas, is a different matter. Both labour and capital are critical inputs in production. Investment can increase land's productivity enormously. Agricultural land as CPRs would be subject to significant management problems, including those due to the temptations to free-ride on investment costs. The lack of incentives to invest and innovate would lead to stagnation, even decay (see Mukhopadhyay, this volume). The fate of collective farms testifies to that. Those regions of sub-Saharan Africa where land has been, or was, held by the kinship were exceptions, but only because land was plentiful and because poor soil quality meant that land had to be kept fallow for extended periods, following only a few years of cultivation. Of course, it may be that agricultural productivity remained low there because land was held by the kinship, not by individuals. As elsewhere in the social sciences, causation typically works in both directions.

---

[5] Steffen *et al.* (2004) is a technical account of the pervasiveness of non-linearities in natural processes. Dasgupta and Mäler (2004) is a collection of essays that develops the welfare economics of non-linear ecosystems.

1.4. Plan of the chapter

In this chapter I present a fairly complete economic theory of CPRs. A timeless deterministic model, taken directly from Dasgupta and Heal (1979), is presented in Section 1.5. The asset under study is a piece of grazing land in which owners of cattle herd their animals. Cattle are assumed to be private property. We first identify the externalities that emerge in an unmanaged CPR (Section 1.5.1). We then confirm that an efficient use of the grazing land involves reduction in the number of cattle. Two regulatory regimes for enforcing that reduction are studied (Section 1.5.2): quota restriction on the number of cattle each herdsman is permitted in the CPR and a tax on each cow introduced into the CPR (paid back lump sum to the herdsmen). As the model is deterministic, the two regulatory regimes are found to be equivalent.[6]

Privatization is an alternative system of property rights to communal ownership in those cases where the resource is divisible without productivity loss. Assuming that pastures are divisible without loss in productivity, we confirm (Section 1.5.3) that the grazing land in the model would be used efficiently if it were divided into private lots.

Irrespective of whether the herdsmen rely on taxes or quotas, managing a CPR involves cooperation. Interestingly, it has been uncommon among social scientists who write about CPRs to ask how cooperative agreements are enforced (Ghate, and Gunawardene and Steele (both this volume) provide documentation in forestry in India and fisheries in Sri Lanka). To say that herdsmen can devise a regulatory regime to implement cooperation (taxes, quotas) isn't enough; we have to ask what incentives the parties have for carrying out their respective sides of the agreement. That raises a far more general question.

Imagine that a group of people have identified a mutually beneficial course of action. Imagine too that they have agreed to follow that course. In what contexts can the group be sanguine that people will do what they said they will do under the terms of the agreement? To put the question in another way, in what contexts are the promises people make to one another credible? In the sixth section we answer that question. The analysis there is based on Dasgupta (1993, 2005). I pay special attention (Section 1.6.5) to the situation where the group faces the problem of cooperation period after period. The theory of repeated games is used to show that agreements can be kept if the parties discount the future benefits from cooperation at a low enough rate. Repeated games are, of course, abstractions. In the world as we know it, the circumstances people face change over time (owing, for example, to

---

[6] Meade (1973) and Weitzman (1974) showed that if the regulator and the herdsmen possess different information, the two regimes are not equivalent. But their finding holds only if the tax is constrained to be constant per cow. The tax-quota alternatives are special cases of non-linear taxes. See Dasgupta, Hammond, and Maskin (1980) and Dasgupta (1982).

changes in the composition of capital assets). However, it can be shown that the conclusions we arrive at from the study of repeated games carry over qualitatively to situations where people face changing circumstances over time.

Writings on CPRs have frequently had a warm glow to them (Bromley *et al.* 1992). And yet, institutions for managing CPRs have been found to be fragile. Moreover, there is a dark side to the institutions that have been built round CPRs. In Sections 1.7 and 1.8 we study those weaknesses.

In Section 1.7.1 the theory of repeated games is applied to the timeless model of the CPR studied in the fifth section to show that it is possible for the benefits of cooperation to be shared unequally even if community members were equally placed to begin with. Economic theory therefore provides a strong account of an empirical observation, that access to CPRs is frequently unequal. In Section 1.7.2 I review a number of empirical findings concerning the deteriorating fate of CPRs in the contemporary world. The theory of repeated games is then applied to the timeless model of Section 1.5 to explain why CPRs are institutionally fragile.

Section 1.8 is about a matter that to the best of my knowledge has not been investigated in the literature. I apply the theory of repeated games to the timeless model of Section 1.5 once again, but this time to show that it is also possible for some members of a community to be worse off under cooperation based on a long-term relationship than they would have been if the community's members hadn't entered into the long-term relationship. The model offers an account of how one group of people in a community could exploit another even while the latter may mistakenly be thought to be enjoying the benefits of long-term relationship. Section 1.9 summarizes the main conclusions.

1.5. CPRs: a formal model

There are N herdsmen, indexed by i (i = 1, 2,..., N). Cattle are private property. The pasture is neither privately owned nor state property, but is communally owned. Outsiders are not permitted to graze their cattle in the pasture, meaning that there is no open access to the land either: the grazing land is a CPR.

The model is timeless. The size of the pasture is S. Cattle intermingle while grazing, so that on average the cows consume the same amount of grass. If X is the size of the herd in the pasture, total output—of milk—is H(X, S), where H is taken to be constant returns to scale in X and S. Assume H(0, S) = 0 for all S ≥ 0. Assume too that the marginal products of X and S are positive, but diminish with increasing values of X and S, respectively. In short, I take H to be a textbook production function. I am modelling the pasture in an

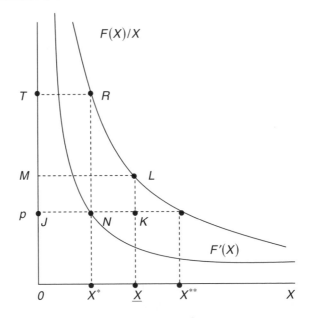

Figure 1.1. Equilibrium grazing in the unmanaged common

orthodox manner for pedagogical reasons. I want to illustrate how, starting from the most conventional of production possibilities, matters concerning human interactions that go far beyond markets and the state can be analysed. Readers can confirm though that excepting for the analysis in Section 1.5.3, every result that I prove in this chapter carries over to cases where the CPR in question displays non-linear dynamics, so that time does not merely involve an indefinite recurrence of a single social situation.

As S is fixed and H is constant returns to scale, we may eliminate S by writing $H(X, S) = SH(X/S, 1)$; by letting $S = 1$ without loss of generality; and by defining $F(X) \equiv H(X, 1)$. From the assumptions made on H, we may conclude that $F(0) = 0$; $F'(X) > 0$; $F''(X) < 0$; and $F(X)/X > F'(X) > 0$ for all $X \geq 0$. Figure 1.1 depicts both the functions $F(X)/X$ (the average product curve) and $F'(X)$ (the marginal product curve).

Herdsmen are interested in the profits they are able to earn from their cattle. We normalize by choosing the market price of milk to be one. Let the market price of cattle be p (> 0), which may be interpreted as a rental price. To have a problem worth studying (see equation (8) below), I assume that $F'(0) > p$.

1.5.1. *An unmanaged CPR*

We first determine the herd size brought into the CPR if the cattle owners have instituted no grazing charges nor any quantity restriction on numbers.

Let x_i be the size of i's herd. x_i is taken to be a continuous variable. Since cattle intermingle, $x_i F(X)/X$ is i's output of milk. Therefore, i's net profit, π_i, is

$$\pi_i = x_i F(X)/X - px_i. \tag{1}$$

We wish to compute the non-cooperative (Nash) equilibrium of the resulting timeless game. Since the model is symmetric, we should expect it to possess a symmetric equilibrium. (It can be shown that equilibrium in this timeless model is unique.)

Without loss of generality, consider herdsman i. If the herd size of each of the other cattlemen is x, equation (1) can be written as

$$\pi_i(x_i, x) = x_i F(x_i + (N-1)x)/(x_i + (N-1)x) - px_i. \tag{2}$$

The profit function $\pi_i(x_i, x)$ reflects the crowding externalities each herdsman inflicts on all others in the unmanaged CPR: π_i is a function not only of x_i, but also of x. Let $\underline{x}$ be the size of each cattleman's herd at a symmetric equilibrium. By definition, $\underline{x}$ would be the value of x_i that maximizes $\pi_i(x_i, \underline{x})$. Therefore differentiate $\pi_i(x_i, \underline{x})$ partially with respect to x_i and equate the result to zero. This yields,

$$F(x_i + (N-1)\underline{x})/[x_i + (N-1)\underline{x}] + x_i F'(x_i + (N-1)\underline{x})/[x_i + (N-1)\underline{x}]$$
$$- x_i F(x_i + (N-1)\underline{x})/[x_i + (N-1)\underline{x}]^2 = p \tag{3}$$

At a symmetric equilibrium x_i in equation (3) must equal $\underline{x}$. Now rearrange terms to confirm that the aggregate herd size in the CPR, which we write as $\underline{X}$, satisfies

$$((N-1)/N)F(\underline{X})/\underline{X} + F'(\underline{X})/N = p, \qquad \text{where } \underline{X} = N\underline{x}. \tag{4}$$

Equation (4) is a beautiful condition. It says that in equilibrium the price of cattle equals the weighted average of the average product of cattle and the marginal product of cattle, with weights $(N-1)/N$ and $1/N$, respectively. $\underline{X}$ is shown in Figure 1.1 as being a point lying between the value of X at which marginal product of X equals p (it is X^* in Figure 1.1) and the value of X at which the average product of X equals p (it is X^{**} in Figure 1.1). It can be easily confirmed that $\underline{X}$ is an increasing function of N.

Notice that aggregate profit, which I denote by $\underline{\pi}$, is

$$\underline{\pi} = [F(\underline{X}) - \underline{X}F'(\underline{X})]/N > 0, \tag{5}$$

implying that rents are not entirely dissipated. In Figure 1.1, $\underline{\pi}$ is the area of the rectangle JKLM.

From equation (5) we conclude that profit per herdsman is

$$\underline{\pi}/N = [F(\underline{X}) - \underline{X}F'(\underline{X})]/N^2 > 0. \tag{6}$$

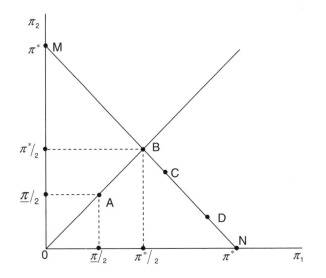

Figure 1.2. Allocation of grazing profits in the managed and unmanaged common

In Figure 1.2 which depicts the case N = 2, the equilibrium pair of profits ($\underline{\pi}/2$, $\underline{\pi}/2$) is the point A.

Although $\underline{X}/N$ is the equilibrium number of cattle per herdsman, it isn't a dominant strategy for the representative herdsman: CPRs do not give rise to the Prisoners' Dilemma game. This is a fact I make use of in Sections 1.7 and 1.8.[7]

If N is large, the unmanaged CPR approximates an open-access resource. To confirm, notice that if N is large, equation (4) becomes

$$F(\underline{X})/\underline{X} \approx p. \tag{7}$$

The approximate equation (7) says that rents are dissipated almost entirely. This is the case studied by Gordon (1954).[8]

---

[7] Recall that a game is called the Prisoners' Dilemma if each player has a dominant strategy (a strategy that is best for him no matter what strategies the others choose) and that playing their dominant strategies results in a collectively inefficient outcome.

[8] Gordon (1954) followed a different modelling strategy, but with the same import. He assumed that H is not constant returns to scale; that, in particular, F'(X) is increasing at small values of X, but decreasing at large values of X. He didn't specify the number of herdsmen; instead he postulated that open access would lead to a complete dissipation of land rents: F(X)/X = p. In Gordon's open-access model, the number of herdsmen is endogenous and finite (because of the increasing returns to scale in F at low values of X). In contrast, the model here regards the number of herdsmen to be exogenously given. The latter is the correct assumption to make on CPRs. If the number of cattlemen is large in our model, each herdsman introduces small numbers of cattle into the pasture, with the result that rents get dissipated almost entirely.

1.5.2. *Regulatory regimes: quotas and taxes*

An unmanaged CPR would be unattractive to the herdsmen: they could increase their profits by managing it together. In their chapter in this volume, Gunawardena and Steele find direct evidence of this in the context of a fishery in the Negambo Lagoon of Sri Lanka.

Imagine that cooperation involves negligible transaction costs (Coase 1960). What would be a reasonable agreement among the herdsmen? As the model is symmetric, it may seem plausible to assume that they agree to maximize aggregate profit and share that profit equally. We assume that here.[9] Maximizing aggregate profit $(F(X) - pX)$ yields the condition

$$F'(X) = p. \tag{8}$$

Equation (8) says that at the optimum the marginal product of cattle equals their price—a familiar result in price theory. Let X^* be the solution of equation (8). At the community optimum, aggregate profit, which I denote by π^*, is

$$\pi^* = F(X^*) - F'(X^*)X^* > \underline{\pi} > 0. \tag{9}$$

In Figure 1.1, π^* is the area of the rectangle JNRT.

From equation (8) we conclude that profit per herdsman is

$$\pi^*/N = (F(X^*) - F'(X^*)X^*)/N. \tag{10}$$

A comparison of equations (4) and (8) shows that $\underline{X} > X^*$. In Figure 1.2, which depicts the case N = 2, the pair of profits $(\pi^*/2, \pi^*/2)$ at the community optimum is the point B (OB is the 45 degree line through 0).

We now study two regulatory regimes for implementing X^*.

With a quota restriction the herdsmen agree to practise restraint by limiting each to at most X^*/N cattle. It is simple to confirm that choosing X^*/N is then the dominant strategy for each herdsman. We conclude that a quota can implement the agreement to limit the aggregate herd size to X^*.

An alternative regime would be to impose an entry tax on each cow and to share the tax revenue equally as a lump-sum income. This is the tax solution to the problem. Let us compute the optimum tax.[10]

In a tax regime the herdsmen are free to graze as many cattle as they like, but have to pay an entry fee per cow. The optimum tax corrects for the externalities each herdsman inflicts on all others when introducing a cow in the CPR. If the tax rate is t, the effective price a herdsman pays is $(p + t)$. The idea therefore is to so choose t that equation (4) reduces to equation (8) and the equilibrium herd size equals X^*.

---

[9] But see Sections 1.7.1 and 1.8.
[10] Wade (1988), Baland and Platteau (1996), Gunawardena and Steele, and Mukhopadhyay (both this volume) have shown how communities do in fact levy user taxes on CPRs.

Let t* be the optimum tax. Routine calculations show that

$$t^* = [F(X^*)/X^* - F'(X^*)](N - 1)/N. \tag{11}$$

Equation (11) is intuitively amiable. The right-hand side measures the externality each herdsman inflicts on others. That externality is the difference between the marginal private benefit of introducing cattle in the pasture (the left-hand side of equation (4)) and the marginal community benefit (the left-hand side of equation (8)). When the tax rate is set equal to that difference (evaluated at the optimum value X^*), cattlemen limit their herds to the right size.

1.5.3. Privatizing the CPR

An alternative to a regulatory regime involves a change in the property rights to the pasture. Consider privatizing the grazing land. The size of the pasture is S. Imagine that S is divided into N equal parts and awarded as private property to the herdsmen. Suppose too that they are able to protect their property rights costlessly (for example, fences are costlessly built). What would be the outcome?

Each cattleman owns S/N amount of land after privatization. If herdsman i were to introduce x_i cows into his own land, his output would be $H(x_i, S/N)$ and his profit would be

$$\pi_i(x_i) = H(x_i, S/N) - px_i. \tag{12}$$

Because H is constant returns to scale, $H(x_i, S/N) = H(Nx_i/S, 1)S/N$. Once again, let us normalize by setting $S = 1$. Now $H(Nx_i, 1) = F(Nx_i)$ in our earlier notation. Therefore equation (12) reduces to

$$\pi_i(x_i) = F(Nx_i)/N - px_i. \tag{13}$$

Notice that unlike equation (2), which represented herdsman i's profit function in the unmanaged CPR, the profit function in equation (13) harbours no externalities: π_i is solely a function of x_i. Privatization removes the crowding externalities among cattle. Differentiating π_i with respect to x_i and setting the result equal to zero, the profit-maximizing size of herd is found to be

$$F'(Nx_i) = p. \tag{14}$$

Comparison of equations (8) and (14) shows that each herdsman introduces X^*/N cows into his private parcel of land. But this is the cooperative outcome in the case where the pasture is a CPR. Thus, privatization also solves the resource allocation problem facing the N herdsmen.

1.6. Trust and credibility

Both privatization of the grazing land and cooperation over the use of that land as a CPR involve trust. If the allocation defined by equation (14) is to be realized, the herdsmen have to trust the 'legal system' to enforce private property rights to their parcels of land. Similarly, if cooperation over the use of the pasture as a CPR is to be achieved, they have to trust one another to enforce the agreement to limit each herd size to X^*/N either by means of a quota (equation (8)) or a tax (equation (9)).

We now use the problem of trust facing our cattlemen to ask a question that goes far beyond the management of CPRs:

Imagine a group of people who have discovered a joint course of action that would lead to a mutually beneficial outcome. Imagine too that they have agreed to cooperate and share the resulting benefits in a specified manner. If the parties don't trust one another, what could have been mutually beneficial transactions won't take place. But what grounds could they have for trusting one another to do what they have undertaken to do?

They would have grounds if promises were credible. So a general question arises: under what circumstances are promises credible? Four come to mind.

1.6.1. Mutual affection

Promises would be credible if the parties care about one another sufficiently. Innumerable transactions take place only because the people involved care about one another and rationally believe that they care about one another (that is, each knows that the others know that they care about one another, each knows that the others know that each knows that they care about one another, and so on) and therefore trust one another to carry out their obligations. Economists model the situation as one where group members have interdependent utilities. The household best exemplifies institutions based on care and affection. As monitoring costs within the household are low (a group of people who cohabit are able to observe and to get to know one another), the institution harbours fewer problems of moral hazard and adverse selection than many other institutions. On the other hand, being few in number, members of a household, as a group, are unable to engage in those enterprises that require large numbers of people of varied talents and locations.

1.6.2. Pro-social disposition

Promises would be credible if it was common knowledge that those making the promises were trustworthy, or that they reciprocated by keeping their promise if others displayed trust in them.[11] Evolutionary psychologists have argued that, because of selection pressures operating among our hunter-gatherer Pleistocene ancestors, we are adapted to have a general disposition to reciprocate. Others have argued that such a disposition is to a greater or lesser extent formed through communal living, role modelling, education, and receiving rewards and punishments, and that the process begins at the earliest stages of our lives.[12]

For our purposes here, we don't have to choose between the two theories; either would do. In any event, they are not mutually exclusive. Thus, evolutionary psychologists have argued that our capacity to have such feelings as shame, affection, anger, elation, reciprocity, benevolence, and jealousy has emerged under selection pressure. No doubt culture helps to shape preferences and expectations (thus, behaviour), which are known to differ widely across societies. But cultural coordinates enable us to identify the locus of points upon which shame, affection, anger, elation, reciprocity, benevolence, and jealousy are put to work; they don't displace the centrality of those feelings in the human make-up. The thought I am exploring here is that, as adults, we not only have a disposition for such behaviour as paying our dues, helping others at some cost to ourselves, and returning a favour; we also practise such norms as those which prescribe that we punish people who have hurt us intentionally; and even such higher-order norms as shunning people who break agreements, on occasion frowning on those who socialize with people who have broken agreements; and so forth. By internalizing specific norms, a person enables the springs of her actions to include them. She therefore feels shame or guilt in violating the norm, and this prevents her from doing so, or at the very least it puts a break on her, unless other considerations are found by her to be overriding. In short, her upbringing ensures that she has a disposition to obey the norm, be it moral or social. When she does violate it, neither guilt nor shame would typically be absent, but frequently the act will have been rationalized by her. For such a person, making a promise is a commitment, and it is essential for her that others recognize it to be so.[13]

Often enough, the disposition to be honest would be toward members of some particular group (clan, or neighbours, or ethnic group), not others. This amounts to group loyalty. One may have been raised to be suspicious of

---

[11] The new behavioural economics emphasizes this aspect of human character. See, for example, Rabin (1993) and Fehr and Fischbacher (2002).

[12] See, for example, Hinde and Groebel (1991), which contains accounts of what is currently known of the development processes through which people from their infancy acquire pro-social dispositions; for example, by learning to distinguish accidental effects from intentional effects of others' actions. Ghate (this volume) examines some of these issues in the forestry sector in India.

[13] In an innovative work, Sethi and Somanathan (1996) have constructed a formal model to ask when a pro-social disposition of the kind I have just sketched in the text is locally stable under selection pressure.

people from other groups, one may have even been encouraged to dupe such others if and when the occasion arose. Society as a whole wastes resources when the disposition for honesty is restricted to particular groups.

Runge (1981, 1986) has asserted that village life in the world's poorest regions involves such close interactions, that people develop pro-social dispositions toward one another. His arguments imply that the timeless CPR game of Section 1.5 would be better modelled as a game where not only is $\underline{X}$ an equilibrium herd size, but so is X^*, because if the herdsmen say to one another they will each introduce X^*/N cattle into the CPR, then they will do just that. A word, or so Runge imagines, is a person's bond; period.[14] But the evidence Runge deploys is not at all transparent. To me his interpretation of villagers' motives is a pleasant assumption, not much more. It may of course be that villagers develop pro-social dispositions toward one another; but it may be that social sanctions are in place on those who break agreements and is the reason why villagers trust one another and their own selves to do what they said they will do (Section 1.6.5). Simply asking people to declare their reason for trusting one another is not enough. Anthropologists have discovered that visitors can easily be misled by the answers inhabitants give about the workings of their local communities. Moreover, Runge's reformulation of the timeless CPR game doesn't seem to be capable of explaining why cooperation over the use of CPRs has broken down in so many instances in recent decades; whereas the modelling I pursue in Section 1.7 is able to do so.

In the world as we know it, the disposition to be trustworthy in both the personal and impersonal spheres exists in varying degrees. When we refrain from breaking the law, it isn't always because of a fear of being caught. When an employee in an unorganized sector works overtime, it may simply be a gesture of benevolence, helping out an employer in unexpected need. Recent work in behavioural economics has reaffirmed that benevolence isn't alien to human nature. On the other hand, if say, relative to the gravity of the misdemeanour the pecuniary benefits from malfeasance were high, some transgression could be expected to occur. Punishment assumes its role as a deterrence because of the latter fact.

1.6.3. *The need for incentives to keep promises*

When the temptation to break one's agreement is so large that neither mutual affection nor pro-social disposition is enough, there is need for socially constructed incentives. The promises the parties have made to one another to keep to their agreement would be credible if they could devise an institution in which keeping those promises would be in the interest of each party if

---

[14] Technically, Runge's (1981, 1986) belief is that CPRs, even when studied in a timeless framework, should be modelled as 'coordination games'.

everyone else kept theirs. The problem therefore is to devise an institution where keeping the agreement is an equilibrium strategy. Gunawardena and Steele (this volume) describe a fishery where the institutional mechanism is able to make honesty economically attractive.

A strategy is a sequence of conditional actions. It involves counterfactuals. Strategies assume the forms, 'I shall choose X if you choose Y', or 'I shall do P if Q happens', and so on. If promises are to be credible, it must be in the interest of those making promises to carry them out if and when the relevant occasions arise. It would follow that the concept we need to track is that of equilibrium beliefs, by which I mean a set of beliefs about one another, one for each party, such that it would be rational for each party to hold his or her belief if everyone else were to hold their respective beliefs.

Societies everywhere have constructed solutions to the credibility problem, but in different ways. What all solutions have in common, however, is their insistence that those failing to comply with agreements without cause will suffer punishment. Broadly speaking, there are two types of situation where parties to an agreement could expect everyone to keep their word.[15] Each gives rise to a set of institutions that capitalize on their particular features. In practice, of course, the types would be expected to shade into one another. (In his study of resource management in Dir-Kohistan's forests, Shaheen Rafi Khan (this volume) refers to one as being based on 'statutory' law, the other on 'customary' law.) In what follows we study them.

1.6.4. *External enforcement*

It could be that the agreement is translated into an explicit contract and enforced by an established structure of power and authority. This is to rely on an external enforcer. We must now assume that whether agreements have been carried out is verifiable, otherwise the external enforcer would have nothing to go on when adjudicating disputes.

By an external enforcer we may imagine the state. (There can, of course, be other types of external enforcement agencies; for example, tribal chieftains, warlords, and so forth.) Consider, as an illustration, that the rules governing transactions in the formal marketplace are embodied in the law. So markets are supported by a legal structure. Firms, for example, are legal entities. Even when you go to a shop, your purchases (paid in cash or by card) involve the law, which provides protection for both parties (the shopkeeper, in case the cash is counterfeit or the card is void; the purchaser, in case the product turns out on inspection to be substandard). The law is enforced by the coercive

---

[15] Of course, none may be potent in a particular context, in which case people would find themselves in a hole they cannot easily get out of, and what could have been mutually beneficial agreements will not take place. The behaviour reported in the Mezzogiorno by Banfield (1958) is an illustration of this possibility. See Section 1.6.5.

power of the state. Transactions involve legal contracts backed by an external enforcer, namely, the state. It is because you and the shopkeeper are confident that the state has the ability and willingness to enforce contracts that you and the shopkeeper are willing to transact. The same confidence would be required among our herdsmen if they are to transact in the market for cows (price p), for milk (price unity), and are to exercise their property rights in the case where the pasture has been privatized.

What is the basis of that confidence? After all, the contemporary world has shown that there are states and there are states. Simply to invoke an external enforcer for solving the credibility problem won't do; for why should the parties trust the state to carry out its tasks in an honest manner? (Mishra (this volume) documents the way 'supra-local' institutions have grown and acted as a counter to the state in the management of forests in Orissa (India).) A possible answer is that the government worries about its reputation. So, for example, a free and inquisitive press in a democracy helps to sober the government into believing that incompetence or malfeasance would mean an end to its rule, come the next election. Knowing that they worry, the parties trust them to enforce agreements, for example in the community forestry programme as described by Kanel (this volume). Even if senior members of the ruling party are getting on in years and therefore don't much care what happens in the future, younger members would worry that the party's reputation would suffer if the government were not to behave.[16]

The above argument involves a system of interlocking beliefs about one another's abilities and intentions. Consider that millions of households in many parts of the world trust their government (more or less!) to enforce contracts, because they know that government leaders know that not to enforce contracts efficiently would mean being thrown out of office. In their turn, each side of a contract trusts the other not to renege (again, more or less!), because each knows that the other knows that the government can be trusted to enforce contracts. And so on. Trust is maintained by the threat of punishment (a fine, a jail term, dismissal, or whatever) for anyone who breaks a contract. We are in the realm of equilibrium beliefs, held together by their own bootstraps.

Unfortunately, cooperation isn't the only possible outcome. Non-cooperation can also be held together by its own bootstrap. In a non-cooperative equilibrium the parties don't trust one another to keep their promises, because the external enforcer cannot be trusted to enforce agreements. To ask whether cooperation or non-cooperation would prevail is to ask which system of beliefs is adopted by the parties about one another's intentions. Social systems have multiple equilibria.

---

[16] Przeworski (1991) has explored this argument.

As the formal analysis of what I have only sketched above is similar to one involving people who expect to face transaction opportunities repeatedly in the future, I turn to the study of such situations.

1.6.5. *Mutual enforcement in long-term relationships*

Let us suppose the group of people in question expect to face similar transaction opportunities over and over again indefinitely. As an example, imagine that the N herdsmen of Section 1.5.1 face the same CPR management problem year after year. Even though each knows that he will die in due course, he would expect his descendants to be round when the future comes. So we may apply the repeatedness of the underlying situation to N dynasties.

I take it that, living as they do in proximity and being as they are a small community, the size of each cattleman's herd is observable by all others. Imagine that the parties aren't able to depend on the law of contracts because the nearest courts are far from their residence. There may even be no lawyer in sight. In rural parts of sub-Saharan Africa, for example, much economic life is shaped outside a formal legal system. Even though no external enforcer may be available, people there do transact. But why should the parties be sanguine that the agreements won't turn sour on account of malfeasance? Returning to our example, why should the herdsmen trust one another to comply with the agreement that each is to limit his herd size to X^*/N in every period?

They would be sanguine if agreements were mutually enforced. The basic idea is this: A credible threat by members of a community that stiff sanctions would be imposed on anyone who broke an agreement could deter everyone from breaking it. The problem then is to make the threat of stiff sanctions credible. The solution to the credibility problem in this case is achieved by recourse to social norms of behaviour.

By a social norm we mean a rule of behaviour (or strategy) that is followed by members of a community. For a rule of behaviour to be a social norm, it must be in the interest of each person to act in accordance with the rule if all others were to act in accordance with it. Social norms are equilibrium rules of behaviour.

To see how social norms work in general contexts, imagine that the private gain to someone from breaking the agreement unilaterally during a period is less than the losses he would suffer if all others were to punish him subsequently in specific ways. The condition can, of course, only hold if the parties discount future benefits at a low rate; otherwise future losses wouldn't look significant when compared to the instantaneous gain from breaking the agreement. Inflicting a punishment could involve refusing to engage in any transactions with the erring person in the following period, shunning him in other ways for suitable numbers of periods, and so on. Call a person 'conformist' if he cooperates with those who are conformists but punishes those who are non-conformists. This sounds circular, but it isn't, because we assume the social norm requires all people to start the process by keeping their agreement. It would then be possible for anyone in any period to determine who is a conformist and who is not. For example, if ever someone were to break the original agreement, he would be judged to be non-conformist. So, the norm would require everyone to punish the non-conformist—perhaps at some costs to themselves. Moreover, the norm would require that punishment be inflicted not only upon those in violation of the original agreement (first-order violation); but also upon those who fail to punish those in violation of the agreement (second-order violation); upon those who fail to punish those who fail to punish those in violation of the agreement (third-order violation); and so on, indefinitely. This infinite chain makes the threat of punishment for errant behaviour credible because, if all others were to conform to the norm, it would not be worth anyone's while to violate the norm. Keeping one's agreement would then be mutually enforcing.[17]

All traditional societies appear to have sanctions in place for first-order violations. That sanctions against higher-order violations haven't been documented much may be because they aren't needed to be built into social norms if it is commonly recognized that people feel a strong emotional urge to punish those who have broken agreements. Anger facilitates cooperation by making the threat of retaliation credible.[18]

How would the idea of social norms apply to groups wishing to cooperate over the use of CPRs? To answer, let us return to the model of N herdsmen. Denote time by t, where t = 0, 1, 2,... We take it that the game studied in Section 1.5.1—which we now call the stage game—repeats itself every period. I assume that the herdsmen discount their future profits at a low rate. (Below we confirm why this is necessary for cooperation.)

Imagine that at t = 0 the herdsmen agree to limit each of their herds to X^*/N cattle, where X^* is the optimum herd size. Under the agreement each herdsman's profit in each period is π^*/N (equation (10)). The question arises as to how the agreement can be enforced.

Consider the following strategy for the representative herdsman: begin by introducing X^*/N cattle into the pasture and continue to bring in X^*/N so long as no herdsman has broken the agreement; but introduce $\underline{X}/N$ cattle

---

[17] For a rigorous proof of this proposition, see Fudenberg and Maskin (1986).

[18] However, on a riverboat ride in Kakadu National Park, Australia, in the summer of 2004, my wife and I were informed by the guide, a young Aborigine, that his tribe traditionally practised a form of punishment that involved spearing the thigh muscle of the errant party. When I asked him what would happen if the party obliged to spear an errant party were to balk at doing so, the young man's reply was that he in turn would have been speared. When I asked him what would happen if the person obliged to spear the latter miscreant were to balk, he replied that he too would have been speared! I asked him if the chain he was describing would go on indefinitely. Our guide said he didn't know what I meant by 'indefinitely', but as far as he knew, there was no end to the chain.

into the pasture in every period following the first violation of the agreement by someone, where $\underline{X}/N$ is the herd size per cattleman in the unmanaged CPR (equation (4)). Game theorists have christened this the 'grim strategy', or simply grim, because of its unforgiving nature.

To see how grim would work, note that since $\underline{X}/N$ is the equilibrium herd size per cattleman in the unmanaged CPR, the threat by someone to switch permanently to $\underline{X}/N$ following the first defection by anyone is credible if all other herdsmen play grim. Since the herdsmen discount their respective profits at a low rate, no one can do better than to choose grim if all others choose grim. We conclude that grim is a Nash equilibrium of the repeated game, meaning that it can function as a social norm.

How low does a herdsman's discount rate have to be if grim is to function as a social norm? Suppose r (> 0) is the rate at which the herdsmen discount their private profits. The date is t = 0. Consider any one of the N herdsmen. Suppose all others play grim. Our herdsman now wonders whether to break the agreement or to keep to it. As all the others play grim, he knows they each will introduce X^*/N cattle into the CPR at t = 0. Let w be the maximum gain in one-period profit he could enjoy by breaking the agreement. (In seeking w, he would be bringing more than X^*/N cattle into the CPR at t = 0.) Obviously, w > 0, which is why he is wondering whether to break the agreement. But our herdsman knows that the others are playing grim. He knows therefore that if he were to break the agreement now, they will each bring $\underline{X}/N$ cattle into the CPR from t = 1 onward. He also knows that the moment they switch to $\underline{X}/N$ cattle, he himself will find it in his own best interest to switch to $\underline{X}/N$ cattle (because $\underline{X}/N$ is a Nash equilibrium of the repeated game that begins at t = 1). But if everyone switches permanently to $\underline{X}/N$ from t = 1, our herdsman's profit flow from then will be $\underline{\pi}/N$. The loss he will suffer from t = 1 onward will be $(\pi^* - \underline{\pi})/N$ per period; the present discounted value of which, when evaluated at t = 0, is $(\pi^* - \underline{\pi})/Nr$. It follows that our herdsman will not find it to his advantage to break the agreement if w $< (\pi^* - \underline{\pi})/Nr$; or, if

$$r < (\pi^* - \underline{\pi})/Nw. \tag{15}$$

It is equally easy to confirm that if r $> (\pi^* - \underline{\pi})/Nw$, cooperation by means of grim is impossible. Readers can confirm too that it isn't possible to enforce cooperation by means of a social norm—grim or otherwise—if r $> \pi^*/Nw$.[19]

Notice how the community's size enters the picture. Inequality (15) says that if N is large, cooperation is possible only if the herdsmen's discount rate is correspondingly low, other things being the same. But other things are not equal: each of π^*, $\underline{\pi}$, and w is a function of N. Nevertheless, it is possible to show that if N is not too small, $(\pi^* - \underline{\pi})/Nw$ is a declining function of N.

---

[19] To do so, use the argument deployed in Section 1.8 below.

Notice also the interesting way the productivity of the CPR enters the picture. Inequality (15) says that if $(\pi^* - \underline{\pi})/w$ is small, cooperation is possible only if the herdsmen's discount rate is correspondingly low, other things being the same. We return to these important facts in Section 1.7.2.

The exercise in comparative statics can be conducted in the reverse way too. Converting a CPR to multiple uses could be a way to raise $(\pi^* - \underline{\pi})/w$, in which case cooperation would be easier, not harder. Senaratne and Karunanayake (this volume) make the point in their study of communal aquaculture in a sample of village irrigation tanks in Sri Lanka.

However, even when cooperation is a possible equilibrium (for example, by means of the grim social norm), non-cooperation is an equilibrium too. If everyone was to believe that all others would break the agreement from the start, then everyone would break the agreement from the start. Non-cooperation would involve each herdsman selecting the strategy, 'choose π/N at all times'. Notice that a failure to cooperate could be due simply to a collection of unfortunate, self-confirming beliefs, nothing else. We usually reserve the term 'society' to denote a collective that has managed to equilibrate at a mutually beneficial outcome, whether by using reputation as an enabling capital asset (as in Section 1.6.2) or by relying on social norms (as in this subsection).

1.7. The dark side of CPRs

After reviewing the economic theory of CPRs (Section 1.5), we went on in Section 1.6 to ask a general question: in what contexts can parties be sanguine that the promises they have made to one another will be kept? Having studied the good news about communitarian institutions, I return to CPRs to report two pieces of bad news. The first concerns inequalities within communities in the access to CPR benefits (Section 1.7.1); and the second records deteriorations in the CPRs themselves (Section 1.7.2).[20]

1.7.1. Inequalities

The first piece of disturbing news about CPRs is a general finding, that entitlements to their products are frequently based on private holdings: richer households enjoy a greater proportion of the benefits. Beteille (1983), for example, drew on examples from India to show that access to CPRs is often

---

[20] In a recent letter Elinor Ostrom has remarked to me that all institutions would be expected to have a dark side; that markets and the state have dark sides as well. True enough, but economists have long studied the dark side of markets (witness the enormous literature on 'market failure') and political scientists that of the state. In contrast, CPRs have enjoyed a relatively comfortable ride in the humanities and social sciences.

restricted to the elite (for example, caste Hindus). Recently, Cavendish (2000) has reported that, in absolute terms, richer households in his sample in Zimbabwe took more from CPRs than poor households. In her work on coastal fisheries and forests products, McKean (1992) noted that benefits from CPRs are frequently captured by the elite. A. Agarwal and Narain (1996) have exposed the same phenomenon in their study of water-management practices in the Gangetic Plain. In their contributions to the present volume, Arun Khatri-Chhetri and Bhim Adhikari document the inequality of access in community-managed forests in Nepal.

That women are excluded has also been recorded (for example, in communal forestry: B. Agarwal 2001). Molians (1998) has noted the way gender inequalities are woven into local collective action in the contemporary setting. In a wider context, Ogilvie (2003) has reported striking differences between the life chances of women in seventeenth-century Germany (embedded in dense networks of social relationships) and the life chances of women in seventeenth-century England (not so embedded in dense networks): English women were better off.

It is an interesting theoretical fact that inequality in groups can emerge even in circumstances that are symmetric to begin with; meaning that you don't need to assume inequality among users of a CPR (for example, elites and non-elites) in order to explain inequality in access to it. To confirm this, we return to the model of herdsmen grazing their cattle in a CPR. The argument that was deployed in Section 1.6.5 can now be used to demonstrate how inequality in the distribution of benefits from the CPR can be sustained under cooperation.

In order to simplify the exposition, suppose $N = 2$ and assume that the stage game is played indefinitely. Denote time by t, where $t = 0, 1, 2, \ldots$ As before, I take it that the herdsmen discount their future profits at a low rate.

Consider an agreement at $t = 0$ that says that in each period, herdsman 1 is permitted to introduce up to aX^* cattle and herdsman 2 up to $(1-a)X^*$ cattle, where a is such that $1 > a > 1/2$ and $(1-a)\pi^* > \pi/2$. If the agreement were kept, the herdsmen's profits in each period would be $a\pi^*$ and $(1-a)\pi^*$, respectively. Notice that under the agreement herdsman 2 earns less than herdsman 1 ($a > 1/2$), but more than what he would earn if the CPR were unmanaged (because $(1-a)\pi^* > \underline{\pi}/2$). Thus, even though the agreement is to share the benefits of cooperation unequally, both parties gain from cooperation. In Figure 1.2, C denotes the pair of profits, $(a\pi^*, (1-a)\pi^*)$, the herdsmen earn in each period under the agreement. C lies to the north-east of A. The question arises as to how the agreement could be enforced.

Let us look at the grim strategy again, but now applied to the unequal division of benefits from the CPR. Let the strategy read: begin by abiding by the agreement and continue to abide by it so long as neither herdsmen has broken it; but introduce $\underline{X}/2$ cattle into the pasture forever following the first violation of the agreement by either herdsman.

To see how grim would work in the social environment of our two herdsmen, notice that $X/2$ is the equilibrium herd size for each party in the stage game (Section 1.5.1). The threat to switch permanently to $X/2$ following the first defection by either of the herdsman is therefore credible if the other herdsman plays grim. Since the pair discount their respective profits at a low rate, neither herdsman can do better than choose grim if the other chooses it.[21] We conclude that grim is an equilibrium of the repeated game, meaning that it can operate as a social norm.

It is important to distinguish a social norm from the state of affairs that is sustained by means of an application of that norm. In those circumstances where grim is an equilibrium strategy in repeated interactions, it can serve as a social norm. But the agreement grim sustains is not uniquely given. In fact we have confirmed that grim can support an infinity of agreements. It can support not only an agreement to share the benefits of cooperation equally (Section 1.6.5), but also a wide range of unequal divisions of that benefit (as just above). The theory I am exploring in this chapter doesn't offer an account of how an agreement is reached; what the theory offers is an account of the way agreements that have been reached can be implemented. Bargaining theory explores the former problem. That pretty much any sharing of the benefits of cooperation can be implemented in long-term relationships is an implication of the Folk Theorem in game theory.[22] For example, any point to the north-east of the origin and in the triangle OMN in Figure 1.2 can be implemented, provided each herdsman's discount rate is small enough (see Section 1.8).[23]

1.7.2. Deterioration of CPRs

The second piece of bad news regarding CPRs is that they have degraded in recent years in many parts of the poor world. Why should this happen now in those places where they had previously been managed in a sustainable

---

[21] What counts as a 'low' discount rate depends on the choice of a: the greater is the value of a (i.e. the greater is the proposed inequality), the lower is the rate the herdsmen must be assumed to use for discounting future profits if the proposed sharing rule is to be enforced by grim. Readers can confirm this by deploying the corresponding argument in Section 1.6.5.

[22] See Fudenberg and Maskin (1986).

[23] It may seem odd that one should pay attention to potential agreements over unequal sharing of benefits in a model that is patently symmetric across the parties. How, one may ask, could the parties have unequal bargaining powers in a world that has been modelled as one where the parties are equally placed to begin with? The answer is that the model reflects only one aspect of the herdsmen's lives; namely, their options as herdsmen. Presumably though, those lives are embedded in a wider set of lives, where the herdsmen are engaged in other projects and purposes and relationships. For example, it could be that the herdsmen are equally placed as herdsmen, but unequally placed as regards their status in society. Unequal bargaining power could be a reflection of that, unmodelled, inequality in status.

manner? Jodha (this volume) returns to some of the sites of his well-known earlier field study (Jodha 1986) to record the changes over this period.

One reason is the kind of deterioration in external circumstances that lowers both the private and collective profitability of cooperative behaviour. There are many ways in which circumstances can deteriorate. Increased uncertainty in property rights is a prime example. You and your community may think that you together own the forest your forefathers passed on to you, but if the community doesn't possess a deed to the forest, its rights to the asset are insecure. In a dysfunctional state of affairs, the government may confiscate the property. Political instability (in the extreme, civil war) is another source of uncertainty: a community's CPR could be taken away from it by force. An increase in such uncertainties as those above translates into an increase in the rate at which people discount the benefits from cooperation. In the context of the CPR we studied, it amounts to an increase in r. But from inequality (15) we know that if r increases sufficiently, cooperation ceases.

Political instability is also a direct cause of environmental degradation: civil disturbance all too frequently expresses itself through the destruction of physical capital. In the context of the grazing land of Section 1.6.5, this amounts to a lowered value of $(\pi^* - \pi)/w$, which, as we noted from inequality (15), makes cooperation more difficult to maintain, other things being the same. I have assumed perfect symmetry among the users of a CPR. This has made the analysis easily tractable.

More generally, when people are uncertain of their rights to a piece of property, they are reluctant to make the investments necessary to protect and improve it. If the security of a CPR is uncertain (owing to whichever of the above reasons), the risk-adjusted returns from collective investment are low. The influence would be expected to run the other way too, with growing resource scarcity contributing to political instability, as rival groups battle over resources. The feedback could be 'positive', exacerbating the problem for a time, reducing private returns on investment further. Groups fighting over spatially confined resources are a frequent occurrence today (Homer-Dixon 1999). Over time, the communitarian institutions themselves disintegrate.

The second reason is rapid population growth, which can trigger resource depletion if institutional practices are unable to adapt to the increased pressure on resources. The CPR then erodes owing to a weakening of cooperation. In Cote d'Ivoire, for example, growth in rural population has been accompanied by increased deforestation and reduced fallows. Biomass production has declined, as has agricultural productivity (Lopez 1998). Moreover, rapid population growth in itself can be the cause of battles over resources (Homer-Dixon 1999). In our analysis of the CPR, it was noted that cooperation is more difficult when community numbers (N) increase (inequality (15)). Since profits decline, whether in the managed CPR (π^*/N) or the unmanaged one

(π/N), the individual temptation to take over the land as private property increases. Economic theory is so much in line with empirical observations that those observations should be believable.

However, rapid population growth in the world's poorest regions in recent decades itself requires explanation. Increased economic insecurity, owing to deteriorating institutions, is one identifiable cause: children yield a higher return in such circumstances than other forms of capital assets (Bledsoe 1994; Guyer 1994; Heyser 1996). This means that even if rapid population growth is a proximate cause of environmental destruction, the underlying cause would be expected to lie elsewhere. When positive links are observed in the data between population growth, environmental degradation, and poverty, they should not be read to mean that one of them is the prior cause of the others. Over time, each could in turn be the cause of the others.[24]

The third reason for a deterioration of CPRs is that management practices at the local level are sometimes overturned by central fiat. (In his contribution to this volume, Mukhopadhyay probes the consequence of populist state measures on agrarian institutions in Goa (India) which could have led to inefficient outcomes.) In recent decades a number of states in the Sahel, for example, imposed rules that in effect destroyed communal management practices in the forests. Villages ceased to have the authority to enforce sanctions on those who violated locally instituted rules. There are now several enumerations of the ways in which state authority can damage local institutions and turn CPRs into open-access resources (Thomson, Feeny, and Oakerson 1986; Somanathan 1991; Baland and Platteau 1996).

And the fourth reason is that social norms of behaviour, founded as they are on reciprocity, can be fragile. Institutions based on reciprocity are especially fragile in the face of growing opportunities for private investment in substitute resources (Dasgupta 1993, 2001; Campbell *et al.* 2001). This is a case where an institution deteriorates even when there is no deterioration in external circumstances, nor population pressure. But when traditional systems of management collapse and aren't replaced by institutions that can act as substitutes, the use of CPRs becomes unrestrained or they are transformed for other uses. In the context of our model of the grazing land in Section 1.6.5, improved economic opportunities elsewhere amount to a reduction in the worth of CPR as a pasture; meaning that both π and π^* decline, relative to the profitability of other forms of activity on the CPR. Balasubramanian (this volume) has found that one of the oldest sources of irrigation—village tanks— have deteriorated over the years in a sample of villages in southern India, owing to a gradual decline in collective investment in their maintenance. The decline has come about because richer households have invested increasingly

---

[24] For the theory, see Dasgupta (1993, 2003); for a recent empirical study on South Africa that tests the theory, see Aggarwal, Netanyahu, and Romano (2001).

in private wells. Since poor households depend not only on tank water, but also on the fuel wood and fodder that grow round the tanks, the move to private wells on the part of richer households has accentuated the economic stress experienced by the poor.

History tells us that CPRs can be expected to decline in importance in tandem with economic development (North and Thomas 1973). Ensminger's (1990) study of the privatization of common grazing lands among the Orma in north-eastern Kenya established that the transformation took place with the consent of the elders of the tribe. She attributed this to cheaper transportation and widening markets, making private ownership of land more profitable. The elders were from the stronger families, and it did not go unnoted by Ensminger that privatization accentuated inequality within the tribe.

The point is not to lament the decline of CPRs; it is to identify those who are likely to get hurt by the transformation of economic regimes. That there are winners in the process of economic development is a truism. Much the harder task is to identify the likely losers and have policies in place that act as safety nets for them.

1.8. Exploitation in long-term relationships

As noted earlier, empirical studies have uncovered inequalities in the distribution of benefits from cooperation. Such inequalities as have been uncovered are however consistent with the possibility that all parties have benefited from cooperation. In the context of cooperation over the use of a CPR, we confirmed in Section 1.7.1 that inequalities in the distribution of the benefits from cooperation can emerge in long-term relationships even if the underlying stage game is symmetrical. However, in the example we studied there, all herdsmen were better off under the agreement than they would have been if the CPR had been unmanaged.

1.8.1. *A question*

Is it possible that someone is worse off in a long-term relationship than he (or she) would have been if the group of which he (or she) is a member hadn't embarked on the long-term relationship? In other words, can there be exploitation in long-term relationships? Empirical studies of communitarian institutions haven't investigated such a possibility.

One reason why they haven't may be that the question is empirically very hard to answer, involving as it does a counterfactual. I believe however that there is another reason. The examples that have motivated thoughts on communitarian institutions in general and CPRs in particular have mostly been conceptualized as the N-person Prisoners' Dilemma, where such a possibility as I am raising here can't arise. However, as we noted in Section 1.5.1, CPRs don't give rise to the Prisoners' Dilemma. I now show that someone could indeed be worse off when engaged in a long-term relationship with others than if the parties had not entered into a long-term relationship.

Lest readers think that one need only to point to bad marriages to provide an affirmative answer to the question posed in this section, we should remind ourselves that people don't enter marriages expecting them to be bad. Marriages go sour because circumstances change in particular ways or because the partners discover aspects of their character they had not recognized before or because they were forced into a bad marriage against their will or desire. The example below is not about such situations. It involves an indefinite repetition of an unchanging CPR game.

1.8.2. The model

Recall the idea of a player's min-max value in a game. It is the largest pay-off a player can guarantee for himself, meaning that he can guarantee it for himself even if the other parties are malevolent toward him. For completeness, I define min-max values in the Appendix 1.1.

The min-max value of a herdsman in the CPR game of Section 1.5.1 is zero. To confirm this, let X^{**} be the herd size at which the average product of cattle equals their price; that is,

$$F(X^{**})/X^{**} = p. \tag{16}$$

Equation (16) says that at X^{**} profits from cattle-grazing are zero. That the min-max value of a herdsman in the CPR game is zero now follows from two observations: (i) each herdsman can avoid earning negative profit by not grazing cattle in the CPR; and (ii) it is impossible for a herdsman to earn positive profit if some other herdsman introduces X^{**} cattle into the CPR. In Figure 1.2, which represents the case $N = 2$, the origin represents the pair of min-max values of the two herdsmen in the CPR game.

As in Section 1.7.1, I simplify the exposition by supposing the number of herdsmen to be two. Assume that the stage game is played indefinitely over time. Denote time by t, where t = 0, 1, 2,... As before, I take it that the herdsmen discount their future profits at a low rate.

Consider an agreement at t = 0 that says that, in each period, herdsman 1 is permitted to introduce up to aX^* cattle and herdsman 2 up to $(1 - a)X^*$ cattle, where a is now so chosen that $(F(\underline{X}) - p\underline{X})/2 > (1 - a)(F(X^*) - pX^*) > 0$. (The above inequality implies that $1 > a > 1/2$.) In our earlier notation, $\underline{\pi}/2 > (1-a)\pi^* > 0$. If the agreement were kept, the herdsmen's profits in each period would be $a\pi^*$ and $(1 - a)\pi^*$, respectively. Notice that under the agreement herdsman 2 not only earns less profit than herdsman 1, but earns less profit than he would if the CPR were unmanaged. Cooperation involves exploitation

45

here, in that herdsman 2 is worse off under cooperation than he would be if there was to be no cooperation over the use of the CPR. In Figure 1.2 the pair of profits $(a\pi^*, (1 - a)\pi^*)$ is depicted as D. Observe that D is to the south-east of A. So the question arises: how can such an exploitative agreement be enforced via a long-term relationship?

Notice first that grim cannot be deployed for the purpose in hand. (Why?) So some other social norm has to be devised. Earlier a conformist was defined as one who cooperated with, and only with, conformists. In our present example, consider the strategy that says that if in any period a cattleman's herd size were not to conform to the agreement, the other party would push him to his min-max value (by introducing X^{**} number of cattle) for a sufficiently large number of periods. If that other person were not to punish the errant, then he would be min-maxed for a suitable number of periods by the person who ought first to have been min-maxed; and so on. The trick now is to choose the periods of punishment to be sufficiently large, so that it would not be in the interest of either herdsman ever to be a non-conformist. When the numbers of periods (for first-order, second-order, and higher-order violations) are so chosen, the strategy can serve as a social norm, meaning that it is in the self-interest of each herdsmen to accept the norm if the other accepts it. Exploitation of one by the other is then enforced mutually.

1.9. Morals

The literature on CPRs has had a warm glow about it. That relationships matter for a person's well-being is no doubt a trite observation; but people writing on communitarian institutions have claimed more. In countries where the law doesn't function well, where officials regard the public sphere as their private domain, where impersonal markets are often absent, communitarian relationships are what keep people alive, if not well. This probably explains their attraction for many contemporary development economists. But we need to bear counterfactuals in mind. It could be that communitarian relationships prevent impersonal transactions from taking place. Moreover, it may be that personal obligations inherited from the past prevent public officials from acting dispassionately. What appears as corruption in the north could well be social obligation in the south.

In this chapter I have offered the economic theory underlying communitarian management of CPRs. The theory is sturdy enough to reveal both the good and bad sides of long-term relationships. Most importantly, the theory tells us what to look for when we study the ways in which CPRs are treated. More importantly, the theory tells us what to look for when we study the way people treat one another.

Appendix 1.1

Let X_1 and X_2 be the set of strategies available to individuals 1 and 2 respectively, in the stage game of a repeated game. Strategies themselves are denoted by x_1 and x_2 for the two individuals. The pay-off function for 1 is denoted by $\pi_1(x_1, x_2)$, for 2 it is denoted by $\pi_2(x_1, x_2)$. Recall that a pair of strategies $(\underline{x}_1, \underline{x}_2)$ is an equilibrium of the stage game if:

$$\pi_1(\underline{x}_1, \underline{x}_2) \geq \pi_1(x_1, \underline{x}_2) \qquad \text{for all } x_1 \in X_1$$
$$\text{and} \qquad \pi_2(\underline{x}_1, \underline{x}_2) \geq \pi_2(\underline{x}_1, x_2) \qquad \text{for all } x_2 \in X_2.$$

The min-max values for individuals 1 and 2, which we write as π_1^{**} and π_2^{**} respectively, are defined as:

$$\pi_1^{**} = [\min_{x_2 \in X_2} \quad \max_{x_1 \in X_1} \quad \pi_1(x_1, x_2)],$$
$$\pi_2^{**} = [\min_{x_1 \in X_1} \quad \max_{x_2 \in X_2} \quad \pi_2(x_1, x_2)].$$

In the CPR game of Section 1.5, $\pi_1^{**} = \pi_2^{**} = 0$.

References

Agarwal, A., and Narain, S. (1989). *Towards Green Villages: A Strategy for Environmentally Sound and Participatory Rural Development*. New Delhi, India: Centre for Science and Development.

—— —— (1996). *Dying Wisdom: Rise, Fall and Potential of India's Traditional Water Harvesting Systems*. New Delhi, India: Centre for Science and Development.

Agarwal, B. (2001). 'Participatory Exclusions, Community Forestry, and Gender: An Analysis for South Asia and a Conceptual Framework'. *World Development*, 29/10: 1623–48.

Aggarwal, R., Netanyahu, S., and Romano, C. (2001). 'Access to Natural Resources and the Fertility Decisions of Women: The Case of South Africa. *Environment and Development Economics*, 6/2: 209–36.

Baland, J.-M., and Platteau, J.-P. (1996). *Halting Degradation of Natural Resources: Is There a Role for Rural Communities?* Oxford: Clarendon Press.

Banfield, E. (1958). *The Moral Basis of a Backward Society*. Chicago, IL: Free Press.

Barbier, E. B. (2004). 'Natural Capital and Labor Allocation: Mangrove Dependent Households in Thailand', Mimeo. Laramie: University of Wyoming, Department of Economics and Finance.

Beteille, A. (ed.) (1983). *Equality and Inequality: Theory and Practice*. Delhi, India: Oxford University Press.

Bledsoe, C. (1994). ' "Children are Like Young Bamboo Trees": Potentiality and Reproduction in sub-Saharan Africa', in K. Lindahl-Kiessling and H. Landberg (eds.), *Population, Economic Development and the Environment*. Oxford: Oxford University Press.

Bromley, D.W. *et al.* (eds.) (1992). *Making the Commons Work: Theory, Practice and Policy*. San Francisco, CA: ICS Press.

Campbell, B., Manando, A., Nemarundwe, N., Sithole, B., De Jong, W., Luckert, M., and Matose, F. (2001). 'Challenges to Proponents of Common Property Resource Systems: Despairing Voices from the Social Forests of Zimbabwe'. *World Development*, 29/4: 589–600.

Cavendish, W. (2000). 'Empirical Regularities in the Poverty-Environment Relationships of Rural Households: Evidence from Zimbabwe'. *World Development*, 28/11: 1979–2003.

Chopra, K., Kadekodi, G. K., and Murty, M. N. (1989). *Participatory Development: People and Common Property Resources*. New Delhi, India: Sage Publications.

Coase, R. (1960). 'The Problem of Social Cost'. *Journal of Law and Economics*, 3/1: 1–44.

Dasgupta, P. (1982). *The Control of Resources*. Delhi, India: Oxford University Press and Cambridge, MA: Harvard University Press.

—— (1993). *An Inquiry into Well-Being and Destitution*. Oxford: Clarendon Press.

—— (2001). *Human Well-Being and the Natural Environment*. Oxford: Oxford University Press.

—— (2003). 'Population, Poverty, and the Natural Environment', in K.-G. Mäler and J. Vincent (eds.), *Handbook of Environmental Economics* (Vol. 1). Amsterdam, Netherlands: North Holland.

—— (2005). 'The Economics of Social Capital'. *The Economic Record*, 81/255 (Supplement): S2–S21.

—— Hammond, P., and Maskin, E. (1980). 'On Imperfect Information and Optimal Pollution Control'. *Review of Economic Studies*, 47/4: 857–60.

—— and Heal, G. (1979). *Economic Theory and Exhaustible Resources*. Cambridge: Cambridge University Press.

—— and Mäler, K.-G. (eds.) (2004). *The Economics of Non-Convex Ecosystems*. Dordrecht: Kluwer Academic Publishers.

Dreze, J., and Sen, A. (1990). *Hunger and Public Action*. Oxford: Clarendon Press.

—— —— (1995). *India: Economic Development and Social Opportunities*. Oxford: Oxford University Press.

Ensminger, J. (1990). 'Co-opting the Elders: The Political Economy of State Incorporation in Africa'. *American Anthropologist*, 92/3: 662–75.

Feeny, D., Berkes, F., McCay, B. J., and Acheson, J. M. (1990). 'The Tragedy of the Commons: Twenty-two Years Later'. *Human Ecology*, 18/1: 1–19.

Fehr, E., and Fischbacher, U. (2002). 'Why Social Preferences Matter: The Impact of Non-selfish Motives on Competition, Cooperation and Incentives'. *Economic Journal*, 112/478: C1–C33.

Fudenberg, D., and Maskin, E. (1986). 'The Folk Theorem in Repeated Games with Discounting or with Incomplete Information'. *Econometrica*, 54: 533–56.

Gordon, H. Scott (1954). 'The Economic Theory of Common-Property Resources'. *Journal of Political Economy*, 62/2: 124–42.

Guyer, J. L. (1994). 'Lineal Identities and Lateral Networks: The Logic of Polyandrous Motherhood', in C. Bledsoe and G. Pison (eds.), *Nupitality in Sub-Saharan Africa: Contemporary Anthropological and Demographic Perspectives*. Oxford: Clarendon Press.

Hardin, G. (1968). 'The Tragedy of the Commons'. *Science*, 162: 1243–8.

Heyser, N. (1996). *Gender, Population and Environment in the Context of Deforestation: A Malaysian Case Study.* Geneva, Switzerland: United Nations Research Institute for Social Development.

Hinde, R. A., and Groebel, J. (eds.) (1991). *Cooperation and Pro-social Behaviour.* Cambridge: Cambridge University Press.

Homer-Dixon, T. E. (1999). *Environment, Scarcity, and Violence.* Princeton, NJ: Princeton University Press.

Jodha, N. S. (1986). 'Common Property Resources and the Rural Poor'. *Economic and Political Weekly,* 21: 1169–81.

Lopez, R. (1998). 'The Tragedy of the Commons in Cote d'Ivoire Agriculture: Empirical Evidence and Implications for Evaluating Trade Policies'. *World Bank Economic Review,* 12/1: 105–32.

Marothia, D. K. (ed.) (2002). *Institutionalizing Common Pool Resources.* New Delhi, India: Concept Publishing Company.

McKean, M. (1992). 'Success on the Commons: A Comparative Examination of Institutions for Common Property Resource Management'. *Journal of Theoretical Politics,* 4/2: 256–68.

Meade, J. E. (1973). *The Theory of Externalities.* Geneva, Switzerland: Institute Universitaire de Hautes Etudes Internationales.

Molians, J. R. (1998). 'The Impact of Inequality, Gender, External Assistance and Social Capital on Local-Level Collective Action'. *World Development,* 26: 413–31.

National Research Council (1986). *Proceedings of a Conference on Common Property Resource Management.* Washington, DC: National Academy Press.

—— (2002). *The Drama of the Commons.* Washington, DC: National Academy Press.

Netting, R. (1976). 'What Alpine Peasants Have in Common: Observations on Communal Tenure in a Village'. *Human Ecology,* 4/2: 135–46.

—— (1985). *Hill Farmers of Nigeria: Cultural Ecology of the Kofyar of the Jos Plateau.* Seattle, WA: University of Washington Press.

North, D., and Thomas, R. P. (1973). *The Rise of the Western World: A New Economic History.* Cambridge: Cambridge University Press.

Ogilvie, S. (2003). *A Bitter Living: Women, Markets, and Social Capital in Early Modern Germany.* Oxford: Oxford University Press.

Ostrom, E. (1990). *Governing the Commons: The Evolution of Institutions for Collective Action.* Cambridge: Cambridge University Press.

Pattanaik, S. K., and Butry, D. T. (2004). 'Spatial Complementarity of Forests and Farms: Accounting for Ecosystem Services'. Discussion paper. Research Triangle Institute, Research Triangle Park, NC.

Przeworski, A. (1991). *Democracy and the Market.* Cambridge: Cambridge University.

Rabin, M. (1993). 'Incorporating Fairness into Game Theory and Economics'. *American Economic Review,* 83/5: 1281–302.

Ray, D. (1998). *Development Economics.* Princeton, NJ: Princeton University Press.

Runge, C. F. (1981). 'Common Property Externalities: Isolation, Assurance, and Resource Depletion in a Traditional Grazing Context'. *American Journal of Agricultural Economics,* 63: 595–606.

—— (1986). 'Common Property and Collective Action in Economic Development', in National Research Council, *Proceedings of a Conference on Common Property Resource Management.* Washington, DC: US National Academy of Science Press.

Sethi, R., and Somanathan, E. (1996). 'The Evolution of Social Norms in Common Property Resource Use'. *American Economic Review*, 86/3: 766–88.

Singh, K. (1994). *Managing Common Pool Resources: Principles and Case Studies*. Delhi, India: Oxford University Press.

Somanathan, E. (1991). 'Deforestation, Property Rights and Incentives in Central Himalaya'. *Economic and Political Weekly*, 26 (Special Issue: January 26): PE37–46.

Steffen, W., Sanderson, A., Tyson, P. D., Jäger, J., Matson, P. A., Moore III, B., Oldfield, F., Richardson, K., Schellnhuber, H. J., Turner II, B. L., and Wasson, R. J. (2004). *Global Change and the Earth System*. Berlin, Germany: Springer.

Stern, N. (1989). 'The Economics of Development: A Survey'. *Economic Journal*, 99/2: 597–685.

Stevenson, G. G. (1991). *Common Property Resources: A General Theory and Land Use Applications*. Cambridge: Cambridge University Press.

Thomson, J. T., Feeny, D. H., and Oakerson, R. J. (1986). 'Institutional Dynamics: The Evolution and Dissolution of Common Property Resource Management', in National Research Council, *Proceedings of a Conference on Common Property Resource Management*. Washington, DC: US National Academy of Science Press.

Wade, R. (1988). *Village Republics: Economic Conditions for Collective Action in South India*. Cambridge: Cambridge University Press.

Weitzman, M. L. (1974). 'Prices vs. Quantities'. *Review of Economic Studies*, 41/3: 477–91.

2

Some Places Again: A 'Restricted' Revisit to Dry Regions of India

Narpat S. Jodha

2.1. Introduction

Between the years 1982 and 1985, an intensive and detailed study of CPRs was carried out in the arid and semi-arid regions of India covering over eighty villages in twenty-one districts of seven states (Jodha 1986). The current chapter is a brief supplement (more like a footnote) to that earlier study. But it also differs from the earlier one in several respects, particularly in terms of the intensity of investigations and coverage (both spatial and CPR dimensions). Firstly, the reference periods of revisits fall between 1996 and 2003, covering thirty-six villages in sixteen districts of seven states. Secondly, while the earlier study focused exclusively on the CPRs, the latter studies CPRs as only *one* of the many aspects of natural-resource management. Thirdly, the second study covers some, but not all geographical areas covered under the first study, and therefore must be seen as a 'restricted revisit to CPRs in the dry regions of India'. Fourthly, the revisit is also 'restricted' in terms of this study's focus on selected units of whole CPRs, and interactions with user groups of the units, rather than total village communities. However, the latter study complements the earlier one by focusing on selected variables barely touched upon earlier, and emerging small group-based strategies to revive and harness degraded CPRs.

The second study, seen through CPR units and their development and usage systems, reveals hitherto unexplored dynamics to CPR transformation and their multiple drivers. These aspects include better protection of the CPR area (including reversal of encroachment); bio-physical rehabilitation of CPRs of different types; emergence of commercially driven, new usage systems revealing clear CPR-PPR complementarities; focus on scale factor; changing rich–poor alliances affecting CPRs; better links between natural-resource-centred

Table 2.1. Number of districts and villages covered by 'restricted revisit' to CPRs in dry regions of India

State with no. of districts	No. of Village	No. of CPR units covered[i]
Andhra Pradesh (2)	5	19
Gujarat (3)	6	22
Madhya Pradesh (3)	6	20
Maharashtra (2)	5	17
Rajasthan (3)	8	30
Tamil Nadu (2)	4	18
Uttar Pradesh (1)[ii]	2	8
Total:	36[iii]	134

[i] Major types of CPR units covered included forest, pasture, wasteland, watershed drainage, watering points, river-rivulet (banks, beds), common spaces for crop-threshing, weekly markets, etc.

[ii] Uttar Pradesh was not a part of the first study; Karnataka, a part of first study, was not covered by the second study.

[iii] Out of 36 villages in the second study 24 were also covered by the first study during (1982–5).

public programmes and CPR management; and evolution of new adaptation systems to the changing situation of CPRs. The positive aspects of such change are summarized in this chapter. We begin by briefly describing the methodology and coverage of the 'revisit', and study the differences as well as links between the past and present studies (summarized in Tables 2.1 and 2.2). The key findings of the two studies are indicated through quantitative details under Tables 2.3, 2.4, and 2.5. In addition to the tables, Boxes 2.1, 2.2, 2.3, and 2.4 report the more concrete actual cases reflecting changes in CPR management and usage.

The value of this exercise lies neither in the quantitative magnitude nor in the generalizability of findings. The study offers new insights into the management of CPRs. More comprehensive, systematic studies should be undertaken to better examine their generalizability. Moreover, in terms of method and evidence, this exercise could be linked to a wider paradigm of research focusing on issues of scales and compatibilities involving links and interactions between nature and society (Shah 1993; Young 1994; Agarwal 1994; Gibson, Ostrom, and Ahn 1998; McKean 1999; Jodha 2000; Sehgal 2001).

2.2. Methodology and approach: focus on CPR units

The 'revisit' is contextualized methodologically as well as in terms of other aspects such as scope and focus of the study, geographical coverage, and intensity of investigation, etc. Accordingly, the differences and similarities between the two studies are indicated in Table 2.2, which presents the comparable details.

Table 2.2. Differences and links between the two studies

Variables	Earlier Study (1982–1985)[v]	'Restricted Revisit' (1996–2003)[iv]
Area coverage	States (7), districts (21), villages (82); arid and semi-arid regions[v]	States (7), districts (16), villages (36) in arid and semi-arid regions[v]
Subject coverage	All aspects of CPR management with focus on changes and impacts	Selected aspect of CPRs (CPR units) and their differentiated management
Study scope and focus	Intensive study exclusively focused on CPRs, their status, changes, and contributions	CPR as subsidiary side-issue of studies/activities focused on natural resources, conducted for different agencies
Field investigation period/intensity	Continuous four years, investigations (including periodical surveys, case studies, physical monitoring, stakeholder participants, 1982–5)	Short-term, area-specific, CPR-unit-specific enquiries, one-shot information gathering in each village at different times during 1996 to 2003
Research mandate and support	Full-fledged CPR study (status and change as well as contributions of CPR), supported for four years by ICRISAT and the Ford Foundation	As side-issue of multiple research cum evaluation exercises supported by the World Bank (Environment Department), WWF (I), SPWD, student research, etc.

[iv] Jodha and Khare (1996); Jodha and Bhatia (1998); Jodha (2000, 2001).

[v] Jodha (1986, 1992).

This paper draws on data from other natural-resource management (NRM) studies conducted during the period 1996–2003. But the data does not represent a continuous set of years for all villages. However, the nature and thrust of investigations were not significantly affected by this.

The primary unit of observation was the CPR unit and a total of 134 CPR units across seven states were covered (see Table 2.1). The CPR was chosen as the focus of study because we had earlier found that villagers often differentiated in their care for CPRs by types as well as by units of the same CPR. The central focus of 'revisits' was not the comprehensive recording of contributions and changes in CPRs but the understanding of the indicators and processes of their revival seen through 'CPR-units'. Hence, the changes in different dimensions of CPRs and the factors behind them are analysed here. This goes beyond issues reported in detail in the earlier study, such as decline of CPR area/productivity, marginalization of traditional systems of CPR management, etc.

2.3. Two studies: similarities and differences

We discuss here some of the similarities and differences in the two studies in terms of their spatial coverage (summarized in Table 2.2). Table 2.2 provides information on the number of states, districts, villages, and CPR units covered by the present study. It is worthy of note that twenty-four villages covered by the present study were also part of the first study. Even though the second study covered only thirty-six villages as compared to eighty-two in the first, the agro-ecological zones indicated by soil and climatic conditions as well as major crops were similar in both the studies. The major types of CPR units covered included village forest pasture, wasteland, watershed drainage, watering points, river/rivulet bed/bank, etc.

The differences in research and policy implications relate to the area and subjects covered, the scope and focus of the studies, the intensity of field enquiries, etc. (see Table 2.2).

2.3.1. *Earlier study: findings and links with the present study*

It would be useful to begin by summarizing the important findings of the earlier study even though they have been widely disseminated through research publications, policy briefs, and training documents. It may also be added that a number of agencies such as the National Wasteland Development Programme, SPWD, Drought Prone Area Programme, and the Planning Commission (during the 9th Plan preparation) have used the findings of this study (Jodha 1995).

The earlier study found that the CPR area constituted 10–24 per cent of the total village area in the early 1980s (see Table 2.3).[1] It recorded a decline of 40–55 per cent in the CPR area in studied villages from 1952–4 to 1982–4. Physical degradation (seen through different indicators) affected 28–85 per cent of the villages. In 88–97 per cent of the villages, the traditional management systems (practices) had been discontinued by 1981–4. Despite their decline, CPRs continued to contribute 17–23 per cent of household incomes of the poor households. Table 2.3 also lists the causes and consequences of decline of CPRs.

2.3.2. *The second study*

Most CPR studies focus on the maintenance and the use of CPRs and their contribution to community livelihoods. This offers usually a generalized picture of CPRs and their dynamics. However, in practice, the same community manages different types of CPRs as well as different units of the same type of CPR differently. This disaggregated dimension to CPRs is seldom captured. The second study attempts to address this aspect.

---

[1] In the 24 villages covered by both studies the corresponding figure was 17–21 per cent.

Table 2.3. Summary of main findings of CPR study 1982–5[vi] and some changes noted during 'revisit'

Items	Details
1. CPRs as a part of total village area in 82 studied villages (1982–5)	10–24% (in different states); (the corresponding figures for the 24 villages covered by both studies are 17–21%)
2. Decline of CPR areas 1950–2 to 1982–4	40–55% in different states. (In the 24 villages covered by both the studies, the corresponding decline ranged between 44–50%; in nearly 75% of CPR units covered by 'revisit' there was no area decline since 1988)
3. Physical degradation of CPRs using different indicators, assessed/observed in the study villages[vii]	28–85% of the villages in different states; (in almost all CPR units covered by 'revisit' conservation measures were adapted)
4. CPR-generated income as part of total annual income of the poor households[viii]	17–23% in different states; (in 24 revisited villages for the CPR-unit users this figure exceeded 50%)
5. Traditional management regulations and user obligations discontinued in the study villages	88–97% of the villages in different states
6. Public policies directly encouraging area decline of CPRs[ix]	54–62% of cases in different villages in different states
7. Public programmes (e.g. infrastructure development, public buildings, etc.) causing decline of CPRs	14–20% of cases in different states; (in contrast during 'revisit' more positive impact of NR-focused public programmes on CPR units was observed. See Table 2.2)
8. CPR-unit-level differentiated management of CPRs	14–39% of CPR units in different villages (in 24 revisited villages the figure ranged between 22–36%)
9. Major causes and consequences of decline of CPRs seen in different villages	• Decline of risk-reducing CPR-PPR (private property resource) complementarities • Disintegration of community's collective stake in CPRs • Increased tendency to grab (privatize) CPR land rather than manage and use it as community asset • Apparent incompatibility between reduced area and productivity of CPRs and the rising demographic and economic pressures • Limited incentive for learning and mainstreaming success stories of CPR management • People trying to evolve their own adaptations to loss of CPRs, including focus on selective CPR units and search for alternative options.

[vi] *Source*: Jodha (1986 and 1992). Total number of states, districts, and villages covered by the study were 7, 21, and 82 respectively. For detailed description and linkages of different aspects, see Jodha (2001).

[vii] The indicators included number and type of physical products collected, per hectare number of trees and shrubs, number of watering points, extent of exclusive grazing space for lactating cattle, etc.

[viii] 'Poor' are defined to include agricultural labourers and small farm (<2 ha. dry land equivalent) households.

[ix] Included interventions such as land distribution and regularization of encroachments of CPRs; new institutions such as village-*panchayat* systems displacing the traditional arrangements for maintenance of CPRs; insensitivity of new technologies to CPR perspective.

In terms of methodology, as mentioned earlier, the revisit was linked to other research/evaluation exercises, where feedback was obtained through a small unstructured questionnaire on well-managed CPR units in the surveyed villages using the participatory/group discussion method. This was supplemented by physical verification visits to some CPR units on a random basis. The purpose was (*a*) to inventorize better managed CPR units, and (*b*) to have a descriptive account (in a broad case-history mode) of the factors and processes responsible for the same.

The important aspects of CPR units focused on during revisits included area protection and biophysical rehabilitation of CPR units; new usage systems of CPR units with focus on high-value products, CPR services, and scale factor; and institutional factors permitting and promoting new adaptations to emerging CPR situations (see Table 2.4). It should be pointed out that the factors and processes described under Table 2.4, column 3, were also observed

Table 2.4. Details on CPR units reflecting positive changes during 1996–2003

Variable (features of CPR units)	Extent (%) of CPR units[x]	Illustrative activities and processes
A. Area protection of CPRs		
• Privatized	9	• Government's land distribution programme, regularization of encroachment, etc.
• Transfer to public utilities	14	• School playground, *panchayat* building, weekly market yard, farming demonstration plots, etc. (New CPRs) in 20 out of 34 villages.
• Recovered from encroachment	3	• Through court case; collective pressure of community, NGO help.
• No decline in area	74	• CPR area protected against encroachment, even by user groups.
B. Biophysical rehabilitation Asset building through:		
• Fencing/trenching/ridging for high productivity	31	• Through relief funding, watershed development activities, self-help.
• Reforestation, reseeding, new plant introductions, etc.	39	• JFM and pasture development programmes; selected pockets under inedible shrubs/trees and fuel-producing facility used with regulation.
• Water-harvesting structures/facility	28	• Percolation tanks supported by NGOs and landowning farmers, exclusive facility of fodder, fuel, water collection for non-well owners.
• Introduction of high-value species/products	32	• Seed collection/multiplication and reseeding of CPR plots; herbs and other plants for sale and new material for handicrafts.
C. New usage systems		
• Focus on high-value products	42	• Local NTFPs, herbs, seeds; with initiatives of local schools, NGOs.
• Reduced emphasis on low cost biomass (fuel, fodder, etc.) as a primary use	60	• Reduced emphasis on open grazing, greater attention to product collection and stall-feeding; fuel-fodder trees and plants on private lands complementing CPR resources.

Table 2.4. (*Continued*)

Variable (features of CPR units)	Extent (%) of CPR units[x]	Illustrative activities and processes
• New approach to CPR services (through better conservation and product marketing)	24	• New crops in plots bordering better-managed CPR plots around percolation tanks; high-value CPR product marketing collectively (including by poor); direct links with urban traders.
• New CPR-PPR links	36	• Through percolation tanks; tree and fodder plantation on private lands, new species and their market links.
• Manageable scale factor (subgroup; selected CPR units)	90	• User groups and CPR-units-focused group action.
• Changing rich-poor alliances	28	• Activities with comparative advantage to poor linked to activities focused on by rich (e.g. basket-making from CPR products for transportation of farm products of rich farmers.
• Short-term visibility of gains	45	• Gains realized within one to two years in many cases (e.g. shrubs).
D. Institutional aspects		
• Contributing agencies/ processes/programmes helping better CPR-unit management	88	• NGOs for community mobilization for NRM, public programmes (e.g. changed focus of relief), selective JFM components, input from watershed project, etc.; role of ex-servicemen, school teachers; market for CPR products.
• Scale factor: user groups and CPR-unit focus	64	• Involvement of smaller, focused user groups rather than whole diverse community; focus on selected CPR units rather than total CPR area.
• New adaptation systems	46	• Focus on scarce resource, i.e., water, high-value NTFPs; linkage with other production/processing and marketing activities.
• Collective response to increased scarcity— vulnerability	33	• Revival of traditional regulations of (more productive) present-day biophysical options, more integrated user groups.
• Positive side-effect of political factionalism	15	• Local factions rather than securing privatization of CPRs for the group, now fight to prevent grabbing of CPR land by rival groups.

[x] The total number of CPR units from the different villages was 134. Since the same CPR unit could fall under different categories (especially under items B to D in Table 2.1), the total of studied units may exceed 100 per cent.

for many more CPR units in many more villages, but could not be probed in depth as it was done in the case of the 134 CPR units.[2]

---

[2] They included exercises/studies related to community forestry programme assessments/evaluation such as the following: preliminary enquiries into institutional aspects of NHES (Natural Habitat and Ecosystem Management); local-level initiatives on rehabilitation of CPRs in India supported by the Environment Department (the World Bank); WWF (I), (World Wide Fund for Nature (India), and SPWD (Society for Promotion of Wasteland Development)-supported NGO enquiries into NRM (natural-resource management) in selected areas; CGIAR (TAC) (Technical Advisory Committee of Consultative Group on International Agricultural Research)-supported work on marginal lands; and drought impact and mitigation assessments by different aid agencies with which I was associated. These activities were carried out during different years over the period 1996–2003.

2.4. The findings of the 'revisit' exercise

CPR-unit-based information collected during the 'revisit' is summarized in Table 2.4, which lists the positive features characterizing the identified (better-managed) CPR units and their contribution (per cent) to the total units probed. These CPR-unit features are grouped under four broad overlapping categories, namely, area protection, biophysical rehabilitation, new usage systems, and institutional aspects. These changes are illustrated by specific activities and processes undertaken by village communities or user groups (Table 2.4, col. 3).[3]

2.4.1. Emerging trends and indicative inferences

The 'CPR-revisit exercise' provided important insights for research methods of CPR dynamics and its policy implications, which are summarized below:

2.4.1.1. DISAGGREGATED APPROACH TO THE STUDY OF CPRs

CPRs are often studied as aggregated wholes (for example, total area of pasture, community forest and total diverse communities as primary stakeholders, etc.) at the village level. Such methods, despite their several advantages, fail to capture the people's differentiated approach to both the different types of CPRs and the different units of the same CPR in the village. Individual CPR-unit-based enquiries, as attempted in the present exercise, demonstrate this. Such studies enable an understanding of why and how people mismanage or better manage the CPRs.

With some variance, the merit of disaggregation of communities, as primary user groups and managers of CPRs, is also clear from the study. While the community as a whole may have almost lost the collective stake in CPRs, the disaggregated user groups of specific CPRs/units exhibit greater commitment to their health and management. The above-mentioned phenomenon is partly reflected through gaps in the aggregated CPR situation and disaggregated CPR-unit-based situation in different villages. In many villages of Rajasthan, Gujarat, and Maharashtra (and others as well), where the grants and relief were received for village pasture as a whole, there was no trace of any activity or improvement (resource upgrading, etc.), while in selected CPR units (reseeded CPR plots often managed by small user groups), one could see rich forage for collection (not open grazing). The same applies to selected parts of dry river beds and river banks managed and used better in villages in Madhya Pradesh, Maharashtra, Tamil Nadu, and Uttar Pradesh (see Box 2.1).

---

[3] For more evidence on these and related issues in different countries, see Shyamsundar, Khan, and Mishra in this volume.

Box 2.1 CPR-UNIT-FOCUSED APPROACH TO CPR MANAGEMENT: CASE OF A RIVULET IN RAISEN DISTRICT (MADHYA PRADESH)

In the villages of Raisen district, a small rivulet feeding some wayside tanks was used mainly as a source of drinking water for animals and casual fishing by tribals and poor households when I visited this area during 1981–2. This has been developed as a livelihood option by different groups of the community. Fishing is well organized and used as profitable enterprise with marketing links; parts of rivulet banks are better shaped and developed as locations for seasonal vegetable and fruit production (for example, melons); more intensively managed parts of the rivulet banks and dry tank-beds are used for off-season production of crop seeds. Impacts and gains from conservation efforts on neighbouring downstream wells (through water percolation as a sort of a bonus) is harnessed by the well owners. The community as a whole could not show any common interest and act in order to rehabilitate and harness the diverse potential of this natural asset of the village. However, once its value was perceived in terms of different units or segments of the CPRs, the situation changed for the better. Groups exhibited a greater stake in specific segments of CPR rather than in its aggregate form.

(*Source*: N. S. Jodha, field notes during visits, 1996.)

The key lesson here is the need for facilitating user-group-based management of CPRs and CPR-unit-based research on the status and dynamics of CPRs in order to complement the conventional aggregate-focused work. This will help us learn, when it comes to CPR management, what works and why. Some of the emerging developments as revealed by such a disaggregative approach followed under the 'revisit' study are discussed below (see Tables 2.4 and 2.5).

2.4.1.2. EMPHASIS ON ECONOMIC CONCERNS AND SHIFTING PRIORITIES FOR CPR PRODUCTS AND USAGES

Economic considerations were important in people's approach to CPRs even under the traditional systems. But the community's collective stake in CPRs was enforced through several social/cultural norms. With modern processes driven by state interventions and market forces, the community's collective stake in CPRs has disintegrated (as several essays in this volume show). In some cases, however, the community stake seems to be re-emerging but in the form of specific user-groups' stakes as revealed by the formation of committed user groups concerned with individual CPRs or rather their units. This could be due to a new sense and manifestation of economic considerations. A few examples are presented below (see Boxes 2.1, 2.2, 2.3, and 2.4):

Table 2.5. Policy-induced factors and processes facilitating improved (CPR-unit-based) management of CPRs

Policies/Programmes	Indicators of role and impacts
(a) Natural Resource Rehabilitation, Development Programmes	JFM and Watershed Development, etc., offered technical input (training, planting material, advice, etc.) selectively used by CPR user groups as per needs and suitability; complemented the people's focus on NTFPs, and high-value CPR products, their collection/processing; facilitated options such as stall-feeding, product-harnessing for market rather than only self-provisioning; helped in productivity growth and regulated use of CPR units.
(b) Drought Relief Policies (long- and short-term focused changes)	Changes in relief policies and programmes focusing on long-term natural-resource capacity building through water-harvesting structures, terracing, trenching, and other conservation measures rather than concentrating on short-term relief supplies and support. These efforts complemented user-group efforts to redevelop CPRs. The short-term relief measures such as cattle camps, fodder banks/depots, etc., substituted some of the non-viable contributions (grazing and fodder collection) of CPRs and prevented their further depletion.
(c) Infrastructural developments	Though not specifically directed to CPRs, the improved accessibility through roads, regular bus facilities, better links to marketplaces, rural electrification, etc., helped in focusing on high-value CPR products and their marketing. A slow shift from bulky biomass for self-provisioning to high-value products; the changes favouring new plants and products that made CPRs economically viable were facilitated by better access.
(d) Thrusts and contributions of agricultural and NR-focused R & D systems	New products including perennial species (for reseeding pastures, reforestation and dry-land horticulture) as well as input for seasonal inland fisheries and their promotion as components of natural-resource regeneration programme created a range of high-value new options usable by CPR-user groups.
(e) Institutional reforms and participatory programmes	The policies and programmes ranging from decentralization through greater autonomy for *panchayats* to enhanced scope and opportunities for NGOs and other social groups on the one hand and gradual growth of political maturity and awareness of rural communities on the other are slowly affecting people's attitudes and the strategies of local factions *vis-à-vis* CPR.
(f) Changing range and quality of adaptation options	Faced with the decline of CPRs, ineffectiveness and non-viability of efforts to harness them, along with the decline of traditional collective concerns for village commons, the people's search for alternative approaches and substitutes for CPR contributions is influenced by the above (i.e. (a–e)) factors. The search led to: (a) Focus on selected CPR units and managing them effectively. (b) Focus on committed user groups (new forms of social capital) rather than waiting for a whole community to engage in the renewed CPR management efforts facilitated by NGOs and other agencies. (c) De-emphasis on largely biomass-based contributions of CPRs and increased attention to high-value options with value-adding activities. (d) The policy-programme changes listed above facilitated search for and use of alternative options to develop and harness CPRs. (e) Sustainability of new adaptation strategies is very much linked to replication of the emerging success stories (including inputs from public policies and programmes) in wider areas and integration of CPRs with new opportunities involving strong user groups and equitable market links.

Box 2.2 PROTECTING, PROMOTING, AND HARNESSING PLANT
BIODIVERSITY IN BANASKANTHA DISTRICT (GUJARAT)

Despite recurrent droughts (during the 1980s) in the district and physical and biological depletion of village commons, the villagers discovered a few spots in common lands that showed survival of shrubs and trees as well as visible sprouting of perennial grasses during post-winter season. A group of villagers (not the whole community) decided to understand and harness the situation. On three CPR units (plots), the indigenous high-value shrubs/grasses and other species were protected and planted. Some desert fruits (for example, *ber*) were also introduced. In some cases, plants were initially watered by bringing water by bullock-cart tankers. The promoters of the initiative immensely benefited from advice and input from watershed programme officials and agricultural researchers. The enterprise focusing on specific CPR units rather than the whole area of CPR lands finally paid off in economic terms. Though at times attacks by stray cattle during the drought/scarcity period damaged their vegetation, loose fencing as well as some trenching and bunding to conserve moisture have been undertaken as necessary capital investment. This had a positive demonstration effect on people from the neighbouring villages who frequently visit this site.

(*Source*: N. S. Jodha, field notes during visits, as part of project activities of the World Bank, WWF (I), SPWD 1994–5.)

- Focus on high-value CPR products, such as NTFPs, medicinal herbs, mushrooms, a variety of lost seeds, and other marketable products with and without processing. These receive priority over low-value, bulky biomass (fodder, fuel, etc.) as part of a subsistence-oriented approach to CPR usage, even in the case of the rural poor. Off-season vegetables or fruits such as melons in place of green fodder in water-harvesting structures and dry river beds/banks in the villages of Andhra, Maharashtra, Madhya Pradesh (MP), Uttar Pradesh (UP), and Gujarat illustrate this new trend.

CPR product plus processing-based direct links to town trader to ensure better prices and share in the value-adding chain.

- Emphasis on new species/plants with marketable products introduced into CPR land (for example, *ber* (*Ziziphus numilaria*) bush, wild mushroom species and fibre items; melons with varying durability, maturity periods, etc.) as seen in the villages of Madhya Pradesh, Andhra Pradesh, Rajasthan, and Uttar Pradesh.
- New gainful alliances between the rich and the poor (for example, basket-making from CPR creepers and plants to market rich farmers' products such as vegetables and fruits; collection, proper bundling, and sale of fuel to urban areas through urban traders, etc.); new variable contract systems for seasonal product supplies with visiting traders helped by NGOs; and

collective sale of high-value CPR products. Mishra (this volume) documents a case in Orissa of a federating structure that has achieved this.

- Indirect and direct gains from percolation tanks to the poor, especially the non-well owners, such as raising short-maturity fish during the season and post-rainy-season vegetables and green fodder for stall-feeding and sale as seen in MP, UP, Andhra, Maharashtra, and Gujarat areas.

To sum up, a mix of the above changes were seen in the villages with relatively better rainfall or groundwater in all the states covered. The factors favouring these changes included a new road or initiation of a regular bus service; NGO encouragement; improved technology and seed provided by (contractor) traders and government agencies including R & D (Research and Development) institutions; and the demonstration effect of isolated success stories in neighbouring areas.

2.4.1.3. NATURAL ASSET BUILDING: IMPACTS OF PUBLIC PROGRAMMES

Governed by the need for higher productivity gains in a short period, selected components of resource-rehabilitating public programmes such as JFM (Joint Forest Management), watershed development projects, drought management, and wasteland revival programmes were used in the CPR units of many surveyed villages. A few examples are cited below (also see Boxes 2.1, 2.2, 2.3, and 2.4).

Box 2.3 DIVERSIFIED, CPR-UNIT-BASED APPROACH TO WATERSHED DEVELOPMENT IN JHANSI DISTRICT (UP)

In Tejpura Watershed area of Jhansi district (Uttar Pradesh), guided and promoted by All India Grassland Research Institute, the collective efforts on water-harvesting, percolation facilities and protection/conservation of vast landscape and water points led to the re-emergence of plant species never seen during the last three decades; availability of water in wells for nine to twelve months in place of one to four months as in the past has reinforced group action and led to economic transformation of the area. This overall ecological revival and economic transformation have also promoted specific small group initiatives focused on specific units of CPRs and specific products of CPRs, particularly production of high-value crops; for example, vegetables, flowers; regulated gathering of herbs and seasonal collection of other biomass items and their complementary role in promoting investment and marketing. Regular bus service, links with town-based traders and technological advice from watershed personnel (some of whom happened to be from the same lower economic and social groups, for example, scheduled castes/tribes) played an important role.

(*Source*: N. S. Jodha's 'back to office Report after project visits'; Internal Document of Social Policy and Resettlement Division, Environment Programme, World Bank, Washington, DC, 1995.)

- Reseeding of CPR units by improved grass varieties using subsidy support and technical training by public agencies and NGOs as in Rajasthan, UP, Gujarat, and MP villages. In selected cases, productivity impacts within two to four years were visible, for example, in reseeded pastures and well-protected forest patches, especially due to the faster growth of shrubs, water-harvesting structures, etc.

- Provision of exclusive areas (wasteland–CPR units) for fuel wood production (using inedible shrubs and trees like *Prosipis julliflora*) for market and local use were also seen in Rajasthan, Maharashtra, and Andhra Pradesh.

- Water-harvesting structures, percolation tanks, rural electrification, and other infrastructural facilities leading to transformation of the CPR landscape with clear orientation towards economic gains is another example seen in most of the areas.

- Reorientation of drought-relief programmes focusing on long-term remedies such as building natural assets for higher productivity, readily usable infrastructure such as market-linked roads, rehabilitation of pastures, etc., also helped in the changing approach to CPRs as seen in different drought-prone areas.

These changes, largely induced by people's concerns about emerging scarcities and search for alternatives on the one hand, and relatively proactive (result-focused) efforts of technical people from government agencies, NGOs, ex-service men, etc., on the other, were observed in all the areas covered by 'revisits'. Faced with these changes, people have adapted the external inputs to suit their own needs and capacities.

Box 2.4 CHANGING CPR SITUATION AND PROCESS OF COMMUNITY ADAPTATIONS THROUGH FOCUS ON DISAGGREGATED CPR UNIT IN NAGAUR DISTRICTS (RAJASTHAN)

CPR decline in the covered villages is reflected through area decline (from 50 per cent of the village territories during early 1950s to about 20 per cent during the late 1990s) as well as depletion of vegetative resources. The story of consequent loss of options and adaptations thereto is as follows:

  (a) The first component of vegetative loss, once CPRs became a casualty (as a side-effect) of land reforms in the early 1950s, was the disappearance of (hardy and slow to grow) desert trees and shrubs from common lands, which were earlier protected through the authority of village elders and feudal landlords (*Jagirdars*) in some villages. This led to the end of camel-raising, which needed top feeds from trees. Some camel-raisers permanently migrated to the better vegetated parts of south Rajasthan.

  (b) Next, in due course, because of the reduced grazing space and feeding material in the village commons (pastures), on the one hand, and because of the closure of seasonal migration routes and destinations in Madhya Pradesh (again

Box 2.4 (*Continued*)

due to large-scale privatization of CPRs there), where cattle from Rajasthan used to migrate, on the other, the proportion of cattle in livestock holdings declined (for example, from average ten cattle per family in the 1950s to three in the 1980s). In some cases, as a side-effect, stall-feeding and a system of cut-and-carry fodder from selected high-productivity and better-protected CPR units picked up. The milk-marketing facility, through 'operation flood' (that is, dairy development programme), also helped in the process.

(c) In terms of the changing composition of animal holdings, the final consequence of depletion of CPRs was the rising prominence of sheep and goat, which could not only sustain better on depleted pastures than cattle but could migrate more easily (without significantly damaging crops en route and at destinations). However, despite these comparative advantages, sustaining sheep and goat in the face of shrinking CPRs became increasingly difficult. This was more so during the post-monsoon periods. In such a scenario, the people responded through the unusual practice of transporting sheep and goats by trucks to the green revolution areas in Punjab and Haryana during the post-*rabi* (wheat crop) season. The sheep-herders were paid by the farmers for penning their animals in post-wheat fallow fields since the manure provided the soil with organic matter. This is a unique example of inter-agro-ecosystem complementarities.

(d) Besides the above responses of adapting the animal economy to shrinking CPRs, the communities also responded to the falling fuel-wood supplies caused by reduced material from CPRs. Accordingly the selected CPR units (especially nearer to village settlements) were used as space for the natural spread of *juliflora* trees. The latter is not consumed by animals (even by goat) and rapidly propagates on its own. However, it does not permit any other plant growth under or around itself. For this reason, in the past people tried to prevent its spread. This is a rather inferior option, yet accepted by communities in limited CPR plots. This trend has been observed in the villages of Sholapur in Maharashtra and Anantpur and Mahabubnagar in Andhra Pradesh.

(e) Besides focusing on some CPR plots as fuel-wood sources, a few CPR plots nearer to the watering points are developed as space for horticulture and seed production. While it was mainly the poorer households of the community that initiated such activity, others 'participated' by not objecting to such efforts.

(*Source*: N. S. Jodha, field work and periodical visits for different projects 1982 to 1994.)

2.4.1.4. CHANGE AGENTS: MOBILIZING PEOPLE AND PROMOTING BETTER MANAGEMENT OF CPRs

Conventional and new agents played a significant role in rehabilitating CPRs. They included:

- Technical personnel of public programmes such as JFM, watershed projects, etc., facilitating change through demonstrations, providing training in new technological components plus subsidies. In most of the districts and villages under study, the increased number of officials with higher technical skills and greater decision-making freedom has changed programme approaches and, in turn, people's responses to them at the grass-roots levels.

- Ex-service men with experience in afforestation activities in the hills and major canal areas (for example, the Indira Gandhi Canal), as well as in water-harvesting and product promotion in military farms have helped the change in some areas, especially in Rajasthan, Maharashtra, UP, and Madhya Pradesh.

- Enlightened village leaders, especially in villages where there was a good equation between formal *panchayats* and informal user groups.

2.4.1.5. PRESSURE REDUCTION APPROACHES/METHODS

Indifference to CPRs as unproductive resources due to their depletion had been the general trend in the dry regions of India (Jodha 1992). The present study found that communities have evolved new approaches to counter the decline in CPRs. They included:

- Reduction as well as structural changes in livestock-holding (for example, a reduced number of cattle and an increase of small ruminants) particularly in Rajasthan and Andhra Pradesh. A rising emphasis on stall-feeding was also observed.

- Increasing supplies for own use and marketing by planting fodder and fuel species on private lands, and adopting new agroforestry systems, especially in Andhra Pradesh, Madhya Pradesh, and the Gujarat villages.

- Seasonal migration of goat/sheep in trucks to green revolution areas (for example, from Rajasthan to Punjab) during the non-crop season with little requirement of CPRs (pasture) en route as well as at the destination locations. Herders in such situations not only have off-season crop lands as rich pastures for their animals but in addition get paid by the farmers for their contribution to organic matter (manuring through penning) for their next crops. This is an important example of an inter-agro-ecosystem link worth promoting.

- Dependence on alternative sources, for example, fodder depots and relief supplies, which seem to be managed better at present than in the past due to interstate movement of supplies, and the involvement of NGOs, the private sector, and the reoriented relief departments. The alternative sources of supplies reduced the crucial dependence on CPRs. Incidentally, as mentioned earlier, drought-relief programmes are increasingly focusing on long-term solutions by promoting asset-building such as water-harvesting structures, fencing/trenching and reseeding of common pastures, forests, etc., which also helped the rehabilitation of CPR units.

2.4.1.6. NEW INSTITUTIONAL ARRANGEMENTS/PRESSURES

The above-mentioned emerging changes were also related to social and institutional aspects. They could be summed up in the following way:

- User groups have been more effective than when whole villages have been involved.
- Links with government agencies at technical programme levels (for example, JFM) rather than at administrative levels, helped in developing better and more functional links between CPR users and government agencies.
- Changes in local factional politics, reflected through local factions fighting to protect CPRs from rivals rather than attempting to grab CPR lands for one's own faction as in the past, was another change. This was partly the result of decentralization and *panchayat* system reform efforts as well as the growth of plural politics at village level.
- Rising awareness of 'green issues' helped by both NGOs and spread by means of mass communication media (radio, TV, etc.) at village level.

Several technological, social, and political factors at grass-roots level have thus reinforced each other in transforming the CPR management system.

2.4.1.7. CONTRIBUTIONS OF FACILITATIVE POLICIES AND PROGRAMMES

There are few clear-cut public policies directly dealing with CPRs. Indeed, some that exist appear detrimental to the survival of CPRs such as (i) the ones contributing to reduction of CPR area by privatization of CPR area through land-distribution programmes, and (ii) the effort to develop/protect natural resources without the CPR perspective (Jodha 1992).

However, there are a few programmes which are relevant for CPR management. We recount below some of the positive impacts in the management of CPR units which could be attributed to changes in technological, institutional, and other policy processes during the recent years. In order to show this, the respective factors/processes are regrouped under different categories in Table 2.5.

2.5. Key lessons and policy implications

Based on the above discussion, the key lessons and policy inferences offered by the 'revisit' exercise could be stated as follows:

- There is a strong need for a disaggregated approach to investigations, through focus on CPR units, in order to complement the conventional aggregated approach where commons including different types of CPRs are seen as aggregated resources. The same argument can be applied to other natural resources and community-centred development interventions such as JFM, wasteland development, watershed development, and various decentralization and participation-focused initiatives (see Shyamsundar—this volume), etc., where the perceived aggregations disregard the issues of diversity and scales, which lead to their ineffectiveness and mixed success in most cases.

- In light of increased socio-economic differentiation in the communities and the rapid disintegration of the community's collective stake in village commons, identification or organization of user groups (often confined to specific CPR units) can better help in mobilizing people for the management of CPRs. It could be hypothesized that the user-group-focused approach through facilitating multiplication of such groups may in the future lead to federating arrangements of user groups and thereby in some way revive the collective stakes of the total village community in CPRs. Examples for such possibilities do exist in South Asia as recorded by Mishra (this volume) on the evolution of micro-level initiatives in forest management gradually leading to cooperative action on a larger scale. This offers leads and insights for user groups in other areas.

- Regarding inducements and motivations for effective management (that is, protection, conservation, and development as well as regulated use) of CPRs, the emergent scenario reveals that high-value products (their yield, markets, etc.) seem to get higher priority over bulky biomass for self-provisioning purposes. It seems that CPR-PPR complementarities are increasingly driven by money-centred rather than biomass-centred options.

Accordingly, the strategies and incentive systems for rehabilitation and promotion of CPRs will need to be more sensitive to emerging commercial dimensions rather than largely focusing on subsistence orientation. However, there is always the risk that, in the process, market agencies may take over the CPRs (through contract systems involving user groups with little decision-making power, etc.). Possible exclusion of the poor and disadvantaged sections from 'user groups' is another risk. Adhikari and Arun (both this volume) discuss this in the context of community forestry in Nepal.

- The key components for an effective and locally acceptable CPR development strategy should include: (i) operational complementarities between different technical programmes involving biophysical elements of CPRs, (ii) involvement of technical people and programmes in natural-resource-building agencies, (iii) encouragement of changes in goals and approaches of local political factions (*vis-à-vis* their approaches to CPRs), and (iv) building on people's understanding of and efforts to find alternatives to the declining CPR situation, using new high-productivity, high-value options.

- Collaboration for joint initiatives by government agencies (especially the technology-oriented ones), NGOs, hitherto unrecognized new change agents/mobilizers such as ex-army personnel and school teachers, promoters of scattered success stories of CPRs, along with local community experts, are some of the most crucial factors that can transform the users' views of and approaches to CPR management and usage.

References

Agarwal, A. (1994). 'Small is beautiful, but is larger better? Group size and collective action in forest management in Indian Himalayas'. Paper presented at Oxford-FAO Forestry Working Group Meetings on Common Property, Oxford Forestry Institute.

Gibson, C., Ostrom, E., and Ahn, T. K. (1998). *Scaling Issues in the Social Sciences.* IHDP Working Paper No. 1. Bonn, Germany: International Human Dimension Programme on Global Environmental Change.

Jodha, N. S. (1986). 'Common Property Resources and the Rural Poor in Dry Regions of India'. *Economic and Political Weekly*, 21/26: 1169–81.

—— (1992). *Rural Common Property Resources: A Missing Dimension of Development Strategies.* World Bank Discussion Paper No. 169, Washington, DC: World Bank.

—— (1995). 'Studying Common Property Resources: Biography of a Research Project'. *Economic and Political Weekly,* 30/11: 556–9.

—— (2000). 'Wastelands Management in India: Myths, Motives and Mechanisms'. *Economic and Political Weekly*, 35/6: 4396–9.

—— (2001). *Life on the Edge: Sustaining Agriculture and Community Resources in Fragile Environments.* Delhi, India: Oxford University Press.

—— and Bhatia, A. (1998). 'Community Management of Commons: Re-empowerment Process and the Gaps'. Paper presented at 7th IASCP Biennial Conference,Vancouver, Canada, June.

—— and Khare, A. (1996). 'Local-level Initiatives on Rehabilitation of CPRs in India: Inferences from Case Studies'. Paper for internal discussion, for limited circulation, Environment Department, World Bank, Washington, DC, July.

McKean, M. A. (1999). 'Designing New Common Property Regimes for New Landscape Futures'. Paper presented at the International Symposium on Landscape Futures, University of New England, Armidale, Australia, September.

Sehgal, S. (2001). 'Joint Forest Management: A Decade and Beyond'. Paper presented at the Workshop on the Policy Implications of Knowledge with respect to Common Pool Resources in India, Institute of Economic Growth, Delhi, India, September.

Shah, P. (1993). 'Participatory Watershed Management Programme in India: Reversing our Roles and Revising our Theories', in *Rural People's Knowledge, Agricultural Research and Extension Practice*, IIED Research Series, 1/3. London: International Institute for Environment and Development, 38–67.

Young, O. R. (1995). 'The Problem of Scale in Human-Environmental Relationship', in R. Keohane and E. Ostrom (eds.), *Local Commons and Global Interdependence: Heterogeneity and Cooperation in Two Domains*. London Sage Publications, 27–45.

3

Decentralization, Devolution, and Collective Action—A Review of International Experience[1]

Priya Shyamsundar

3.1. Introduction

In the natural resources area, profound changes are occurring in terms of who has access to and control over resources. Over the last decade, the rights of local communities over natural resources have been strengthened either through power-sharing agreements with the state, increased legal access to natural resources, or decentralization within national agencies (World Resources Institute 2005). Understanding the impacts of these institutional changes is important both for governments and other stakeholders.

A number of policies are often clubbed together under the term 'decentralization of natural resource management.' While many of these policies seek to reduce the extent of public-sector management of natural resources, there are important differences among them (see Box 3.1). At one extreme is privatization, which is generally the least practised policy change. At the other end of the spectrum is deconcentration, which is simply a form of administrative decentralization (Knox and Meinzen-Dick 2000). In this paper, our focus is on devolution of resource rights, a process wherein state control over the use of natural resources is gradually and increasingly shared with local communities. Such policy processes are generally accompanied by the creation or strengthening of a subset of communitarian institutions. Our aim is to examine the implications of such institutional changes on natural

[1] This paper builds on analyses undertaken at the World Bank with support from the Trust Fund for Environmentally and Socially Sustainable Development (see Shyamsundar, Araral, and Weeraratne 2005). The results and analyses in this paper cannot be attributed to the World Bank or the donors who supported this work.

Box 3.1 DEVOLUTION AND DECENTRALIZATION—SOME DEFINITIONS

Decentralization has been used to characterize devolution of power within state bureaucracies, privatization, and increased political power to local authorities. Knox and Meinzen-Dick (2000) discuss decentralization as part of a group of policies that are closely related to each other. These different policies include:

- Administrative deconcentration—the transfer of decision-making authority to lower-level units of government.
- Decentralization—the transfer of administrative and financial responsibility to lower levels of government.
- Privatization—the transfer of public-sector functions to the private sector or private individuals.
- Devolution—the transfer of rights and responsibilities to user groups at the local level.

The focus of this study is devolution, which can happen with or without bureaucratic or political decentralization.

---

resources and the people who depend on these resources. In the rest of the paper, we treat the phrases 'devolution of resource rights to communities' and 'community-based natural resource management' (CBNRM) interchangeably.

CBNRM, whether it is endogenous or policy-driven, is often a response to a felt need for managing a resource.[2] Devolutionary policies assume that communities are willing to manage local resources either because of their utilitarian and/or intrinsic benefits or because communities are promised a reward for taking on management tasks. There is a rich theoretical and empirical literature on the conditions underlying collective action to manage natural resources (Ostrom 1990; Baland and Platteau 1996; Agrawal 2001; Dasgupta, this volume). Many of these conditions contribute to the success (or failure) of devolutionary policies. In general, as Dasgupta (this volume) discusses, there is no escaping the economic analytics underlying community decisions—whether devolutionary policies meet their goals or not depends on the returns from local-resource management to communities and the communities' own supply response to the changes and incentives presented by devolutionary policies.

In this chapter, we seek to understand the scope and scale of devolution in natural resource management in three different resource areas—wildlife management, forestry, and irrigation.[3] We ask how and in what

---

[2] There is considerable evidence worldwide of CBNRM that is endogenous, evolving locally with little support through state or private non-profit actors.

[3] In South Asia, wildlife and forestry issues tend to be clubbed together in terms of natural resource policy and practice. We treat them separately because of the large number of examples drawn from wildlife management in Africa, where it raises a separate set of challenges from forestry.

way decentralization has contributed to improved livelihoods, better resource management, and to government revenues. What factors contribute to success? What are some emerging challenges? We seek to address these issues in the context of many recent policy interventions to devolve natural resource management to local communities and to identify synergies between poverty reduction goals and resource management (Vermillion 1992; A. Wily 2000; Khare *et al.* 2000; Kanel 2004; Shackleton and Campbell 2001).

This paper draws on a large number of case studies on devolution in wildlife management, irrigation, and forestry in developing countries (see Shyamsundar, Araral and Weeraratne (2005) for the full review). While we have tried to examine recent peer-reviewed literature on CBNRM, our review is clearly not exhaustive. Furthermore, our cut-off year (1998) is not strictly adhered to and is of course somewhat arbitrary. Nonetheless, it allows us to examine impacts of devolutionary programmes that were started in the eighties and nineties.

3.2. Community-based natural resource management: a global phenomenon

Decentralization and devolution have enjoyed considerable momentum in the last two decades. While the most historically and geographically advanced forms of devolution are arguably in the irrigation sector, there is significant evolution in the other fields as well.

In wildlife and biodiversity management, decentralization appears to be characterized by two overlapping phases. Integrated Conservation and Development Programmes (ICDPs), a popular biodiversity management programme in the eighties that often sought to reduce community dependence on natural resources (Wells and Brandon 1992), exemplifies the first phase. A good South Asian example is the eco-development programme that was supported by the World Bank/Global Environment Facility and implemented in several national parks and reserves in India. A second phase is what is currently known as community-based natural resource or wildlife management, which has a stronger focus on devolving authority to local communities. Typically, community-based wildlife management (CBWM) programmes attempt to provide communities with benefits and rights over wildlife and wildlife-based tourism.

Much of the experimentation in CBWM has been in Africa. Devolution has typically occurred either by increasing management powers of local government; creation of new local conservation institutions; or enhanced authority to traditional leaders. One of the earliest and best known of such efforts is Zimbabwe's CAMPFIRE programme.[4] Here, authority was devolved

---

[4] Communal Areas Management Programme for Indigenous Resources.

to local government agencies known as rural district councils, which retained rights over wildlife management and tourism revenue distribution (Jones and Murphree 2001). A different type of example is ADMADE in Zambia,[5] where decentralization was at two levels: a management authority headed by the district governor managed wildlife areas; and traditional chiefs controlled sub-areas within each wildlife area (Gibson 1999). A third type of model is found in Namibia, where communities can establish a conservancy and gain exclusive rights to commercial tourism operations if they define a geographical area, define membership, develop operating rules, and so on (Jones 1999). In all these cases, community institutions or local government agencies are empowered to varying degrees to negotiate contracts with tourism agencies, manage guards and game-hunting activities, and make decisions about revenue sources and uses.

In the irrigation sector, the process of transferring irrigation management from government to farmer organizations started in the United States, France, Taiwan, and other countries during the 1950s to the 1970s. Many developing countries followed in the eighties and nineties and currently some twenty-five countries in Asia, Latin America, and Africa practise some form of decentralized irrigation management (Vermillion 1992). The centrepiece of reforms has been the transfer of management of irrigation systems—wholly or in part—to non-governmental agencies, combined with a reduced role for government agencies in operation and maintenance (O & M), fee collection, water management, and conflict resolution. Typically, the transfer is from public irrigation agencies to water users' associations (WUA) or irrigators' associations (Araral 2005). This is the case in many countries including India, Pakistan, Nepal, and Sri Lanka (see Herath—this volume, for a longer discussion on Sri Lanka).[6]

Of the 3.9 billion hectares of global forest estate, an estimated 11 per cent is owned by or reserved for community and indigenous groups (White and Martin 2002). If only developing countries are considered, this number doubles to 22 per cent. Thus, a sizable tract of the forest estate in poor countries is identified as being controlled by communities. Not surprisingly, over the last two decades, community forestry as a forest-management strategy has graduated from being a somewhat experimental strategy to being more integrated into conventional national forestry efforts (Arnold 2001).

---

[5] Administrative Management Design for Game Management Areas.

[6] Other types of governance structures exist but are not the norm. For instance, in Turkey, municipal governments became the new management unit. In Vietnam, parastatal organizations assumed responsibility, while in Sudan and New Zealand, private / mutual companies assumed responsibility (Araral 2005). In the United States, Japan, South Korea, Mexico, and Taiwan, farmer-elected boards of directors oversee the new institution, while professionals undertake actual management.

The importance of community forestry is clear in South Asia, where Joint Forest Management (JFM) in India and community forestry in Nepal has transformed the relationship between the forestry department and rural households.[7] In South Asia, as in many other regions community-based forest management is often undertaken through the creation of new village-level institutions. Several chapters in this volume (Ghate, Mishra, Kanel, Arun, and Adhikari) discuss the role of institutions that govern community forests in India and Nepal. Devolution to lower levels of government is also seen in parts of Latin America, especially Guatemala and Bolivia, where forest laws passed in the mid-1990s delegate authority to municipal governments (Andersson 2003). In Africa, traditional leaders have established themselves as important stakeholders and there is evidence of parallel local authority systems consisting of traditional leaders on the one hand and government-established structures on the other (Weeraratne 2005).

In general, decentralization in natural resource management results in the creation of a community user group to manage a common pool resource. However, there is some ongoing devolution to a local-level government or a parastatal entity, as well as allocation of new powers to traditional leaders. In some cases, the links between local government and the decentralized NRM authority are indistinguishable; however, often, local user groups function with minimal supervision from the state.

3.3. Understanding impacts

Measuring the impacts of the many global experiments in decentralized natural resource management is fraught with difficulties associated with understanding ongoing biophysical changes and the effects of overlapping policies and their implementation (Ribot 2002). Lack of careful 'before and after' studies make it difficult to link specific outcomes to decentralization. Thus, the conclusions we draw about the impacts of decentralization represent *impact observations* and should be treated as a mapping of likely outcomes rather than as definite results.

Table 3.1 summarizes some of the impacts of CBNRM. Impacts can be categorized into livelihood impacts, natural resource impacts, and empowerment impacts. There are also various impacts on government finances and personnel requirements.

---

[7] As of 2001, some 22 Indian states had adopted JFM and some 45,000 groups were protecting nearly 12 million hectares of government forests (Agarwal 2001, GOI, 2001 in Kumar 2002). The total land area under community management is likely to be much higher as the above figures do not include many self-initiated groups. In Nepal, some 13,000 forestry user groups (FUGs) manage 25% of Nepal's forests (Kanel 2004).

Table 3.1. Impacts of decentralized natural resource management

Issue		Wildlife	Forestry	Irrigation
Livelihood Impacts	1	Public (infrastructural) benefits not directly linked to resource use		Public infrastructural benefits that compliment private farm income and resource use
	2	Private benefits (jobs, tourism ventures) mainly linked to resource protection	Private benefits mainly linked to resource use (NTFPs, timber)	Private benefits also from additional activities undertaken through cooperative efforts (extension)
	3	Opportunity costs in terms of loss of land, possible increases in crop predation, and loss of subsistence food/fodder uses	Opportunity costs mainly linked to current protection of forests and loss of subsistence fuel/fodder/NTFP uses	
	4	Transaction costs in terms of time in creating and sustaining new forms of group interaction and also in terms of fees		
	5	Significant monitoring costs	Production costs possible when timber and non-timber resources are used for forest enterprises.	Significant costs of infrastucture maintenance
				Production costs in terms of increase in water fees
Empowerment Impacts	6	Communities have regained limited traditional control over resources		
	7	Where control remains mostly in the hands of the state or is devolved to local government, community empowerment is limited		
	8	Lack of secure tenure, limited rights to punish infractions, lack of bureaucratic support contribute to limited community empowerment		
	9	Heterogeneity in power, assets, and preferences result in winners and losers		
Natural Resource Impacts	10	Anecdotal and case-study evidence of improvements in resource health and stock		Water-use efficiency limited—observed only in cases where other conditions (such as volumetric pricing) are met
	11	Scale issue remain unresolved		Less problematic because of government system-wide control
Government Impacts	12	Monitoring costs are reduced		
	13	Some operational costs are reduced		
	14	Staff costs may be reduced		Redction in staff a kay component of reforms

3.3.1. *Livelihood and empowerment impacts*

CBNRM seeks to strengthen rural livelihoods by providing access to local public goods through development of infrastructure and by offering community services; by expanding private income opportunities through jobs, access to credit, and self-employment possibilities; and by increasing avenues to legally use natural resources.

Community benefits are a trademark of natural resource management programmes. Some of these benefits are from direct international assistance, while the rest comes from programme earnings. Many of the wildlife management programmes in Africa, for instance, have resulted in local infrastructure such as roads and schools.[8] Community forestry has also frequently resulted in village-level assets. For example, in Nepal, community management of forests has led to the creation of community funds, which raise revenues from forest-user fees, penalties, and by obtaining donor assistance. Data from the Nepal Swiss Community Forestry Project shows that in 2003, forestry user groups in Nepal spent 21 per cent of their community fund income for local construction projects, 8 per cent on education, and 6 per cent on health services (Pokharel, Nurse, and Tembe 2004). In the irrigation sector, successful transfer of management to farmer groups often involves investments in the maintenance of irrigation infrastructure.

A pertinent concern is whether community infrastructural benefits create the right incentives for sustainable resource use, particularly in forestry and wildlife. Infrastructural benefits (such as schools or community halls) are rarely directly tied to prudent use of resources. They equally benefit households who follow community rules as well as households that defect. Household benefits are the most important incentive mechanism for motivating successful natural resource management. Household-specific benefits from community-oriented wildlife management in Africa include wildlife dividends, guide and scouting jobs, employment in lodges and tour agencies, possibilities of selling handicrafts and tourism-related services, and availability of meat from culling operations.[9,10] Similarly, household benefits in community forestry accrue from management-related jobs, increased control over timber and non-timber resources, and revenue sharing with the government. Employment in forest-related enterprises is another common source of revenue. For example, in Beharoonguda in Andhra Pradesh, India, income

[8] For instance, between 1989 and 1992, ADMADE in Zambia resulted in approximately sixty projects, including twenty-three houses for teachers, nine maize-grinding mills, and seven rural health centres (Gibson 1999).

[9] CAMPFIRE in Zimbabwe is among the few programmes that offer wildlife dividends (Bond 2001).

[10] A high-end example is the Torra Conservancy in Namibia. Community members are documented to have earned $70,000 in wages from 1996 to 1998 through an agreement with a photographic safari company (Jones 1999).

from forest-related employment schemes (coppicing, singling, etc.) accounted for nearly 43 per cent of household income in 1998.[11]

In irrigation, management transfer to communities is expected to increase farm productivity in the long run. However, the relationship between irrigation management transfer (IMT) and agricultural and economic productivity is unclear. Much of irrigation management transfer has focused on decreasing the burden on government budgets rather than on increasing farm productivity. Evidence of increased farm productivity is found mainly in cases where robust farmers' organizations have earned revenues through diverse sources and by providing better extension services to members (see details in Araral 2005).

The poverty impacts of CBNRM are as much a result of the benefit stream that occurs as of the costs that are incurred. The most important costs associated with CBNRM are opportunity costs stemming from loss of access to land, forests, and wildlife. While estimates of opportunity costs are limited, in specific cases these costs can be large and result in negative short-term returns. For example, many state-supported community forestry programmes result in forest closures or loss of access to non-timber forest products in the short run. This can impose immediate costs on poor households who are dependent on forests for fuel wood and other subsistence products.[12] However, short-terms costs can be minimized through careful planning (see Box 3.2). Long-term costs of land loss are more difficult to address.

Another set of costs associated with community-based activities is transaction costs resulting from participation in meetings, monitoring, providing labour for maintenance of infrastructure, and membership fees. Few studies actually document the burden placed by these costs, but monitoring costs, in particular, can be significant (Adhikari, Arun, Gunawardena, and Steele, this volume). Community management can increase production costs as well. Participatory irrigation management, for example, can lead to an increase in the cost of irrigated water when significant subsidies existed before IMT and these subsidies are simultaneously dismantled. Further, high-cost systems such as pump irrigation may significantly increase the cost of water to farmers (Vermillion 1997). In areas with wildlife, animal predation-related costs are another major difficulty.

In addition to direct economic benefits and costs, devolutionary policies also change the relationship between the state and communities. In fact, many of these policies are driven by the goal of empowering local communities relative to the state. CBNRM strengthens local rights over resources

[11] Villagers received additional income of a total of Rs. 359,500 from the sale of teak poles (D'Silva and Nagnath 1999). JFM, in fact, reduced the need for migration from Behroonguda for employment purposes.
[12] Such opportunity costs can result from many different forms of natural resource management and are not specific to community-based management.

Box 3.2 COMPENSATORY STRATEGIES TO REDUCE THE OPPORTUNITY
COSTS OF INCOME LOSS FROM FOREST CLOSURES

Wage income through forest-related activities

The JFM programme in Buldhana forest division in Maharashtra, India was started in twelve villages and expanded to 100. Success here can be partly attributed to income-generation strategies adopted by the Forest Department and the communities. The Forest Department generated wage income for villagers by enabling them to undertaking forestry work like plantation, transporting dead wood from inside of forests, and carrying out activities of coppicing, singling, and dressing of tree stumps in the forest area adjoining these villages (Ghate 2000).

Self-employment through collection, marketing, and sale of forest products

In the Buldhana forest division, Ghate (2000) reports that Forest Protection Committees took up large-scale collection and marketing of Anjan (good fodder). They also encouraged self-employment, small business ventures, and cooperative dairy development. Committees sought loans from cooperative banks to buy their own trucks to transport forest produce to the market. Some bought cattle and engaged in dairy business privately, while some committees initiated cooperative diaries with their own funds.

Decreasing dependence on fuelwood

The use of appropriate alternative fuel technologies in Behroonguda reduced fuelwood consumption and decreased pressure on forests. The distribution of subsidized smokeless *chullas* (stoves) to half the households in the village cut down firewood needs by 25 percent. Eight families that received bio-gas generators operating on animal dung ceased collecting firewood altogether. These measures have resulted in a decline in annual firewood consumption by 20 percent (D'Silva and Nagnath 1999).

Alternative resource collection/use mechanisms

The community of San Antonio in Mexico imposed many restrictions on individual uses, but also succeeded in redirecting traditional rights. For example, firewood gathering was coordinated with logging activities to decrease fire hazards and favour pine regeneration. Community members also agreed to forgo cutting pine trees for traditional roofing shingles, but as compensation, the forestry business supplies free tin roofing materials and lumber when needed. Some other communities maintain designated areas for cutting fuelwood (Klooster 2000). An example from the Terai region in Nepal shows how local people satisfied their needs for fuelwood and other essential forest products through illegal extraction from a nearby government-owned forest (Chakraborty 2001).

Compensation for lost rights

Nuevo San Juan community also of Mexico integrated individual tenure rights with community interests. All forests in the area are parcelled out to community members for resin tapping. Leaders establishing the community logging business choose to respect individual usufruct rights to forest plots, and resin collection continues in these plots. When logging plans slate an area for cutting, communal interests take over, but possessors of resin-tapping plots get a stumpage payment as an incentive for protecting trees (Klooster 2000).

Source: Weeraratne 2005.

to the extent that devolution increases access to local government officials, allows communities to regain traditional control over resources, brings management decisions to the local domain, and improves access to information about natural resource changes. Further, there are a number of non-financial benefits as well. For example, in Namibia, community management of wildlife has resulted in development of new skills, pride, a sense of control, and experience and confidence in dealing with outsiders—outcomes that go beyond initial development objectives (Ashley 1998). Similarly, authors such as Pokharel, Nurse, and Tembe (2004) argue that community forestry in Nepal contributes to growth in social capital (by increasing participation of women and weaker castes in decision-making) and human capital (through training programmes). Another important result of many community-oriented wildlife management and forestry programmes is improved relations over time between authorities managing protected areas and local households, and a decrease in conflicts.[13] Some of these changes are a product of strategies that try to empower *both* communities and government officials to work together to meet common goals.

Ribot (2002) has suggested that successful decentralization depends on (*a*) how accountable local institutions are to communities; (*b*) whether these institutions have adequate discretionary power; and (*c*) whether the transfer of this power is secure. All of these factors appear to make the difference between whether or not decentralization empowers local communities. In many small-scale irrigation systems in west and central Java in Indonesia, for instance, water users' associations have a mandate for operations and maintenance, but they do not have formal rights over water and infrastructure. This makes them powerless to settle disputes, enforce fee collection, or enter into business contracts (Samad *et al.* 2000). The least empowerment also seems to occur in instances where local government agencies are perceived to promote natural resource management instead of economic development or where decentralized structures recreate traditional hierarchies with some members having more and others less 'voice'. In India for instance, JFM is sometimes viewed as a burden to poor women because it can reinforce traditional patterns of gender discrimination (Agarwal 2001; Sarin 2001).[14] Institutional change can have a differential effect on households depending on how they use natural resources. Arun's work in Nepal in this volume, for example, suggests that

[13] Among many such examples is evidence in the 1990s from national parks in western Uganda (Mgahinga, Bwindi, and Kibale), which suggests that community relations with park authorities have improved as a result of community outreach efforts (Infield and Adams 1999; Archbald and Naughton-Treves 2001).

[14] Despite the general trend of low female participation in formal groups, there are also exceptions in South Asia of user groups made up exclusively of women or mixed groups with a high female presence. All women user groups are found primarily in the hills of UP and parts of Nepal. In Nepal, all women FUGs are said to constitute 3.8% of all FUGs (Government of Nepal, 2000 in Agarwal 2001).

poorer households can be hurt when their access to forests is curtailed as a result of formal adoption of a community forestry programme.

3.3.2. Resource and revenue implications

There is some evidence that community-management programmes are meeting their conservation goals. Increases in the number of animals and a decline in signs of poaching are evident in many parts of Africa, including Tanzania, Namibia, and Uganda, either because of improved monitoring and enforcement or because of changed preferences (Songorwo 1999; Jones 1999; Infield and Adams 1999).[15] In some cases, however, community management may be contributing to changes in terms of which animals are hunted rather than fully stemming hunting (Gibson 1999). In forestry, there is demonstrable evidence of community forestry resulting in healthier forests. Tanzania is perhaps the best example of positive natural resource impacts in Africa (Wily 1999). Existing studies from Mexico also suggest that community management may have contributed to stabilization or expansion of forest cover (Bray *et al.* 2003). There is also evidence from India and Nepal that community forestry is contributing to improved tree cover (Khare *et al.* 2000; Kanel 2004; Kanel, this volume).

Interestingly, in the irrigation sector, there is little to show that irrigation user groups influence water use or conservation. For example, in a well-known study of the Alto Rio Lerma Irrigation District in Mexico covering over 100,000 hectares, little evidence was found that increasing farmer control over water has led to changes in water allocation or distribution (Kloezen, Garces-Restrepo, and Johnson 1997). In the case of irrigation, conservation appears to be more closely tied to infrastructural developments and water-pricing reform (where it exists) rather than to increases in efficiency as a result of institutional changes.

A final important aspect of the impact of devolution in natural resource management is changes that occur in the state's net revenue stream. Much of the case-study literature on community management reports an increase in benefit-sharing between the state and communities as a result of devolution. Increased attention to wildlife management has meant that the state can tax rural communities for a resource (wildlife) that may have been previously untaxed. In popular parks and protected areas, revenue-sharing with communities may actually decrease government revenues in the short run.

---

[15] For example, animal census results from 1991 and 1994 show that the Selous Conservation Programme in Tanzania may have increased animal populations (Songorwo 1999). Such evidence is found in other areas such as the Kunene region of Namibia, where the community-guard programme has resulted in the recovery of flagship species such as the desert elephant and the black rhino (Jones 1999).

However, to the extent that community participation results in conservation and better opportunities for tourism, government revenues are likely to increase over time. The state also gains because of reductions in monitoring costs and decreased conflicts between frontline guards and communities.

In community forestry, the impact on the state is somewhat similar. In India, most JFM state orders ensure participating villagers between 25–50 per cent share of the net income from timber on 'final felling' of mature trees. This usually entails a minimum of five to ten years of protection of the forests before the benefits are reaped. For example in the state of West Bengal, by 1998 poles worth Rs. 40 million had been harvested and 25 per cent of the net proceeds shared with the members of the concerned forest protection committees (Khare *et al.* 2000).[16] To the extent that community control increases forest cover (as appears to be the case in several countries), devolution results in assets that are then shared between the state and communities. Improved relations between forest departments and communities, a potential decrease in corruption, and decreased monitoring costs are other benefits.

In irrigation management, there is a more direct and significant link between government finances and devolution. Devolution does seem to lead to a decrease in government subsidies and it improves the budget solvency of irrigation agencies (Araral 2005; Table 3.1). An early study from India, for example, reports that IMT resulted in a 25 per cent decrease in government subsidies for tube wells in Uttar Pradesh (Pant 1994). In Sri Lanka, Government O & M spending decreased from $14.8/ha in 1985 to $6.50/ha in 1994 as part of its irrigation management transfer programme (Kloezen 1996). Improvements in government finances result mainly from decreased spending on O & M, increased fee collection, decreased subsidies, and a gradual decline in staff in national irrigation agencies.

It is difficult to summarize the net impacts of devolutionary policies. By and large, the case-studies literature suggests that CBNRM can economically empower poor people by providing both community and household-specific benefits. Decentralization, however, is not costless. What is hard to say is whether the aggregate impacts are mainly positive or not. This is mainly because: (*a*) studies often do not distinguish between gross and net benefits; (*b*) impact evaluations rarely consider before- and after-programme results; (*c*) programmes differ in their distributional implications; and (*d*) trade-offs between short-term and long-term benefits are generally ignored.

The case studies also suggest that devolution creates the space for communities to have a 'voice' in how forests, water, and wildlife are managed. Voice, however, depends on contractual agreements between the state and

---

[16] Recent amendments to the orders of two states, Andhra Pradesh (AP) and Tamil Nadu now entitle the partner village institutions 100% of the final produce. However, in AP's case, at least 50% of the income has to be reinvested in the JFM forest (Khare *et al.* 2000).

communities and on inherent inequalities within communities. Devolution of natural resource rights to local user groups invariably changes the roles and functions of government agencies. Overall, for cash-strapped governments in developing countries there are some significant advantages to decentralizing resource management. There is also anecdotal evidence, at least in the forestry and wildlife sectors, that devolution is contributing to the health of resource stocks.

3.4. From devolution to local governance

The success of devolutionary efforts depends on the resource under consideration, the community dependent on the resource and the type of institution created to govern the use of the resource. Collective action amongst and within communities is at the core of CBNRM programmes. In fact, the effectiveness of devolutionary policies is directly related to their ability to foster cooperative behaviour to manage resources.

Scholarly discussions identify several group and resource characteristics that can contribute to successful collective use of natural resources (Ostrom 1990; Baland and Platteau 1996; Agrawal 2001).[17] Partha Dasgupta in this volume identifies conditions under which long-term cooperation may emerge as an equilibrium strategy. In this section, we examine CBNRM in light of some of these theoretical and empirical conditions. Table 3.2 outlines key attributes of the three resources under consideration and identifies factors associated with commons-dependent communities that are likely to influence the outcomes of devolutionary processes.

As Table 3.2 shows, the three resources under discussion are quite different in terms of their inherent characteristics. Wildlife and forests are *divisible*; they can be individually extracted. This has two implications: subunits of the resource can be managed separately depending on need and circumstance, but this can also increase the costs of monitoring the use of the resource. Water, though divertible for individual uses, is not divisible in the same sense. Thus, theft is more easily monitored locally. A related key characteristic is the *diversity* of ways in which the resource is used. Forests, in particular, may need to be managed for multiple local, let alone national and international uses. These multiple uses make the task of local management complicated and institutional change can have distributional implications. However, they also favour decentralized management over centralized control.

[17] There is considerable theoretical and empirical literature on conditions for durable commons institutions and why cooperation in managing natural resources occurs in some cases and fails in others. Agrawal (2001), for example, identifies 24 conditions (see Table 3.1) based on a synthesis of three books by Wade (1988), Ostrom (1990), and Baland and Platteau (1996).

Table 3.2. Differing characteristics of resources and communities and implications for governance and benefits distribution

Resource and Institutional Characteristics	Wildlife	Irrigation	Forestry
Resource characteristics with differing management requirements			
Divisibility	Selective extraction of game can increase costs of managing the entire system	Not divisible in the traditional sense	Selective extraction can contribute to degradation and to private ownership of trees or forest patches
Diversity of uses	Some diversity of use (local game meat, hunting safaris and viewing/photo safaris) with different management requirements	Diversity of uses mainly at the sectoral allocation level	Diverse uses can support a variety of local, national and international needs
Management scale and system-level needs	Large to support required animal population	Large to maintain system level integrity. Can be managed at different scales with smaller subsystems more easily managed by farmer organizations	Large to support upstream and downstream services; but smaller systems can support extractive uses
Scarcity	Scarcity provides important motivation for collective action		
Factors affecting net returns to cooperation			
Salience	Extractive use important for most households, while tourism benefits salient for subset of households	Important to most agricultural/landed households	Extractive uses (fuelwood, non-timber forest products etc.) depend on opportunity costs of labour, alternate income, etc.
Stakeholder size	Large groups result in declining net benefits	Large groups increase transaction costs associated with collective action; social norms to reinforce collective decisions are weaker	
Secure Rights—clear boundaries	Varying and limited rights over resources and infrastructure can create uncertainties and disincentives. Boundary conflicts problematic; resolution can have distributional implications		

(cont.)

Table 3.2. (Continued)

Resource and Institutional Characteristics	Wildlife	Irrigation	Forestry
Participation, monitoring and enforcement (M&E)	M&E the most significant component of community management costs; local monitoring can signal for scarcity and conservation.	Maintenance of infrastructure key local activity; can significantly increase costs of community management	M&E significant component of community costs, but can signal scarcity and lead to better conservation.
Homogeneity in endowments, preferences, and information	Benefits from devolution vary based on heterogeneous use prior to institutional change		
Type of institutional arrangement	Local user groups most likely to allow communities to exercise direct control over resources, direct M&E likely to increase compliance to rules as well as conservation, evolution of rules possible to match diverse uses of resource and heterogenous stakeholders.		

Another factor that adds to the complexity of managing these three resources is the scale at which resources need to be managed. Some wildlife, for example, may need a large habitat to thrive—an area that may include the jurisdictions of several groups. In such cases, management will require intercommunity collaboration. In the case of water and forests, upstream activities may have downstream impacts—posing significant challenges to decentralized management.

A problem that supporters of devolutionary policies have to address is that communities have little incentive to undertake collective management if there is no evidence of scarcity. For example, if irrigation water is abundant, farmers are unlikely to bear the transaction costs of creating and sustaining user groups. Similarly, in forest communities in India, scarcity is likely to be an important motivation for putting the time and resources into management activities (Bandyopadhyay and Shyamsundar 2004). In fisheries too, the case study by Gunawardena and Steele (this volume) reveals that monitoring is stricter in the group where scarcity and dependence are greater.

What is critical for successful CBNRM is the salience of the resource to locals, which affects the net returns to cooperation. With irrigation and forestry, practically every household has a stake in ensuring sustainable use; irrigated water is vitally important to farm households and firewood and non-timber forest products together serve energy, food, and medicinal needs. Salience may be more problematic for wildlife management. While most households are dependent on wildlife for food, only a smaller number directly benefit from ecotourism and associated commercial ventures that are the mainstay of CBWM.

The literature on common property resources suggests that successful cooperative action is often characterized by small group size, which enables members to interact with each other and prevent people from defaulting on cooperative agreements. This is true in irrigation management, where it is often easier for a small number of large farmers to agree to rules (as is the case in many developed countries) than for a large number of small farmers (as seen in the experience of smallholders in South Africa and elsewhere (Shah *et al.* 2002)). In wildlife management, group size impacts community success through high *per capita* revenues rather than through increased group interaction and trust.[18]

Certainty over rights to the resource can increase the returns to cooperative management (Dasgupta, this volume). This makes lack of secure rights over resources a vital concern since governments rarely hand over complete control to communities. In forestry, for example, decentralization is characterized by two different approaches: the 'user-centred' approach, found in India,

---

[18] Murombedzi (2001), for example, argues that in Zimbabwe's CAMPFIRE, benefits are highest where human populations are low and animal populations are high.

which recognizes communities as forest users and secures their cooperation by granting legal access to certain products or a share in forest-derived benefits; and the 'power-sharing' approach, found in Tanzania and the Gambia, where communities gain varying degrees of managerial power (Wily 2002a; Weeraratne 2005).[19] There is some indication of a gradual trend away from the user-based to a manager-oriented system, which should increase incentives amongst communities to make long-term resource investments. A practical subcomponent of challenges associated with assigning property rights is the problem of boundary identification. Communal boundaries are often ambiguous and boundary identification is a first step towards strengthening local property rights over natural resources. One promising strategy to resolve boundary problems is the 'incentive' system used in Namibia, where community conservancies cannot register themselves and make use of associated rights unless they resolve their boundary disputes (Jones 1999).

Local monitoring and enforcement of resource use contribute to a sense of ownership over resources, can supply superior information on illegal resource use, and provide more reliable signals of scarcity. In wildlife management, hundreds of local guards, who have better information about local hunting, are held responsible for controlling poaching and are accountable to users (Gibson 1999). Similarly, Araral (2003) finds that successful irrigation associations in the Philippines conduct internal audits at least every two months and external audits regularly, and have a system of checks and balances to avoid nepotism between auditors and treasures. Indicators such as volumetric water pricing can also provide the right signals for farmers. The most effective monitoring systems include penalties for failure to cooperate. In Behroonguda's community forestry programme in India, patrolling duty is mandatory and failure to comply results in a penalty and even loss of membership (D'Silva and Nagnath 1999). Monitoring of participation is also useful for building community confidence.

The case-study literature shows that communities engaged in natural resource management are rarely homogeneous entities that harmoniously agree to conserve. Differences in initial endowments, location, and power relations within communities can lead to unequal costs from institutional change and affect the poverty impacts of CBNRM. As Arun Khatri-Chhetri shows in this volume, poor households can be excluded and hurt by local decisions regarding resource management. This story fits with Dasgupta's (this volume) argument that a long-term cooperative equilibrium can emerge with some people being worse off than if they had not cooperated in the first place.

---

[19] These countries have supported legal processes that encourage communities to bring unreserved forest areas under their own jurisdiction and to apply to manage nationally owned forests (Wily 2002a).

A final practical question related to the implementation of devolutionary policies is what form of local governance is likely to increase cooperation. For example, is the most common form that is currently practiced, that is, management by local user groups, better than passing this mandate on to local governments? Decentralization to local government agencies has distinct advantages in terms of implementation because it increases the possibility of linking to different arms of the government that can help resolve issues related to revenues, resources, and conflict management. However, collective action problems may not be resolved unless local governments are strongly accountable to communities and there is mutual trust. On the other hand, community-level organizations are typically more likely to result in locals exercising control over natural resources and these actions are likely to be sustained as norms are internalized. Perhaps the least favoured outcome is increased power to local leaders—there are numerous problems with corruption and elite capture with this form of decentralization.

3.5. Challenges ahead

Community-based NRM is not a panacea for managing natural resources in developing countries. The resources under consideration differ considerably and the communities that depend on them are each unique. However, the case-study literature is able to point to different conditions that contribute to successful devolutionary policies. It also identifies a number of key challenges (see Table 3.3), which we discuss below.

3.5.1. Getting household incentives right

Critical to the success of CBNRM programmes is that they are incentive-compatible at the household level. CBNRM programmes, for obvious reasons, focus on creating community user groups, establishing community rules, and providing community infrastructure. While these are important mechanisms to put in place, they do not necessarily make CBNRM an attractive prospect for the individual household.[20]

In wildlife management, for example, there are several reasons why community investments may not be incentive-compatible at the household level: (a) household benefits from wildlife management are often small relative to agriculture;[21] (b) wildlife related ecotourism benefits are often limited to a small number of residents, while a large number of households are affected

[20] Note Mukhopadhyay's chapter in this volume, which discusses how exit options affect incentives to manage a resource collectively.
[21] Agricultural crop production may be subsidized: An issue often beyond the control of communities.

Table 3.3. Some challenges and solutions associated with decentralized natural resource management

Challenges	Actions Contributing to Solutions
1 Improve household incentives	• Public infrastructural services • Private services such as insurance, credit, marketing, etc. • Role for private sector–community partnerships (ecotourism) • Short-term compensatory strategies to reduce costs • Stronger property rights • Reduction in perverse policy incentives that may reduce relative returns to natural resource activities
2 Strengthen property rights	• Legal recognition of rights (changes in policies and bureaucratic procedures) • Improved local monitoring of resource use • Improved state's ability to enforce contracts
3 Reduce distributional conflicts	• Early identification of stakeholder conflicts and needs • Conflict resolution capacities within communities and state agencies • Benefits from institutional change linked to conflict resolution
4 Solving the scale problem	• Creation of federated or nested agencies • Role for state as a coordinating and monitoring agency
5 Resource and capacity building	• Training for communities and state agencies • NGO engagement • Long-term policy changes
6 Sustainability	• Long-term role for the state in capital (natural and human) investments with operations and maintenance devolved to communities • Clear division of responsibilities between state and communities over capital investments before they are made • Monitoring of resource use with incentives/disincentives tied to scarcity triggers

by wildlife predation; (c) community benefits are publicly available—they are neither tied to conservation improvements, nor do they deter illegal actions; and, (d) lack of tenure creates limited 'ownership' over programmes and wildlife. A next step in the evolution of CBNRM has to be to more carefully identify and invest in private incentives for wildlife management.

In irrigation, because of the close connection between water and broad-based household dependence on agriculture, there is a greater incentive to participate in collective management. Nonetheless, it appears that successful irrigation associations in the Philippines provide a host of other incentives to members and officers such as credit, scholarships, health insurance, and transport allowances. These incentives, while unrelated to irrigation, are specifically tied to household well-being.

In community forestry, given the dependence of poor households on forests, trade-offs between short-term and long-term benefits can be a major challenge. However, as shown in Box 3.2, there are many examples of strategies that increase short-term returns. Short-term returns occur mostly as a result of improvements in governance or because of careful compensatory mechanisms that decrease negative impacts of forest closure. Attention to mechanisms that decrease household-level costs and increase household benefits will underscore success in CBNRM.

3.5.2. *Addressing heterogeneity and distributional issues*

Communities engaged in natural resource management are rarely homogeneous entities that harmoniously agree to undertake resource conservation. As previously stated, collective action programmes have to deal with distributional impacts from institutional changes. Elite capture and gender discrimination are specific aspects of this problem.

Koppen, Parthasarathy, and Safiliou (2002), comparing the differential impacts of irrigation management transfer on poor and non-poor farmers, note that it has often been assumed that the interests of the poor sufficiently overlap with the general interest in the irrigation scheme, and that rich and poor farmers alike have equal access to canal water. However, the evidence from Andhra Pradesh and Gujarat, India, suggests the strong possibility of elite capture of the IMT process, particularly in large-scale canal irrigation where land ownership and locational advantages are skewed in favour of big landlords. Small farmers, who participate in repair and rehabilitation work may be unaware of the existence of the water user association, while large farmers make crucial decisions based on their involvement in executive committees. Thus, the challenge of making participatory irrigation and other forms of devolution pro-poor still remains.

The presence of heterogeneity in communities and the possibility of elite capture do not necessarily argue for scaling down the current enthusiasm for CBNRM. Rather, there may be a case for adopting a more flexible approach that builds on existing conflicts and strategies. This would require many steps, including (*a*) early identification of stakeholder conflicts and needs; (*b*) linking benefits from institutional change directly to conflict resolution; and (*c*) development of conflict-resolution mechanisms, including a role for the state to mediate conflicts. Community 'public' investments can also counter the inherent inequalities that may be reproduced in CBNRM projects.

3.5.3. *Strengthening property rights*

Rights extended by the state to communities to help manage natural resources cover a broad range and can generally be categorized into rights of access, withdrawal, management, exclusion, and alienation of natural assets (Agrawal and Ostrom 2001). The literature on wildlife management suggests that communities invariably have access and withdrawal rights, but there is considerable diversity in management rights.[22] Even in 'best practice' cases, communities cannot really exclude others from using their lands for grazing purposes (Jones 1999). In almost all the cases reviewed, the right of alienation or the right to buy and sell natural resources is held by the state.

In many cases, CBNRM programmes confer responsibilities on communities without commensurate rights (Meinzen-Dick and Di Gregorio 2004). Clear rights enable communities to respond to local circumstances, creating the right conditions for success. This is the case with irrigation associations in the Philippines that have the right to devise and change operational rules within the ambit of their charters. Such associations are deemed to be among the more successful associations in the country (Araral 2003).

Issues of authority and control are closely tied to legal recognition and land-tenure security. As Kanel points out in this volume, the community forestry programme in the Terai region in Nepal owes much of its success to the fact that local forest legislation has created a legal basis for forest user groups there.[23] Tenure is important for successful CPR institutions, but it is not always a sufficient or even necessary condition for success (Morrow and Hull 1996). Tenure needs to be backed by the state's ability to enforce contracts. Thus, strengthening property rights needs to go hand-in-hand with strengthening the state's ability to arbitrate and enforce contracts.

3.5.4. *Solving the scale problem*

Fugitive resources, such as wildlife in Africa, need to be managed at a large ecological scale. Decentralization can lead to a mismatch between what is required from an ecological perspective and what is known to work better from a social management perspective. Logan and Mosely (2002), for example, discuss the case of the Bulima CAMPFIRE district, where elephant forage can cause considerable crop damage in the wet season. By the dry safari-hunting season, these elephants migrate to Tsholotsho district and benefit resident communities there. This is a clear example of decentralized management resulting in inequitable impacts and overlapping claims.

In irrigation, the issue of scale plays out in the form of group size, and raises the question of whether user-group management is feasible in irrigation systems characterized by a large number of poor subsistence farmers. In forestry too, it is important to consider issues of upstream and downstream coordination, and what kinds of institutions are required to ensure this within

[22] In CAMPFIRE, for example, decisions are made by local government and benefits are conferred upon community members. In Namibian conservancies, on the other hand, a great deal more management authority is held by communities themselves.

[23] Tanzania and the Gambia are two other countries that have transferred legal ownership of unreserved forestlands to local communities and provide ample testimony of the benefits of legal recognition.

a decentralized context. Ostrom's (1990) solution of nested institutions is beginning to emerge with the creation of federated organizations. An example of such a process is documented by Mishra (this volume).

In the irrigation sector, federations of irrigation associations sometimes form a mid-level link between the state and smaller user groups. Also, partly because of the crucial importance of water resources, and partially because of personnel and infrastructure already invested in irrigation, the state plays a much more significant role as a meta-institution that can coordinate between smaller groups. Should intermediate institutions be crafted to complement decentralized user groups and play the role of the 'coordinator'? Or should 'leaner' government bureaucracies play this role? This question needs further exploration in each of the three sectors reviewed for this chapter.

3.5.5. *Providing adequate support*

Local institutions, whether government on community-run, need to be equipped with resources to implement management plans, training so they can make informed decisions, and the policy and legal tools that can make them downwardly accountable. An enabling policy and legal framework is a first step forward.[24] Progress has been made in decentralized forest management, especially in Africa, where new forest laws have been passed in more than thirty countries since 1990 (Wily 2002b). Tanzania and the Gambia have led the way in creating legal processes to support decentralization. Policy reforms in forestry in India and Nepal have also been significant, but are arguably incomplete (see Kanel and Ghate, this volume).

Donors have played a critical role in facilitating decentralized natural resource management. Non-governmental organizations are another important actor. As Herath's paper on irrigation institutions in Sri Lanka (this volume) indicates, progress is often linked to programmes where donors or non-profit organizations provide significant and steady assistance to communities. Decentralized NRM needs to be equipped with policy and legal changes. However, critical to this effort is consistent support and skill enhancement of communities and to some extent of government agencies as well.

3.5.6. *Enhancing sustainability*

CBNRM programmes are generally not self-sustained. Support for these programmes usually comes from the state, commercial activities, and from international donors. Community conservation programmes are dependent on tourism revenues, which vary depending on economic and political circumstances, while development assistance is often a function of agendas that are

[24] A detailed discussion of the legal aspects of devolution is beyond the scope of this chapter.

far beyond the control of local communities. Further, revenues earned only partly accrue to local communities because of cost-sharing arrangements with the state.

Looking beyond the financial sustainability of current programmes, we need to question whether CBNRM promotes future investments in natural resource stocks. In other words, does CBNRM provide the right mix of information, empowerment, and financial incentives to enable households and communities to invest in natural resources? Wildlife investments may only become attractive to farm households if (a) revenues from wildlife increase relative to revenues from agriculture; (b) insurance schemes can reduce the costs of wildlife predation; and (c) wildlife is seen more as a private resource over which households have much more control. Until these conditions emerge, local communities may well treat wildlife as an asset that is available to be run down and utilized for greater 'development'.

In irrigation, the sustainability issue surfaces in two forms. First, without other measures such as volumetric pricing, water-use efficiency may remain unaffected even when irrigation systems are under community management. Second, maintaining irrigation systems remains a pervasive problem. The problem seems to be one of moral hazard and co-dependency—farmers need the irrigation agency for irrigation maintenance, and they know the agency will bail them out because the agency depends, in part, on irrigation fee collections and because dilapidated systems are used as a justification for donor support. One solution is to make user associations assume responsibilities for future rehabilitation as a precondition for current rehabilitation. However, given the financial frailties of most small-scale water user associations and their very limited capacity to provide for capital expenditures, it is unlikely that this issue will be resolved soon. A more practical approach may be to bundle management transfer with a package of current and future infrastructure improvements.

Our review suggests that decentralization may reduce some operational and monitoring costs to the state, but long-term investments in restoring capital assets (natural and physical) may remain a government responsibility. There are many examples of current benefit-sharing schemes between the state and resource-dependent communities. Contractual arrangements that outline and enforce long-term sharing of investment costs need further exploration.

3.6. Conclusions for managing devolution in South Asia

This chapter differs from most of the others in this volume, because its focus is global rather than South Asia. Yet, some of the lessons drawn from the global experience are relevant for managing the commons in South Asian countries.

Increased local control motivates local interest in long-term investments, creates space for local decision-making, and can increase accountability and management performance. Devolution also contributes to improved interaction between sector agencies and communities and helps decrease hostility between government officials and local households. All of this enhances environmental outcomes and can empower local communities and reduce poverty. For these outcomes to be fully realized in South Asia, however, supra institutions that can play a coordinating role may be required. Also needed are stronger mechanisms for increasing household returns to CBNRM. Furthermore, getting incentives right for bureaucracies may be as important as getting them right for households and communities, recognizing that external circumstances and political and market uncertainties can frequently change these incentives.

References

Agarwal, B. (2001). 'Participatory Exclusions, Community Forestry, and Gender: An Analysis for South Asia and a Conceptual Framework'. *World Development*, 29/10: 1623–48.

Agrawal, A. (2001). 'Common Property Institutions and Sustainable Governance of Resources'. *World Development*, 29/10: 1649–72.

—— and Ostrom, E. (2001). 'Collective Action, Property Rights, and Devolution of Forest and Protected Area Management', in R. Meinzen-Dick, A. Knox, and M. D. Gregorio (eds.), *Collective Action, Property Rights and Devolution of Natural Resource Management: Exchange of Knowledge and Implications for Policy Proceedings of the International Conference*. Puerto Azul, the Philippines. 21–25 June, 1999. Deutsche Stiftung für Internationale Entwicklung/Zentralstelle für Ernährung und Landwirtschaft (DSE/ZEL), Feldafing, Germany.

Andersson, K. (2003). 'What Motivates Municipal Governments? Uncovering the Institutional Incentives for Municipal Governance of Forest Resources in Bolivia'. *Journal of Environment & Development*, 12/1: 5–27.

Araral, E. (2003). 'Capacity Assessment of Irrigator's Associations'. Project Preparation notes prepared for the World Bank-funded Philippines, Riverbasin, and Watershed Management Project.

—— (2005). 'Water User Associations and Irrigation Management Transfer: Understanding Impacts and Challenges', in P. Shyamsundar, E. Araral, and S. Weeraratne (eds.), 'Devolution of Resource Rights, Poverty and Natural Resource Management: A Review'. Environment Department Paper No. 104. Washington, DC: World Bank.

Archbald, K., and Naughton-Treves, L. (2001). 'Tourism Revenue-Sharing around National Parks in Western Uganda: Early Efforts to Identify and Reward Local Communities'. *Environmental Conservation*, 28/2: 135–49.

Arnold, J. (2001). *Forests and People: 25 Years of Community Forestry*. Rome: Food and Agricultural Organization of the United Nations.

Ashley, C. (1998). 'Intangibles Matter: Non-financial Dividends of Community-based Natural Resource Management in Namibia'. Windhoek: WWF LIFE Program.

Baland, J.-M., and Platteau, J.-P. (1996). *Halting Degradation of Natural Resources. Is there a Role for Rural Communities?* Oxford: FAO and Oxford University Press.

Bandyopadhyay, S., and Shyamsundar, P. (2004). 'Fuel Wood Consumption and Participation in Community Forestry in India'. Policy Research Working Paper No. 3331, World Bank, Washington, DC.

Bond, I. (2001). 'CAMPFIRE and the Incentives for Institutional Change', in D. Hulme and M. Murphree (eds.), *African Wildlife and Livelihood: The Promise and Performance of Community Conservation*. Oxford: James Currey, 227–43.

Bray, D., Merino-Perez, L., Negreros-Castillo, P., Segura-Warnholtz, G., Torres-Rojo, J., and Vester, H. (2003). 'Mexico's Community-managed Forests as a Global Model for Sustainable Landscapes'. *Conservation Biology*, 17/3: 672–7.

Chakraborty, R. (2001). 'Stability and Outcomes of Common Property Institutions in Forestry: Evidence from the Terai Region of Nepal'. *Ecological Economics*, 36: 341–53.

D'Silva, E., and Nagnath, B. (1999). 'Local People Managing Local Forests: Behroonguda Shows the Way in Andhra Pradesh, India'. Working Paper Series No. 3, Asia Forest Network, California.

Ghate, R. (2000). 'Joint Forest Management: Constituting New Commons—A Case Study from Maharashtra, India,' Paper presented at the Eighth Biennial Conference of the International Association and Society for Common Property, 'Constituting the Commons: Crafting Sustainable Commons in the New Millennium', Indiana University, Bloomington, Indiana, 31 May–4 June.

Gibson, M. (1999). *Politicians and Poachers. The Political Economy of Wildlife Policy in Africa*. Cambridge: Cambridge University Press.

Infield, M., and Adams, W. M. (1999). 'Institutional Sustainability and Community Conservation: A Case Study from Uganda'. *Journal of International Development*, 11: 305–15.

Jones, B. T. (1999). *Rights, Revenues and Resources: The Problems of Potential Conservancies as Wildlife Management Institutions in Namibia*. Discussion Paper No. 2. London: Evaluating Eden Series, International Institute for Environment and Development (IIED).

Jones, B., and Murphree, M. (2001). 'The Evolution of Policy on Community Conservation', in D. Hulme and M. Murphree (eds.), *African Wildlife and Livelihoods. The Promise and Performance of Community Conservation*. Oxford: James Currey, 38–58.

Kanel, K. R. (2004). 'Twenty-five Years of Community Forestry: Contribution to Millennium Development Goals', in Proceedings of the Fourth National Workshop on Community Forestry, Community Forestry Division, Department of Forest, Kathmandu, Nepal, 7: 4–18.

Khare, A., Sarin, M., Saxena, N., Palit, S., Bathla, S., Vania, F., and Satyanarayana, M. (2000). *Joint Forest Management: Policy, Practice and Prospects*. London: World Wide Fund for Nature, India and International Institute for Environment and Development (IIED).

Kloezen, W. H. (1996). 'Going Beyond the Boundaries of Water User Groups: Financing Operations and Management in Sri Lanka'. Paper prepared for the Internal Programme Review, International Irrigation Management Institute, Colombo, Sri Lanka.

—— Garces-Restrepo, C., and Johnson, S. (1997). 'Impact Assessment of Irrigation Management Transfer in the Alto Rio Lerma Irrigation District, Mexico'. Research Report 15, International Irrigation Management Institute, Colombo, Sri Lanka.

Klooster, D. (2000). 'Community Forestry and Tree Theft in Mexico: Resistance or Complicity in Conservation?' *Development and Change*, 31: 281–305.

Knox, A., and Meinzen-Dick, R. (2000). 'Collective Action, Property Rights, and Devolution of Natural Resource Management: Exchange of Knowledge and Implications for Policy—A Workshop Summary Paper'. CAPRi Working Paper 11, International Food Policy Research Institute, Washington DC.

Koppen, B., Parthasarathy, R., and Safiliou, C. (2002). 'Poverty Dimensions of IMT in Large-scale Canal Irrigation in Andrah Pradesh and Gujarat, India'. Research Report 61, International Irrigation Management Institute, Colombo, Sri Lanka.

Kumar, S. (2002). 'Does "Participation" in Common Pool Resource Management Help the Poor? A Social Cost-Benefit Analysis of Joint Forest Management in Jharkhand, India'. *World Development*, 30/5: 763–82.

Logan, B. I., and Mosely, W. G. (2002). 'The Political Ecology of Poverty Alleviation in Zimbabwe's Communal Areas Management Programme for Indigenous Resources (CAMPFIRE)'. *Geoforum*, 33: 1–14.

Meinzen-Dick, R., and Di Gregorio, M. (2004). 'Collective Action and Property Rights for Sustainable Development'. Overview. 2020 Vision for Food, Agriculture, and the Environment, Policy Brief No. 1, International Food Policy Research Institute, Washington, DC.

Morrow, C., and Hull, R. (1996). 'Donor-initiated Common Poll Resource Institutions: The Case of the Yanesha Forestry Cooperative'. *World Development*, 24/10: 1641–57.

Murombedzi, J. (2001). 'Committees, Rights, Costs and Benefits: Natural Resource Stewardship and Community Benefits in Zimbabwe's CAMPFIRE Programme', in D. Hulme and M. Murphree (eds.), *African Wildlife and Livelihoods. The Promise and Performance of Community Conservation*. Oxford: James Currey, 244–55.

Ostrom, E. (1990). *Governing the Commons: The Evolution of Institutions for Collective Action*. Cambridge: Cambridge University Press.

Pant, N. (1994). 'The Turnover of Public Tube Wells in Uttar Pradesh: A Case Study of a Successful Cooperative Society'. Paper presented at the International Conference on Irrigation Management Transfer, Wuhan, China, September.

Pokharel, B., Nurse, M., and Tembe, H. (2004). 'Forests and People's Livelihoods: Benefiting the Poor from Community Forestry'. Discussion Paper, 1/04, NSCFP (Nepal Swiss Community Forestry Project), Kathmandu, Nepal.

Ribot, J. (2002). *Democratic Decentralization of Natural Resources. Institutionalising Popular Participation*. Washington, DC: World Resources Institute.

Samad, M., Vermillion, D., Pusposotardjo, S., Arif, S., and Rochdyanto, S. (2000). 'An Assessment of the Small-scale IMT Program in Indonesia'. Indonesia Country Paper, International Irrigation Management Institute, Colombo, Sri Lanka.

Sarin, M. (2001). 'Disempowerment in the Name of "Participatory" Forestry?—Village Forest Joint Management in Uttarakhand'. *Forest, Trees and People Newsletter*, 44: 26–35.

Shackleton, S., and Campbell, B. (2001). 'Devolution in Natural Resource Management: Institutional Arrangements and Power Shifts: A Synthesis of Case Studies from Southern Africa'. Report, Centre for International Forestry Research, Bogor, Indonesia.

Shah, T., Koppen, B., Merrey, D., Lange, M., and Samad, M. (2002). 'Institutional Alternatives in African Smallholder Irrigation: Lessons from International Experience with IMT'. Research Report 60, International Water Management Institute, Colombo, Sri Lanka.

Shyamsundar, P., Araral, E., and Weeraratne, S. (2005). 'Devolution of Resource Rights, Poverty and Natural Resource Management: A Review'. Environment Department Paper No. 104, Washington, DC: World Bank.

Songorwo, A. (1999). 'Community-based Wildlife Management (CWM) in Tanzania: Are the Communities Interested?' *World Development*, 27/12: 2061–79.

Vermillion, D. L. (1992). 'Irrigation Management Turnover: Structural Adjustment or Strategic Evolution?' *IIMI Review*, 6/2: 3–12.

—— (1997). 'Impacts of Irrigation Management Transfer: A Review of the Evidence'. Research Report 11, International Water Management Institute, Colombo, Sri Lanka.

Wade, R. (1988). *Village Republics: Economic Conditions for Collective Action in South India.* Cambridge: Cambridge University Press.

Weeraratne, S. (2005). 'Assessing Decentralized Forest Management', in P. Shyamsundar, E. Araral, and S. Weeraratne (eds.), *Devolution of Resource Rights, Poverty and Natural Resource Management: A Review*. Environment Department Paper No. 104. Washington DC: World Bank, 65–90.

Wells, M., and Brandon, K. E. (1992). Planning for People and Parks: Design Dilemmas. *World Development*, 20/4: 557–70.

White, A., and Martin, A. (2002). 'Who Owns the World's Forests? Forest Tenure and Public Forests in Transition'. Report, Forest Trends and Centre for International Environmental Law, Forest Trends, Washington, DC.

Wily, A. (2000). 'Land Tenure Reform and the Balance of Power in Southern and Eastern Africa'. Natural Resources Perspectives Newsletter No. 58. Overseas Development Institute, London.

Wily, L. (1999). 'Moving Forward in African Community Forestry: Trading Power, Not Use Rights'. *Society & Natural Resources,* 12: 49–61.

—— (2002a). 'The Political Economy of Community Forestry in Africa—Getting the Power Relations Right'. *Forest, Trees and People Newsletter,* 46: 4–12.

—— (2002b). 'Participatory Forest Management in Africa: An Overview of Progress and Issues'. Draft manuscript. <http://www.cbnrm.net>.

World Resources Institute (WRI) in collaboration with the United Nations Development Programme, United Nations Environment Program, and the World Bank. (2005). *The Wealth of the Poor—Managing Eco-systems to Fight Poverty*. Report. Washington, DC: WRI, 55–70.

Part II

Evolution and Transitions

4

Does Afforestation Ensure Sustainability? A Study of the *Haors* of Bangladesh[1]

A. K. Enamul Haque

4.1. Introduction

The publication of Hardin's seminal article on 'The Tragedy of the Commons' in 1968, it might be said, has generated much interest in common property resources in the fields of resource and environmental economics as well as poverty analysis and law. The research mostly focuses on the overexploitation of fisheries, forests, grazing land, air and water pollution among other resources. In essence the research demonstrates how the absence of a clear demarcation of property rights when it comes to these resources leads to overexploitation. This, in general, could be categorized under the problem of 'free riding' in economics. Presented in the form of the 'prisoner's dilemma' using a game-theoretic framework, it could be shown that a competitive equilibrium might lead to overexploitation of resources. However, those who critique the 'tragedy of the commons' argue that such open-access resources are not truly the commons. Many of these commons are traditionally used by rural communities within a framework of communal property rights and there are no rules of engagement for access and for joint use. Consequently, the absence of such rules has led to overexploitation (McCay and Achenson 1987; Bromley 1992).

Ostrom, Gardner, and Walker (1994) further analysed the situation of CPR and laid down a detailed typology of CPR problems in terms of two broad

[1] The author gratefully acknowledges the financial support provided by UNDP and IUCN Bangladesh to do the fieldwork for this study. The study went through several rounds of discussion and the author has immensely benefited from these discussions at various stages. Furthermore, the report was internally reviewed by Ms Lucy Emerton of IUCN regional office, Bangkok and the author appreciates her comments at different stages of the study.

classes: appropriation and provision. Appropriation deals with issues relating to the flow of resources whereas provision deals with maintenance or enhancement of the stock (or base) of resources. The argument is that if individuals have the right to the resource then they will take care of its quality and quantity of services. In fisheries, this is often done using a long-term leasing contract for the wetland. In other words, 'appropriation' looks at the output produced each year and provision looks at ensuring a growing resource base that increases the possibility of greater extraction (or appropriation) in subsequent periods. Solving these two aspects simultaneously could be problematic in the sense that what may be efficient in a static framework may not be efficient in a dynamic framework.

To solve this puzzle, the literature has suggested three broad arrangements: (a) creation and enforcement of private property rights in the commons (Demsetz 1967; Johnson 1972; Smith 1981; Cheung 1970). This entails building new institutions with the authorities responsible for creating rules and regulations for management of the resource like private property; (b) transfer of management right to an external agency to regulate the access and use of the resources (Hardin 1968); and (c) decentralized collective management using voluntary compliance rules and an 'assurance approach' (Berkes 1989; Wade 1987; Jodha 1986; Chopra, Kadekodi, and Murthy 1989). But the question is whether these approaches can solve the sustainability puzzle? In other words, if the resource in question is to be managed in a sustainable way, is it possible to achieve it only through refixation of rights for the resources using institutional changes? The first approach suggests creating private property rights on the resources; the second proposes creating a public good to benefit the people; while the third argues for community ownership of the resource. From the literature on CPR, it is evident that CPR management ultimately results in institution-building and rule-making. At least, this has been the experience when it comes to forestry resources. In the book *Governing the Commons*, Ostrom (1990) describes a series of CPR institutions where rules in use had enabled individuals to utilize the resource over a long period of time. In Nepal, community forestry institutions evolved from the failure of the state ownership of forestry to benefit the people who are dependent on forest resources. The community forestry movement in Nepal, which began in 1978 and went through several phases, has today settled into basic community forestry institutions known as forest user groups (FUGs) (see Kanel, this volume). In 1993, these new institutions received legal recognition in order to ensure sustainable management of forests. However, Adhikari (this volume) shows that such institutions have benefited the wealthier section of the community more than the poorer sections. Ghate's study (this volume) on the Joint Forest Management institutions in India also suggests that absence of well-defined property rights over communally managed forests adversely affects the long-term sustainability of local institutions.

Therefore, the two problems of CPR management can be stated as follows: (*a*) the problem of institutionalizing the access and use rights to the resource by the community, and (*b*) the problem of ensuring ecological sustainability of resources for future generations. It can be hypothesized that an efficient solution may not necessarily guarantee sustainable management of the resource. Consequently, before undertaking institutional change it is important that dynamic efficiency is studied in terms of the sustainable use of the resource. In this chapter, we study the *haor* system of Bangladesh and examine the outcome of proposed state interventions with the help of simulations based on a simple bio-economic model.

4.2. The *haor* ecosystem

The *haors*, in Bangladesh, are unique ecosystems which have conjunctive uses as wetland, cropland, and fallow land. A *haor* is a bowl-shaped low-lying land that usually goes under water during the early monsoon months (April–May) and remains a water body until the end of the rainy season in September. In these months it provides freshwater fish for the people. Environmentally, the *haor* through its storage capacity protects lower floodplains (mostly agricultural cropland) from flash floods. The lower floodplain areas benefit through the successful harvest of *boro*[2] rice. It also regulates the flow of water in the rivers flowing out of the *haor*. In the dry season (commonly know as *rabi*), on the other hand, as the water recedes, the *haor* splits into hundreds of small natural water bodies (locally known as *beels*) and the dry land is used either for rice farming or is left fallow for grazing. In terms of ecological services, the *haor* provides shelter to mother fishes during dry months, provides a fertile spawning ground during monsoon months, generates agricultural income in the dry season and/or becomes pasture land for the cattle and buffalo herds. The vast plains of the *haor* are very thinly populated and are, therefore, a landing ground for migrating winter birds from the north.

4.2.1. *Property rights regimes in the* haor *ecosystem and the land-use pattern*

Land rights in a *haor* are quite complex. Three types of land use exist in a *haor*: (*a*) the cropland, (*b*) the water body; and (*c*) the reed-cum-grass-cum-swamp forest land, also known as *kanda* land. The cropland is generally privately owned land located inside the *haor* basin. It is cultivable during the dry months—from October to April. The cropland is gently sloped and the farther

[2] There are three cropping seasons in Bangladesh agriculture. The *boro* season starts in November and lasts until April, the *aus* season starts in April–May and lasts till July, and the *amon* season starts in August–September and lasts until November–December.

the land is away from the water bodies, the *beels*, the more productive it is in terms of agricultural output because it is the longer cropping season and is less likely to be inundated in the beginning months of the monsoon. Human settlements in a *haor* basin are sparse and they are either located outside the main *haor* basin or on small hilltops inside the *haors*. During monsoon months many of these settlements are like islands in a large water body. Agricultural land in a *haor* is generally single-cropped and *boro* is the main rice season in a *haor*. Furthermore, there is a greater likelihood of flooding of agricultural land inside a *haor* than outside it. The reed-cum-grass swamp forest land (*kanda*) in a *haor* is generally located near the water bodies (the *beels*).

Kanda land is government land by default and remains a *de facto* common property resource. During the dry season people use the *kanda* as their common pasture. Poor people living in the villages manage the cattle herds (called *bathan*) for the whole dry season. However, there are areas in *kanda* where reeds and swamp forests are grown, which are collected by local people freely. During the early monsoon days, the *kanda* becomes a rich spawning ground for fishes and provides shelter and feed to fish larvae. The swamp forests in the *kanda* also function as a major source of fuelwood for people living in the *haor* area.

Beels, the water bodies inside the *haor*, are mixed in terms of ownership pattern. The bigger *beels* are government property, the middle-sized *beels* are owned by the village community, and the smaller *beels* are privately owned. During the dry winter months, the *beels* also become the home of thousands of migratory waterfowls and other local birds which take refuge there. The state often leases out the *beels* to local fish lords for fishing activities for a specific time period.

In sum, the land-use pattern in a *haor* is a mixture between rice, fish, grass, reed, and forests (swamp). At the same time, productivity in private lands (mostly cropland) is not independent of the quality of open and common properties in the *haor*.

4.2.2. *Ecological services of* haors

Haors provide important ecological functions such as the following: spawning ground for fish; shelter for mother fishes; landing ground for thousands of migrating birds during the winter months; and grazing field, housing materials, and fuelwood for the community. The appropriation and provisioning rights in each of these lands differ significantly because the benefits from activities in the *haor* have both spatial and temporal dimensions. As the *haor* retains water during early monsoon months, low-lying areas benefit through successful crop harvests. Many *beels* in the *hoar* are natural mother fisheries while the *kanda* is the natural spawning ground, which ultimately benefits the whole country in terms of an increased supply of freshwater fishes. In addition, the *haors* also benefit local people through fish and rice production.

4.2.3. *Spatial land-use conflicts*

The distribution of such benefits and their relative share depend on the land-use system of the *haor*. There is interdependence in the quality of the ecological services provided by the three major resources in the *haor*—agricultural land, *beel*, and *kanda*. An increase in the rice area generally reduces the *kanda* area, an increased fish harvest reduces future fish availability, and reduced *kanda* reduces fish harvests in future years, and so on. The competition to use these resources by several agents in the absence of an active institution to conserve both the state and community (common) properties in the *haor* results in the deterioration of its ecological conditions and makes the resource unsustainable.

4.3. The Hakaluki *haor* case study

This study concerns the biggest *haor* system in Bangladesh: the Hakaluki *haor* located in the Sylhet and Moulvi Bazaar districts of north-eastern Bangladesh (Figure 4.1). The *haor* has been identified as an ecologically critical area by the Department of Environment of the government of Bangladesh and has been considered a good candidate for sustainable management by the government and also by the international agencies. For example, UNDP has agreed to finance part of its activities through Global Environment Facility fund. Therefore, it makes sense to study the management options for the sustainable use of the *haor*.

Hakaluki *haor* lies between the latitude 24° 35′ N to 24° 44′ N and longitude 92° 00′ E to 92° 08′ E. Hakaluki *haor* is a complex ecosystem, containing more than 238 interconnecting *beels/Jalmahals* (Choudhury 2005).[3] The total area of the *haor* is about 18,000 ha, including the area which is completely inundated during the monsoon and is designated as the ECA. Of this total area, *beels* (permanent wetlands) cover an area of 4,635 ha. This 18,000 ha area represents the Ecologically Critical Area (ECA) declared by the government of Bangladesh in the Hakaluki *haor*. More than 200,000 people live in the area surrounding Hakaluki *haor*.

---

[3] Information related to the number of *beels* in the Hakaluki *haor* is not very accurate. The UNDP project known as the Coastal and Wetland Biodiversity Management Project (CWBMP) has claimed that there are eighty interconnecting *beels* in the *haor* basin, the CNRS census data provided names of forty-seven major *beels* and an unknown number of small *beels* whereas Choudhury (2005) has claimed that there are more than 125 interconnecting *beels*, while other studies show that there are 238 *beels*.

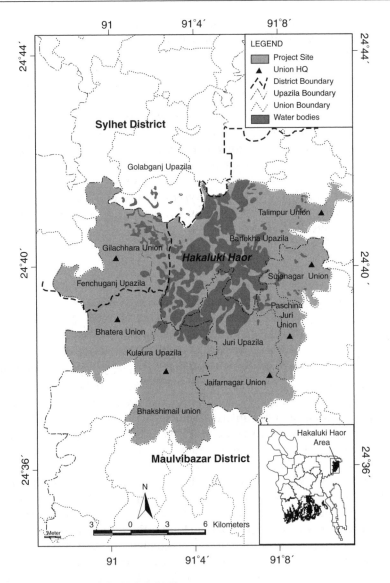

Figure 4.1. Location of the Hakaluki *Haor*
Source: GIS Mapping by CNRS.

4.3.1. *Estimating the economic value of wetland goods and services*

To understand the nature of dependence of the people on the *haor* resources and to estimate the use value of *haor* resources, a survey of 837 randomly chosen households was conducted between January–April 2006. A modular questionnaire was developed to elicit information from these households. To value the productivity of the Hakaluki *haor*, a structured questionnaire was used to collect data.

Data from the household survey was used to estimate the economic value of wetland resource use and wetland services. The benefit transfer method was used to value wetland services such as watershed, flood control, biodiversity, carbon sink, and aesthetic benefits. This involved extrapolating the results of a valuation exercise carried out in a similar wetland elsewhere in Bangladesh, which had established values for wetland services. The resulting values discussed later in this study are expressed in per hectare.

4.3.2. The beels

Most of the large *beels* in the Hakaluki *haor* are *de jure* owned by the government. There are 13,595 ha of land under 238 *beels* in the *haor* and 67 per cent of them are government-owned. Table 4.1, however, also shows that 50 per cent of the *beels* are *de facto* open-access. Nearly 17 per cent of the government-owned *beels* are leased out for fishing. Similarly, 11 per cent are community-owned (either owned or operated by fisher communities or by neighbouring villages) and about 22 per cent are under private ownership.[4]

Table 4.1. Fishing rights in the *Beels*

Rights for Fishing	per cent
Cooperative	9.60
Leasing	16.70
Open fish catch	50.00
Village-based right	1.20
Individual ownership	22.00
Others	0.50

Source: IUCN Survey 2006.

While ownership and operating rights in the *beels* have significant bearing on the fish harvests, *beels* are also naturally threatened due to silt deposits during monsoon months. This is an active natural degradation process that reduces the volume of water and therefore stock of fish. GIS data shows (Table 4.2) that majority of the *beels* in the Hakaluki *haor* suffers from silt deposits. The average rate of silt deposits in these *beels* is about 10.9 per cent.

4.3.3. The demand for alternative uses

In the dry season, there are nearly 13,408 ha of cropland in the Hakaluki *haor*. All croplands are privately owned and are used mainly for *boro* season

---

[4] For detailed survey information, see Haque (2006*a*).

Table 4.2. Rate of silt deposits in the *Beels* of Hakaluki *Haor*

Rate of silt deposits	No. of *Beels*	Area (acre)
0–10%	87	5903.26
11–25%	34	1759.5
26–50%	70	3133.62
51–75%	25	1330.01
Above 75%	22	220.75
Total	238	12347.14

Source: Collected by the author from GIS database of CNRS (unpublished data).

rice production. Rice harvests in the *haor* are prone to flood risks due to flash floods in the pre-monsoon days. As a result, there is strong political demand to build embankments for the protection of the rice crops. This demand by the farmers is in direct conflict with the interests of fishermen and environmentalists. The *haor* has already been declared an ecologically critical area. There is strong opposition among the environmentalist to building embankments. Similarly ecologists and fisheries experts also oppose construction of embankments because it would restrict fish migration during the spawning seasons and hence reduce the fish population. It is also important to note that while silt deposits in *beels* were found to be harmful for fisheries, the silt deposits in cropland are beneficial for agricultural producers for the following two reasons: (*a*) it naturally replenishes the soil fertility and therefore increases productivity of rice; (*b*) silt deposits in the *beels* reduce the depth of water and therefore help the process of conversion of wetland into agricultural land. Siltation thus increases private benefits but reduces the community/social benefits from fisheries.

4.3.4. *The* kanda

There are 7,116 ha of *kanda* land in the Hakaluki *haor*. *Kanda* refers to fallow land used for grazing by the local people and also as a source of supply of fuelwood, housing materials, medicinal plants, and several kind of fruits (usually low-value crops consumed by the poor) for local inhabitants. Furthermore, it is used as a landing ground for fishing activities. During monsoon months, *kanda* provides feed and shelter to fish larvae. *Kanda, de jure,* is owned by the government. The expansion in irrigation facilities, and embankments would put pressure on *kanda* and in the absence of an effective control on the use of *kanda* by the government, it is likely to be converted into agricultural land. Due to the open-access nature of *kanda*, the quantity and the quality of the reed, swamp forests, and other plants have deteriorated significantly. As a result, the fish stock is under threat in the *beels* of the *haor*.

4.3.5. *Produces of the Hakaluki* haor

4.3.5.1. FISH

Fishing is the major economic activity in the *haor*. In fact, the *beel*s in the *haor* are directly responsible for generating employment in fishing, fish trading, and hatchling supplies for aquaculture. Because of the seasonality in fishing activities, people in the *haor* area have multiple sources of income. Nearly 48 per cent of people are engaged in harvesting fish from the *beel*s, 3 per cent engaged in hatchling supplies to the aquaculture farms, and 9 per cent in fish trading. Overall, 52 per cent of the people earn their income from fish or fish-related activities. The average annual income from these activities amount to 21,463 taka or $311 per household (Haque 2006*b*). According to fish-landing centre records 1,800 tons of fish produced from the *haor* comes to the landing centres annually. However, there might be a similar amount of fish which may not come to the landing stations because they are consumed locally.

4.3.5.2. FARMING

Rice farming is another major activity in the *haor* area. In Hakaluki, nearly 66 per cent of households that surround the *haor* are engaged in rice cultivation in the *haor* area. Gross income from rice cultivation from the *haor* area is 5,931 taka or $85 per household or 7,050 taka per hectare per year (survey data).

4.3.5.3. OTHER INCOME-GENERATING ACTIVITIES (IGA)

Several other types of economic activities were reported in the survey besides fishing and farming, although they were dependent on the quality of the *kanda* land. Plants and aquatic fruits, duck keeping, cattle and buffalo rearing, and fuelwood and reed collection are some of them. Nearly 42 per cent of the people are involved in these activities. Most of these incomes are earned by the poorer families from the use of the CPR (in general the bottom 40 per cent of the population in Bangladesh live below the poverty line) while their annual collection came to only about 9,780 taka or $140 per household. In terms of per acre of production such activities produce nearly 13,872 taka per ha or $198 per ha.

4.3.5.4. ECOSYSTEM SERVICES

Hakaluki *haor* provides four major types of environmental benefits. These are: watershed and flood-control benefits to the lower riparian areas, biodiversity benefits (in terms of birds, migratory birds, aquatic flora and fauna, non-aquatic flora and fauna), acting as a carbon sink, and providing aesthetic benefits to visitors.

4.3.6. *The concept of sustainable management in Hakaluki* haor

Primary survey findings indicate that as far as distribution of benefits is concerned, nearly 40 per cent of benefits come from fisheries, and 15 per cent from rice farming. Roughly 28 per cent of benefits (mainly by NTFP collection from the commons) go to the poor. The remaining 17 per cent accrue as environmental benefit.

We now turn to the notion of sustainability in the context of this fragile ecological system. We use the concept of sustainability which suggests that a management system is sustainable if the current production possibility set is growing (Arrow, Dasgupta, and Maler 2004). Using this notion one can obtain two possible scenarios. First, there is the efficiency hypothesis, where the present value of all future resource extractions is maximized. Second, there is the sustainability hypothesis where the objective is to maximize the growth in the flow of services from the CPR. These hypotheses are presented below using mathematical notations.

4.3.7. *The theoretical framework for efficiency and sustainability hypotheses*

The activities in the *haor* are summarized using the following system of equations:

Let, $y_{1t} = y_1(S_1, S_3, S_4, e_1)$, $y_{2t} = y_2(S_2, S_3, e_2)$, and $y_{3t} = y_3(S_2, S_3, e_3)$

$$\frac{dS_1}{dt} = (\delta_1 - \delta_2)S_1 \text{ and } S_1(0) = S_1^0 + S_4$$

$$\frac{dS_2}{dt} = (\delta_2 + \delta_3)S_2; \text{ and } S_2(0) = S_2^0$$

$$\frac{dS_3}{dt} = (\delta_5 - \delta_4 - \delta_3)S_3; \text{ and } S_3(0) = S_3^0$$

Where, yi = Output and Si = Stock, and i = 1 is fishing, etc.

Subscript (of *y*) and S runs from 1 to 3 with 1 meaning fishing, 2 meaning agriculture (land area), and 3 meaning goods and services from the commons. *y* is the production value of *i*th activities (in constant prices) at time *t*, S is the stock of *i*th resources at time *t*.

e_1, e_2, e_3 are the level of efforts per unit of Ss.

δ_1 the rate of silt removal from the land (measuring the effectiveness of silt removal activities).

δ_2 the rate of silt deposits in the land/water (per cent of *beel* bed under silt cover).

δ_3 the rate of expansion in the rice fields done by farmers due to adoption of irrigation facilities and other means.

δ_4 the decay in the *kanda* land's productivity

and δ_5 the growth in *kanda* land's productivity due to afforestation activities. S_i^0 is the initial stock of *i*th resource. $i = 1$ means *beels*, 2 means agricultural land, and 3 means *kanda* land. S_4 is the size of the sanctuary area. Fish sanctuary is a designated area in the wetland (*beels*) where harvest does not take place for a specific period of time to allow parent fishes to live safely.

Based on the explanation provided above, we can derive two propositions:

Proposition I. *Efficiency hypothesis*: For a given level of effort per unit of stock of the resource, the reassignment and reprovisioning procedure is efficient if $\int_0^T (y_1 + y_2 + y_3)e^{-rt}dt$ is maximized, where T is the planning horizon in years.

Proposition II. *Sustainability hypothesis*: For a given level of effort per unit of stock of the resource, the reassignment and reprovisioning procedure is sustainable if $\frac{d(y_1+y_2+y_3)}{dt} \geq 0$.

4.3.8. *Sustainable management of Hakaluki* haor

Since Hakaluki *haor* is already labelled as an ecologically critical area and has both national and international benefits, the UNDP has agreed to finance the development of a management regime in the *haor* that would make it sustainable. The Bangladesh government has been working on a management plan for the sustainable use of the Hakaluki *haor* that consists of four options which are feasible and have received popular support from the local people. These are: (*a*) the construction of submergible embankments to protect rice farming from early floods; (*b*) removal of silt deposits from the *beel* beds; (*c*) setting up of fish sanctuaries; and (*d*) afforestation in *kanda*. Due to the existing conflicts between different resource users, all four options were in high demand from the local people. Our focus here is whether the implementation of the options would result in the sustainable and efficient management of the *haor*.

4.3.9. *Reassignment of rights*

As part of the resource management strategy, the government has been actively working with local people in the *haor* area to devise a strategy for the reassignment of resource rights in the *haor*. This includes provision for leasing out land to fisher communities, increasing access to resources through making roads, management of the resources by the local communities through user groups, etc.

4.3.10. *Provisioning of rights*

The designation of the *haor* as an ecologically critical area by the government of Bangladesh illustrates the following: (*a*) that the environment in the *haor* might already be in such a state of irreversibility that the government is interested in preserving it for future generations; or (*b*) that the condition is moving towards a state of irreversibility and so the government of Bangladesh has resorted to a pre-emptive policy using the 'precautionary principle' of environmental protection. The government is, therefore, considering reprovisioning of rights through (*a*) afforestation of the *kanda* land for use by the poor; (*b*) developing a fish sanctuary in some of the *beels* for the fisher community; (*c*) building embankments to reduce risk from flash floods to the rice crop; and (*d*) removing silt formation from the *beel* beds. As discussed above, there are conflicts between these management strategies because each has consequences for the others. Hence, there has arisen a conflict of interests between the use rights of the fisher, farmer, and the poor communities around the *haor*.

4.4. The bio-economic model

The biological process models designed to simulate agro-ecological processes can be used to examine changes in the biological and anthropogenic processes on an ecosystem. These models are quite useful in understanding the process of interlinkages and also to determine impacts of different policy options.

Most bio-economic models use 'mechanistic' or 'theory-driven' relationships to study the 'biological processes'. Very few of these models include human components explicitly in the model specification beyond the part played in specifying the management regime for the scenario under simulation (Peng 2000; Bossel and Krieger 1991; Olmsted, Alvarez-Buylla 1995; Brian *et al.* 2003). However, these models use a set of accounting equations to determine benefits and costs (economic and biological) associated with various strategies or scenarios. These models do not explicitly optimize any variables but they do provide an analysis from which it is possible to take decisions which are welfare-enhancing.

In Bangladesh, no bio-economic models have been previously developed that link the economy and the bio-physical world. We attempt to fill this gap in the context of the *haor* system and to examine possibilities for sustainable management outcomes of the *haor*. We examine the interaction between resource stocks, ecological services, and resource flows.

The bio-economic model presented here examines the four management interventions proposed by the government as strategies for achieving sustainability in the *haor*. Here we consider three economic goods and services and four ecological goods and services. Fishing and related activities, rice

Table 4.3. Economic and ecological services from Hakaluki *Haor*

	Land Area in ha	BDT per ha	Total value (Tk mill) per year	% total
Economic Goods and Services				
Fish harvest	13,595.10	13, 586.43+	184.71	28%
Fish hatchlings supplies	13,595.10	761.69+	10.36	2%
Fish trading	13,595.10	5,010.90+	68.12	10%
Rice production	16,102.19	7,050.00+	113.52	15%
Non-fish and non-rice products—mainly poor households receive this	7,115.87	5,330.37+	37.93	11%
Duck rearing—mainly poor households receive this	13,595.10	11.89+	0.16	0%
Cattle and buffalo rearing—mainly poor households receive this	7,115.87	5,466.82+	38.90	11%
Other benefits—mainly poor households receive this	7,115.87	3,063.27+	21.80	6%
Ecological Services				
Watershed benefits	13,595.10	1,020.93*	13.88	2%
Flood-control benefits	13,595.10	2,242.04*	30.48	5%
Biodiversity benefits (birds, migratory birds, aquatic flora and fauna, non-aquatic flora and fauna)	13,595.10	4,174.63*	56.75	9%
Aesthetic benefits	13,595.00	671.91*	9.13	1%
Total		48,390.89	585.75	100%

Source: + Haque (2006); * USAID 2002, values are adjusted for 2006 using CPI.

cultivation, and non-fish non-rice goods and services come under the category of economic goods and services; while flood protection service, watershed services, biodiversity services, and aesthetic services fall under the category of ecological services of the *haor*. The field-survey results provided some values of the services which have been factored into the model (see Table 4.3).

The model used a thirty-year planning period to understand the effect of management interventions on sustainability and on the total value of services from the *haor* (in present value terms).

4.4.1. *Impact of afforestation on sustainability and efficiency*

The bio-economic model presented in the Appendix (4.1 and 4.2) is used to understand the impact of changes in the management policies on (*a*) economic productivity of the *haor* with regard to fish and rice production (labelled as 'Fisheries' and 'Rice' lines in Figure 4.2 and thereafter); (*b*) production of goods and services commonly appropriated by the poor (shown in Figure 4.2 as 'Poor's Benefit'); and (*c*) ecological services from the *haor* in terms of wetland benefits, watershed benefits, etc. (shown in 'Environmental Benefit' line). Each of these management options were included as binary parameters in the model. For simulation exercises the model compared the 'with' and 'without' scenarios under different management options. The 'Total Benefit' line shows the sum of economic and ecological benefits under a

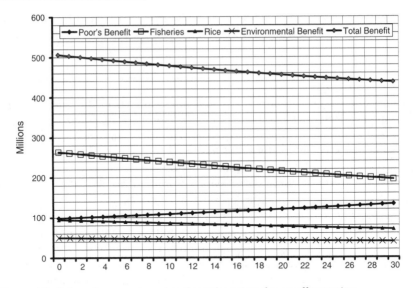

Figure 4.2. Value of economic and ecological services due to afforestation

Note: Simulation results using the bio-economic model. STELLA Output.

defined management option. Figure 4.2 illustrates the impact of afforestation on the value of services of the *haor*. It has been assumed that the afforestation policy is implemented along with the provision for reassignment of rights on *kanda* for the poor.

The sustainability hypothesis makes it clear that the total benefit from the *haor* will continue to fall if only afforestation is chosen as the management intervention. The model shows that the total value of the *haor* goes up by 362 million taka or $5.25 million in terms of 'Present Value' (compared with the business-as-usual scenario) in thirty years' time (see Table 4.4).

Table 4.4. Comparative analysis of benefits from Hakaluki *Haor* management policies and their impact

	Changes in the PV of benefits from Hakaluki *haor* in BDT millions (for 30 year lifetime with a 5% rate of discount)			
	Total Benefits	Economic Benefits	Environmental Benefits	Poor's Benefit
Afforestation	362.09	347.76	14.32	347.76
Sanctuary	854.95	827.85	27.10	—
Sediment control	651.90	578.20	73.69	—
Embankment	(230.47)	(230.47)	—	(468.69)
Sediment Control + Sanctuary	1,323.30	1,249.61	73.69	—
Sed con. + Sanct. + afforestation	1,685.39	1,597.37	88.02	347.76
Sed. Con. + Sanct. + Affor. + Embankment	1,454.92	1,366.90	88.02	(120.93)

Note: — means no change, numbers in parenthesis means negative effect.

4.4.2. *The impact of the fish sanctuary*

Figure 4.3 illustrates the impact of the fish sanctuary on the value of services of the *haor*. The total benefit from this intervention goes up by 855 million taka or $12.39 million in thirty years' time in present value terms at a 5 per cent rate of discount. A 5 per cent discount rate is used which is close to the real rate of interest (= nominal interest rate – rate of inflation) in Bangladesh. A fish sanctuary is also implemented with corresponding changes to the rights of fishers who have access to fish production in future years if they agree to restrict their current right to fishing on selected *beel*s.

The simulation exercise shows that the total benefit still decreases. Hence, it could be asserted that this intervention too will not ensure the sustainability of the *haor*. In other words, the sustainability hypothesis fails when only the fish sanctuary is established. However, the overall efficiency has increased significantly and it is shown in terms of increase in the value of goods and services produced from the *haor*. Table 4.4 shows the changes in value of various services due to management interventions.

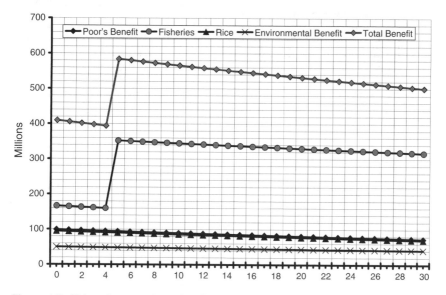

Figure 4.3. Value of economic and ecological services due to establishment of the fish sanctuary

Note: Simulation results using the bio-economic model. STELLA Output.

4.4.3. *The impact of sediment control on* beels

The impact of the policy intervention on sediment control in the *beels* is also similar to that of previous management options. The model shows that the total benefit increases by 651.9 million taka or $9.45 million if this is implemented. This amount is less than that of the sanctuary but higher than that of afforestation. However, Figure 4.4 shows that this management step too failed to survive the sustainability test as the future flow of total benefit continues to fall.

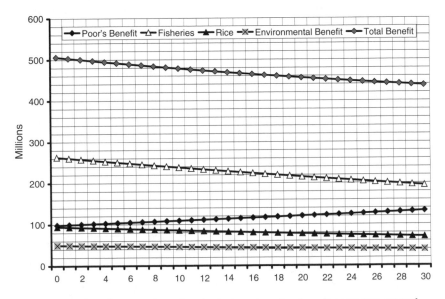

Figure 4.4. Value of economic and ecological services due to sedimentation control

4.4.4. *The impact of embankment*

Table 4.4 has already indicated that the embankment is clearly inefficient and that the present value will decrease if this policy is implemented (compared to the business-as-usual scenario).

4.5. The sustainable management option

Using the management interventions and the simulation model built in STELLA, Table 4.5 summarizes whether these interventions passed the sustainability and efficiency test. A sustainability test is considered to be

Table 4.5. Sustainability and efficiency trade-offs for *Haor* management

Scenario	Management Option	Sustainability test	Efficiency test
Scenario 1	Afforestation	Not passed	Not passed
Scenario 2	Sanctuary	Not passed	Not passed
Scenario 3	Sediment control	Not passed	Not passed
Scenario 4	Embankment	Not passed	Not passed
Scenario 5	Sediment control + sanctuary	Not Passed	Not passed
Scenario 6	Sedimentation control + sanctuary + afforestation	Passed	Passed
Scenario 7	Sedimentation control + sanctuary + afforestation + embankment	Passed	Not passed

passed if the future flow of services continues to grow or at least stay constant. An efficiency test is said to have passed if the present value of services is higher than that of the business-as-usual scenario. Figure 4.6a shows cases when efficiency test is passed. For projects below eight years, business-as-usual is the best management option (NPV is the maximum) while for projects above eight years of lifetime, scenario 6 is the best management option. On the other hand, when considering the sustainability test, Figures 4.2, 4.3, 4.4, 4.5a, and 4.5b show that except for scenario 6 and scenario 7 (shown in Figures 4.5a and 4.5b) and their associated management plans the future flow of services from the *haor* resources decreases over time. At the same time, Figure 4.6b shows that NPV is the maximum under

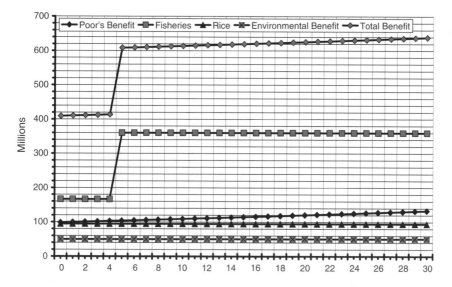

Figure 4.5a. Value of economic and ecological services due to sedimentation control, afforestation, and establishment of the fish sanctuary (Scenario 6)

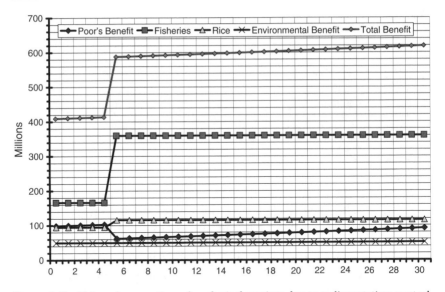

Figure 4.5b. Value of economic and ecological services due to sedimentation control, afforestation, establishment of the fish sanctuary, and construction of the embankment (Scenario 7)

scenario 6. Hence, if we want to guarantee both sustainability and efficiency, management option 6 becomes the ultimate choice.

4.6. Concluding observations

Simulations based on real-life data from the Hakaluki *haor* in Bangladesh show that sustainable management of resources requires a multi-pronged strategy. The current government strategy of promoting afforestation is important but cannot guarantee sustainability. Afforestation, along with reassignment and reprovisioning of rights for resources, is also not enough for the sustainable development of CPRs. This is perhaps the link which is the missing from much of the empirical literature that has shown how reallocation of rights and creating new institutions for the management of forest resources in Nepal, and India, for example, did not guarantee sustainable development of CPRs. It has been shown in this study that of the seven independent but popular management options suggested by both the local inhabitants and the institution managing the resources, six passed the efficiency test while only two passed the sustainability test. Of them, option 6 (see above), a combination of establishing sanctuary, removing sediments from the *beel*-beds, and afforestation, provides the highest total benefits. Between management

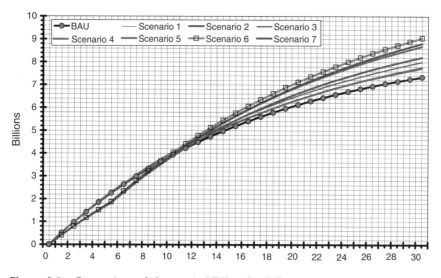

Figure 4.6a. Comparison of changes in NPV under different management options for 30 years of life of the management plan

options 6 and 7, it appears that net present value under option 6 is higher than that under option 7 (see Figure 4.6b). Hence, option 7 is less efficient that option 6. Thus, option 6 is the best choice to guarantee the biggest benefits which is both sustainable and efficient. Incidentally, under this policy the benefits to the poor are also the maximum (Table 4.4).

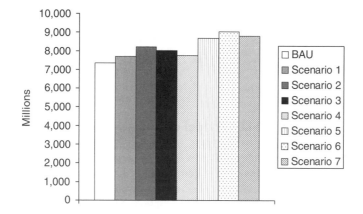

Figure 4.6b. NPV under different management options

Appendix 4.1 The Schematic Model used for Simulation

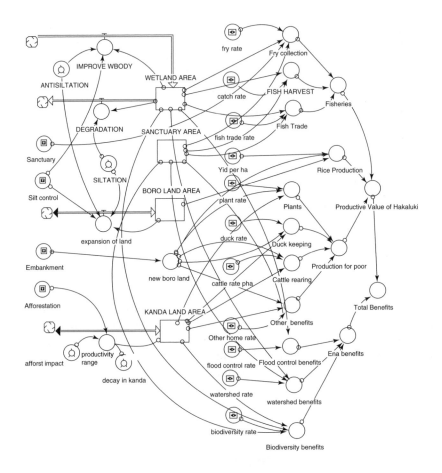

Appendix 4.2 The STELLA Model on Hakaluki *Haor* Management

BORO_LAND_AREA(t) = BORO_LAND_AREA(t − dt) + (expansion_of_land)*dt

INIT BORO_LAND_AREA = 13418+new_boro_land

INFLOWS:

expansion_of_land = Silt_control*BORO_LAND_AREA*ANTISILTATION-SILTATION *BORO_LAND_AREA

*KANDA*_LAND_AREA(t) = *KANDA*_LAND_AREA(t − dt) + (productivity_change) * dt

INIT *KANDA*_LAND_AREA = 7116
INFLOWS:
productivity_change   =   Afforestation**KANDA*_LAND_AREA*afforst_impact-*KANDA*_
   LAND_AREA*decay_in_*kanda*
SANCTUARY_AREA(t) = SANCTUARY_AREA(t − dt)
INIT SANCTUARY_AREA = 5000*Sanctuary
WETLAND_AREA(t) = WETLAND_AREA(t − dt) + (IMPROVE_WBODY−DEGRADATION)
   *dt
INIT WETLAND_AREA = 13595-SANCTUARY_AREA*Sanctuary
INFLOWS:
IMPROVE_WBODY = WETLAND_AREA*ANTISILTATION*Silt_control
OUTFLOWS:
DEGRADATION = WETLAND_AREA*SILTATION
Afforestation = 1
afforst_impact = .02
ANTISILTATION = .01
Biodiversity_benefits = (SANCTUARY_AREA+WETLAND_AREA + *KANDA*_LAND_AREA)
*biodiversity_rate
   biodiversity_rate = 571.19
catch_rate = 13586
cattle_rate_pha = 5466
Cattle_rearing = *KANDA*_LAND_AREA*cattle_rate_pha-
new_boro_land*cattle_rate_pha
decay_in_*kanda* = .01
Duck_keeping = *KANDA*_LAND_AREA*duck_rate-new_boro_land*duck_rate
duck_rate = 11.89
Embankment = 1
Env_benefits = watershed_benefits+Flood_control_benefits+Biodiversity_benefits
Fisheries = Fry_collection+Fish_Trade+FISH_HARVEST
FISH_HARVEST
WETLAND_AREA*catch_rate+DELAY(SANCTUARY_AREA*catch_rate *2,5,0)
Fish_Trade
WETLAND_AREA*fish_trade_rate+delay(fish_trade_rate*SANCTUARY_AREA*2,5,0)
fish_trade_rate = 5010
Flood_control_benefits = (SANCTUARY_AREA+WETLAND_AREA)*flood_control_rate
flood_control_rate = 1905.95
Fry_collection = WETLAND_AREA*fry_rate+delay(SANCTUARY_AREA*fry_rate*2
   *Sanctuary,5,0)
fry_rate = 761
new_boro_land = delay(3000*Embankment,5,0)
Other_benefits = *KANDA*_LAND_AREA*Other_bene_rate-new_boro_land*Other_bene_
   rate
Other_bene_rate = 3063
Plants = *KANDA*_LAND_AREA*plant_rate-plant_rate*new_boro_land
plant_rate = 5330
Production_for_poor = Cattle_rearing+Duck_keeping+Plants+Other_benefits

Productive_Value_of_Hakaluki = Fisheries+Production_for_poor+Rice_Production
Rice_Production = Yld_per_ha*BORO_LAND_AREA+new_boro_land*Yld_per_ha
Sanctuary = 1
SILTATION = .01
Silt_control = 1
Total_Benefits = Env_benefits+Productive_Value_of_Hakaluki
watershed_benefits = (WETLAND_AREA+SANCTUARY_AREA)*watershed_rate
watershed_rate = 878.89
Yld_per_ha = 7050

References

Arrow, K. J., Dasgupta, P., and Maler, K.-G. (2004). 'Evaluating Projects and Assessing Sustainable Development in Imperfect Economies', in P. Dasgupta and K.-G. Maler (eds.), *The Economics of Non-Convex Ecosystems*. London: Kluwer Academic Press.

Berkes, F. (ed.) (1989). *Common Property Resources—Ecology and Community-based Sustainable Development*. London: Belhaven Press.

Bossel, H., and Krieger, H. (1991). 'Simulation Model of Natural Tropical Forest Dynamics'. *Ecological Modelling*, 59/1-2: 37–71.

Brian, D., Richter, R. M., Harrison, D. L., and Wigington, R. (2003). 'Ecologically Sustainable Water Management: Managing River Flows for Ecological Integrity'. *Ecological Applications*, 13/1: 206–24.

Bromley, D. W. (ed.) (1992). *Making the Commons Work: Theory, Practice and Policy*. San Francisco, CA: Institute of Contemporary Studies.

Cheung, S. N. (1970). 'The Structure of a Contract and the Theory of a Non-exclusive Resource'. *Journal of Law and Economics*, 113: 49–70.

Chopra, K. C., Kadekodi, G., and Murthy, M. (1989). 'People's Participation and Common Property Resources'. *Economic and Political Weekly*, 24: A.189-A.195.

Choudhury, G. A., and Nishat, A. (2005). *Hydro-Meteorological Characteristics of Hakaluki Haor*. IUCN-The World Conservation Unition, Dhaka.

CNRS (2003). 'Biophysical and Socioeconomic Characterization of Hakaluki *Haor*: Steps towards Building Community Consensus on Sustainable Wetland Resources Management'. Unpublished monograph. Center for Natural Resources Studies, Dhaka.

Demsetz, H. (1967). 'Towards a Theory of Property Rights'. *American Economic Review*, 52/2: 347–79.

Haque, A. K.-E. (2006a). *Natural Resource Economic Evaluation at Hakaluki Haor*. Monograph, Bangladesh: IUCN.

—— (2006b). 'Field Survey conducted in 10 Unions Surrounding the Hakaluki Haor'. Personal communication. Financial support from IUCN Bangladesh.

Hardin, G. (1968). 'The Tragedy of Commons'. *Science*, 162/1: 243–8.

Jodha, N. S. (1986). 'Common Property Resources and the Rural Poor in Dry Regions of India'. *Economic and Political Weekly*, 21/27: 169–81.

Johnson, O. E. G. (1972). 'Economic Analysis, the Legal Framework and Land Tenure Systems'. *Journal of Law and Economics*, 15: 259–76.

IUCN (2006). 'Inception Report: Economic Evaluation of Hakaluki *Haor*'. Unpublished report. World Conservation Union (IUCN) Bangladesh, Dhaka.

McCay, B. J., and Achenson, J. M. (1987). *The Question of the Commons: The Culture and Ecology of Common Resources*. Tucson: University of Arizona Press.

Olmsted, I., and Alvarez-Buylla, E. R. (1995). 'Sustainable Harvesting of Tropical Trees: Demography and Matrix Models of Two Palm Species in Mexico'. *Ecological Applications*, 5/2: 484–500.

Ostrom, E. (1990). *Governing the Commons: The Evolution of Institutions for Collective Action*. Cambridge: Cambridge University Press.

—— Gardner, R., and Walter, J. (1994). *Rules, Games and Common-Pool-Resources*. Ann Arbor, MI: University of Michigan Press.

Peng, C. (2000). 'Understanding the Role of Forest Simulation Models in Sustainable Forest Management'. *Environmental Impact Assessment Review*, 20/4: 481–501 (21).

Smith, R. (1981). 'Resolving the Tragedy of the Commons by Creating Private Property Rights in Wildlife'. *CATO Journal*, 1: 439–68.

USAID (2002). 'Hail Haor MACH Project Study'. Management of Aquatic Ecosystems through Community Husbandry (MACH) project, USAID, Bangladesh.

Wade, R. (1987). 'The Management of Common Property Resources: Collective Action as an Alternative to Privatisation or State Regulation'. *Cambridge Journal of Economics*, 11: 95–106.

5

A Tale of Three Villages: Practised Forestry in India

Rucha Ghate

5.1. Introduction

The Indian government took a major step by adopting a policy of partici-patory forest management in 1988, which was a major deviation from the British legacy of centralized forest management. To operationalize this policy of 'inclusion', Joint Forest Management (JFM) was implemented in a number of states. The three subsequent Government Resolutions[1] in this direction, and a recent decision to create a two-tier system for federating JFM commit-tees into Forest Development Agencies (FDA), are indicative of 'participation' becoming an integral part of government's forest management policy. At the ground level also there is evidence of JFM becoming popular amongst forest-dwelling communities. In twenty-eight states that have adopted JFM, 8.4 mil-lion families in 84,632 JFM committees are managing around 17.33 million hectares of forestland in India (annual report of Ministry of Environment and Forest (2004–5)). A programme that got started in response to pressure from donor agencies as well as recognition of the failure of the past approach of the state agencies (Thompson 1995), is today being accorded some credit for improvement in forest cover (Baalu 2002; Bahuguna 2001). However, it has been critiqued that in most places protection committees created under JFM do not last long (Matta and Kerr 2004), or end being unequal partners. They become dysfunctional either after initial enthusiasm dies down or after the incentive money is exhausted. In some cases village-level JFM committees exist only on paper, and are ineffective in protecting the resource (Ghate and Nagendra 2005). Concerns are being increasingly expressed over the efficiency and sustainability of this approach (Sundar 2001; Lele 2000). If JFM is to

[1] No. 6.2/89-Forest Policy, 1 June 1990; No. 22-8/2000-JFM (FPD), 21 February 2000; Strengthening of JFM Programme, Guidelines, by MoEF, on 24 December 2002.

be the new institutional arrangement, to ensure its effectiveness it needs to become a 'peoples' programme'. But the question is, in the given scenario, does the 'participation' envisaged under JFM ensure collective action? Is the arrangement flexible enough to suit local conditions?

In the Indian context, 'collective action'-based 'community' management has a long history, although 'participatory' forestry is a relatively modern concept. Until the end of the nineteenth century, at least 80 per cent of India's natural resources were common property (Singh 1986). Despite the fact that there existed vast tracts of seemingly inexhaustible forests with low population pressure, restrictions on reckless and indiscriminate exploitation have always been the foundation of the social and cultural institutions developed by people in various forest areas of India (Guha 1983; Roy Burman 1985; Gadgil and Berkes 1991; Gadgil and Subhash Chandra 1992). This situation changed with the first policy statement in 1894, which termed forest communities as 'intruders' and 'aliens over the state property'. Forestlands were transformed into mere sources of revenue for the British Government (Rangarajan 1996) even at the expense of forest areas allocated to villagers' use (Guha and Gadgil 1989), resulting in the erosion of localized institutions.

This situation started changing again much before the government of independent India realized that unless the large number of biomass-dependent communities were accepted as stakeholders of the forest resource, its protection would be extremely difficult. Once again community-initiated and NGO-promoted 'collective action'-based resource management started emerging sporadically throughout the country almost two decades before JFM (Sarin 1996). Studies in different parts of the country (Gadgil and Berkes 1991; Gadgil and Guha 1992; Gadgil and Subhash Chandra 1992; Ghate 2004a; Guha 1983; Sarin 1996, to cite just a few) point to the existence of communities that have been consciously maintaining and managing forests within their village boundaries at their own initiatives. They have been forming their own rules of the game and have developed strong sanctioning mechanisms including social fencing.

5.2. Present study

This study analysis alternative outcomes in the institutional structures, that is, the self-initiated, NGO-promoted, and government-sponsored JFM programmes in Maharashtra, India, and compares them with the help of three case studies. All the case-study villages are from Gadchiroli, one of the eleven districts in Maharashra that has forest cover. The villages were chosen so that they do not vary much in terms of population size and composition, distance from market, and forest type. The three institutional structures are different, in their strengths and weaknesses too. This paper tries to identify factors that may ensure the sustainability of collective action in each of these institutions. The data for the study was collected through ten research instruments developed by the International Forestry Resources and Institutions (IFRI) research programme,[2] and through informal group discussions. Group discussion and observation are necessary methods of information gathering, especially in rural/tribal set-ups where the population tends not to be very forthcoming in giving information.

Beginning with a discussion on 'participation' and 'collective action', we proceed to describe the three institutional structures, and provide a brief summary of documentation of the three case studies. With the objective of understanding strengths and weaknesses of the three institutional structures, we conclude with some suggestions for reorientation of the forest management policies.

5.3. Participation or collective action?

Is 'participation' different from 'collective action'? Collective action is voluntary and evolves due to commonality of objectives. It is based on unity of a community as well as freedom to take decisions regarding issues that directly affect the community. Naturally, since the communities own such decisions, acceptability and adherence levels are high. On the other hand, 'participation', especially between unequal partners as in JFM, may not have these characteristics. It is alleged that the participatory management approach of the government under the JFM programme is not necessarily based on 'collective action'. 'Participation' should be determined by rules, norms and perceptions, endowments and attributes of all the partners (Agarwal 2001), and not be forced by one on the other. But under the existing model of JFM, the Forest Department's autonomy over allocation and demarcation of forestlands, its control over micro-plans and the disposal of forest produce leaves no room for 'people's participation' (Ballabh, Balooni, and Dave 2002). If the JFM committees are looked at not as a people's organization but as a creature that works under the thumb of a forester (Shah 2003), participation by local communities can only be 'puppetish' (Lele 2000). More often JFM is showcased by the Forest Department as an example of 'bottom-up' development by a sympathetic government structure 'from above', with the government extending support to the most vulnerable sections of the

---

[2] IFRI, based on a Workshop in Policy Analysis, at Indiana University in USA, has developed a set of ten research instruments to facilitate collection of information about the demographic, economic, and cultural characteristics of communities dependent on forests. The set of ten pre-structured questionnaires is filled in using rapid appraisal and in-person interview methods.

community. Many studies indicate that this is not 'participation' in a true sense (Hill 2000). It seems that 'participation' under JFM is relegated to a paper theory or a suboptimal-level approach with no real interest in the community, and therefore in 'collective action'.

In the beginning JFM suffered because in many instances both partners— Forest Department and communities—were not ready for the new institutional arrangement. The Forest Department staff, with a long history of 'command and control', were not oriented to the changed approach. Similarly, the communities found it difficult to acclimatize to the idea of being an equal partner in managing a resource from which they were strictly kept away for all these years and whose use invited punishment. This scenario has changed over the last decade to some extent but JFM is still treated as a palliative to appease villagers so that they will not erode the potential timber harvest (Jodha 1998). Although 'participation' has been accepted at the policy level, it is sometimes completely missing in spirit at the grass roots. Therefore 'participation' of communities in a real sense, seems to be a difficult contention.

On the other hand, we argue that the success of self-governing community institutions, (either self-initiated or NGO-promoted), lies in voluntary 'collective action' (Mishra, this volume). In these institutions, rule formation, benefit-sharing arrangements, conflict resolution mechanisms, sanctioning, monitoring, etc., are more or less collectively determined indigenously by the community. The one thing they lack is legal recognition by formal law. That probably explains why despite the apparent limitations of JFM, an ever-increasing number of communities seem to be keen to form Forest Protection Committees under JFM. Even the self-initiated or NGO-promoted efforts of forest management are keen to join the JFM programme to achieve some legal recognition for their efforts (Ghate and Mehra 2004). At the same time, it is important to note that the effectiveness of JFM depends on the quality of implementation of the programme. If it fosters only bureaucratic participation, and 'fails to account for the specific characteristics of the local context within which these partnerships are to be developed' (Vira 2005: 5074), its success would be limited despite soaring numbers.

5.3.1. Self-initiated efforts

'A self-governed forest resource is one where actors, who are the major users of the forest, are involved over time in making and adapting rules within collective choice arenas regarding the inclusion or exclusion of participants, appropriation strategies, obligations of participants, monitoring and sanctioning, and conflict resolution' (Ostrom 1999: 2). Apart from its effect on forest condition and optimum resource use, a shared understanding of social norms plays a crucial role in community-initiated management regimes. The writings of scholars regarding the commons, with historical and contemporary evidence, have shown that resource users often create institutional arrangements and management regimes that help them allocate benefit equitably, over long time periods, and with only limited efficiency losses (Agrawal 1999; Gunawardena and Steele, this volume; McKean 1992; Ostrom 1992*a* and 1992*b*). It is also found that when the users of a common property resource organize themselves to devise and enforce some of their own basic rules, they tend to manage local resources more suitably than when the rules are externally imposed on them (Baland and Platteau 1996; Khan, this volume; Mishra, this volume; Tang 1992; Wade 1994).

Usually communities organize themselves for collective action in the case of resources that are scarce as well as salient for the community (Gibson and Becker 1999). A huge amount of literature has come up in recent times in search of an answer to the perennial question, why do some communities organize themselves to solve the problems of institutional supply, while others in similar circumstances are not able to do so (Agrawal 2002). Another important issue that has been widely discussed is about the factors that are conducive for collective action. In the Indian context as well, despite hostility from forest authorities, some communities have opted for self-governance of forests basically to meet their sustenance needs. Forests are a 'lifeline' for the biomass-dependent millions of Indians living in rural areas in general and those living in and around forests in particular. Realizing the fact that they themselves are the primary sufferers of forest degradation, these more 'enlightened' communities have taken it upon themselves to protect forests that are within their village boundaries by restricting use within the community. Some such attempts have been informal and merely based on mutual understanding while others have been much more explicit.

However, it is important to take note of the fact that not all efforts on behalf of the community to manage its resources are successful. Caste hierarchies, the domination of the economically better-placed individuals or the elite within the community, etc., can easily mar the well-intended self-initiated efforts of the communities.

5.3.2. NGO-promoted efforts

In India, NGOs have played an important role in encouraging communities to manage their own resources. These NGOs are characterized by their diversity. Most are private, voluntary, or non-profit organizations, but not all. Some are based in urban areas while others are in rural areas. Their areas of operation too vary from international to local. While some NGOs focus on a particular issue, others attempt a holistic approach to overall development. Some may only provide technical and financial support for various activities, or remain in an advisory capacity while others may be involved directly in developmental activity. Like the local communities and states in which they operate, NGOs too differ widely in ideology, political and economic power, and organizational capacity (Isager, Theilade, and Thomsen 2002).

In the Indian forestry sector, NGOs have gained credibility, mainly because of the unpopular regulatory role of the Forest Department (FD). The transition from community ownership of the resource to the policing of the FD has put the FD in a bad light amongst the forest-dependent communities. Even after the FD adopted participatory approaches, in the initial stages the local communities found it hard to believe that the FD was willing to accept them as partners in forest management. Similarly, the FD was sceptical about NGO involvement in JFM and NGOs faced non-cooperation from the FD for assisting village communities (Arul 1998; Balooni 1998). However, in many places NGOs have played a crucial role as facilitator in bridging the credibility gap as well as in providing assistance on the non-technical and social aspects of participatory forestry (Varalakshmi and Kaul 1999). Despite their own limitations and constraints, there is potential for the involvement of NGOs in practically every aspect of common property resource (CPR) management and in making decentralized forest management a reality. The next step after JFM is community forest management in which NGOs will have an important role to play, be it building community stakes in CPRs, rebuilding institutional mechanisms to facilitate CPR management, promoting bottom-up approaches to natural resource management strategies, or in facilitating the devolution process in general (Jodha 2002). The state too has recognized the positive role of NGOs in natural resource management. The recognition has come in the form of the mandatory involvement of an NGO representative in the JFM committee (via. the GoI circular no. 6.21/89-FP-dt.1.6.1990). Extending their role further, NGOs are now increasingly involved right from the first stage of the micro-plan preparation at village level, followed by monitoring and project evaluation. Due to the diversity of the nature, purpose, reach, and working of NGOs, it is not possible to evaluate the role of NGOs *en bloc* but the fact remains that NGOs often play a critical role in successful negotiation and co-management between people and governments (Isager, Theilade, and Thomsen 2002). The presence of capable and environmentally concerned NGOs indicates that efforts to resolve the increasing conflicts over natural resources can be made at multiple levels.

As in the case of self-initiated efforts, NGO initiative to prompt collective action amongst communities to manage their own resources may not always be successful. NGOs could lack accountability and may fall into the role of 'benevolent paternalism' (Gupta 1990). The credibility of the NGOs concerned, resources available, level of motivation, acceptability to a community, attitudes of the concerned forest officials can be cited as some of the factors that determine success or failure of such efforts.

5.3.3. *Joint forest management*

The reasons for the government's shift from a century-old, centralized, command and controlled management system to decentralization in the form of participatory JFM intrigued scholars initially. Environmental activists and rural communities have been sceptical about the government's intentions in sharing power with the forest users, as it is one of the revenue-generating sectors of the state. Their apprehensions are based on past experience as well as the limitations of the initial provisions of the JFM scheme. Earlier, in all government forestation programmes, participation of the rural poor was largely limited to wage employment because the poor were seen as destroying forests through overuse and overgrazing. The forest-poverty relationship was defined such that if people continue to be poor they will destroy forests. In fact, although JFM talks about the positive role that forests can play in poverty alleviation and the role that people can play in forest protection, the implementing agency (FD) was apprehensive in the beginning.

Criticisms against JFM have been manifold and are now well recorded in the literature. Although JFM was expected to increase the collective ability of the communities adjacent to forests to manage, grow, and equitably share common resources, there have been few efforts to involve people in the planning process or to identify priorities. Communities cannot decide which species are to be taken up for plantation and there has been little correlation between the amount of land that is brought under JFM and what is required to meet the biotic requirements of the users. JFM does not take into consideration the fact that the management objectives of the locals could be very different and may not coincide with those of the state (Ligon and Narain 1999). While the JFM agreement talks about sharing long-term benefits from timber, the fate of the forests after being successfully regenerated remains hazy (Arora and Khare 1994). Another major limitation mentioned is that the important question of 'tenure' that includes clear, secure, and exclusive rights of access to the resource is kept ambiguous in the JFM scheme (Lele and Rao 1996). Absence of legal status to Forest Protection Committees (FPCs'), the government's right to dissolve FPCs, unilateral decision-making, and inappropriate sharing of forest produce are some of the other aspects criticized by scholars (Pattnaik and Dutta 1997).

Many of these issues were dealt with in the two subsequent resolutions in the years 2000 and 2002, as mentioned at the start of this chapter. Two states in India, Andhra Pradesh and Madhya Pradesh, have taken a step forward by decentralizing decision-making and by granting limited financial autonomy to the JFM communities.[3] One is not sure whether the government

[3] Incidentally, both these states have been recipients of large funding from the World Bank while it is a well-known fact that 'decentralization' has been on the Bank's agenda when it comes to dispersal of funds.

is interested in expanding this shift from 'joint management' to 'community management' for the whole nation but one thing seems clear: it will now be difficult to go back to the days of unilateral decision-making and total control by FD (see Mishra, this volume, for an example where community groups have increased their strength by forming supra-local institutions).

5.4. Process documentation

'Process documentation/analysis' is a method used to understand how the communities or their institutions have developed, what were the aims and motives behind coming together, and how the process was initiated. In other words, it tries to understand the ways through which their objectives were achieved, aims were fulfilled (or why they were not fulfilled), and what the potential areas of intervention are for achieving wider, common goals. The participatory process inevitably varies from institution to institution and from one community to another within the category of an institutional structure. In the three case studies presented here, since all three are covered under JFM now, the focus here is on the process of collective action through an investigation of its genesis, leadership initiatives, interest-holder analysis, local land-use history, institutional analysis (rule structure, infractions, compliance), legal rights and privileges, and strengths and weaknesses. Sustainability of each institutional structure has been evaluated on the basis of its perceived strengths and weaknesses. The three case-study villages are predominantly tribal villages with comparable forest dependence. The first village was chosen to represent the category of self-initiated participatory forest management as 'collective effort' for forest protection and management. It was only after eight years of self-initiated protection that JFM came to the village. The second village is the one that was able to initiate forest management with the guidance of a local NGO. JFM was introduced here two years later. The third case study is of a village where collective action was JFM-initiated. Field visits for primary data collection were made in the year 2001.

5.4.1. Case study 1

Village *Deulgoan*, situated 18 kilometres from the *taluka* (subdistrict) headquarters, has around 600 hectares of forestland in its revenue boundary. A village of thirty-three households with population of 175, it is even today dependent on the surrounding forest for fuelwood, fodder, grass for thatching houses, bamboo for fencing houses, timber for housing and making agricultural implements, and non-timber forest products for supplementing nutrition and income from agriculture. Gradual degradation of the forest, caused by multiple factors like increase in population, overharvesting and poaching, and lack of attention from Forest Department officials despite the area being under their jurisdiction, had been experienced by the Deulgoan community for a couple of decades. Believing that forest degradation was affecting water availability in the village wells, the community decided to undertake collective action.

5.4.1.1. BEGINNING OF COLLECTIVE FOREST PROTECTION

Forest protection activities started in Deulgoan to stop indiscriminate felling by neighbouring villagers. Immediately following a land survey in 1988, the villagers decided that all the forest that was in their revenue boundary would be protected from outsiders. The decision was also influenced by the spurt of forest-protection activities taking place in a nearby village. The villagers came together in an informal meeting in 1990. The *sarpanch* and the police *patil* at that time, who often have to travel to other villages and thus have more exposure, took the lead in organizing this meeting. Long discussions identified two areas where action was needed—restricting neighbouring villagers to harvest from Deulgoan's forest and restricting use by the community itself. As a consequence daytime patrolling started to curtail poaching by outsiders, and it was decided by consensus that each household would harvest according to its genuine requirement, and would not sell any forest product. These were two simple rules introduced by the community at the outset. No formal forest association was formed.

5.4.1.2. PROTECTING AUTONOMY

With no access to funding or technical know-how for increasing the stock and quality of the resource, the informal efforts of the community continued in the form of 'protection' work allowing only natural regeneration. However, the community used to meet often to discuss various issues related to forest protection. This is a practice that continues even now. Hearing of the good work being done by the people of Deulgoan, the local forest officer urged the community to join JFM. The villagers took their time to decide: they held frequent meetings amongst themselves, discussed the pros and cons of joining JFM, and only after consensus was reached was it decided that they would register under JFM. In 1998 the Forest Protection Committee (FPC) was formed, the executive committee and general body (which included two adults from each household) were also constituted. The committee was eventually registered in 2000. Importantly, the persons who had taken a lead in the forest-protection work were made members of executive body as well. The norms set by the JFM regulation regarding representation of caste, gender, and landholding, did not dictate the constitution of executive committee.

To this day the community continues to work according to its own rules wherein all members are eligible to participate in the meetings that are held once a month, and on an average are well attended. The decisions related to forest are taken only at the meetings of the general body as no separate executive committee meetings take place, although mandatory under JFM. Decisions taken at these meetings normally relate to daily wages for plantation work, punishments, and fines related to infractions. Suggestions from all members are invited. For example, night patrolling was started along with day patrolling on the basis of a suggestion made by one member. The suggestions are incorporated only if all the members accept them unanimously, which is a costly preposition (Ghate 2000).

5.4.1.3. FLEXIBILITY IN RULE FORMATION

The association, independent of the rules under JFM, has developed a rule structure for the harvesting of forest products, determining who is authorized to harvest from this forest, monitoring forest condition and conformance to rules, and the punishment of rule breakers. There are restrictions on felling certain trees even for self-consumption, for species like *Tendu (Diospyros melenoxylon)*, *Moha (Madhuca longifolia)*, gums that have traditional value and are regular suppliers of leaves, flowers, and fruits. Similarly, only trees of a certain minimum girth can be harvested, thus ensuring protection to smaller trees and saplings as a basis for sustaining forest stocks. Only dead wood and fallen branches can be gathered for fuel. Sale of timber, fuelwood, and fodder is not allowed. In case anyone needs to harvest more than the legitimate requirement because of a special occasion, one has to submit the request at the monthly meeting, which is mostly a general body meeting, where the decision is taken unanimously.

No full-time or part-time employees have been appointed for the village forest association to carry out its various forest-related activities. Forest patrolling is on a voluntary basis; two persons are sent from two households every day, throughout the year, on rotational basis. The association is now looking into activities such as harvesting of forest products, distribution of forest products to local users, determining the quantity of forest products that can be harvested sustainably, determining who should be authorized to harvest these forest products, monitoring compliance to rules, sanctioning the rule breakers, arbitrating in disputes among local users, restricting areas of forest for harvesting, monitoring of forest condition, and interaction with higher authorities.

Infractions to these rules are few and have subsided over the years with the growing clarity of purpose and provisions. Since the rules have been strictly implemented, with monetary sanctions, right from the beginning, compliance has been increasing. A sliding-scale penalty structure, ranging from a day's income for the first infraction to approaching the police after subsequent infractions, is in place. The community does not approach the FD, since communication and coordination between the village and the FD are not very good. There is also a provision for 'public apology' to restore harvesting rights if under exceptional circumstances any member loses them. Almost everyone in the community is aware of these rules and considers them easy to understand, responsive to the needs of the people, fair, and legitimate. During informal discussions it became clear that no one from the user group has been deprived of the benefits from this forest or become worse off due to the rules of the association.

5.4.1.4. COSTS AND BENEFITS OF FORMAL SET-UP

Under the wings of JFM, the self-initiated attempt at forest management got a boost in the forms of technical know-how and funds. After accepting JFM, a plantation on 85 hectares of forestland has been established with FD assistance, where species that the forest lacked or the villagers desired have been planted. Encouraged by this support, the community was also expecting further cooperation from the FD, which has not been forthcoming. Deul- goan community is upset over the way the Department deals with poachers apprehended by the guards of Deulgoan. During group discussion, several instances were quoted when offenders were taken to the forest office but the officials would only confiscate the products that were caught and let off the offenders. The tools used by the offender were released after a few days without informing the villagers of Deulgoan, nor was the amount paid as penalty shared with the village. Despite such discouragement, the people of Deulgoan continue to protect 'their' forest with their own rules.

We next look at the second case where an NGO had prompted a community to take up forest protection.

5.4.2. Case study 2

Ranvahi village is spread over 924 hectares of which 641 hectares is forest- land. There are 393 who populate eighty-one households. Of these, nineteen households do not own any land. The village is located 25 kilometres away from the subdistrict town of Kurkheda. It has 96 per cent of its population belonging to an indigenous tribe called Gond and yet more than 62 per cent of the population is literate.

5.4.2.1. AN NGO INITIATIVE

An NGO, *Amhi Amchya Arogya Sathi* (AAA) located in a nearby town, intro- duced the idea of the community protecting the forest in the vicinity of its village. The NGO has been working in this village, especially amongst women in forming their self-help groups, for quite some time. Inspired by the NGO, women in the Ranvahi community started protection work, concentrating on the poachers who were mainly from the neighbouring villages. In the cluster of villages around, Ranvahi has the most forest area. Therefore, these nearby villages were habituated to collecting fuelwood and grazing their cattle in the forest area within the jurisdiction of Ranvahi. With determined efforts, the community was successful in preventing poaching of its forest by outsiders. However, excessive harvesting by the Ranvahi community itself continued for some time. Encouraged by the suggestions from the NGO (AAA), some villagers tried to estimate the usage of forest products by each household. They found that households were using forest products like timber and fuelwood much more than was necessary. It was then decided that the community members would be allowed to collect only what was genuinely required. This was the first rule formed by the informal association. AAA not only encouraged the participation of women in forming rules during community meetings, but also suggested round-the-clock vigilance. Protection of the forest from external use and internal 'over'-withdrawal was the only activity taken up by the community.

During a meeting of self-help groups, an AAA representative introduced the JFM scheme to the Ranvahi community, and explained the advantages of joining the programme. He urged the community members to contact the Forest Department and send in their application. After reaching a consensus, the community sent its application to the FD in 1995. The Deputy Conservator of Forest (Dy CF) on receiving the application sent the Range Forest Officer (RFO) of *Malewada* to hold a meeting with the people of Ranvahi to test their commitment. In 2001 Ranvahi was formally registered under the JFM programme.

5.4.2.2. RULE FORMATION WITH NGO'S HELP

Under its JFM status, an executive committee was formed with five men and two women, elected for a term of five years. In keeping with the government regulations, Ranvahi community has prepared its own rules. Almost everyone in the community is aware of the rules that govern the association, as they are easy to understand. The rules are kept flexible in the interests of the community, taking into consideration times of emergency or urgent needs of the members of the user group. This has resulted in the rules being perceived by the members as fair and legitimate. Specific rules regarding felling are: no trees can be felled for fuelwood; in case of timber for construction of houses, ten poles per year per household are permitted; if the requirement is up to fifty poles, permission can be sought by applying to the committee. Any harvesting over fifty poles is on the basis of a payment of fees. There is no limit fixed on the quantity of fodder that can be harvested and open grazing is generally practised. Only certain parts of the forest, such as the 60 hectare plantation set up under JFM, are closed for grazing, but even here evidence of grazing was found at the time of our study.

All the executive committee members work on a voluntary basis without any pay or material compensation. All members of the general body are eligible to participate in the meetings that are held once a month, and due to a high level of general awareness, most of the members of the association attend these meetings. The meetings normally discuss requisites for timber made by members for house construction and decide whether full or part requirement is to be approved. Similarly, distribution of money received from the FD for forest activities undertaken by members of the community also takes place at these meetings. Conventionally, all decisions are taken unanimously. The level of conflicts within the user group has decreased over the years, but this is reportedly due to leniency shown in imposing penalties. Forest patrolling is taken very seriously.

5.4.2.3. LENIENCY IN DEALING WITH INFRACTIONS

The members of the user group generally follow these rules, but infractions do take place as fuelwood or timber is often collected in excess of the limit. Guarding of the forest is done on a voluntary basis by lots, where two persons from two houses go on patrol every day. Yet, evidence of grazing and lopping of branches in restricted areas is evident in the forest that the community is protecting (Ghate and Nagendra 2005). For such infractions the community decided to pardon the offender on the first and second occasions either with a warning or with a small penalty. On the third occasion the member has to be expelled from the association. But despite several infractions, sanctions have never been imposed. All the penalties have been decided by a vote in the user group, and it is the members of the executive committee who are responsible for imposing the fines. If a violator refuses to pay the fine his harvesting rights are to be totally withdrawn. For restoring harvesting rights, one has to apologize publicly in one of the association meetings. In spite of such elaborate rule structures, there has not been one instance of penalizing any community member. Apparently it was at the behest of the NGO that the community adopted a lenient stance in dealing with offenders within the community. Probably the NGO does not want to antagonize anybody in the community, which could affect its other activities in the village. Therefore, to avoid conflicts within the community, infractions are often neglected. This has adversely affected collective action as the rule abiders resent leniency shown to violators. They feel that this is resulting in iniquitous sharing of benefits (Ghate 2004*b*).

Although FD officials are not called in to enforce penalties on the community members, Ranvahi community is very strict in dealing with outsiders poaching in its forest. Whenever the neighbouring villagers are caught stealing, they are taken to the Malewada forest office where a fine is imposed, and a certain percentage is given to the association of the Ranvahi.

We now discuss the third case where a forest protection committee was formed at the behest of the Forest Department, under its JFM programme.

5.4.3. Case study 3

Markegaon is a small tribal village with easy access to forest due to the low density of its population and the good quality of the forest surrounding the village. Although the total area of forest within the revenue boundary is less than the other two case-study villages, Markegaon community uses many more forest products because of its better quality of forest (Ghate, Chaturvedi, and Mehra 2003).

5.4.3.1. UNWILLINGNESS TO HAVE FOREST PROTECTION

Due to abundance of the resource, the need for forest protection and the restrictive use of forest products never made sense to the majority of the people unlike the case in Bhutan, where despite abundance a new institutional arrangement developed to protect the forest (Webb and Dorji, this volume). People's participation in forest management got introduced here in 1997 when the Forest Department set up a Forest Protection Committee (FPC) under its JFM programme. Few felt the need for forest protection and the community, as a whole was not united on this issue even though difficulties in harvesting forest products and conflicts with intruders were increasing. Markegaon community was also facing difficulties because the forest guard had started demanding some kind of payment to allow people to take out anything from the 'government forest'. This led to a simmering discontent among the people. Yet the community did not do much towards forest protection till 1997 resulting in indiscriminate felling both by the community members and the neighbouring villagers. With JFM already working in a neighbouring village, and its benefits being visible, a small group of people from Markegaon finally decided to contact the FD to set up an FPC. At the first meeting of the FPC, which was not attended by all the households, those who were present decided to restrict grazing and ban tree felling. The FD in turn, promised to provide funds for plantation and soil conservation.

5.4.3.2. FOLLOWING THE RULE-BOOK

In keeping with the provisions under JFM an executive committee of the association was formed where eight men and three women were elected from the general body (formed of one male and one female member from each household). According to the rules, each term is fixed for a period of five years for the members who work on a voluntary basis, and can be removed by a majority vote of the general body. The general body meetings of the association are called once a month where all members are eligible to participate. The attendance at these meetings is normally poor despite the provision for a small fine for members who do not attend two consecutive meetings. In these meetings decisions are made regarding poaching in the forest and thefts in the plantation areas and suggestions are taken for imposing extraction rules. But, reportedly, no suggestion has come from any member in last eight years. Payments of fines are also supposed to take place at these meetings. An emergency meeting can be held under special circumstances—for example, to address theft, but no such meeting has ever been held.

Few interested members of Markegaon community have formed the rules of the forest association: no new trees can be cut to meet the requirement of timber, especially valuable trees like *Tendu, Awala (Phyllanthus officinalis)*, and *Moha*, which are more important for their leaves, flowers, and fruits. Only one pole per year per family is allowed for house construction. For fuelwood, only fallen wood and stems can be harvested. Infractions of these rules do take place as people collect more than what the limit defines, yet penalties are not strictly imposed and the offender is let off even after ensuing infractions.

5.4.3.3. ADVANTAGES AND LACUNAE

The villagers feel that registration under JFM has been beneficial to them mainly because now they have rights over usufructs and they do not have to bribe the forest guard. They are also aware of the limited tree tenure and the benefits that would follow after ten years of the JFM programme. The small group of individuals, which had initiated protection activities, feels that the setting up of FPC under JFM has validated its efforts. However, the community is not efficiently protecting the forest since it still lacks strong will and positive support from the FD (Ghate and Nagendra 2005). Although relations with the FD are cordial, there is little help coming from the FD in helping the community to develop rule structures and enforce those rules. Meetings of the forest association are rarely attended by any representative of the FD, not even by the Forest Guard who is an ex-officio member of the Executive Committee. As a result, meetings do not take place regularly. The community continues to remain unaware of all the provisions of JFM; nor is the ex-officio secretary who is the forest guard of the Forest Department aware of the decisions taken by the FPC. In other words, the 'jointness' in day-to-day decision-making is totally missing.

Table 5.1 presents a summary of the process analysis. Without intending to compare the three institutional structures, the effort is to determine positive and negative aspects of the three, to understand what could make 'participatory' JFM more acceptable and encourage collective action.

Table 5.1. A summary of process analysis

Institutional Structure	Self-Initiated—Deulgoan	NGO-promoted—Ranvahi	JFM—Markegaon
Genesis	Scarcity felt, threat of accentuation of scarcity. Concern for external threat to forest resource. Community brought together by village *sarpanch* and police *patil* in 1990. **Endogenous initiative.**	Driven by the need to protect forest from outsiders. Passing of information, awareness-building by NGO in 1996. Encouragement to control overharvesting by the community itself. **Endogenous initiative.**	Lack of community consensus on need to protect and manage forest. Inclusion in JFM in 1997 at the behest of a small group of villagers. **Exogenous initiative.**
Evolution	**Voluntary** collective action, consensus-building, gradual evolution of flexible rule structure, therefore total compliance. More egalitarian make-up of association. Even after accepting JFM, original set-up maintained.	**Encouraged by NGO,** rapport building through self-help groups, support in evolving rule structure. Leniency towards rule breakers.	**Incentives provided by FD** in the form of plantation, community hall, etc. No role in building of rule structure. Slow community response in actively taking up protection work.
Planning	Protection from outsiders, regulating self-consumption, which encouraged natural regeneration. **No technical inputs.**	Just protection at first. Support from NGO in approaching and pursuing with FD. **Technical support from FD.**	No help or suggestion from FD regarding rule structure. Community taking initiative only recently, but no unanimity. **Investment by FD through plantations.**
Structure of Association	**Informal,** dominated by men.	**More formal.** Women encouraged to participate	**Formal** membership to men and women in accordance with rulebook. In reality only few persons participate in decision-making.
Democracy	Unanimity in decision-making. Regular reformation of rule structure in accordance with suggestions.	In coordination with the NGO and FD.	Irregular meetings, low participation, two women included in executive committee in accordance with the JFM regulations. Rule adherence not very strict.

(*cont.*)

Table 5.1. (Continued)

Institutional Structure	Self-Initiated—Deulgoan	NGO-promoted—Ranvahi	JFM—Markegaon
Important aspects	**Leadership:** Local, tribal (dominant tribe), literate but without formal education, self-motivated, belonging to middle class of village.	**Leadership:** Provided by the NGO, worked towards empowerment of women.	**Leadership:** Local—influenced by outsiders, tribal, average economic background.
	Salience: Scarcity of forest products due to low forest availability for neighbouring villages.	**Salience:** Basically from economic point of view, emphasized by the NGO.	**Salience:** Strong non-economic reason, fear of scarcity in future.
	Internal Unity: To stop outsiders from poaching and regulating internal use.	**Internal Unity:** Restricted to stop outsiders from poaching. Weak internal regulation.	**Internal Unity:** Weak internal as well as external monitoring, lack of common understanding regarding need to protect forest despite homogeneous population.
Results	Little help from FD in forest management, technical know-how, and funding. Community determined to continue on its own. Lack of coordination with FD as major hindrance in dealing with external poachers.	JFM formalized association and procedures and provided incentives for forest protection. Leniency in dealing with internal infractions, and high dependence on the NGO has negative impact on the working of FPC.	Community interest half-hearted. Expected initiative and support not coming from FD, no partnership in real sense.
Sustainability of collective action	**Possible** but with stunted opportunities unless FD extends active cooperation. Needs to be stricter with poachers, needs to improve coordination and support from FD.	**Likely.** Support from NGO and FD, Good coordination with FD due to mutual understanding and respect, no unasked-for interference. Gaining forest revenue. Dealings with internal infractions needs to be stricter. Dependence on NGO needs to go down gradually.	**Unlikely.** Control on illegal harvesting weak. Lack of will in the FPC as well as FD. Unless FD takes keen interest in helping the FPC in rule formation and monitoring, the forest will continue to deteriorate.

5.4.4. *Strengths and weaknesses under each system*

From the three case studies it can be surmised that the self-initiated efforts, including the NGO-backed efforts, induce a sense of ownership, belonging, and responsibility in the community. By developing its own rule structure for using the resource, a community is able to take care of its needs. The autonomy creates a sense of responsibility leading to better compliance as well as monitoring. Since the rules are collectively developed through consensus-building during frequent meetings, they are transparent, known to all, and are considered easy to understand by all members. Also, the rules being endogenously evolved according to villagers' perceptions, infractions are fewer.[4] This reduces the cost of conflict resolution and monitoring, since the settlement is reached within the community and infractions are fewer. The community also enjoys the advantage of flexibility in rule formulation at an operational level. There are serious limitations of the community when it comes to technical skills and finance, and this kind of collective action cannot go beyond regulated use by community members. It is ineffective against protection from outside encroachers, in the absence of legal backing from the state. In the long run, therefore, collective action limited to the community may have limited success and become unsustainable.

In the case of the NGO-promoted collective action, the study shows that the major advantages to the community are the conscious efforts in establishing rapport with the community. Also, the NGO may prove to be helpful in awareness-building, supporting the community with necessary information, introducing it to modern values like gender equality, helping it in decision-making and developing the skills of the community members. The NGOs can groom a community to become equal partners with the FD in schemes like JFM where there is lack of self-evolved active leadership. However, it can result in long-term reliance of the community on NGO support, without making it independent. Some NGOs may have their own agenda and may not act in the larger interest of the community. This could result in non-fulfilment of community's needs and suboptimal outcomes. The positive aspects of NGO intervention like awareness-building and skill enhancement, found in the study are in fact meant to be intrinsic to the JFM programme, which is also posed as a rural development programme.[5] But the case of Markegaon is indicative of what is found in most of the JFM villages, that is, lack of interest of the implementing agency despite JFM's 'participatory' nature. Bureaucratic participation neither ensures the concern of forest officials nor their efforts to make the community actually participate in forest management. Although

---

[4] Gunawardena and Steele's study in Sri Lanka, in this volume, finds a similar effect.

[5] According to a letter (no. MSC/2004/20/F-2, dated: 21 June 2004) issued by the chief secretary, GOM, the villages that are registered under JFM are to be given priority in the implementation of rural development schemes.

JFM provides for liberty in rule formulation by the community itself, the proactive role of a concerned forest official becomes necessary in cases where (*a*) there is external encroachment, (*b*) communities lack internal leadership, or (*c*) the community is not able to manage the resource due perceived relative abundance. Importantly it is the legal backing that JFM provides that strengthens collective action outcomes. It reduces ambiguity in intracommunity benefit sharing, gives authority in dealing with poachers, encourages women's participation by making it mandatory to include women members in executive committees.

5.5. Conclusion

The growing popularity of JFM offers an excellent opportunity to bring in a new institutional arrangement that is effective in curtailing deforestation and is acceptable to communities living in forest areas as well. It is the legal sanctity given to usufruct use by the members, which has worked as a major incentive for even self-initiated communities to adopt JFM arrangement. This is despite the fact that JFM is a quasi-legal arrangement, with limited transfer of resource ownership. The communities that have been managing their own resources know that their autonomous collective efforts could result in stagnation and non-sustainability in the absence of legal backing, 'credibility', as Dasgupta terms it in this volume, by government institutions. At the same time it would be wrong for the government to assume that there exists a large number of communities as cohesive units that would always be willing to take control over common lands—a control that the communities had supposedly exerted in pre-British times. Therefore, mere floating of participatory programmes like JFM and allowing the communities to formulate their own rule structure would not necessarily result in effective forest protection. It is a ground reality that not all rural communities are well-knit and homogeneous. Strong social stratification in rural India implies that participation and sharing of benefits are open to elite capture. Therefore self-initiated or NGO-promoted efforts can neither be replicated nor be expected to bring in countrywide change within a reasonable period of time.

Carefully designing of institutions, in a manner that will ensure fairness, without taking away autonomy to develop own rules, is required—a requirement which is more likely to be, and can be, provided by the state. For that purpose, government-backed efforts at larger scale are essential. The 'participatory approach' that the government wishes to promote should lead to 'collective action', which is indigenous, flexible, and provides developmental opportunities. Echoing Ostrom (1992*c*), the study concludes that neither community nor enforcers are sufficient, both are needed and can enhance the other.

References

Agarwal, B. (2001). 'Participatory Exclusions, Community Forestry, and Gender: An Analysis for South Asia and a Conceptual Framework'. *World Development*, 29/10: 1623–48.

Agrawal, A. (1999). *Greener Pastures: Politics, Markets and Community among a Migrant Pastoral People*. Durham, NC: Duke University Press.

—— (2002). 'Common Resources and Institutional Sustainability', in E. Ostrom, T. Dietz, N. Dolšăk, P. C. Stern, S. Stovich, and E. U. Weber (eds.), *The Drama of the Commons*, National Research Council, Committee on the Human Dimensions of Global Change. Division of Behavioral and Social Sciences and Education. Washington DC: National Academy Press, 41–85.

Arora, H., and Khare, A. (1994). 'Experience with the Recent Joint Forest Management Approach'. Paper prepared for the International Workshop on India's Forest Management and Ecological Revival, New Delhi.

Arul, M. J. (1998). 'Participatory Management of Forests'. IRMA Working Paper 119. Institute for Rural Management (IRMA), Anand, India, <http://www.irm.ernet.in/pub/wp119/html>

Baalu, T. T. R. (2002). Speech by Hon'ble Minister Of Environment And Forests, Government Of India, at a function for 'Launching of Ecology of Hope Initiative', Johannesburg, South Africa, 30th August.

Bahuguna, V. K. (2001). 'Production, Protection and Participation in Forest Management: An Indian Perspective in Achieving the Balance'. Keynote address. Conference proceedings of the 16th Commonwealth Conference. Perth, Australia, <http://www.envindia.com/FORBAHUGV.htm>.

Baland, J.-P., and Platteau, J.-M. (1996). *Halting Degradation of Natural Resources: Is There a Role for Rural Communities?* New York: Food and Agriculture Organization of the United Nations and Oxford University Press.

Ballabh, V., Balooni, K., and Dave, S. (2002). 'Why Local Resources Management Institutions Decline: A Comparative Analysis of Van (Forest) Panchayats and Forest Protection Committees in India'. *World Development*, 30/12: 2153–67.

Balooni, K. (1998). 'Financing of Afforestation of Wastelands'. Ph.D. Dissertation. Department of Economics, Vallabh Vidyasagar, Sardar Patel University.

Gadgil, M., and Berkes, F. (1991). 'Traditional Resource Management Systems'. *Resource Management and Optimisation*, 8/3–4: 127–41.

—— and Guha, R. (1992). *This Fissured Land: An Ecological History of India*. New Delhi, India: Oxford University Press.

—— and Subhash Chandra, M. D. (1992). 'Sacred Groves'. *Indian International Centre Quarterly*, 19/1–2: 183–7.

Ghate, R. (2000). 'The Role of Autonomy in Self-Organizing Process: A Case Study of Local Forest Management in India'. Working paper. Workshop in Political Theory and Policy Analysis, Indiana University, Bloomington.

—— (2004a). *Uncommons in the Commons: Community-initiated Forest Resource Management*. New Delhi, India: Concept Publishing Company.

—— (2004b). '"Equity" in Decentralized Forest Management in India'. Paper presented at the 10th Biennial IASCP conference on 'The commons in an age of global transition, challenges, risks and opportunities' at Oaxaca, Mexico, August.

Ghate, R., Chaturvedi, A., and Mehra, D. (2003). 'Bio-Diverse Economic Dependence of Indigenous Population: A Study from Gadchiroli District of Maharashtra State', Paper presented at the 3rd Biennial Conference of the Indian Society for Ecological Economics (INSEE), at the Indian Institute of Management, Kolkata, 18–20 December.

—— and Mehra, D. (2004). 'The Land on Which Forest Stands is Not Ours, So What? Forest Products are Ours! A Study of Three Collective Action-based Forest Regimes Operating without Land Tenure'. *Forest, Trees, and Livelihoods*, 14: 91–108.

—— and Nagendra, H. (2005). 'Role of Monitoring in Institutional Performance: Forest Management in Maharshtra, India'. *Conservation and Society*, 3/2: 509–32.

Gibson, C., and Becker, D. (1999). 'The Lack of Institutional Demand', in C. C. Gibson, M. A. McKean, E. Ostrom (eds.), *People and Forests: Communities, Institutions and Governance*. Cambridge, MA: MIT Press, 135–62.

Guha, R. (1983). 'Forestry in British and Post-British India—A Historical Analysis'. *Economic and Political Weekly*, 28/44: 1883.

—— and Gadgil, M. (1989). 'State Forestry and Social Conflicts in British India'. *Past and Present*, 123: 141–77.

Gupta, A. K. (1990). 'Politics of Articulation, Mediating Structures and Voluntarism: From "Chauraha" to "Chaupal"'. Working paper no. 894. Indian Institute of Management, Ahemdabad, India.

Hill, D. (2000). 'Assessing the Promise and Limitations of Joint Forest Management in a Era of Globalisation: The Case of West Bengal', Paper presented at the Eighth Biennial Conference of the IASCP, 'Constituting the Commons: Crafting Sustainable Commons in the New Millennium', Indiana University, Bloomington, 31 May–4 June.

Isager, L., Theilade, I., and Thomsen, L. (2002). *People's Participation and the Role of Governments in Conservation of Forest Genetic Resources*. Guidelines and Technical Notes No. 62. Humlebæk, Denmark: Danida Forest Seed Centre.

Jodha, N. S. (1998). 'Poverty and Environmental Resource Degradation: An Alternative Explanation and Possible Solutions'. *Economic and Political Weekly*, 5–12: 2389.

—— (2002). 'Natural Resource Management and Poverty Alleviation in Mountain Areas: Approaches and Efforts'. Conference Paper Series No. 11. International Conference on Natural Assets, Political Economy Research Institute (PERI) and Centre for Science and Environment, Tagaytay City, Philippines, 8–11 January. <http://www.peri.umass.edu/fileadmin/pdf/conference_papers/CDP11.pdf>.

Lele, S. (2000). 'Godsend, Sleight of Hand, or Just Muddling Through: Joint Water and Forest Management in India'. *ODI Natural Resource Perspectives*, 53: 1–6. Available online at <http://www.odi.org.uk/NRP/53.pdf>.

—— and Rao, R. J. (1996). 'Whose Co-operatives and Whose Produce? The Case of LAMPS in Karnataka'. Paper presented at the National Seminar on 'Rediscovering Co-operation', Institute of Rural Management, Anand, India, 19–21 November.

Ligon, E., and Narain, U. (1999). 'Government Management of Village Commons: Comparing Two Forest Policies'. *Journal of Environmental Economics and Management*, 37/3: 272–89.

Matta, J. R., and Karr, J. (2004). 'Selling Environmental Services—Challenges and Opportunities for Sustaining Local Resource Management: Lessons from Joint Forest Management Experience in Tamil Nadu, India'. Paper presented at the 10th Biennial

IASCP Conference on 'The Commons in an Age of Global Transition, Challenges, Risks and Opportunities' at Oaxaca, Mexico, August.

McKean, M. A. (1992). 'Management of Traditional Common Lands (Iriaichi) in Japan', in D. Bromley (ed.), *Making the Commons Work: Theory, Practice and Policy*. San Francisco, CA: Institute for Contemporary Studies, 63–93.

Ostrom, E. (1992*a*). *Crafting Institutions for Self-Governing Irrigation Systems*. San Francisco, CA: ICS Press.

—— (1992*b*). 'Policy Analysis of Collective Action and Self-governance', in W. N. Dunn and R. M. Kelly (eds.), *Advances in Policy Studies since 1950*, Policy Studies Review Annual, 10. New Brunswick, NJ: Transaction Publishers, 81–119.

—— (1992*c*). 'Community and the Endogenous Solution of Commons Problems'. *Journal of Theoretical Politics*, 4/3: 343–51.

—— (1999). 'Self-governance and Forest Resources'. Occasional paper No. 20. Centre for International Forestry Research (CIFOR), Bogor, Indonesia. <http://www.cgiar.org/cifor>.

Pattnaik, B. K., and Dutta, S. (1997). 'JFM in South-West Bengal—A Study in Participatory Development'. *Economic and Political Weekly*, 32/50: 3225–32.

Rangarajan, M. (1996). *Fencing the Forest: Conservation and Ecological Change in India's Central Province—1860–1914*. New Delhi, India: Oxford University Press.

Roy Burman, B. K. (1985). 'Issues in Environmental Management Centring Forest and Role of Tribal Communities'. *South Asian Anthropologist*, 6/1: 41–8.

Sarin, M. (1996). 'From Conflict to Collaboration: Institutional Issues in Community Management', in M. Poffenberger and B. McGean (eds.), *Village Voices, Forest Choices*, reprinted, 1998. Delhi, India: Oxford University Press, 165–203.

Shah, A. (2003). 'Fading Shine of the Golden Decade: The Establishment Strikes Back'. Paper presented at GIDR national seminar on 'New Developmental Paradigms and Challenges for Western and Central Regional States in India', Gujarat Institute for Development Research, Ahemdabad, India, 4–6 March.

Singh, C. (1986). *Common Property and Common Poverty: Indian Forests, Forest Dwellers and the Law*. Delhi, India: Oxford University Press.

Sundar, N. (2001). 'Is Devolution Democratisation?' *World Development*, 29/12: 2007–23.

Tang, S. Y. (1992). *Institutions and Collective Action: Self-Governance in Irrigation Systems*. San Francisco, CA: ICS Press.

Thompson, J. (1995). 'Participatory Approaches in Government Bureaucracies: Facilitating the Process of Institutional Change'. *World Development*, 23/9: 1521–34.

Varalakshmi, V., and Kaul, O. N. (1999). 'Non-governmental Organisations: Their Role in Forestry Research and Extension'. *The Indian Forester*, 125/1: 37–44.

Vira, B. (2005). 'Deconstructing the Harda Experience—Limits of Bureaucratic Participation'. *Economic and Political Weekly*, 40/48: 5068–75.

Wade, R. (1994). *Village Republics: Economic Conditions for Collective Action in South India*. San Francisco, CA: Institute for Contemporary Studies Press.

6

The Stake-Net Fishery Association of Negombo Lagoon, Sri Lanka: Why Has It Survived over 250 Years and Will It Survive another 100 Years?

Asha Gunawardena and Paul Steele

6.1. Introduction

Heavy involvement of the state in managing natural resources has been widespread due to the strategic importance of resources, market failures, and other externalities. However, there has been growing awareness in recent years of the poor performance of government agencies in managing resources, especially at the local level (Rasmussen and Meinzen-Dick 1995). Community-based management of common property resources (CPRs) is receiving more attention in natural resource management in developing countries as a potential mechanism for increasing the efficacy, legitimacy, and sustainability of natural resources management (Olson 1965). Many studies on the commons have shown that resource users have the capacity to create institutional arrangements and management regimes by themselves that help equitable allocation of resources over long time periods with limited efficiency losses (Agrawal 1999; Ostrom 1990).

In the case of open-access natural resources, the exclusion of beneficiaries through physical and institutional means is costly while exploitation by one user reduces the availability of resources for others. These two characteristics make them difficult to manage effectively and they can easily become degraded through excessive use. In many cases, communities have been able to address the above-mentioned exclusion and substractability problems by devising collective action (Lobe and Berkes 2004). Local collective action is important to develop rules for resource use, monitor compliance with rules and sanctions, and mobilize necessary resources. According to Bromley (1991), the main difference between open-access and common property is that in an open-access situation, every potential user has a privilege with respect to use of the resource since no one has the legal ability to exclude others. In a common property regime, on the other hand, there are rules defining who is included in the resource management group and who is not. Only group members have access to the resource.

This study analyses the determinants of the success of the Stake-Net Fishery Association (SNFA) of Negombo Lagoon in Sri Lanka using Agrawal's (2001) critical enabling conditions for sustainability of the commons as a framework. The chapter proceeds as follows: Section 6.2 provides an overview of the fishery sector in Sri Lanka. Section 6.3 describes the stake-net fishery in the Negombo lagoon. Section 6.4 elucidates data collection while Section 6.5 presents the conceptual framework, which is used for analysis. Section 6.6 analyses the determinants of the success of the SNFA under seven major themes. Section 6.7 presents the future challenges to the SNFA. Section 6.8 ends the chapter with conclusions.

6.2. Fishery sector in Sri Lanka

Fish and coastal resources are vital for many poor people in Sri Lanka. In the pre-tsunami period, about one million people depended on the fishing industry for their livelihood (MENR 2003). Subsistence fishers generally fall into the poorest category of the population, suffer from livelihoods dependent on a depleting resource, poor housing and, in some areas, limited access to basic amenities such as sanitation (ADB 1999).

One of the main challenges facing any fishery is open access. Open-access fisheries exhibit free entry with the result that fishing efforts lead to overharvesting and declining profits. For example, in the Chilaw lagoon, the number of traditional craft doubled from 1981 to 1996 (SDC 1998). In Negombo, the number of traditional craft more than doubled between 1981 and 1996 (SDC 1998). The Fisheries and Aquatic Resource Act was introduced in 1996 to focus on fisheries conservation and management by emphasizing the importance of community-based fisheries management and introducing licenses for fishing vessels. However, there has been no real attempt to tackle the problem of open access by limiting the number of licences issued. Any new fisherman who applies is given a licence. What is worse, there are many fishermen who fish without a licence.

This paper focuses on fishery issues in the Negombo Lagoon (3164 ha) which is located on Sri Lanka's west coast—about 30 km north of the capital Colombo. This lagoon also suffers from the problem of open access as mentioned earlier. Currently, there are over 3000 lagoon fishers using ten different fishing methods in the Negombo Lagoon.

The most common methods are push-net, trammel or disco-net, grill-net, drag-net, cast-net, brush pile, hook and line, and fishing by trawl. Some of these methods such as trawl and push-net are harmful and destructive (Hoogvorst 2003). This diversity when it comes to the types of fishers and the large size of the lagoon has made it impossible to tackle the problem of open access.

During the past several decades there has been visible degradation in the lagoon environment. This is the result of inadequately planned settlements, expansion of prawn farms, the growth of the Negombo town, industrial and municipal pollution, intensification of fishing, deforestation, and general habitat destruction.

In addition, the property rights of the Negombo lagoon and the surrounding land are held by multiple government agencies such as Department of Fisheries and Aquatic Resources, Department of Forest, Department of Wildlife Conservation, National Aquatic Research Agency, several divisional secretaries, and some private owners (Ranasinghe 2001). Poor coordination among these organizations has made the sustainable management of the Negombo lagoon more complicated.

6.3. Stake-net fishery in the Negombo lagoon

Community-initiated common property management regimes have been in existence in Sri Lanka in fisheries and in small-scale irrigation tanks (Senaratne and Karunanayake, this volume) for a long time. In addition, the Sri Lankan government has taken initiatives to promote collective action by farmers in the management of major irrigation schemes (Herath, this volume).

This study discusses a community-initiated common property regime in the fishery sector in Sri Lanka—the Stake-Net Fishery Association in the channels of the Negombo lagoon. The SNFA is an example of a long-standing collective arrangement for successfully limiting open access in contrast to all other fisheries operating in the Negombo lagoon.

6.3.1. Technical features of stake-net fishery

There are several islands close to the mouth of the Negombo lagoon so that the northern part of the lagoon is divided into a number of channels. The three main channels (*ela*) are Kongaha, Munkuliya, and Ambalanpitiya. Stake-net fishing takes place in the locations known as 'stations' along these channels. There are twenty-two fishing stations. Each station has a specific name, which is related to adjoining physical features such as trees. Only 1–2 nets can be fixed in most of the stations at a time. However some stations in Munkuliya and Kongaha channels can accommodate 4–5 nets. The total number of nets that can be fixed is 50–7.

Stake-net fishery uses large conical-bag-shaped nets attached to stakes, which are tied across channels. The net can only be operated in channels of about 3.5 m depth and about 15–25 m wide. The net is fixed at night with the onset of the ebb tide targeting sub-adults of penaeid shrimps migrating from the lagoon towards sea. The net is removed after about 4–6 hours depending on the tide. On average, a member can operate his net 5–10 days a month based on complex rules for rotating access to the fishing sites.

6.3.2. History of the management regime

This management regime has existed since 1721 as attested to by deeds preserved in the local Roman Catholic Church. According to the fishers, the fishing rights (*Pelle*) were originally given to three families by the name of Kurukulasooriya, Warnakulasooriya, and Mihindukulasooriya that lived close to the channels of the Negombo lagoon. Later, members from these three families formed the three major groups of stake-net fishery: Grand Street, Sea Street, and Duwa-Pitipana respectively. The Duwa-Pitipana group consists of two separate societies called Duwa and Pitipana Street although fishing is undertaken as one group.

Each society has a special mandate, rules and regulations as determined by the fisher folk themselves although codified in 1956 via a government regulation. Members of the SNFA own a *Pelle* or share of the fishery, which provides the legal right to undertake stake-net fishing. In the past, each society had separately attempted to control access to this fishery resource by outsiders. In more recent times, there has been informal cooperation among the three groups in terms of preventing access by outsiders, conflict resolution, and also communicating fish-yield information since all three fishing societies undertake fishing in the same channels of the lagoon rotationally. In 1986, the leadership of Grand Street took the initiative to conduct an integrated annual general meeting in order to formalize cooperation among the societies.

This membership-based organization has been in existence for over two hundred and fifty years (Lobe and Berkes 2004) and appears to have managed the shrimps in a way that is equitable for its members without noticeably depleting the resource (ADB 1999). The association holds valuable lessons about indigenous self-organized and self-governed common property management for Sri Lanka and other countries. During its long history, this management regime survived major conflict and crisis situations by being able to reorganize and adapt to dynamic conditions (Lobe and Berkes 2004).

6.3.3. *The Stake-Net Fishery Association (SNFA)*

The stake-net fishers are currently organized into four separate (but affiliated) societies (Grand Street, Sea Street, Duwa, and Pitipana Street) totalling about 270 fishermen located around Negombo town (see Table 6.1). Grand Street has the highest number of members (101). All members of SNFA are from the adjoining villages of the Negombo lagoon channels.

Table 6.1. Membership of the SNFA

Society	Grand Street		Sea Street		Duwa—Pitipana	
Subgroups	Grand Street A	Grand Street B	Sea Street A	Sea Street B	Duwa	Pitipana Street
Number of members	50	51	40	40	41	48

The stake-net fishers are a culturally homogeneous group—Sinhala Roman Catholics—who share a common set of norms and beliefs. The Catholic religion plays an important role in the traditions; for example, meetings start with prayers and the rotational calendar is decorated with the Virgin Mary.

6.4. Data collection

The primary data was collected from fishery societies of the SNFA in the Negombo lagoon. Four focus-group discussions (10–12 members per group) were conducted in order to collect information from the four societies. In addition, key informant interviews were conducted with fishery group leaders and officials of the Department of Fisheries.

6.5. Conceptual framework

Rasmussen and Meinzen-Dick (1995) develop a conceptual framework for examining the role of local organizations in natural resource management. They analyse studies by key authors (Ostrom 1990; Ostrom 1992; Wade 1988; Bardhan 1993; Nugent 1993; Tang 1992) using this framework and categorize factors affecting the success of local organizations for natural resource management into four: physical and technical characteristics of the resource system, characteristics of the user groups, institutional arrangements, and social relationships.

Agrawal (2001) adapts a similar approach by reviewing three major studies on the conditions under which a group of self-organized users are successful in managing their resources in a sustainable manner over time (Baland and Platteau 1996; Ostrom 1990; Wade 1988). These studies have focused on small-scale community-based user groups. Agrawal (2001) combines all the conditions enabling successful CPR management that each of the three studies mentions (which are not mutually exclusive) with other relevant studies and comes up with a more comprehensive list of conditions called *critical enabling conditions for sustainability of the commons*. However, these conditions are not independent. Agrawal emphasizes the fact that some of these conditions are empirically correlated.

Agrawal categorizes all these conditions into six broader classes:

- Resource system characteristics;
- Group characteristics;
- Relationship between resource system characteristics and group characteristics;
- Institutional arrangements;
- Relationship between resource system and institutional arrangements;
- External environment.

6.6. Determinants of the success of the SNFA

This study uses Agrawal's critical enabling conditions as a framework. Therefore, the study discusses determinants of the success of SNFA under six main themes that Agrawal used. However, the study is not restricted to Agrawal's critical enabling conditions and takes further steps to identify another condition—positive net benefits—which contribute to the success of the SNFA.

6.6.1. *Resource system characteristics*

The physical features of the resource system such as size, definition of boundaries of the resource system, predictability of the flow of the benefits, low mobility of the resource, etc., are described under this category (see Table 6.2).

Wade (1988) finds that relatively smaller resource systems are likely to be better managed under common property regimes. However, Agrawal (2001) argues that the effect of the resource size is dependent on the state of one

Table 6.2. Application of Agrawal's critical enabling conditions listed under resource system characteristics with respect to SNFA

Resource system characteristics	Availability
Small size	?
Well-defined boundaries	Y
Low level of mobility	N
Possibilities of storage benefits	N
Predictability	Y

or more variables such as group size, level of authority relationships, etc. In this study, it is difficult to judge whether the resource system is small or large and/or its contribution to the success of the SNFA.

As described in Section 6.3.1, this lagoon fishery is captured in fishing stations in the channels, which connect the lagoon to the sea. The boundaries of this resource are well defined and well known to all the members. This is proved by the lack of any boundary conflicts.

Fish are a mobile resource. But the stake-net fishing method is arranged in such a way as to capture this mobile resource in fixed places (fishing stations) along the channels.

The fish catch varies significantly over the year depending on the tide and monsoon. Harvests are high during the onset of the rains in April/May and October/November. However, there can be variation in the fish yield in-between due to various reasons (ADB 1999). In spite of these variations, harvests of different seasons and different fishing stations can be predictable up to a certain extent. For example, fishers know what the most productive months are, the most productive stations are, and what the less productive stations are.

6.6.2. Group characteristics

The features of the local community which manages the resource system such as group size, level of wealth and income, types of heterogeneity, shared norms, appropriate leadership, interdependence among group members, and past experience of collective action are discussed under group characteristics (See Table 6.3).

Some studies have shown that smaller groups are more likely to engage in collective action than those larger in size (Oslon 1965; Baland and Platteau 1996). However, Ostrom (1997) shows that the impact of group size on successful collective action is mediated by several variables. In this study, what is interesting is the appropriateness of the allocation of the resource

Table 6.3. Application of Agrawal's critical enabling conditions listed under group characteristics to the SNFA

Group Characteristics	Available
Small size	Y
Clearly defined boundaries	Y
Shared norms	Y
Past successful experience—social capital	Y
Appropriate leadership	Y
Interdependence among group members	Y
Heterogeneity of endowments	Y
Homogeneity of identities and interest	Y
Low levels of poverty	Y

system among different subgroups and also among members within each subgroup (Section 6.6.4.1.2 gives detailed information on resource allocation and boundaries among subgroups and also among members).

The SNFA has a long history of existence. This long history is proof that SNFA is rich in local social capital. The stake-net fishers are mostly related and are culturally a homogeneous group—Sinhala Roman Catholics—who share a common set of norms and beliefs. For example, possession of fishing rights (*pelle*) is a privilege.

The SNFA benefits from a charismatic overall leadership. The President of Grand Street Society, for instance, is someone who has a comparatively high education level, long experience, and the ability to converse in the three main languages used (Sinhala, Tamil, and English) in Sri Lanka. The remarkable features of this leadership are flexibility, fairness, and equity considerations. Meinzen-Dick, Raju, and Gulati (2002) indicate that having local social capital and leadership potential are likely to lead to more active organizations. Therefore, the strong local leadership explains partly the success of the SNFA.

Since all three fishing groups (four societies) undertake fishing in the same three channels rotationally, the interdependence among group members is high in terms of preventing access by outsiders, conflict resolution, and communicating fish-yield information.

In addition to the above-mentioned features, it is interesting to note that there are differences too among the four societies. The four societies belonging to SNFA have four separate constitutions. Members of one society do not directly influence rules and regulations of other societies. In other words, society members have autonomy to change, modify, or form new rules. Ostrom (1999) emphasizes that the autonomy of the members in determining their own rules reduces the cost of organizing. However, most of the basic rules are similar. Sea Street Society, for instance, has been restricting its membership and implementing more restrictive rules compared to other societies. The differences in the education levels of members, characteristics of the leaders, and dependence on the resource have also resulted in differences among the groups in implementing rules (see Table 6.13 in Appendix 6.1 for further details).

6.6.3. *Relationship between the resource system and group characteristics*

This section manifests (as shown in Table 6.4) a high level of dependency of users on the resource system, proximity of the residential location of the user group to the resource system, fairness in the allocation of resources, and different levels and changes of user demand.

Table 6.4. Application of Agrawal's critical enabling conditions listed under relationship between resource system and group characteristics to the SNFA

Relationship between resource system characteristics and group characteristics	Available
Overlap between user group residential location and resource location	Y
High level of dependence by group members on resource system	Y
Fairness in allocation of benefits from common resources	Y
Low levels of user demand	N
Gradual change in levels of demand	Y

Fifty per cent of the members of the SNFA totally depend on stake-net fishing. However, the night-time nature of the fishery allows some members to undertake additional jobs during the daytime. Some fishers do part-time jobs such as sea fishing, carpentry, three-wheeler driving, and manual labour work for larger sea vessels. But the limited availability of alternative unskilled job opportunities in the area has kept some fishers dependent on stake-net fishing. The chapter by Balasubramanium in this volume too finds higher dependency on the common property resource as one of the driving forces for active participation in collective action.

Several studies show that the richer members or elite members of management regimes benefit from collective action more than the poorer marginalized members (Dasgupta, this volume). However, in the case of the SNFA, each member of the society has an equal chance at accessing the fishing sites due to the rotational lottery system. Hence, nobody can purposely plan and obtain a higher benefit than others (details on mechanisms to allocate the resource equitably among members are given in Section 6.6.4.1.2.3 under institutional arrangements).

6.6.4. *Institutional arrangements*

This section describes the institutional regimes concerning monitoring, sanctions, adjudication, and accountability (see Table 6.5).

Table 6.5. Application of Agrawal's critical enabling conditions listed under institutional arrangements to the SNFA

Institutional Arrangements	Available
Rules are simple and easy to understand	Y
Locally devised access and management rules	Y
Ease in enforcement of rules	Y
Graduated sanctions	Y
Availability of low-cost adjudication	Y
Accountability of monitors and other officials to users	Y

The SNFA shows all these enabling conditions in its institutional arrangements. The following subsection explains the institutional arrangements of the SNFA in detail since these arrangements are a major contributing factor to its long-term success.

6.6.4.1. MANAGEMENT RULES

The rules and regulations are basically similar in all four societies although there are minor differences in rules among them (see Table 6.13).

6.6.4.1.1. *How rules are made*

The special feature of the SNFA is that rules and regulations are made by the fisher folk themselves although these have been codified in 1956 by a government regulation. Rules and regulations can be introduced, modified, or removed at the annual general meeting of each society with the consent of the majority. This, it could be said, is in line with Ostrom's design principle on collective choice agreement (Ostrom 1990). However, some rules and regulations, which are relevant for the whole association, are made at the integrated annual general meeting. While being relatively fixed, the management regime is not rigid. For example, in May 1999, it was decided by Grand Street members one morning to increase the number of nets allowed at Keerikaduwa Ela site from three to four.

6.6.4.1.2. *Access rules for SNFA members*

There are four levels of resource rights to access the fishing sites (see Table 6.6).

A right to undertake stake-net fishing is given only for SNFA members. The following section explains the rules for membership, how membership is passed on, and how membership is cancelled.

Table 6.6. Resource rights and allocation methods

Resource Right	Allocation Method
a) **Right to fish** in stake-net fishery (*Pella*)	Currently about 270 members exercise these rights.
b) **Access to three channels** in the Negombo lagoon	Rotations are six days among six different subgroups of four societies: 1) Grand Street A 2) Grand Street B 3) Sea Street A 4) Sea Street B 5) Duwa 6) Pitipana Street
c) **Free access to fishing stations** within allocated channels (*Padu*)	Annual auction—'Big number' Daily auction—'Small number'
d) **Bidding access to fishing stations**	For society members only. For example, the day Grand Street A undertakes fishing, Grand Street B members can have bidding access if any additional fishing sites are left after allocation among Grand Street A members.

6.6.4.1.2.1 *Rules for membership*

Table 6.7. Rules for membership

Members of the SNFA have fishing rights—access to fishing stations—called *Pelle*	Only fishers who belong to the SNFA member families are eligible Membership is given for life. Membership is passed primarily by inheritance to the youngest son of the family after the death of the head of the household	This controls the free-riding on reproductive side and limits entry of one member from a family to the society.
Other rules for membership	Each fisher must possess the necessary tools (stake-net, an outrigger canoe and pillars) for fishing. No hiring or borrowing from others is allowed	This rule helps to prevent free-riding of others' canoes and fishing tools
Rules for new membership	New membership has been limited to two per year since 1972. Married males who are descended from Association members are eligible. New applicants must demonstrate their understanding of the fishery by fishing for six months on probation	This rule also helps to limit the membership to one member per family.
Cancellation of membership	The membership is for life and automatically comes to an end when a person dies if he has no son to take over. In addition, there are rules for forfeiting membership. Sea Street Society: If a member does not undertake fishing at least ten times per year his membership will be cancelled. Grand Street: The membership will be cancelled if a member does not undertake fishing for five years continuously. Duwa and Pitipana societies have no such rules.	

6.6.4.1.2.2. *Rules of access to three channels by SNFA members*

For the purpose of accessing the stake-net sites, these societies have the following rules. Since the number of members at Grand Street and Sea Street societies is more than fifty, each society has two subgroups called A and B. Each of the six subgroups has access to fishing once in six days in rotation in the three main channels. In other words only one subgroup undertakes fishing per day. Each subgroup consists of 40–5 members and there are about 50–7 fishing sites (see Table 6.8).

Table 6.8. Distribution of channels among stake-net fishery subgroups

	Subgroup		
	Kongaha ela	Munkuliya ela	Ambalanpitiya ela
Day1	GS-A	GS-A	GS-A
Day2	SS-A	SS-A	SS-A
Day3	D	D	Pitipana [1]
Day4	GS-B	GS-B	GS-B
Day5	SS-B	SS-B	SS-B
Day6	PS	PS	Pitipana [1]

GS-A—Grand Street A   GS-B—Grand Street B
SS-A—Sea Street A   SS-B—Sea Street B
D—Duwa   PS—Pitipana Street

[1] There is a separate group of fishers who undertake stake-net fishing but do not belong to the Stake-Net Fishery Association. This group has been given legal rights from the courts to fish in Ambalanpitiya channel once in three days only when Duwa—Pitipana group's turn comes

6.6.4.1.2.3. *Mechanisms for equitable access to fishery resource by members* As mentioned earlier in the section on resource system characteristics, different fishing sites produce different prawn yields. Hence, designing an equitable system of access to all members is complex and challenging due to

- Harvest of the fishery resource being seasonal and sometimes varying between years;
- Three channels which is unique and the number of stations per channel also being different;
- The total number of members in the SNFA being higher than the available fishing stations (50–7).

However, the fishers employ the following three methods to allocate fishing stations/sites among members.

- **Annual auction—'Big number system'**

This is a rotational access system based on a lottery that takes place once a year at the annual general meeting where all society members are present. This method allows each member to have a chance at accessing the best fishing stations during the specified year. This method is used more by Grand Street, Duwa, and Pitipana Street. Fishers implement this system for ten months per year when the fish harvest is comparatively high. This method assures that every fisher gets access to high-yielding fishing stations during these ten months.

According to the fishers, this method allows them to know when they have access to good fishing stations during the ten-month period. This gives them the flexibility to attend only when they have access to good fishing stations and to plan ahead to undertake other employment. It seems this method is preferred by the fisher societies whose members are comparatively less dependent on fishing.

On the other hand, some fishers who are highly dependent on fishing do not prefer the 'big number' approach since they go fishing every three–six days. They argue that there are days that are less productive even within the ten-month period. If a fisher gets the first priority to access the best fishing station on such a day, he may not be able to obtain the expected good harvest.

From the point of view of the administration, most leaders argue that implementing the 'big number' has lower administrative costs for those societies that have more flexible rules such as Grand Street, Duwa, and Pitipana.

• Daily auction-'small number system'

This is the implementation of a daily lottery system to allocate fishing sites among its members at each *Padu* meeting (each society conducts a *Padu* meeting once in three days). This system is implemented by most societies during the unproductive periods of fishing, which lasts for two months. However, Sea Street Society has been implementing this method continuously for five years. Fishers of this group mostly depend on fishing and prefer the 'small number' as it gives access to the better fishing sites each and every day. Since this society is less flexible in implementing rules, the administrative cost of implementing this method is not as high as for other societies.

• Sharing of resources among active members

A challenge to collective management is the opportunity cost of time with regard to participation at meetings. The societies have developed a self-financing solution to this problem by compensating members who participate at meetings through funds raised from auctioning some fishing sites. For example, in Sea Street, Duwa, and Pitipana societies, every fifth turn (that is, number) is kept for the society. In other words, when allocating the lottery they add 7–8 numbers in excess of the number of members. These additional numbers are auctioned at every *Padu* meeting. Half of the auctioned money is kept for the maintenance of the society while the other half is distributed among the members who attend the *Padu* meeting. Grand Street adopts a slightly different method. They distribute half of the auctioned money among the members who went fishing on that particular day.

Given the nature of the resource and the number of users, a combination of the three methods seems the best way to handle the resource while maintaining equity. However, whatever the method or combination of methods, a society's choice is based on the consent of the majority of that particular society.

Implementation of a combination of the three methods was to be observed in all but one society. These methods are chosen by the members of each society at the annual general meeting. Irrespective of the method or combination of methods chosen, each society conducts a meeting once in three days called *Padu* to allocate the fishing stations among the relevant members. These meetings are conducted in the morning and take half to one hour. Each society has a society-owned meeting place except Sea Street Society, which conducts its meeting in the Church premises.

The complex rotational rules described above reduce social conflicts over access to the fishery. For example, one of the best fishing sites is at Kongaha, located in the upper reaches of the eastern part of the lagoon. This is more than twice as profitable as the other sites allowing up to US$600 to be earned a single night during the most productive times. It is evident that there would be major conflicts to access this rich resource without this kind of management regime.

6.6.4.1.3. *How rules are enforced*

Table 6.9 explains the mechanisms for enforcing rules.

6.6.4.1.4. *Monitoring*

The association, in addition to fishing, has also engaged in a monitoring procedure that has successfully prevented entry by outsiders. Although fishing takes place during the night, fishers have to fix their nets in specific sites across the channels beforehand. While fixing their own nets, they notice if any outsiders fix nets. In addition, all the fishers live in close proximity to channels, which makes monitoring easy. If any fisher finds outsiders engaged in fishing, he will complain to the SNFA. Leaders of the association, in turn, inform the Fisheries Office in Negombo. However, according to the members such cases are very rare. Therefore, the SNFA has been able to minimize the cost of monitoring and preventing open access.

6.6.4.1.5. *Mechanism to resolve conflicts among members*

The SNFA has evolved through a series of conflicts and compromises over many years. Conflicts have been resolved mainly by the Roman Catholic

Table 6.9. Enforcement of rules

Monetary fines and punitive actions for non-compliance	There are standard fines or punitive actions for rule breaking and free-riding. There are slight changes in the fines imposed by different societies In some cases penalties are implemented on a case-by-case basis. Some rules have changed over time. Fines are decided according to the gravity and the context of the offence. The last major problem was in 1970 when an extremely troublesome stake-net member was denied fishing rights for five years and fined Rs 20,000. He appealed to the District Court against this fine, but the court upheld it. He was forced to find alternative employment in the public sector. Since his son grew up with no experience of the fishery, his *Pella* was lost. However, after this incident, fishing out of turn has not occurred. Graduated sanctions are also in place. For fishing out of turn, the penalties are higher. A first-time violator will lose two turns to fish (i.e. twelve days without fishing) and US$5. If caught again, he will lose four turns and so on.
Incentives for not cheating	If a fisher uses any other fisher's canoe for fishing, two turns of fishing will be cancelled. If a fisher's canoe is damaged and if he informs the society, he will be given a period within which he has to get his canoe repaired. During this period he can use another fisher's canoe. If he fails to have it repaired during the grace period and continues to use another's canoe, he will be fined via a loss in fishing turns. However, the fine will be less if the fisher himself informs the society. This also shows that rules are flexible for justified reasons. It is also interesting to see incentives given for honesty.

Church and, in some cases, by the Courts. However, currently the role of the Church is minimal in terms of conflict resolution because there are hardly any major conflicts. What minor conflicts arise are resolved by the members themselves. Government involvement has been limited to legalizing the foundation of fisheries management in order to reduce conflicts. They have survived many crisis situations by their ability to reorganize and adapt to dynamic conditions.

Usually, overall association decisions are taken at the annual general meeting. Decisions taken depend on the consent of the majority. However, members do not have to meet additionally to resolve conflicts since each society meets once in three days in *Padu* meetings. Thirty minutes, just after the *Padu* meeting, are utilized to resolve conflicts if there are any. This appears a low-cost mechanism to resolve conflicts.

6.6.4.1.6. *Arrangements to mobilize funds in order to strengthen a supportive social network*

The funds mobilized through various means such as collection of membership fees, auctioning of additional fishing sites, payments gained from fines, etc., are used to provide welfare benefits to its members (refer to Table 6.10 for further details).

Table 6.10. Social supportive work

Arrangement	Description
Death donation	Usually the membership fee is charged to cover part of this expenditure. However, Sea Street society does not charge a membership fee and covers this cost by auctioning the additional fishing turns.
Payment for widows of members	Grand Street society has recently started to pay an allowance (US$3.5/month) to the widows of its fishery members.
Payment for disabled and old members	Their turns (*Padus*) are auctioned at the *Padu* meeting and 2/3 is paid for the member while other 1/3 is kept for the society maintenance. The same procedure is followed when a member is sick and informs the society. Grand Street pays a fixed allowance of US$12 for the disabled/old fishers instead of paying 2/3. However, selling of a turn is not allowed under any other circumstance.
Loan scheme to buy new boats	Pitipana Street society is implementing a loan scheme without interest for the members who want to buy new canoes. Initially, the fisher shall pay one third of the cost of the canoe and the other 2/3 will be paid by the society. Fishers can settle the loan by paying monthly instalments.
Donations to the Church	Fishers of Duwa and Pitipana Street societies pay 3 per cent of their income to their respective Churches. Grand Street and Sea Street pay a considerable amount of money from society funds for their Church feast.

6.6.5. Relationship between resource system and institutional arrangements

Arrangements to restrict the harvest in order to regenerate the resource are considered under this category.

Table 6.11. Application of Agrawal's critical enabling conditions listed under relationship between resource system and institutional arrangements to the SNFA

Relationship between resource system and institutional arrangements	Available
Match restrictions on harvest to regeneration of resources	Y

There are restrictions on the harvest to assure the future sustainability of the fishery resource. The species captured by the stake-nets are mostly shrimps. These shrimp species reproduce at sea and enter the estuary as larvae and grow up to the juvenile stage. Stake-nets which are tied across the channels capture these juvenile species which migrate back to the sea to reach adulthood. The mesh size of the stake-net is larger than one inch which assures that the catch mostly contains mature shrimp. In addition, there is a limitation on the length of the net a fisher can use in order to make sure they do not exploit the resource. The maximum length of a net when other nets are operating at the same station is 15 m, which can be increased to 25 m if there are no other nets. The fine for flouting this is Rs 100 for each 0.5 m net in excess of 15 m.

Hence, it can be concluded that the stake-net is an ecologically sound fishing gear which does not overexploit the fishery resource.

6.6.6. Conditions of External Environment

The conditions of the external environment depend on technology, demography, markets, and different levels of governance (see Table 6.12).

Table 6.12. Application of Agrawal's critical enabling conditions listed under conditions of external environment of the SNFA

Conditions of external environment	
Low-cost exclusion technology	Y
Low levels of articulation with the external market	N
Gradual change in articulation with external market	Y
Central government should not undermine local authority	Y
Appropriate level of external aid to compensate local users for conservation activities	N
Supportive external sanctioning institutions	Y
Nested level of appropriation, provision, enforcement, and governance	Y

Government involvement in SNFA has been limited to the legalization of the fisheries management regime. In fact, legalization is also one of the factors explaining the success of the SNFA. Although the central government does not undermine the SNFA, there has been little help from the government to solve the wider problems of the Negombo lagoon which indirectly affects the fish yield of stake-net fishing.

6.6.7. Total positive net benefits: another determinant of success of the SNFA

6.6.7.1. FINANCIAL BENEFITS

Individuals sustain membership in organizations basically to obtain private benefits in terms of increased production, improved marketing, or insurance (McCarthy, Dutilly-Diane, and Drabo 2004). If people are to organize themselves into or continue cooperative action, they must perceive that the personal benefits and joint benefits that they gain exceed the costs (Ostrom 1997).

The SNFA members appear to accrue positive net benefits by minimizing their costs in different ways. It is very difficult to estimate the fishers' monthly income due to the fluctuations in the yield. The income gained from one fishing term varies from US$1 to US$600. According to the fishers, the fish yield has been decreasing over the years. However, this has been largely compensated by increasing shrimp prices. In addition to the individual fish yield, fishers who attend *Padu* meetings or who undertake fishing earn an income from auctioning additional fishing turns.

6.6.7.2. COSTS

The major initial capital costs are entrance fee (although Sea Street does not have such a fee), cost of a canoe (US$35–50), complete net (US$35), and pillars (US$35) to fix the net. The operational costs are annual membership fee (only Grand Street levies this fee), cost of fuel (US$1/day), maintenance cost of the canoe, and the opportunity costs of time for management (time spent on meetings). The latter are kept low by using a system of clearly defined, well-understood rules. In addition, the time spent for meetings is also compensated by paying a sitting allowance. Members undertake monitoring during laying and removing of nets. Hence, no additional time is needed for this activity. In comparison, the benefits of membership in terms of income, reduced conflicts, and social support networks are high.

6.7. Future challenges

This association is now facing challenges due to declining productivity of the fishery as a result of loss of fishing sites (known as stations) and other external threats to the lagoon. This has stimulated the society to try to work with other fishing groups in the Negombo lagoon to limit open access to the wider lagoon as a whole. This attempt to replicate the association's success within the stake-net fishery across the many diverse fisheries of the lagoon is a major undertaking whose success or failure may determine whether the SNFA can continue to provide benefits to its members in the future. In fact, whether it can face the challenges of the larger issue of open access to the lagoon as a whole and its resources will determine its continuing success.

6.8. Conclusions

The stake-net fishery of Negombo has sustainably managed common property resources through collective action. Its success is explained by a combination of factors such as characteristics of the resource system, characteristics of the user group, their institutional arrangements, that is, a well-defined and agreed-upon code of conduct, and some conditions of the external environment. In addition, this study argues that the success of the SNFA is also explained by the positive net benefits gained by the members.

Appendix 6.1

Table 6.13. Common features of and differences between the societies of SNFA

Society	Grand Street	Sea Street	Duwa—Pitipana	
Subgroup	Grand Street (A & B)	Sea Street (A & B)	Duwa	Pitipana Street
Number of members	101	80	41	48
Dependence on stake-net fishery (approximately)	50%	95%	30%	20%
Entrance fee-	Rs 15,000	No entrance fee	Rs 5000	Rs 5000 in instalments
Annual membership fee	Rs 500 (from last 2 years) the day you get the first priority the fee should be paid	No annual fee	No annual fee	No annual fee
Distribution of income of additional fishing turns auctioned in *Padu* meeting	50%—divided among the members who undertake fishing on respective day. 50%—for the maintenance of the society	50%—divided among the members who came for the respective day *Padu* meeting 50%—for the maintenance of the society	50%—divided among the members who came for the respective day *Padu* meeting 50%—for the maintenance of the society	50%—divided among the members who came for the respective day *Padu* meeting 50%—for the maintenance of the society
Rotational System to access fishing stations	10 months/year	Not implemented for 5 years	10 months/year	10 months/year
Daily lottery system to access fishing stations	Only for 2 months (unproductive period)	This has been implemented for 5 years	Only for 2 months (unproductive period)	Only for 2 months (unproductive period)
Death Donation	Rs 15,000	Rs 10,000	Rs 5000	Rs 5000
Payments for disabled/old fishers	Pays a fixed allowance Rs 1200	Auction their 'Pella' in the meeting and pay 2/3 to the owner and keep 1/3 for the society	Auction their 'Pella' in the meeting and pay 2/3 to the owner and keep 1/3 for the society	Auction their 'Pella' in the meeting and pay 2/3 to the owner and keep 1/3 for the society
Benefits for widows	Recently introduced Rs 350 per person	—	—	—

References

ADB (Asian Development Bank) (1999). *Report of the President to the Board of Directors, Coastal Resource Management Project, Ministry of Fisheries and Ocean Resources, Sri Lanka.* Manila: Asian Development Bank.

Agrawal, A. (1999). *Greener Pastures: Politics, Markets and Community among Migrant Pastoral People.* Durham, NC: Duke University Press.

—— (2001). 'Common Property Institutions and Sustainable Governance of Resources'. *World Development,* 29/10: 1649–72.

Baland, J.-M., and Platteau, J.-P. (1996). *Halting Degradation of Natural Resources: Is There a Role for Rural Communities?* Oxford: Clarendon Press.

Bardhan, P. (1993). 'Symposium on Management of Commons'. *Journal of Economic Perspectives,* 7/4: 87–92.

Bromley, D. W. (1991). *Environment and Economy: Property Rights and Public Policy.* Cambridge: Blackwell.

Hoogvorst, A. (2003). *Survival Strategies of People in Sri Lankan Wetland: Livelihood, Health and Nature Conservation in Muthurajawela.* Ph.D. Dissertation. Wageningen University. ISBN 90–5808–859–6.

Lobe, K., and Berkes, F. (2004). 'The *padu* System of Community-based Fisheries Management: Change and Institutional Innovation in South India'. *Marine Policy,* 28: 271–81.

McCarthy, N., Dutilly-Diane, C., and Drabo, B. (2004). 'Cooperation, Collective Action and Natural Resources Management in Burkina Faso'. *Agricultural Systems,* 82: 233–55.

Meinzen-Dick, R., Raju, K. V., and Gulati, A. (2002). 'What Affects Organization and Collective Action for Managing Resources? Evidence from Canal Irrigation Systems in India'. *World Development,* 30/4: 649–66.

MENR (Ministry of Environment and Natural Resources) (2003). *Caring for Environment 2003-2007—Path to Sustainable Development.* Colombo, Sri Lanka: Ministry of Environment and Natural Resources.

Nugent, J. B. (1993). Between State, Markets and Households: A Neo-institutional Analysis of Local Organizations and Institutions. *World Development,* 21/4: 623–32.

Olson, M. (1965). *The Logic of Collective Action: Public Goods and Theory of Groups.* London: Harvard University Press.

Ostrom, E. (1990). *Governing the Commons: The Evolution of Institutions for Collective Action.* Cambridge: Cambridge University Press.

—— (1992). *Crafting Institutions for Self-governing Irrigation Systems.* San Francisco, CA: Institute for Contemporary Studies.

—— (1997). 'Self-governance of Common Pool Resources'. Working paper W97-2. Workshop in Political Theory and Policy Analysis, Indiana University, Bloomington.

—— (1999). 'Self-governance and Forest Resources'. Occasional paper No. 20. Centre for International Forestry Research, Bogor, Indonesia.

Ranasinghe, D. M. S. H. K. (2001). *Conservation of Mangroves in Muthurajawela Marsh and Negombo/Chilaw Lagoon.* Report. Sri Jayewardenepura University, Nugegoda.

Rasmussen, L. N. and Meinzen-Dick, R. (1995). 'Local Organizations for Natural Resource Management: Lessons from Theoretical and Empirical Literature'. EPTD Discussion Paper. International Food Policy Research Institute, Washington, DC.

SDC (Sustainable Development Consultants) (1998). *Study on Economic Environmental Linkages of Lagoon and Near-shore Fishing.* Report. Sri Lanka: Ministry of Environment.

Tang. S. Y. (1992). *Institutions and Collective Action: Self-governance in Irrigation Systems.* San Francisco, CA: ICS Press.

Wade, R. (1988). *Village Republics: Economic Conditions for Collective Action in South India.* Oakland: ICS Press.

7

Transaction Costs and Institutional Innovation: Sustainability of Tank Aquaculture in Sri Lanka

Athula Senaratne and Kalpa Karunanayake

7.1. Introduction

Both rural poverty and malnutrition are common and widespread problems in the dry zone of Sri Lanka. The main source of animal proteins for an average Sri Lankan is fish and nearly 90 per cent of the supply comes from marine sources (Ministry of Fisheries and Aquatic Resources 2004). The supply of fish from marine sources to inland dry-zone areas is restricted, however, due to reasons such as limited surplus available after meeting the demand from coastal areas, inadequate cold transport facilities, and the poor keeping quality of products. Therefore, only a limited supply of animal proteins is available to residents in the inland dry-zone areas, leading to high incidence of protein malnutrition among them.

The most sensible strategy to address this problem is to increase the production of freshwater fish in inland areas using the vast endowment of village irrigation tanks. Village tanks are basically rainwater-harvesting devices established for paddy cultivation under water scarcity conditions. They have helped achieve the food security goals of successive generations over a period of over two millennia and continue to play an important role in irrigated agriculture even today. Similar structures are also found in other areas of the South Asian region, particularly in Southern India and Balasubramanian discusses the problem of decline of traditional irrigation institutions associated with them in Tamil Nadu in the present volume. In addition to irrigation, village tanks fulfil a variety of other rural agrarian needs, which include fisheries, domestic water uses, bathing and washing, and animal husbandry. Village irrigation tanks are common property resources (CPR) and all user rights are defined with respect to an identified community of villagers. Hence, utilization of village-tank resources invariably requires collective action.

Even though village irrigation tanks have the natural potential to support a fish population, a vast majority of them are seasonal reservoirs (Thayaparan 1982). As a result, very low productivity levels have been observed due to intermittent disturbance to life cycles during the annual drying-up (Chakrabarty and Samaranayake 1983). As a measure to improve fish productivity in village tanks, scientists have proposed carrying out community-based aquaculture that would recruit fish fingerlings artificially (see Appendix 7.1 for details).

Community-based aquaculture in village irrigation tanks has a number of features that appeal to policy makers and development workers. Among the major policy advantages are: (a) involvement of local resources that directly deals with the rural poor; (b) obligatory need for community participation due to common ownership; (c) ability to cater to a larger section of the population due to widespread distribution of the resource base; (d) the low-cost nature of the technologies involved and their successful demonstration; and (e) the potential to address the problems of poverty, malnutrition, and unemployment together. As a result, community-based aquaculture has gradually captured the attention of stakeholders such as the central government agencies, provincial governments in the tank areas, donor-funded projects, and NGOs.

Community-based aquaculture in village tanks is introduced through a local institution called 'farmer organizations' (FO). An FO is an institution established primarily for irrigation water management for paddy farming. The objective of this model is to promote aquaculture as a rural enterprise undertaken by community groups, with only the initial catalytic support by the government. As FOs are community-based organizations, aquaculture in village irrigation tanks is essentially a collective action venture.

Collective action demands cooperation among resource users. In the case of community-based aquaculture however, the issue of cooperation among resource users is complicated by a number of factors. Village tanks and associated institutional arrangements have evolved historically in the context of subsistence, family-based farming systems, which depended on commonly held rights over a majority of other village resources too (Somasiri 2001; Ulluwishewa 1997). This traditional subsistence farming system is currently being replaced by a commercialized system where associated resource ownership patterns too are transforming themselves to predominantly privately owned resources. Simultaneously, agriculture technologies used by farmers are also being fast 'modernized'.

Further, community-based aquaculture is a non-traditional use of the resource. Even though small-scale capture fishing has been in existence since ancient times, aquaculture itself is not a familiar practice in village tanks.

Collective action for this non-traditional use therefore has to be rallied through an institutional arrangement that developed for irrigation water management. Due to these reasons, the process of adoption of community-based aquaculture by community groups has been exceedingly slow despite the favourable policy climate and positive technical demonstrations.

Researchers have examined the collective action problem in a variety of contexts that involve common property resources (Meinzen-Dick and Knox 1999; Agrawal and Ostrom 1999). Among the most frequently asked questions are why collective action is successful in certain CPR while it fails in others, and what conditions would likely ensure successful cooperation among community groups (Wade 1988; Ostrom 1990). Collective action however is not a costless phenomenon (Abdullah, Kuperan, and Pomeroy 1998; Kuperan et al. 1998, Hanna 1995). Dasgupta (this volume) clearly anticipates that individual efforts at collective action are determined by the cost involved in initiating and maintaining collective action. On many occasions, collective action involves transaction costs (TC) for information, negotiations and making agreements, and ensuring compliance and monitoring. Hence, some scholars have proposed the concept of transaction cost as a useful tool to explain certain aspects associated with collective action (Birner and Wittmer 2000). Adhikari, in the present volume, examines the relationship between transaction cost and collective action in community forestry in Nepal. The concept of transaction cost has the potential to elucidate the circumstances under which costs associated with collective action may or may not permit the evolution of institutions (contracts) managing CPRs.

In the present paper, we utilize the concept of transaction cost to examine the institutional aspects to community-based aquaculture in village irrigation tanks. The system of village irrigation tanks has managed to survive over a period of two millennia as CPR through its ability to continuously adjust institutional arrangements to adapt to new realities (Panabokke 2001). Given such a time-tested record of collective action, there is great potential to develop community-based aquaculture in village irrigation tanks in a sustainable manner if suitable institutional arrangements were espoused. This study therefore, attempts:

- To assess the importance of costs associated with institutional factors that in turn affect collective action when it comes to community-based aquaculture in village irrigation tanks;
- To identify suitable institutional arrangements and management strategies that would help ensure collective action among resource users for sustainable community-based aquaculture in village irrigation tanks.

The next section of the chapter provides background information on the evolution of institutional arrangements in village tanks and community-based aquaculture. It is followed by a description of the study site and sources of data used in the study. The methodology and conceptual framework for the study are discussed in the next section. It is followed by a discussion of the results of the empirical investigation. The final section discusses conclusions and policy implications that can be derived from the entire exercise.

7.2. Background

The last one and a half centuries have been an era of regular experiments when it comes to institutional arrangements *vis-à-vis* village irrigation tanks that have meant shifting responsibilities from the state to community and vice versa very frequently (Panabokke, Shakthivadivel, and Weerasinghe 2002; Aheeyar 2001). In the past, a village in the dry zone consisted of the following basic components: (*a*) the village tank; (*b*) the housing area (or *gangoda*); (*c*) the tank command area (that is, the paddy-field area serviced by the tank); (*d*) the rain-fed upland crop area (*chena*); and (*e*) the tank catchment (Somasiri 2001). Of these components, common ownership included not just the tank but the lands in the catchment area and rain-fed upland crop areas while the villagers used goods and services extracted from them in usufruct (Ulluwishewa 1997). Households usually held private rights to plots in the village paddy field and the homestead area.

These traditional resource ownership patterns are presently under transformation. The Crown Lands Encroachment Act, a piece of legislation enacted by the British rulers in the first half of the nineteenth century, catalyzed this process initially (Abeysinghe 1978; Government of Sri Lanka 1990). The process is further influenced by: (*a*) commercialization of local economies; (*b*) 'modernization' of agriculture; and (*c*) increasing population (Aheeyar 2001; Leach 1971; Panabokke, Shakthivadivel, and Weerasinghe 2002; Ulluwishewa 1997). Accordingly, most communally held lands allocated for highland crops and tank catchments have been converted to permanent, private land tenure patterns (Ulluwishewa 1997). These changes in ownership and tenure patterns were closely followed by ensuing changes in institutional arrangements. After a number of experiments with regard to various institutional arrangements, the village tanks, during the last two decades, settled to their present arrangement where FOs have to play a major role. This has opened up a wide scope for community participation and collective action.

Parallel with these transformations was a village-tank aquaculture programme that the former Inland Fisheries Division of the Ministry of Fisheries launched in the late Seventies (Chakrabarty and Samaranayake 1983; Thayaparan 1982; Chandrasoma 1986). This programme was carried out as a promotional activity of the state with the support of a few individuals selected from the tank sites who were provided with fish fingerlings from the government breeding centres as a form of state patronage for stocking in tanks. It was the experience gained from this programme that helped establish the technical feasibility of aquaculture in seasonal village tanks. Despite early signs of success, however, the aquaculture programme in village irrigation tanks faced total collapse in 1990 when the government decided to withdraw support for the inland fisheries and aquaculture sector. This revealed the vulnerability of the initially adopted model where no significant attempt was made to instigate a suitable institutional arrangement at the local level. The programme was resumed again in 1994 when the government reinstated support to the inland fisheries and aquaculture sector. Taking lessons from the earlier experience, this time it was introduced as a community-based venture organized under the patronage of FOs with the government providing only the initial catalytic support.

The outcome of the community-based aquaculture programme since the resumption of state support however has been mixed. While a handful of communities have succeeded in completing a few cycles of production on their own initiative, the programme has faced problems in many tanks after external support was lifted. In management circles, these failures are usually attributed to reasons such as the lack of an adequate number of extension staff, poor dedication of extension workers, scarcity of fish fingerlings, poor coordination among relevant stakeholders, etc. Although these reasons no doubt explain the slow progress of the state programmes carried out to provide initial catalytic support, they have limited explanatory potential from an overall policy perspective. It is highly unlikely that initial catalytic support from the state would be provided to all feasible village irrigation tanks even in the long run. At the final count, the success of interventions like this depends largely on the voluntary adoption of collective action by community groups on a large scale who would ensure its feasibility by setting an example of success to neighbouring locations.

7.3. Study area and data

The study was conducted in the Anuradhapura district, which is located in the heart of the dry zone. It is the district with the highest inland fish production in the country and houses 2,334 inland water bodies covering a total inland water area of 51,500 ha. It ranks first in the country in terms of consumption of freshwater fish with 2,482 g/month per household. It is the area where community-based aquaculture has also been practised in the highest number of village tanks. Hence, Anuradhapura district naturally becomes first choice for the study area.

The study was carried out using primary data collected in two surveys, which separately gathered data on community (tank) and household levels.

Community-level data was collected using a checklist whereas an interview schedule was used to elicit household information.

Information from a total of forty-one tanks was collected using the tank checklist. These tanks covered a majority of locations where community-based aquaculture had been practised during the recent past. The cross-section of selected sites included tanks where community-based aquaculture had been practised continuously for a few cycles by community groups after initial catalytic support was lifted as well as tanks where programmes were abandoned after one or two cycles. Information about each tank and the community it supported was collected from a number of sources, which included official records, village officers, agriculture and irrigation officers, members of FOs, and village elders. The tank checklist collected data on the following major aspects: (a) physical information on the seasonal tank; (b) details on agricultural activities and irrigation; (c) details on fish production in tanks (that is, details of past culture cycles, economic cost/return details on last culture cycle, organizational arrangements, group characteristics, funding of fish-culture programmes, organizational activities/meetings, time allocation, supporting organizations/extension services, marketing, etc.).

Household-level data was collected using an interview schedule, which was administered to gather information from 340 households. These households were selected randomly from forty-one tank sites covered by the tank checklist. Of the total number of households, 208 households had participated in community-based aquaculture at least once while the remaining 132 households were non-participants. The sample included a total population of 1,632 of which 50.5 per cent were females. The average family size was 4.8. The household survey covered information on the following aspects: (a) general household information; (b) living conditions/facilities and ownership of assets; (c) location and infrastructure facilities in the village; (d) income earning activities and income; (e) household expenditure and credit; (f) details on agriculture activities; (g) the nature of involvement in fish-culture activities (that is, contribution, labour use, organizational involvements, sharing of benefits, etc.).

Table 7.1 provides a social profile of the households covered in the survey. As evident, the sample represented a somewhat homogeneous social group consisting mainly of households coming from the Sinhala-Buddhist ethno-religious background. On the whole, households were related to each other through kinship. In the case of participants, the overall income recorded a significant contribution (35 per cent) from seasonal sources whereas non-participant households had a higher share of income from regular sources (74 per cent). However, no significant difference was observed in the total income of the two groups.

Table 7.1. A socio-economic profile of households surveyed

Household Parameter	No. of Households	Percentage
Head of the household		
Male	330	97.0
Religion		
Buddhists	309	91.0
Hindu	1	0.0
Islam	28	8.0
Christian	2	0.0
Education (Head of HH)		
No formal education	6	2.0
Grade 1–5	85	25.0
Grade 6–11	150	44.0
O/L passed	71	21.0
A/L passed	24	7.0
University	4	1.0
Major occupation (Head of HH)		
Farming	266	78.0
Government service	26	8.0
Trader	14	4.0
Self-employed	13	4.0
Private sector	11	3.0
Labourer	07	2.0
Fish farmer	03	1.0

7.4. Methods

Any productive venture, despite type of ownership, involves activities pertaining to input-output transformation and exchange of (property) rights (Eggertson 1990). Costs involved with input-output transformation are the usual 'production costs'. Exchange of property rights gives rise to 'transaction costs' for collecting information, making negotiations, reaching agreements, and enforcement and monitoring of agreements. The concept of transaction cost has been developed as a major tool for the analysis of institutions by the economic schools known as 'Neo-institutional Economics' (NE) and 'New Institutional Economics' (NIE) (Eggertson 1990; Williamson 1973 and 1998; North 1989 and 1991). These schools promote comparative analysis of institutions, taking 'transaction' as the basic analytical unit. Accordingly, different institutional arrangements are considered as outcomes of the interplay between the behavioural attributes of agents, nature of transactions involved, and associated institutional environments (Birner and Wittmer 2000). The framework is guided by the basic premise known as 'Discriminating-Alignment Hypothesis', which asserts that transactions that differ in their cost and competence tend to align with 'governance structures' (that differ in their cost and competence), which help minimize transaction costs (Williamson 1998).

In a common property regime where no one owns exclusive private rights for the resource, exchange of property rights usually requires the creation of institutional arrangements (governance structures) that provide a mechanism for the organization of collective action among stakeholders (co-owners). A given institutional arrangement is usually associated with a corresponding structure of transaction costs. Kuperan *et al.* (1998) attempted to estimate the major types of transaction cost involved in the context of fisheries co-management, namely, ex-ante and ex-post transaction costs. Ex-ante costs are information and collective decision-making costs whereas ex-post transaction costs include enforcement and monitoring costs. They have pointed out that different management regimes (that is, co-management versus the regulatory approach) tend to enlist different types of transaction costs while the burden of those costs to government and community partners may vary accordingly.

When an existing institutional arrangement is transformed to a new one, changes usually take place in the transaction cost structure as well. Hanna (1995) suggested that the introduction of co-management in place of regulatory approaches tends to shift the high ex-ante transaction cost from the state to the communities. Further, co-management has the potential to increase the ex-ante transaction costs while achieving gains from ex-post transactions as well (Abdullah, Kuperan, and Pomeroy 1998; Kuperan *et al.* 1998).

The burden of the transaction cost could vary among individual households in a given community group too in addition to that between the government and community groups. Adhikari and Lovett (2005) and Adhikari (this volume) have shown that the transaction cost for community forest management in Nepal is higher for wealthier households compared to poorer households on average though the burden for poorer households as a percentage of resource appropriation costs is higher than that for richer households. Further, the transaction cost varies among different community groups (villages) too.

Based on a study conducted in two co-managed wildlife dispersal areas in Kenya, Mburu, Birner, and Zeller (2003) show that the magnitude of transaction costs incurred by (individual) landowners is influenced by a number of factors. Among them are: (*a*) attributes of transactions; (*b*) biophysical and ecological characteristics of resources systems; (*c*) human, social, and financial capitals of landowners; (*d*) losses from human-wildlife conflicts; (*e*) tenure security; and (*f*) benefits from conservation. They further suggest that the influence of these factors is not the same in different locations and that individual transaction costs are determined by a combination of factors specific to a local site.

7.4.1. *Transaction costs for community-based aquaculture*

As a productive venture, community-based aquaculture also has production costs and transaction costs. Assuming that there are no significant costs or

Table 7.2. Transactions in community-based aquaculture in village irrigation tanks

Type	Transactions
Searching and information	Accessing scientific methods and species for culture
Collective decision-making	Organizing meetings, reaching agreements, coordinating with authorities
Enforcement and monitoring compliance	Collective organization of tank preparation actions, stocking, etc.
Prevention of free-rider activity	Protection from poaching
Distribution of benefits	Organizing collective harvesting
	Monitoring the distribution of benefits

benefits generated due to the interaction of activities, a simplified model of the overall economic benefit structure in a village irrigation tank can be given as follows.

$$Bt = Bi + Bf + Bo \qquad (1)$$

Bt = Total Economic Benefits of the Seasonal Tank
Bi = Net Benefits from Irrigation
Bf = Net Benefits from Rural Aquaculture
Bo= Net Benefits from Other Uses

Given that benefits from aquaculture are conditional upon collective action, the decision rule to adopt community-based aquaculture in a given seasonal tank can be stated by:

$$Bf > TC \qquad (2)$$

TC = Transaction cost of organizing collective action

Table 7.2 summarizes the major types of transactions associated with organizing collective action for community-based aquaculture. Each of the activities mentioned involves a certain level of transaction cost, which may or may not be accounted in terms of monetary value. These categories are somewhat similar to those recorded by Adhikari and Arun (both this volume) in the community forestry in Nepal.

In any collective action context, decision-making takes place at least on two levels, namely, collective (community-level) decisions on adopting the action and individual (household-level) decisions on whether to participate in it. The transaction cost structure associated with a given institutional arrangement has a variable impact over the decisions of individual agents and collective groups. The abandonment of collectively adopted decisions on the grounds of poor participation by individual members is a familiar circumstance in rural development.

As discussed, collective action for community-based aquaculture in village tanks is usually the responsibility of FOs. Accordingly, certain elements of

Table 7.3. Methods of estimating transaction costs

Transaction	Nature of Transactions	Nature of Cost	Approach
Organization of collective action	Meetings/dealing with agents	Time for meetings/action	Value of time (WR × time)
Ensuring the implementation of decisions	Meetings/dealing with agents	Time for meetings/action	Value of time (WR × time)
Avoiding free-rider activities	Watching/dealing with officers	Cash payments/time cost for watching	Wage cost/Value of time (WR × time)
Organizing the sharing of benefits	Meetings	Time for meetings	Value of time (WR × time)

WR = average wage

transaction costs are incurred by FOs, which are taken care of by collective decision-making. In addition to these, there are elements of transaction cost that are borne individually by members of the community. Such household contributions to community-based aquaculture come mainly as a share of labour-time. While a part of this contribution accounts for usual 'production costs', share of labour used for collecting information, negotiation, reaching agreements, and monitoring activities represent transaction costs. Regardless of whether something is a part of transaction costs or production costs, all contributions from households have opportunity cost implications in relation to the economic strategy of a given household. Hence, the opportunity cost of individual contributions is a deciding factor that influences participation in community-based aquaculture.

Table 7.3 presents the major types of transaction costs involved and methods adopted to measure them in our study. Most transaction costs are forfeited in terms of opportunity cost of time and only a limited amount of direct cash payments are involved. In rural economies, time costs incurred by households are not always backed by observable 'monetary values' that are determined by market-based prices. Instead, such decisions are often backed by 'shadow prices', which reflect the opportunity cost to the household of an activity, taken (Sadoulet and De Janvry 1995). In estimating transaction costs, general wage rates available in the area for agricultural labour were used as a proxy for the opportunity cost of time. As participation by females was practically negligible, the issue of gender difference in wage rate did not arise. However, watching for protection from poachers was an activity usually undertaken during the night-time. Application of general wage rates in this case was hence not appropriate. However, this activity was carried out by hired watchers in seven tanks and the average wage rate paid for these watchers was applied to estimate the cost of watching by unpaid community members in other tanks too. In all other cases, TC was measured in terms of the average wage in the specific community multiplied by the total time spent on the transactions plus any cash payments.

The preceding section has described the conceptual foundation that applies to the empirical analysis of the transaction cost in community-based aquaculture. Based on this framework, a comparative analysis of the transaction cost was undertaken for the different institutional (contractual) arrangements adopted for community-based aquaculture in different tanks. The results of this analysis and their implications are discussed in the forthcoming sections.

7.5. Results and discussion

In this section, an empirical analysis of the transaction cost is presented, highlighting its implications for the actions of individuals and collective groups. In the analysis, the transaction cost under each different contractual arrangement is compared with another, with the objective of deriving associated policy implications.

7.5.1. Institutional arrangements for community-based aquaculture

In the sample of tanks, collective action for community-based aquaculture has been organized under three types of contractual arrangements: (*a*) organizing of culture operations by the FO itself (ten tanks, 26 per cent); (*b*) forming of a separate Fisheries Sub-Committee (FSC) under the FO (twenty-seven tanks, 67 per cent); and (*c*) contracting of rights to culture fish in tanks to another party by the FO (three tanks, 7 per cent). In one tank, the government had stocked fingerlings without the support of any local institution. In the first two arrangements, a subgroup of FOs had taken on the operational responsibility of the aquaculture programmes while in the third non-members of FO were also involved.

7.5.1.1. FISHERIES SUBCOMMITTEES

Establishing an FSC is the dominant contractual arrangement observed in two-thirds of the sample. The average number of members in an FSC is nineteen (range 6–54). The FSC, always a subgroup of the FO, has been contracted by the FO to carry out aquaculture in return for a share of benefits, usually in cash. The remaining income is shared between the members of the FSC, principally on equal terms but with minor adjustments to reflect contributions by different members. The major feature of this arrangement is that FO members who are not in the FSC do not have any ownership claim for fish harvested after the stocking of tanks. Hence the members of the FSC usually carry out their activities more independently while meetings and other organizational arrangements record participation by limited numbers.

7.5.1.2. FARMER ORGANIZATION

The basic difference between this arrangement and that of the separate FSC is that under the FO the entire membership has an equivalent claim for the final harvest, the income earned from which is usually credited to the FO's fund. In addition, a portion of harvest is also distributed among the membership, usually a small quantity of fish for each household. As far as collective action is concerned, other than meetings to decide on arrangements at which there is participation by a majority of the members, a subgroup of members usually organizes and carries out aquaculture operations on behalf of the entire membership. The average size of the fish-culture group was thirty-one (range 3–60), which is significantly larger than that of the FSC. While members who make a greater contribution are paid by the FO, a significant amount of labour comes as unpaid minor contributions from other members. This is an advantage from the point of view of the organization.

7.5.1.3. OTHER CONTRACTUAL PARTIES

This arrangement was found only in tanks where the FO is non-functional or quite weak. In the sample, this arrangement was found only in three tanks. This is similar to a private rental arrangement as the contracted parties did not have any ownership claim to the resource base (that is, village tanks) derived from common ownership unlike in the other two cases. The smallest size groups were observed under this arrangement averaging eight (range 5–13).

7.5.2. *The transaction cost for community-based aquaculture*

Figure 7.1 and Table 7.4 provide details on the three types of transaction cost that have been reported. The costs given in the table are aggregates of individually incurred costs computed for a given tank. The cost for searching and gathering of information is relatively low due to the specific circumstances found in village tanks. Firstly, members of fish-culture groups already possess substantial knowledge, both on resource conditions and contracting parties as they have already taken part in activities based on the same resource with the same group. Secondly, groups are usually small. As per acquiring technical know-how, however, participants have to incur some cost as they have to participate in awareness and training programmes conducted by government extension officers on aquaculture operations. It should be noted that this does not include the expenses incurred by the government in order to conduct training and awareness programmes.

However, groups have to incur transaction costs for making collective decisions and for enforcing and monitoring them. The most important fact is that these costs are borne individually by members of the active group, except in

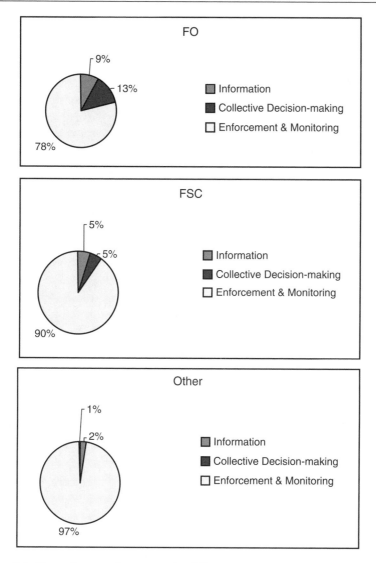

Figure 7.1. Share of transaction cost under different institutional arrangements

eight tanks where hired watchers were recruited using organizational funds. Many communities hold meetings to decide on organizational matters of community-based aquaculture on a few occasions (2.5 times on average in the range of 0–4). Usually, costs were appropriated in terms of time and they were valued using a uniform wage rate, which does not reflect the real opportunity cost with respect to a given household. In all three institutional arrangements,

Table 7.4. Transaction cost under different institutional arrangements (land per cycle of production)

Institutional arrangement	Information cost (Rs)			Collective decision-making cost (Rs)			Enforcement and monitoring cost (Rs)			Total transaction cost (Rs)		
	Average	Max	Min	Average	Max	Min	Average	Max	Min	Average	Max	Min
Farmer Organization	2,179 (8.6%)	9,010	—	3,187 (12.7%)	8,116	—	19,722 (78.6%)	77,520	1,520	25,088	79,620	3,420
Fisheries Subcommittee	1,854 (5.2%)	9,450	—	1,793 (5.0%)	9,075	—	32,069 (89.8%)	136,800	2,280	35,717	138,750	2,280
Other	375 (0.06%)	1,500	—	1,150 (2.6%)	1,600	—	53,010 (97.2%)	168,720	—	54,535	168,720	500
Overall	1,744	9,450	—	1,998	9,075	—	30,319	168,720	—	34,012	168,720	—

work is distributed among members of the active group in a uniform manner (76 per cent in FSC, 70 per cent in FO, and 100 per cent in others) while in the case of two tanks there were penalties for neglect of work.

Compared with information and collective decision-making costs, enforcement and monitoring costs were substantial. Enforcement and monitoring costs basically imply the cost of watching to prevent poaching measured in terms of the imputed value of labour and/or actual payments made for the task. Poaching used to be the most important problem faced by community-based aquaculture in many village tanks. While poaching is an act of theft when engaged in by outsiders, on most occasions the poachers came from the same community. Hence, it can be construed as a form of free-riding as well. On a few occasions, litigation was pursued via calling on the police for redress.

Table 7.4 also indicates the transaction cost under the three different institutional arrangements. As evident, the lowest average aggregate TC is reported in FO-managed village tanks while the tanks managed by other parties contracted by the FOs recorded the highest TC. The average aggregate TC of FSC-managed tanks lie in between these two. This result is clearly indicative of the influence exerted by the three institutional arrangements on the behaviour of the village community. In the tanks where the FO itself organized aquaculture, the TC incurred for training and collective decision-making is relatively high as more participants were involved in collective action. Yet, given the fact that a wider section of the village community claims ownership of the fish cultured in tanks, the TC for protection of the harvest is relatively low. When the FO contract the rights of fish culture to a subgroup of it (FSC) or other party from outside, they have to incur more TC to protect the harvest from theft, or free-riders, in successively high amounts. This reflects the villagers' perception of ownership of fish cultured in tanks under the three different institutional arrangements.

7.5.3. Production and efficiency of community-based aquaculture

Production and returns from the tanks were highly variable. As Table 7.5 shows, on average, the value of fish relative to agriculture in the selected villages is only about 5 per cent. This relative value is 4.1 per cent in FO-managed tanks whereas in the case of FSC managed tanks it is 5.6 per cent. Given the magnitude of benefits involved, it is apparent that the values generated by aquaculture are not in a scale capable of providing a major livelihood for all members of a given community. As a result, in all three institutional arrangements, the organizational responsibilities of community-based aquaculture have been passed on to a smaller subgroup of stakeholders of the tank.

A net-benefit analysis was conducted in order to assess the economic viability of the system. It shows that nearly 60 per cent of tanks managed by the

Table 7.5. Relative contribution by community-based aquaculture

Value parameter	Total annual value of irrigated paddy (Rs)	Total annual value of cultured fish (Rs)	Avg. share of value of fish (%)
Average	4,883,842	74,654	4.8
Max	125,537,665	540,000	33
Min	96,925	—	—

FOs as well as the FSCs indicate positive net margins. Tanks managed by the FSCs have recorded the best performance in terms of average production, fish productivity per unit area, and total value of production and net margin, compared with the other two arrangements (Table 7.6). Even though higher average revenues were indicated for a few tanks managed by other contracted groups, they experienced higher average costs, too, particularly for the harvesting of fish using hired labour which resulted in a net loss overall. Tanks managed by the FOs indicated a moderate situation as far as economic returns are concerned. The results of the net-benefit analysis indicate that village-tank aquaculture has the potential to qualify as an economically efficient system in a significant number of tanks.

However, the net-benefit analysis was conducted using conventional criteria and the TC was not taken into account in the analysis. Therefore, an attempt was made to assess the efficiency of the system using the net-margin analysis extended to test the impacts of TC as well. Here the extended net benefit is defined as net benefit minus TC. A culture programme in a tank was taken as a single unit and all costs, including TC borne by individual members, were subtracted from returns. Table 7.7 presents the outcome of the analysis.

Once the transaction costs too are taken into consideration, particularly the cost incurred for monitoring (that is, watching the actions of poachers), community-based aquaculture loses its appeal. As Table 7.7 shows, only 34 per cent of forty-one tanks indicate a positive net benefit from aquaculture once all TCs are taken into account. This fact becomes particularly important when the associated institutional aspects are also taken into consideration. As indicated in Table 7.4, the burden of transaction costs is higher in FSC-managed

Table 7.6. Economic performance of three institutional arrangements

Institutional arrangement	Average Production (kg)	Average Productivity (kg/ha)	Average Value of Total Product (Rs)	Average Cost (Rs)	Average Net Margin
Farmer organization (FO)	1,816.4	132.3	50,732.8	45,841.0	4,891.8
Fisheries Subcommittee (FSC)	2,387.8	255.0	87,733.9	44,630.3	43,103.6
Other	1,966.7	206.7	61,559.9	102,566.7	−(41,006.8)
Overall	2,196	218.2	74,654.2	48,447.7	26,206.6

Table 7.7. Results of the extended net margin analysis in tanks

Criteria	No. of tanks with positive net margins			
	FO managed	FSC managed	Other	Overall
Net benefit under pure 'production costs'	06 (60%)	16 (59%)	01 (33%)	23 (58%)
'Extended' net benefit including aggregate decision-making and information costs	05 (50%)	15 (55%)	01 (33%)	21 (53%)
'Extended' net benefit including aggregate monitoring costs as well	05 (50%)	09 (33%)	– (0%)	14 (35%)

tanks than in FO-managed tanks and therefore the impact of TC on net bene-fits too. According to Table 7.7, despite high relative returns in FSC-managed tanks, only 33 per cent of tanks show a positive net margin once TC is taken into account, compared with 50 per cent of FO-managed tanks. This is with-standing the fact that FO-managed tanks have recorded relatively low average returns. Overall, the outcome of the extended cost benefit points to a few very important facts, namely, (a) that the transaction cost of community-based aquaculture has a substantial economic impact on a significant number of tanks; (b) that the impact of the TC is particularly significant in FSC-managed tanks, which is the dominant and more productive institutional arrangement for community-based aquaculture; and (c) that this could create a negative impact on the adoption and sustainability of the activity in the long run.

Given the fact that community-based aquaculture is a risk-prone activity, a sensitivity analysis (without subtracting TC) was carried out under three scenarios, namely, (a) reduction of benefits by 5 per cent; (b) increase of costs by 5 per cent; and (c) a and b together. The results indicate that on average, net benefits decreased by 24 per cent, 19 per cent, and 43 per cent respectively under the three scenarios. In one tank where positive net benefits were reported earlier, returns were reversed into a negative margin. This indicates that returns from community-based aquaculture in village tanks are vulnerable to uncertainties that could cause production losses or price drops even when TC is not included.

Despite the vulnerable situation revealed in the financial analysis, how-ever, community-based aquaculture has usually been reported as a financially viable venture from the perspective of FOs as seed fish has been provided either freely, or on a subsidized basis, as a promotional encouragement from a state agency or an NGO in many tanks. Besides, organizational cash flows consider conventional costs and benefits only. On a number of occasions, revenues remitted from fish-culture activities claimed a significant portion of the organizational funds of FOs, which usually have a limited portfolio of other income-generating activities. This could lead to misleading implications unless the cost of subsidized inputs and transaction costs are also taken into consideration.

7.5.4. *Distribution of benefits from community-based aquaculture*

Table 7.8 shows the average benefits divided (in cash and kind) among individual members and organizations under the three institutional arrangements separately. In a majority of tanks, a certain amount of returns were retained with organizations while the remaining benefits were distributed to individual members in the form of fish, money, or both. Returns have been transferred to FOs in twenty-eight (70 per cent) tanks and in over 60 per cent of the cases this portion amounted to less than 40 per cent of total returns. Aquaculture ventures failed completely in three tanks, which left no benefits to distribute among either individual members or organizations.

In 70 per cent of the tanks, benefits were distributed to individuals as well. These included seven (70 per cent) of the FO-managed tanks and twenty-one (75 per cent) of the FSC-managed tanks. However, in many cases, individual benefits were restricted to a portion of the unsold fish harvest and cash returns were distributed in only nineteen (46 per cent) of the tanks. In sixteen of them, income was uniformly distributed among active members while in others benefits were distributed according to work done in a proportionate manner. In addition to benefits distributed among participants, during the event of harvesting, many non-participant community members also benefited from the harvest in terms of small quantities of fish, which could amount to a substantial portion of the harvest in aggregate.

The distribution of benefits differed widely among the three institutional arrangements. Such variations were observed in the amount of cash retained by the organizations (FO or FSC) as well as in the benefits distributed to individuals. In a few tanks, a complete portfolio of benefits (that is, cash for FO and FSC and fish and cash for individuals) has been offered to all stakeholders involved. Of the three institutional arrangements, the FSC is relatively more successful in terms of organizational benefits as well as in the magnitude of individual benefits (see Table 7.8). However, contribution to village food security was high in FO-managed tanks as the number of beneficiaries was higher in those tanks.

On the whole, community-based aquaculture has helped village communities in two important ways. First, these ventures have helped earn some amount of cash returns for FOs in a majority of tanks. This income, though moderate in magnitude, seems to provide relief for many FOs with poor cash flows as a means of overcoming their financial difficulties. This can be considered a benefit to the respective communities with indirect advantages to individual households too.

The second major contribution is support for village food security. Table 7.8 shows that an average of 6.5 kg of fish has been distributed among participant members. In margin, this can be considered a significant increment to household nutrition given the fact that average fish consumption in the area has

Table 7.8. Distribution of benefits of community-based aquaculture among participants and organizations

Institutional arrangement	Individual benefits				Benefits retained by organizational group					
	Fish (kg)		Money (Rs)		By FSC		By FO		By Others	
	No. Tanks	Average	No. Tanks	Average	No. Tanks	Average	No. Tanks	Average	No. Tanks	Average
Farmer Organization (FO)	8	6.43	4	2236	—	—	8	27,071	—	—
Fisheries Subcommittee (FSC)	26	6.54	15	2813	9	14,492	20	8,623	—	—
Other	1	2.0	—	—	—	—	—	—	3	23,333
Overall	35	6.45	19	2691	9	14,492	28	13,893	3	23,333

been estimated as 25 kg per household per annum. Once the unaccounted-for fish output distributed among village communities during the harvesting event is also taken into consideration, it could be said that the system has helped increase the supply of animal proteins to the rural poor in a significant manner.

However, despite the cash-flow support for organizations and contributions to village food security, the direct cash benefits to individual participants seem relatively low and hence cannot be considered as providing a strong incentive to attract participation. Given the magnitude of benefits involved, it is apparent that productivity improvements generated by community-based aquaculture are not on a scale that is adequate to provide a major livelihood for all members of a given community. More equitable distribution of benefits, although contrary to the expectations of policy makers, therefore, runs the risk of further thinning out incentives for the active group. This essentially has implications for the sustainability aspect of the enterprise.

7.5.5. Participation in community-based aquaculture and poverty

According to the household survey, incidence of poverty (that is, percentage of households in the sample with a per capita income lower than the official poverty line) among participant and non-participant households is 26 per cent and 20 per cent respectively. Despite this slight gap in poverty in favour of non-participants, other income parameters do not indicate a significant difference between the two groups. The average annual household income is slightly higher in the case of participants with a higher contribution from seasonal sources (33 per cent) compared with non-participants (26 per cent). Variation of income is significantly high among participant households (CV = 103 per cent) than non-participants (CV = 59 per cent). Overall, it seems that households with variable, seasonal sources of income are more attracted towards community-based aquaculture than households which depend more on regular sources of income. This is quite understandable given the fact that the opportunity cost of time is usually higher for regular income earners than for seasonal earners.

7.5.6. Sustainability

The data collected in the survey does not allow for an objective assessment of the sustainability of community-based aquaculture in terms of future continuity. Out of forty-one tanks studied, only seven tanks have continued activity for more than one cycle while one tank has entered into its fourth cycle of operation. Many tanks were in their inauguration stage.

The survey gathered information on the last complete production cycle, usually for the year 2003. Many tanks had not stocked up for the ongoing

2004 cycle due to the extended drought that prevailed at the time of the survey. In tanks where the inaugural cycle of production was being undertaken, inputs had been given on a free or subsidized basis as a promotional measure. Hence, it is premature to draw any conclusions on the sustainability of the venture based on the limited information currently available.

As far as preparedness for forthcoming cycles are concerned, only in the case of nine (33 per cent) out of twenty-seven tanks managed by the FSC were a part of returns (extended up to 60 per cent of total returns) retained to finance future cycles. In these tanks, a share of returns was left aside to purchase fingerlings for the next cycle. Overall, it seems that the returns that had been set aside as institutional deposits to continue aquaculture operations in forthcoming years are quite low, which is against the expectations of policy makers who advocate promoting community-based aquaculture on a large scale.

However, the survey helped to recognize a set of constraints that could affect the sustainability of the activity based on opinions expressed by the participants. Farmers identified a list of constraints, which can be categorized as technical, institutional, and other physical problems. A majority of constraints that were seen to affect the culture operations in tanks were institution-related (Table 7.9). Among them, the problem of free-riders is the most prominent. This problem was reported in two-thirds of tanks in the sample. The situation was aggravated in a few tanks to a crisis level where authorities had to be called in for redress. Hence, the free-riders problem has the potential to cause a significant impact on the sustainability of the system, making it difficult to rally necessary cooperation among community members. It seems that other major institutional problems, namely, conflicts in FOs and mismanagement of benefits, are also more or less interlinked with the free-riders problem.

In addition, the poor supply of fish seeds, natural disasters, and predators also have the potential to affect the success of programmes. However, their impact on the sustainability of the system is largely due to productivity fluctuations with indirect implications on institutional factors such as group cooperation and individual participation. Hence, future sustainability of community-based aquaculture depends on a few major factors among which institutional factors assume an important place.

7.6. Conclusions and Policy Implications

Community-based aquaculture in village irrigation tanks has been organized under three institutional arrangements. In these arrangements, either the FOs have retained the organizational responsibility for themselves or have contracted it out to another party. Forming an FSC, a subgroup of an FO, is the dominant contractual arrangement observed in two-thirds of the sample.

185

Table 7.9. Constraints for community-based aquaculture

Type of constraint	Constraint(s)	Number of tanks reported	Percentage
Technical	Poor supply of fish seed	16	39
	Poor tank selection	2	04
	Unsuitability of cultured species	8	20
Institutional	Problem of free-riders (poaching and other problems from villagers)	27	66
	Poor participation		
	Political influence	8	20
	Ambiguous legal status	3	07
	Conflicts in FO	3	07
	Mismanagement of benefits	10	24
	Problem of marketing	13	32
		6	15
Other physical	Natural disasters	15	37
	Predators	14	34
	Premature harvest due to water supply uncertainty	1	02

The major advantage of this arrangement is that it helps delimit the claims for relatively moderate returns from the activity to a manageable number of beneficiaries. Further it allows for activities to be undertaken by a limited number of active participants in a more independent manner.

All three institutional arrangements involve transaction costs which are variable in their magnitude. There are three major types of transaction cost for information, collective decision-making, and protection of the fish harvest from poachers. While the costs for information and collective decision-making are relatively low under all three arrangements, significant differences could be observed when it comes to the cost of protecting the harvest. As shown above, the lowest average aggregate transaction cost is reported in FO-managed village tanks, indicating the influence of the collective perception of ownership by the entire membership. When the FO has contracted the right to culture fish in tanks to a restricted group, they have to incur more transaction cost to protect the harvest from theft or free-riders.

On the whole, community-based aquaculture has helped generate much-needed cash returns to FOs in a majority of the tanks, though at moderate levels, simultaneously helping to increase the supply of animal proteins to the rural poor too. Of the three institutional arrangements concerned, FSC is the most successful in terms of generating benefits to individual members as well as to organizations. Despite these achievements, however, individual benefits to members of collective action groups are low, providing only a limited incentive to attract participation.

Sustainability of community-based aquaculture therefore depends largely on its ability to attract and sustain the participation of members of farming communities. The transaction cost for protecting fish from poaching is likely to have a large impact on sustaining the participation of households. These costs are usually borne by individual members and are substantial in their magnitude. Drawing from the example of the community forestry in Nepal presented in this volume by Adhikari, forest user groups with higher individual transaction costs appear to have lower level of collective action.

Limited rewards for participation as well as the presence of significant transaction costs for individuals place the sustainability of the system at stake. Even if the programmes are found cost-effective in terms of cash flow to FOs, the sustainability of operations may not be ensured if active participation could dissipate gradually due to inadequate incentives to participants. Hence, the sustainability of collective action for aquaculture relies to a large degree on the ability to minimize transaction costs and on enlarging the share of benefits for an active group of participants who bear these costs.

In the backdrop, three factors merit special attention. The first is a tank's ability to achieve adequate returns for its members. According to the data, this could be quite variable among selected tanks. Hence, selecting tanks with adequate productivity levels is important. The second is how the unaccounted-for, individually borne transaction costs would be taken care of and what impact they have on the decisions to participate in community-based aquaculture by individual members. It has been indicated that these transaction costs are highly variable among tanks while adjustments in institutional arrangements are also taking place in tanks, which have entered subsequent cycles of operation. The final factor is how successful the ongoing experimenting with institutional arrangements to minimize associated transaction costs are, which simultaneously help to achieve substantial improvements in the productivity of tanks as well. These points are particularly important from the point of view of the long-term sustainability of community-based aquaculture in village irrigation tanks and therefore are highly policy-relevant.

Appendix 7.1. A brief note on community-based aquaculture

In Sri Lanka, reservoir-based freshwater fish production takes place under two major subsystems, namely, (*a*) inland fisheries in relatively large perennial reservoirs; and (*b*) seasonal village-tank fisheries where community-based aquaculture is practised. Even though both systems of production practically deal with the same species of freshwater fish, resource-use contexts in the two systems are different from each other. Inland fisheries in large perennial reservoirs have continuous, self-recruited fish populations exploited by regular, full-time fishermen. These fisheries have been identified among the most productive artisanal inland fisheries in Asia (de Silva 1989). In contrast, less productive seasonal fisheries in village tanks cannot support a regular fishing community, under natural conditions and, therefore, annual stocking of fish fingerlings is necessary to achieve higher levels of productivity.

Typically, an aquaculture system involves a three-stage sequence, namely, (*a*) hatchery operations; (*b*) nursery operations; and (*c*) grow-out operations. Seasonal tank aquaculture is basically a grow-out operation and, usually, the other two stages of the operation are fulfilled outside the reservoir site. However, procurement of inputs (fingerlings) from the nursery and immediate disposal of harvested output from the tank site are also two essential steps in a seasonal tank aquaculture programme. Seasonal tank aquaculture can be described as an extensive type of aquaculture practice due to the fact that fish are stocked in relatively low densities and external inputs are scarcely used other than fish fingerlings. Once stocked, the fish are left entirely for natural feeding for their growth. Hence, the natural fertility in a tank is an important parameter that affects the final fish output. As a measure to exploit natural foods available in different niches in an optimal manner, a polyculture combination of species is usually stocked.

Given the associated conditions, aquaculture in seasonal tanks is a task left for the surrounding agrarian communities rather than fishermen as the scope for involvement of full-time regular fishing communities is quite low. Hence, in the case of the community-based aquaculture, the major rural institution involved is FOs. However, it is mainly a rural institution established for the management of minor irrigation structures for paddy-based agriculture.

References

Abdullah, N. M. R., Kuperan, K., and Pomeroy, R. S. (1998). 'Transaction Cost and Fisheries Co-management'. *Marine Resource Economics,* 13: 103–14.

Abeysinghe, A. (1978). *Ancient Land Tenure to Modern Land Reforms,* Vols. 1 and 2. Colombo, Sri Lanka: Centre for Society and Religion.

Adhikari, B., and Lovett, J. C. (2005). *Transaction Cost and Community-based Natural Resource Management in Nepal.* York: University of York. Environment Department.

Agrawal, A., and Ostrom, E. (1999). 'Collective Action, Property Rights and Devolution of Forest and Protected Areas Management', in R. Meinzen-Dick and A. Knox (eds.), *Collective Action, Property Rights and Devolution of Natural Resource Management.* Germany: German Foundation for Economic Development (DSE), 75–110.

Aheeyar, M. M. M. (2001). 'Socio-economic and Institutional Aspects of Small Tank Systems in Relation to Food Security', in H. P. M. Gunasena (ed.), *Proceedings of the Workshop on Food Security and Small Tank Systems in Sri Lanka.* Colombo, Sri Lanka: National Science Foundation, 64–78.

Birner, R., and Wittmer, H. (2000). 'Co-management of Natural Resources: A Transaction Cost Economics Approach to Determine the Efficient Boundaries of the State'. Paper presented at the International Symposium of New Institutional Economics, Tubingen, Germany, 22–4 September. <http://www.isnie.org/ISNIE00/finalprogram.htm#Panel4A>.

Chakrabarty, R. D., and Samaranayake, R. A. D. B. (1983). 'Fish Culture in Seasonal Tanks in Sri Lanka'. *Journal of Inland Fisheries,* 2: 125–40.

Chandrasoma, J. (1986). 'Primary Productivity and Fish Yield in Ten Seasonal Tanks in Sri Lanka'. *Journal of Inland Fisheries*, 3: 56–62.

De Silva, S. S. (1989). *Reservoirs of Sri Lanka and their Fisheries*. FAO Fisheries Technical Paper 298, FAO, Rome.

Eggertson, T. (1990). *Economic Behavior and Institutions*. Cambridge: Cambridge University Press.

Government of Sri Lanka (1990). *Report of the Land Commission—1987*. Sessional Paper No. III. Colombo, Sri Lanka: Government of Sri Lanka.

Hanna, S. (1995). 'Efficiencies of Users' Participation in Natural Resources Management', in S. Hanna and M. Munasinghe (eds.), *Property Rights and the Environment—Social and Ecological Issues*. Washington, DC: Beijer International Institute of Ecological Economics and World Bank, 59–67.

Kuperan, K., Abdullah, N. M. R., Pomeroy, R. S., Genio, E., and Salamanca, A. (1998). 'Measuring Transaction Cost of Fisheries Co-management'. Paper presented at the 7th Biennial Conference of the International Association for the Study of Common Property, Vancouver. <http://www.indiana.edu/~iasap/Drafts/kuperan.pdf>.

Leach, E. R. (1971). *Pul Eliya, A Village in Ceylon: A Study of Land Tenure and Kinship*. Cambridge: Cambridge University Press.

Mburu, J., Birner, R., and Zeller, M. (2003). 'Relative Importance and Determinants of Landowners' Transaction Costs in Collaborative Wildlife Management in Kenya: An Empirical Analysis'. *Ecological Economics*, 45/1: 59–73.

Meinzen-Dick, R., and Knox, A. (1999). 'Collective Action, Property Rights and Devolution of Natural Resource Management', in R. Meinzen-Dick and A. Knox (eds.), *Collective Action, Property Rights and Devolution of Natural Resource Management*. Germany: German Foundation for Economic Development (DSE), 41–74.

Ministry of Fisheries and Aquatic Resources (2004). 'Fisheries Statistics-2003'. Report. Ministry of Fisheries and Aquatic Resources, Colombo, Sri Lanka.

North, D. C. (1989). 'Institutions and Economic Growth: A Historical Introduction'. *World Development*, 17/9: 1319–32.

Ostrom, E. (1990). *Governing the Commons*. Cambridge: Cambridge University Press.

Panabokke, C. R. (2001). 'Small Tank Systems in Sri Lanka: Summing and Issues', in H. P. M. Gunasena (ed.), *Proceedings of the Workshop on Food Security and Small Tank Systems in Sri Lanka*. Colombo, Sri Lanka: National Science Foundation, 3–4.

—— Shakthivadivel, R., and Weerasinghe, A. D. (2002). *Small Tanks in Sri Lanka: Evolution, Present Status and Issues*. Report. Colombo, Sri Lanka: International Water Management Institute (IWMI).

Sadoulet, E., and De Janvry, A. (1995). *Quantitative Development Policy Analysis*. Baltimore, CO: John Hopkins University Press.

Somasiri, S. (2001). 'Strategies for Optimizing Food Security under Small Tank Systems in Relation to the High Variability of the Resource Base,' in H. P. M. Gunasena (ed.), *Proceedings of the Workshop on Food Security and Small Tank Systems in Sri Lanka*. Colombo, Sri Lanka: National Science Foundation, 48–63.

Thayaparan, K. (1982). 'The Role of Seasonal Tanks in the Development of Freshwater Fisheries in Sri Lanka'. *Journal of Inland Fisheries*, 1: 133–67.

Ulluwishewa, R. (1997). 'Searching Avenues for Sustainable Land Use: The Role of Indigenous Knowledge between Market Forces and State's Intervention: A Case Study from Sri Lanka'. Sri Lanka Studies, 6. Department of Geography, University of Zurich, Zurich.

Wade, R. (1988). *Village Republics: Economic Conditions for Collective Action in South India.* Cambridge: Cambridge University Press.

Williamson, O. E. (1973). 'Markets and Hierarchies: Some Elementary Considerations'. *American Economic Review*, 63/2: 316–25.

—— (1998). 'The Institutions of Governance'. *American Economic Review*, 88/2: 75–9.

8

Irrigation Management—Does Bottom Up Work Better than Top Down in Sri Lanka?

Gamini Herath

8.1. Introduction

The management of irrigation water in developing countries is a critical issue for policy makers. However, recent government interventions into irrigation water management have largely resulted in increasing subsidies for water use and creating perverse incentives for farmers, bureaucrats and politicians to engage in rent-seeking activities (Lam 2001; Gulati and Narayanan 2002). Available evidence indicates that market-based approaches may not be appropriate at least in the short term to provide a satisfactory outcome to irrigation water management problems because of the common-property characteristics of water (Lam 2001; Saleth and Dinar 1999; Montginoul and Ranault 2003). Further, neoclassical economics appears to provide only limited insights into the question of improving irrigation efficiency. It cannot provide a satisfactory explanation for the presence of a wide range of irrigation institutions such as rotational irrigation and informal farmer groups in developing countries.

Many scholars argue that institutional deficiencies are at the root of irrigation water management problems (Ostrom 1990). The literature on development provides evidence of a continuing effort by economists to gain a better understanding of the role of institutions in irrigation water management. The New Institutional Economics (NIE) provides a framework to analyse the structure of transactions and their governing institutions that influence economic behaviour and performance (Williamson 1985). NIE recognizes that the allocation of rights and responsibilities depends on the nature of the transaction, costs of monitoring and enforcement, and the relationship between economic agents. These insights offer a new array of tools for managing irrigation.

This chapter focuses on the evolution of irrigation management institutions and their impact on efficiency, equity, and environmental issues in Sri Lanka over the past fifty years. It identifies the types of institutional innovations undertaken, and their successes and failures as well as lessons for the future based upon published studies.

The paper is organized as follows. Section 8.2 describes Sri Lanka's experience when it comes to institutional reforms in the irrigation sector—the major schemes (command area greater than 80 ha), minor irrigation schemes (command area less than 80 ha, especially village tanks and *anicut* schemes), and groundwater programmes. The main focus is on the performance and problems of water user associations (WUAs) and the recent experiences in Irrigation Management Transfer (IMT). The last section discusses the lessons and limitations of institutional approaches to irrigation development.

8.2. Institutional evolution in irrigation water management in Sri Lanka

8.2.1. *The three phases of modern irrigation development*

Irrigation development in Sri Lanka has played a critical role in increasing production, productivity, and extension of the cultivated area. Out of approximately 500,000 ha of land under irrigation, 350,000 ha are under major irrigation schemes which are under the Irrigation Management Division (IMD) and the Irrigation Department (ID). Groundwater resources which cover around 0.065 million ha are mostly privately owned (Saleth and Dinar 1999).

Until the 1980s, new irrigation construction accounted for 20 per cent of total public investment in the country but the expansionary trend changed due to escalating costs and management failures (Aluvihare and Kikuchi 1991).[1] Since the 1980s, the focus has been on rehabilitation and upgrading of irrigation systems. The rehabilitation and modernization phases were followed by an emphasis on maximizing the use of scarce water resources in the country through improved management.

A conspicuous feature of irrigation development in Sri Lanka is the significant increase in groundwater development in recent years (Kikuchi *et al.* 2003). After the 1980s, agro-wells were rapidly adopted particularly in the dry zones which had high private as well as social benefit-cost ratios. The most predominant examples are the lined dug wells and irrigation pumps. Private individual investment is high in agro-wells. Well-water is used mainly to grow subsidiary crops and, occasionally, paddy.

---

[1] The expenditures on operation and maintenance (O & M) of irrigation systems were very low at around 5 per cent of total expenditure during the early construction period. There is some evidence that this has reduced the efficiency and lifespan of most major irrigation schemes.

8.2.2. *Policies to improve water management*

The organizational structure for irrigation management can be viewed both from a macro and micro perspective. The macro environment of the water sector in Sri Lanka is dependent on a number of *ad hoc* ordinances introduced at various times (Samad 2005). These ordinances, developed over time, are largely from outside the water sector and ignore the common-property characteristics of water. Further, the absence of orderly development when it comes to specific water policies has led to partial solutions. For example, there are nearly fifty Acts that influence the management of the water sector in Sri Lanka since the 1950s (Saleth and Dinar 2004). Consequently, lack of clear rules for water allocation, poor recovery of operation and maintenance (O & M) costs, equity problems in water distribution, environmental concerns, and unplanned groundwater development reflect the major management failures in the irrigation water sector.

These problems have forced a search for new policy options for effective water management. A comprehensive water policy was in fact prepared in the early 1990s. This new water policy identified two major aspects for reforms, namely (*a*) water entitlements, and (*b*) irrigation water pricing, which created major conflicts in policy circles (Gunatilake and Gopalakrishnan 2002). The idea of pricing water and rights over water was not acceptable to many and the policy was not implemented. Some have also argued that increasing irrigation charges may not lead to efficient allocation and financial viability unless the institutional features governing water rights and land rights are properly aligned (Gandhi, Crase, and Herath 2006).

8.2.3. *Institutional innovations in irrigation management*

As previously noted, over the last two decades, emphasis has moved from irrigation development to improving irrigation water management. Beginning in the 1980s, the government of Sri Lanka sought to achieve higher returns to irrigation investment through the involvement of user groups in operation and management (Samad and Vermillion 1999).[2] These institutions are based on the understanding that collective action is required in irrigation management. The trust and reciprocity present in these communities decrease transaction costs and increase the probability of success of collective action. Some of these initiatives emerged from farmers themselves with no governmental intervention while some WUAs were introduced through government involvement. The initial motive for introducing farmer participation was to make the irrigation systems financially viable (Raby 1991). The IMT programme however goes beyond that and also aims to empower farmers through greater participation.

[2] Water user groups are organizations that are made up of local farmers or irrigators.

IMT has gained popularity in recent years as a mechanism to reduce the role of government agencies in irrigation management. In many countries irrigation systems have been handed over to farmer groups to enhance equity and efficiency (Shyamasundar, this volume). In 1988, the government adopted IMT for major irrigation schemes and in the following year management responsibilities were transferred to legally registered WUAs. The government irrigation agency was responsible for the headwork and the main canal system while the WUAs were responsible for the O & M activities below the distributory channel (Samad and Vermillion 1999). The WUA concept spread rapidly. By March 1997, there were 757 WUAs although this number needs to be interpreted with caution (Saleth and Dinar 1999).

The WUAs can formulate farm plans for the area, market local produce and distribute farm inputs, formulate rules for the maintenance of irrigation infrastructure, devise procedures for the distribution of water, and impose and collect irrigation fees (Samad 2002). The O & M (excepting the tank and the main canals) was the responsibility of the WUA although some of them had limited financial autonomy and could undertake contracts of up to Rs 50,000 only (Raby 1991).[3] It is envisaged that the ownership of the irrigation network will be transferred to WUAs when they are ready but to date no such transfers have taken place. Sri Lanka's irrigation sector has a poor record of cost recovery. Less than 50 per cent of the maintenance costs have been collected from farmers at any time (Herath 2002). With the introduction of the WUAs, full recovery of O & M costs from members was expected. This does not appear to have happened and the government frequently subsidizes maintenance costs (Herath 2002; Samad 2002).

While the broad direction of the necessary institutional arrangements for local irrigation management is reasonably clear, working out the details and implementing them are far from easy. The design of appropriate institutions in the face of variations in the environment, agrarian structure, and other related aspects is complex and, hence, engineering the reforms is difficult (Herath 2002). Thus the performance of a select sample of institutional initiatives (reflecting top-down, bottom-up approaches) and their achievements form the focus of the following sections.

8.2.3.1. THE IMPACT OF INSTITUTIONAL DEVELOPMENTS IN THE MAJOR IRRIGATION SCHEMES IN SRI LANKA

This section examines institutional developments in the major irrigation schemes. For this purpose, we use a sample of published case studies. These include (*a*) Irrigation Management Transfer (IMT) in fifty WUAs, (*b*) the

---

[3] US$1 = Rs 100 in 2005.

farmer-run Gal Oya project, (c) the Rajangana and Mee Oya projects, and (d) multiple-use commons in Kirindi Oya.[4]

8.2.3.1.1. *The IMT programme*

Four different types of schemes were studied: (1) schemes rehabilitated and transferred with IMT; (2) schemes that were transferred with IMT but not rehabilitated; (3) schemes that were rehabilitated but not transferred; and (4) schemes that were neither rehabilitated nor transferred (Samad and Vermillion 1999; Samad 2002) (see Table 8.1 in Appendix 8.1).

In order to understand the impact IMT has on productivity, the pre- and post-transfer situations need to be examined. It was found that IMT has not led to any reduction in government expenditure on O & M. Paddy yields which had shown a declining trend in the pre-IMT period have shown an increasing trend in the post-IMT phase after the schemes were rehabilitated and transferred although cropping intensity has not increased. The increase in yield is significant where both rehabilitation and IMT have occurred. This implies some degree of complementarity between rehabilitation and management—that is, rehabilitation alone is not sufficient in the absence of better management after rehabilitation. Those schemes that were transferred but not rehabilitated and those which were rehabilitated but not transferred did not show a significant increasing or decreasing trend in yield.

In the Nachchaduwa and Hakwatuna Oya schemes, it was found that in general water fee collections have not been well developed and that only a minority of farmers paid any irrigation fee. Paddy yields, however, have increased after transfer. Around 60 per cent of the farmers were dis-satisfied with the maintenance work undertaken after rehabilitation in the Nachchaduwa scheme. The quality of the irrigation service was examined in terms of farmers' perception of adequacy, timeliness, and fairness of water distribution, and the incidence of irrigation-related conflicts before and after IMT. The two schemes showed that there is no difference in the quality of water supply both in the dry and the wet seasons before and after IMT. In Nachchaduwa, about 33 per cent of the farmers in the head-end and

[4] The first case is based on a study undertaken by IWMI of WUAs in 50 irrigation schemes and in-depth studies of the Nachchaduwa and the Hakwatuna Oya schemes (Samad 2002). The financial performance was examined using piecewise linear regression for the period 1985–90 (before IMT) and 1990–5 (after IMT) (Samad 2002). The WUAs in these schemes were introduced by the Government and reflect the 'top-down' approach *vis-à-vis* WUAs. In addition, in-depth studies were carried out in two major schemes. The aim of the study was to assess the impact of IMT on productivity, cost recovery, irrigation services, and maintenance of the schemes. The Gal Oya project had WUAs but they were of the 'bottom-up' type because they were initiated by the farmers themselves (Uphoff and Wijayaratna 2000). The Rajangana system's evaluation is based on a study conducted by HARTI and managed under the PISMP (Aheer 1999). The Kirindi Oya study was conducted by IWMI but focused on multiple use of the commons unlike the other studies which concentrated only on irrigation water (Meinzen-Dick and Bakker 2001).

25 per cent at the tail-end reported a worsening water supply. This worsening was attributed to poor rehabilitation before IMT. In general, timeliness of water supply, fairness of distribution, and occurrence of conflicts has remained unchanged after IMT. Hence, IMT as practised has not produced the desired impacts.

8.2.3.1.2. *WUAs and social capital in the Gal Oya project*

The Gal Oya project in south-eastern Sri Lanka is an example of successful management of the commons through social capital and WUAs/FOs.[5] This scheme was studied for a long period to explore the potential for increasing water-use efficiency, productivity, and maintenance of infrastructure. Local farmer organizations (FOs) were initiated in the 1980s. By 1985, nearly 12,000 farmers were involved in cooperative organizations. The farmers created the organizational roles and rules with assistance from the Hector Kobbakaduwa Agrarian Training and Research Institute (HARTI) and Cornell University (Uphoff 1996; Uphoff and Wijayaratna 2000). Each unit would constitute 10–12 farmers who were cultivating from a common source of water. They gradually worked out informal agreements until their members were ready for a formal structure. The new roles made it easier for farmers to undertake collective action.

There was significant improvement in the efficiency of irrigated rice production after the FOs were introduced. Farmers reported a higher yield of 4,360 kg/ha which is 10 per cent higher than that reported in government statistics (Uphoff and Wijayaratna 2000). A net profit of Rs 24,000 (US$375) per hectare was obtained. A simple analysis indicates that in 1997 the value of rice output achieved through collective action was US$7.4 million more than that of the proposed government scenario.

There was also an extension in the area cultivated. In the 1997 cropping season, the WUAs/FOs were able to bring nearly 25,000 ha under cultivation through collective action where, according to the Irrigation Department, not more than 10,800 ha could be cultivated. For example, in the dry season of 1997, 25,000 ha were cultivated with around 0.3 ha-metre of water per crop, which is one-third the norm. Prior to the introduction of FOs, around 2.4–2.7 ha-metre of water per crop were released in the dry season. In 1985, this number was down to 1.65 ha-metre and reached 1.35 ha-metre in the late 1980s. This means that the institutional arrangements introduced were able to distribute very limited water sparingly yet effectively and to obtain a better yield with a fraction of the earlier amount of water supply (Uphoff and Wijayaratna 2000).

---

[5] The complex social relationships which include social norms, cultural values, and institutions are collectively referred to as social capital. They create trust, reciprocity, or positive emotions among the individuals (Libby and Sharp 2003).

Moreover, collective action was used to clean some irrigation channels not cleaned for nearly twenty years. The available water is distributed on a rotational basis in the dry years with any surplus water distributed to downstream farmers (Uphoff and Wijayaratna 2000). According to Uphoff and Wijayaratna (2000), although initial analysis focused more on structural social capital, cognitive forms of social capital such as commitment to equitable distribution, etc., were evident thirteen years after the experiment. This shows that institutions based on community social capital are robust and sustainable (see Table 8.1). For further innovative ideas on social capital and collective action, see the chapter by Dasgupta in this volume.

8.2.3.1.3. *Rajangana and Mee Oya Schemes*

The two other major WUA-managed schemes selected, the Rajangana and the Mee Oya irrigation schemes in the north-central and the north-western provinces, were examined in 1999. These schemes were managed by the Provincial Irrigation System Management Programme (PISMP) and had had WUAs for more than ten years, which is longer than most other schemes (Aheer 1999). The PISMP failed to delineate institutional rules and to clarify farmers' rights and responsibilities. There were competing demands for the finances of the FOs including construction of buildings, purchase of capital equipment, working capital for service provision, and advances for rehabilitation and maintenance.

A study to assess the impact of WUAs on irrigation efficiency and productivity found that WUAs did not increase the efficiency of irrigation water use. WUAs failed to mobilize adequate (cash and labour) resources. The O & M was unsatisfactory and wastage of water was reported. The failure of PISMP is attributed to the premature transfer of irrigation responsibilities to farmers, and poor training, which led to inadequate commitment of resources by farmers. Moreover, lack of experience led to poor fee collection and financially weak FOs. These problems have occurred because the transfers had been made more for budgetary reasons and due to donor pressure than any readiness on the part of farmers for a genuine transfer (Aheer 1999). A similar experience when it comes to tenants associations has been noted in Goa by Mukhopadhyay (this volume).

8.2.3.1.4. *Multiple-use commons in the Kirindi Oya irrigation project*

The Kirindi Oya irrigation system in the South provides water for irrigation and other uses such as fishing, livestock production, and home gardening. The provision of drinking water is important since many areas lack safe drinking water.[6] While it is likely that water allocation for irrigation will still dominate

---

[6] Safe drinking water is water that is free of contaminants that can undermine the health of the user.

use in the foreseeable future, the demand for other uses is important and rational allocation of water needs to focus on these uses as well.

Meinzen-Dick and Bakker (2001) examined the Kirindi Oya system to assess its potential to bring users together for organizing a platform for the better management of irrigation water. The study interviewed seventy-eight households, held ten focus-group discussions, and also undertook direct observations. It was found that many users did not have any statutory rights and the presence of parallel or multiple government agencies created hurdles with regard to developing WUAs. Currently, the irrigation department controls the water releases. The evolution of WUAs for multiple users can ensure participation of all relevant stakeholders in the allocation of water from irrigation to other uses. Multiple use is important not only for better allocation but also for equity reasons (Meinzen-Dick and Bakker 2001).

8.2.3.2. THE IMPACT OF WUAs/FOs IN MINOR IRRIGATION

8.2.3.2.1. *Village tanks and anicut schemes*

Another important source of irrigation in Sri Lanka is the minor irrigation systems which typically have less than 80 ha of command area fed by a major reservoir, harvest rain, or are of the run-of-the-river systems, and are used for economic as well as non-economic activities such as washing, bathing, and aquaculture (Senaratne and Karunanayake, this volume). Although studies of minor irrigation schemes are not as abundant compared to major schemes, several detailed studies have been conducted, mainly by the International Water Management Institute (IWMI) (Somaratne *et al.* 2005; Jinapala *et al.* 2005; Molen 2001). There are two main types of minor irrigation schemes in Sri Lanka, namely, village tanks and *anicut* schemes. Village tanks are small reservoirs which store water for varying periods. *Anicut*s are small-scale weirs/dams or notches in the riverbanks that divert water from canals to command areas to grow crops. It is estimated that there are about 60,000 small tanks and 12,353 *anicut*s in Sri Lanka. Most of the minor irrigation schemes are located in the dry zone but a wide range of village tanks is also found in the wet zone of Sri Lanka. These schemes are used particularly during the dry period (that is, the *yala* season). They also help in recharging the groundwater table (Madduma Bandara 1985). These tanks are the main source of income for a majority of the people living in these areas (see Balasubramanian, this volume, for a detailed study of tanks in south India).

8.2.4. *Evolution of water management institutions in minor irrigation systems*

The minor irrigation systems have a long tradition of user management from very early times (Herath *et al.* 1989). The traditional institution for managing irrigation water was the *Vel Vidane* (that is, the water headman) system. In this system, a distinguished person from the village is nominated as the *Vel Vidane* who is responsible for water allocation, investigating complaints, and resolving conflicts. The farmers pay the *Vel Vidane* generally in kind although non-payments have been reported.

The responsibility for the maintenance of minor irrigation systems was taken over by the Ministry of Agriculture and Food in 1958 and the *Vel Vidane* system replaced by cultivation committees (CC) (Somaratne *et al.* 2005). Further changes were introduced in the 1960s with the introduction of the cultivation officer (CO), a political appointee, which led to a serious deterioration in leadership.

The minor irrigation systems managed under the Agrarian Services Act of 1979 were later transferred to the Provincial Irrigation Departments under the Provincial Councils (Samad 2005). Since the PIDs were of recent origin and lacked technical competence, the Agrarian Services Department continued to provide support. In 1992, the FOs were introduced, which liaise with government institutions to perform maintenance activities of the tanks/*anicuts*. It is noteworthy that the IMT programme, which is so explicit in major irrigation schemes, is missing under minor irrigation because they were traditionally managed by users.

These minor schemes were rehabilitated under the World Bank-sponsored Village Irrigation Rehabilitation Project (VIRP). The VIRP reported that there was a reduction in maintenance work due to rehabilitation and permanent structures, but a concomitant decline in collective action too in certain cases. The VIRP, completed in 1990, showed lower returns to rehabilitation compared to some others such as the Gal Oya project because the VIRP focused more on technical development and less on institutional development (Kikuchi *et al.* 2002). The typical head-tail problem has been observed in most minor schemes, especially in the dry (*yala*) season (Herath *et al.* 1989). The uncertainty when it comes to water availability in minor tanks constrains the effective performance of FOs. Three case studies of minor tanks are briefly reviewed below to highlight their principle features, as well as the problems constraining their effective utilization by WUAs/FOs.

8.2.4.1. STUDY OF A CASCADE SYSTEM IN THE WALAWE RIVER BASIN

A study of seven small tank cascade systems in the Walawe River Basin in Sri Lanka provided valuable insights into the evolution of minor tanks in response to socio-economic, agro-ecological, and institutional dynamics in dry-zone agriculture. The study was made via a review of existing literature, formal and informal interviews, focus-group discussions, and a questionnaire survey.

The study found collective action in farmer-managed schemes where the FOs manage O & M activities of tanks jointly with ASD. The study further showed that the command areas of minor tanks have increased in most tanks due to encroachment associated with population growth. This led to a limited distribution of water to farmers, reducing the sustainability of tank communities. Many tanks have been abandoned due to this reason. Where tanks are owned individually, operation and management activities are carried out successfully by the farmers themselves (Somaratne *et al.* 2005). Numerous problems have been reported in the minor tanks in the Basin such as poor maintenance of tank bund, regulatory structures, and the canal system. Establishment of FOs based on village boundaries and not hydrological boundaries has weakened the FOs because under these circumstances the FOs cannot impose full authority on the system (Aheer 2001). Population growth too has contributed to the decline in institutional capacity and commitment in the community.

8.2.4.2. STUDY AT DEDURU OYA

The Deduru Oya Basin as a whole has approximately 3,228 small tank systems, of which 1,560 small tanks servicing nearly 12,000 ha are registered in the Department of Agrarian Services. Water management in the minor schemes is done by community groups or the FOs and the Agrarian Services Department is responsible for institutional development activities. In the Deduru Oya Basin, O & M activities in some minor irrigation systems are inadequate partly due to lack of resources at the Agrarian Centre and with the committees as well as political interference and lack of commitment by officials. These factors further constrain efficient delivery of institutional services.

The minor tanks experience shortage of water in the dry season. The cropping intensity varies from 150 in Bingiriya to 100–20 in the Kobeigane, Wariyapola, and Kotawehera areas. Thus, unlike the major schemes, the greater variability of water availability and severe shortages in the dry season imply that water management institutions find it difficult to produce efficient outcomes and, consequently, the institutions themselves become weak. The study shows that paddy farming has become less profitable and that many youths migrate to the cities for better-paid employment. Such migration of youth can lead to a weaker leadership as well as unsustainability of farming activities. Most farmers hold less than one hectare of paddy land and the yields range from 2,100 to 2,900 kg/ha which is lower than that of the major schemes (Jinapala *et al.* 2005). While the small farm size may be conducive to collective-action institutions, uncertainty in critical water inputs can undermine collective action.

8.2.4.3. THE STUDY OF *ANICUTS* IN THE UPPER WALAWE

Molle, Jayakody, and de Silva (2003) engaged in an exploratory study of twenty-five streams with 120 *anicuts* in the Upper Walawe Basin in southern Sri Lanka in order to identify agrarian changes in *anicut*-based communities. These constitute 59 per cent of the total number of *anicuts* in the basin and 43 per cent in terms of the irrigated area (Molle, Jayakody, and de Silva 2003). Around 66 per cent of the selected *anicuts* were constructed during the time of the kings and have been an important source of water for a long time.

These *anicuts* were rehabilitated under the VIRP. While farmers reported benefits, numerous problems too were created in the process. Before rehabilitation, the *anicuts* were often washed off in the rains and farmers resorted to collective action to repair the broken structures. Under the VIRP, the *anicuts* were redone with concrete and canals were lined, making regular collective action redundant. Better structures have allowed farmers at the upper end of the canals to efficiently divert water, sometimes depriving water to tail-end farmers. Similar observations have been made for other countries such as Nepal (Lam 1996; Ostrom 1990).

In 1992, the FOs were established which elect their board members every year and set up the water schedules for rotational irrigation. The FOs perform multiple functions, including maintenance of *anicuts* and canals, and coordination with government institutions such as the Department of Agriculture (Molle, Jayakody, and de Silva 2003). The membership fees are very low (between Rs 5 and Rs 12), and can be paid in kind (Molle, Jayakody, and de Silva 2003). During the *yala* (dry) season when water deficits are common, they adopt rotational irrigation and the *bethma* system in order to reallocate water. Collective action embodied in FOs implies that conflicts are often minimal. Molle, Jayakody, and de Silva (2003) find that collective action is efficient in maintaining the canals and *anicuts*.

8.2.5. *Groundwater exploitation in Sri Lanka*

Since the 1980s, there has been a rapid diffusion of agro-wells in certain dry-zone districts, especially in the north-central, north-western, and southern provinces (Kikuchi *et al.* 2003). The wells are of various kinds: unlined/lined tube wells and pumps. The lined wells were promoted by the government through subsidies for construction and are found mainly in the north-western part of the dry zone, especially in the Kurunegala and Anuradhapura districts. Most water pumps are operated with diesel and kerosene (Herath and Gulati 2006). Tube wells are widespread in minor irrigation schemes in the Puttalam district, Deduru Oya in the north-western province, and Kirindi Oya in the south (Kikuchi *et al.* 2003). Around 16 per cent of the farmers use agro-wells to irrigate non-paddy crops such as chillies, onions, and bananas. The low cost of drilling and subsidies has led to a rapid development of wells.

Most of the wells are shallow, approximately 4.8 metres deep, and can irrigate only a limited amount of land, generally less than 1 ha. Hence, there is no surplus water to sell. Factor use is intensive and efficient in these farms (Herath and Silva 1988). The labour intensity was inversely related to farm size in the Mulankavil Tube Well Scheme (Herath 1986). The private rate of return is high at more than 100 per cent for unlined dug wells and pumps. Investment in pumps for lifting water from surface water schemes has yielded benefit-cost ratios that are above 100 per cent in most cases. The private as well as the social benefit-cost ratios in the Mulankavil Tube Well Scheme in Northeast Sri Lanka were found to be high (Herath and Nagendran 1984).

There is no groundwater market in Sri Lanka because the capacity of the agro-wells and pumps in Sri Lanka is small. The average size of a farm is about 0.2–0.4 ha. However, trade liberalization has made pumps cheaper and their diffusion has become rapid. A rental market for pumps has emerged instead of a water market. The rapid diffusion of agro-wells in Sri Lanka is a concern because of the common property nature of groundwater although serious environmental problems have not yet emerged (Kikuchi *et al.* 2003).

8.3. The future of irrigation institutions in Sri Lanka—some lessons

The above review of institutional intervention in irrigation provides considerable insights into water management. But we need also to be aware of certain limitations, presented below before drawing general conclusions on replicability, and future challenges as a result of institutional changes in irrigation.

8.3.1. *Limitations of evaluative studies*

In the IMT study by Samad (2002), there is a selection bias since only what were perceived to be successful schemes were chosen for analysis while failures had been left out which obscures important causes of institutional failure. Further, the methodology used does not clearly delineate the impact of institutional change. The impacts of WUAs were not captured properly in the estimated equations which may include the impact of other factors such as technology, climate, labour inputs, and ownership. Unless these factors are separated out, the impact of institutional change cannot be precisely determined. For example, the failures or successes attributed to institutions may partly be due to other factors. Hence, a more methodologically rigorous evaluation is necessary.

In some of the other studies reviewed, only certain aspects of institutions were examined such as multiple use. They ignored aspects such as the characteristics of users and user groups that can affect institutional sustainability. In particular, it is important to identify the adverse distributive consequences of IMT, especially with reference to the well-publicized head-tail problem, elite capture, and vulnerable groups such as the very poor and women farmers. The equity effects of IMT are of fundamental importance in providing policy direction to design cost-recovery strategies. A holistic approach could have yielded more robust results to evaluate institutional change.

8.3.2. *Insights for strengthening impacts*

The Samad (2002) study shows that rehabilitation prior to transfer is a prerequisite for success in IMT. Those schemes that were transferred but not rehabilitated and those which were rehabilitated but not transferred, had no significant increasing or decreasing trend in yield. This implies that there is some degree of complementarity between rehabilitation and IMT. This important insight, regarding the sequencing of institutional change, needs to be incorporated to minimize the poor performance of WUAs. The study is especially useful in showing how farmers should be involved in the rehabilitation process to ensure better performance and that the need for matching these prerequisites such as rehabilitation has to be considered at the planning stage because any post-construction change is not easy.

The study supports the view that social capital can play an important role in the evolution of water management institutions. For example, the emergence of true institutional leadership through social capital is key to the success and greater sustainability of the impacts of institutions at Gal Oya (Uphoff and Wijayaratna 2000). Policy makers should consider social capital as a resource and use it for promoting collective action in the social dynamics of the farmer community. Local social capital can form the foundation for use rules, monitoring, and enforcement mechanisms for irrigation water management. The government should play the role of the facilitator in establishing institutions. This can only be achieved by working with the institutional organizers.

There is a need to strengthen WUAs so that they deal with not just water allocations but undertake the complex tasks of financial management and technical support to communities to ensure sustainable management of irrigation resources. Admittedly, these capacities may not be present in most WUAs, as shown by the Gal Oya and other studies discussed. Hence, governmental agencies have a critical role to play in enhancing capacity. Policy effort must be directed towards improving and facilitating the development of local administrative, managerial, and financial capacities of WUAs through training to identify products, markets, and production techniques and technology as has been done in Taiwan and China (Lam 2001).

In general, existing property rights over water may not be the most appropriate from equity and efficiency perspectives. Any new water right should guarantee that the farmer gets water of the desired quality and quantity at the required time. As the WUAs are strengthened, it is essential to revise the enabling framework and water-rights systems in order to secure efficient and equitable water allocations. For example, property rights to groundwater in Sri Lanka need to be revised before excessive extraction creates serious negative externalities.

IMT by itself is not a winning strategy. Therefore, attention needs to be paid to the undoubtedly significant differences in the different schemes. The rural environment is a complex, dynamic socio-cultural system with many stakeholders. The success of the IMT will be influenced by these factors and understanding them is essential to better conceptualizing the type of institution for a given situation.

8.3.3. Challenges

The links between rural institutions and welfare outcomes need to be more intensively studied. Evidence of institutional impacts is currently based upon indicators which fail to take into account broader indicators of development. Often, the success of WUAs is gauged by quantitative measures such as the number of WUAs established or the extent of financial disbursements—not the impact on indicators of development. This approach has serious limitations. As has been noted, in these cases, often the benefits disappear as soon as financial support for the project ends.

A stakeholder may have many uses for water and not necessarily irrigation. Such multiple-use situations are common. Hence, different user groups must be brought into the decision-making process. Recognition of multiple uses will be complicated but if water is to be allocated efficiently for multiple purposes, water rights need to be moved to centre stage. This is a complicated issue but is a challenge that needs to be faced.

A major aim of IMT is cost recovery and reduction of subsidies. In a mature water economy, efficient pricing would be used but in Sri Lanka the water-pricing strategy is still in its infancy. Market pricing of water is a politically sensitive issue and can raise fierce opposition as was the case with the Water Policy statement. Nevertheless, efficient pricing is inevitable in the long run and can be facilitated by removing institutional imperfections (Sampath 1992). Future research should investigate the conditions necessary to establish successful water markets, identify potential problems, and develop mitigating strategies.

There is no significant groundwater market in Sri Lanka but groundwater extraction can increase due to increase in the demand for water in the future. Such an increase is a concern because of the potential damage to delicate underground aquifers. It is necessary to monitor groundwater development in order to ensure that adverse effects are minimized and appropriate institutional safeguards are introduced.

Financial independence, accountability, and training should lead to better fee collection which can be used for system maintenance. Appropriate mechanisms for user-fee collection require better understanding of the farmers' problems and production processes. Uncertainty and variability of water allocation is the most important hindrance to user-fee collection. Irrigation fees can also raise equity issues.

Water institutions need to be dynamic in order to successfully face emerging trends and circumstances. Training and education activities geared towards improving the skills and knowledge of participants to improve water allocation practices are essential ingredients for success. Training and education support prepares institutional participants to face emerging circumstances. They disseminate information on current and pending legislation as well as rules and obligations.

8.4. Conclusion

This chapter shows that institutional initiatives for improved irrigation water resources management in Sri Lanka have not been an unqualified success. The results indicate that there are many factors that affect the outcomes of IMT. Farmers should be involved in the design of both technical and managerial changes. Participatory management should provide greater autonomy to local groups and incorporate social norms and cultural values. The greater success of some of the major and minor schemes testifies to the importance of local cultural and social factors when it comes to management.

Furthermore, the failure of top-down arrangements in WUAs in some of the major irrigation schemes in Sri Lanka needs to be examined more critically. Training on different aspects of participatory irrigation management, including financial management, can increase the potential of local people to orient their futures towards more financially autonomous institutions. WUAs can change the existing pattern of income distribution. Governments should ensure that vulnerable groups (for example, tail-enders and women farmers) are fully incorporated into the decision-making process to ensure better distribution of benefits. Progress towards markets will improve as the technical, socio-economic, and institutional features evolve, removing imperfections and making efficiency a more realistic goal. Undoubtedly, political factors will still constrain progress towards efficiency but, with the changes proposed above, the ubiquity of the political process can be reduced.

Appendix 8.1

Table 8.1. Summary of achievements in the case studies presented

Scheme/type of classification	Government expenditure after IMT	Cost recovery	Quality of irrigation	Maintenance of irrigation facilities	Agricultural productivity (paddy yield)	Equity	Multiple use
Major schemes							
Group 1	No difference				Increased	—	—
Group 2	No difference				No change	—	—
Group 3	No difference				No change	—	—
Group 4	No difference				No change	—	—
Nachchaduwa		Poor	No change	Worse	No change		—
Hakwatuna Oya		Poor	No change	Poor	No change		—
Gal Oya		Good	Major improvement	—	Increased by 10%	Improved	—
Rajangana		Poor	Worse	Poor	No significant change	—	—
Mee Oya		Poor	Worse	Poor	No significant change	—	—
Kirindi Oya	—	—	—	—	—	Gender bias	Significant
Minor Schemes		Good	—	Mixed	—	—	—
Ground Water	N/A	N/A	Good	N/A	high	N/A	N/A

Sources: Samad 2005; Aheer 1999; Meinzen-Dick and Bakker 1999; Molen 2001; Uphoff and Wijayaratna 2000; Kikuchi *et al.* 2003.

Group 1: Rehabilitated and transferred.

Group 2: Rehabilitated but not transferred.

Group 3: Transferred but not rehabilitated.

Group 4: Not rehabilitated and not transferred.

References

Aheer, M. M. M. (1999). 'Impact of Irrigation Management Policy on Environment: Lessons from Sri Lanka'. *Asia-Pacific Journal of Rural Development*, 9: 71–8.

—— (2001). 'Socio–economic and Institutional Aspects of Small Tank Systems in Relation to Food Security', in H. P. M. Gunasena (ed.), *Food Security and Small Tank Systems in Sri Lanka*, Proceedings of the Workshop Organized by the Working Committee on Agricultural Science and Forestry. Colombo, Sri Lanka: National Science Foundation, 64–78.

Aluvihare, P. B., and Kikuchi, M. (1991). *Irrigation Investment Trends in Sri Lanka: New Construction and Beyond*. Research Paper. Colombo, Sri Lanka: International Water Management Institute.

Gandhi, V., Crase, L., and Herath, G. (2006). 'Comparing Indian Irrigation Institutions: What Determines Institutional Behaviour and Performance? Preliminary Empirical Observations'. Paper presented at the AARES Conference, Sydney, Australia, February.

Gulati, A., and Narayanan, S. (2002). 'Subsidies and Reforms in Indian Irrigation', in D. Brennan (ed.), *Water Policy Reform: Lessons from Asia and Australia*. Canberra: Australian Centre for International Agricultural Research, 131–48.

Gunatilake, H. M., and Gopalakrishnan, C. (2002). 'Proposed Water Policy for Sri Lanka: The Policy versus the Policy Process'. *Water Resources Development*, 18: 545–62.

Herath, G. (1986). 'Inverse Relationship between Productivity and Farm Size: Some Empirical Results'. *Sri Lankan Journal of Agricultural Sciences,* 23: 92–7.

—— (2002). 'Issues in Irrigation and Water Management in Developing Countries with Special Reference to Institutions', in D. Brennan (ed.), *Water Policy Reform: Lessons from Asia and Australia*. Canberra: Australian Centre for International Agricultural Research, 149–60.

—— and Gulati, A. (2006). 'Public Institutions: The Case of Infrastructure'. Working Paper. International Food Policy Research Institute (IFPRI), Washington, DC.

—— and Nagendran, A. (1984). 'A Present Social Cost Analysis of Groundwater Technologies in the Mulankavil Tube Well Scheme'. *Sri Lankan Journal of Agricultural Sciences*, 21: 92–107.

—— and Silva, L. (1988). 'Study of Factor Use Intensity in Tube Well Irrigation'. *Sri Lankan Journal of Agricultural Sciences*, 25: 165–72.

—— Sivayoganathan, S., Pinnaduwage, S., and Bogahawatta, C. (1989). *Socio-economic Evaluation of the Village Irrigation Rehabilitation Project*. Report No. 2. Sri Lanka: Department of Agricultural Economics, University of Peradeniya.

Jinapala, K., Somaratne, P. G., Ariyaratne, B. R., Perera, L. R., and Makin, I. (2005). *Contextual Challenges of Developing Effective Water Management Institutions: The Deduru Oya Basin, Sri Lanka*. Research Paper. Colombo, Sri Lanka: International Irrigation Management Institute.

Kikuchi, M., Barker, R., Weligamage, P., and Samad, M. (2002). *Irrigation Sector in Sri Lanka: Recent Development Trends and the Path Ahead*. Research Report No. 62, Colombo, Sri Lanka: International Irrigation Management Institute.

Kikuchi, M., Weligamage, P., Barker, R., Samad, M., Kono, H., and Somaratne, H. M. (2003). *Agro-well and Pump Diffusion in the Dry Zone of Sri Lanka: Past Trends, Present Status and the Future Prospects*. Research Report No. 66. Colombo, Sri Lanka: International Water Management Institute.

Lam, W. F. (1996). 'Improving the Performance of Small-scale Irrigation Systems: The Effects of Technological Investments and Governance Structure on Irrigation Performance in Nepal'. *World Development*, 24: 1301–15.

—— (2001). 'Coping with Change: A Study of Local Irrigation Institutions in Taiwan'. *World Development*, 29: 1569–92.

Libby, L. W., and Sharp, J. S. (2003). 'Land Use Compatibility, Change, and Policy at the Rural-Urban Fringe: Insights from Social Capital'. *American Journal of Agricultural Economics*, 85: 1194–200.

Madduma Bandara, C. M. (1985). 'Catchment Ecosystems and Village Tank Cascades in the Dry Zone of Sri Lanka: A Time-tested System of Land and Water Resources Management', in J. Lundquist, U. Lohm, and C. Falkenmark (eds.), *Strategies for River Basin Management*. Dordrecht, Holland: D. Reidel, 99–113.

Meinzen-Dick, R., and Bakker, M. (1999). 'Irrigation Systems as Multiple-use Commons: Water Use in Kirindi Oya, Sri Lanka'. *Agriculture and Human Values*, 16: 281–93.

—— —— (2001). 'Water Rights and Multiple Uses'. *Irrigation and Drainage Systems*, 15: 129–48.

Molen, I.-V. (2001). *An Assessment of Female Participation in Minor Irrigation Systems in Sri Lanka*. Working Paper No. 8. Colombo, Sri Lanka: International Water Management Institute.

Molle, F., Jayakody, P., and de Silva, S. (2003). *Anicut Systems in Sri Lanka: The Case of the Upper Walawe River Basin*. Working Paper No. 61. Colombo, Sri Lanka: International Water Management Institute.

Montginoul, M., and Renault, D. (2003). 'Economic Instruments for Water Management in the Presence of Positive Externalities: The Case of Rice-based Irrigation in Sri Lanka', in P. Koundauri, P. Pashardes, T. M. Swanson, and A. Xepapadeas (eds.), *The Economics of Water Management in Developing Countries: Problems, Principles and Policies*. UK: Edward Elgar, 116–33.

Ostrom, E. (1990). *Governing the Commons: The Evolution of Collective Action*. Cambridge: Cambridge University Press.

Raby, N. (1991). 'Participatory Management in Large Irrigation Systems: Issues for Consideration'. *World Development*, 19: 1767–76.

Saleth, M., and Dinar, A. (1999). *Water Challenges and Institutional Response: A Cross-country Perspective*. Policy Research Working Paper No. 2045. Washington, DC: World Bank.

—— —— (2004). *The Institutional Economics of Water*. UK: Edward Elgar.

Samad, M. (2002). 'Impact of Irrigation Management Transfer on the Performance of Irrigation Systems: A Review of Selected Asian Experiences', in D. Brennan (ed.), *Water Policy Reform: Lessons from Asia and Australia*. Canberra: Australian Centre for International Agricultural Research, 161–70.

—— (2005). 'Water Institutional Reforms in Sri Lanka'. *Water Policy*, 7: 125–40.

——— and Vermillion, D. (1999). *Assessment of Participatory Management of Irrigation Schemes in Sri Lanka: Partial Reforms, Partial Benefits*. Research Report No. 34. Colombo, Sri Lanka: International Irrigation Management Institute.

Sampath, R. K. (1992). 'Issues in Irrigation Pricing in Developing Countries'. *World Development*, 20: 967–77.

Somaratne, P. G., Jayakody, P., Molle, F., and Jinapala, K. (2005). *Small Tank Cascade Systems in the Walawe River Basin*. Working Paper No. 92. Colombo, Sri Lanka: International Water Management Institute.

Uphoff, N. (1996). *Learning from Gal Oya: Possibilities for Participatory Development and Post-Newtonian Social Science*. London: Intermediate Technology Publications.

——— and Wijayaratna, C. M. (2000). 'Demonstrated Benefits from Social Capital: The Productivity of Farmer Organizations in Gal Oya, Sri Lanka'. *World Development*, 28: 1875–90.

Williamson, O. E. (1985). *The Economic Institutions of Capitalism*. New York: Free Press.

Part III

Livelihoods and Distribution

9

Heterogeneity, Commons, and Privatization: Agrarian Institutional Change in Goa

Pranab Mukhopadhyay

9.1. Introduction

This chapter attempts to address two related questions in the context of agrarian transitions in Goa, a small western state in India. At the time of Goa's independence from Portuguese colonization in 1961, a major part of Goa's agrarian lands was owned and regulated by a community institution called the *communidades*. In 1964, the government brought in land reforms through the Tenancy Act (1964) and Rules (1965 and 1975) which gave security of tenure to tenants and attempted to make land occupancy equitous. Subsequently, tenants were given the right to purchase land at fixed rates to convert their tenancy claim to ownership rights. This applied not only to private lands but also to the *communidade* lands and amounted to virtual privatization of the community lands, which were till then common property in the classic sense of the term.

This chapter addresses the following two questions:

- What is the impact of heterogeneity in asset ownership on cooperation? Does a more equal ownership of (agricultural) land make agents (cultivators) more amenable to cooperate on matters pertaining to productivity improvement?

- Does privatization of commons lead to greater sustainability? By ecological sustainability we mean the maintenance of recovered lands in their current ecological status of agricultural land use and by conservation we imply undertaking protective measures (embankment maintenance) from unintended flooding by tidal waters (similar to Holden, Shiferaw, and Wik 1998). Will privatization of commons lead to better soil conservation measures and maintenance of agricultural lands? By soil conservation we mean measures to control soil salinity particularly embankment maintenance in this case.

In Goa, most of the paddy cultivation is on 'recovered' lands (*khazans*) and a large section of these lands in the coastal zones was under the control of the *communidades* prior to 1961 when Goa joined the Indian union. In 1964, tenancy legislation was introduced which gave security of tenure to tenants but in the process also paved the way for privatization of the *communidade* lands. The empowerment of the tenants and disenfranchisement of the *communidades* had ecological implications since embankment maintenance which had been done by this institution was now neglected, leaving the fields open to salinity ingress.

We find that on the one hand the new resource owners were unable to cooperate to finance public investment and on the other there was an exit mainly of *Gaunkars* who were the resource managers under the previous dispensation. The increase in reported fallows due to salinity indicates declining sustainability in this region.

In Section 9.2, which follows, we examine the existing theory on cooperation and sustainability followed by a discussion in Section 9.3 of transition in local institutions in Goa. Section 9.4 presents results of the primary survey with an econometric model of exit and sustainability. Section 9.5 concludes the chapter with a discussion on the findings.

9.2. Heterogeneity, cooperation, and sustainability

Communities with extreme inequalities or very homogenous distributions of wealth are often seen to exhibit greater cooperation than others and a Kuznets(-like) relationship could exist between inequality and conservation.[1] The so-called 'Olson effect' is valid to the extent that threshold effects exist in wealth holding. Anyone below a certain threshold level of wealth will not cooperate, irrespective of what others do. Beyond the threshold level of wealth holding, cooperation could emerge if agents find others cooperating too. However, cooperation would break down if the proportion of those below the threshold is high (Dayton-Johnson and Bardhan 2002).

On normative grounds asset redistribution may be desired, but what is also of concern are the ecological consequences when endogenous institutions are

---

[1] The Kuznets curve (relationship) originally examined the problem of inequality and economic growth of nations. Empirical evidence collected by Simon Kuznets suggested that at very high and low levels of inequality the rate of growth was lower than in the intermediate range. The Kuznets inverted-U relationship has since been borrowed for use in debates on environment and a similar pattern is suggested *vis-à-vis* the relationship between inequality and conservation of natural resources especially in the context of common property resources.

replaced by new inorganic ones wherein the incentives for conservation may not be optimally configured (Jodha 1980; Mukhopadhyay 2002*b*).

The impact of such changes is compounded when there are strong incentives and opportunities for exit. For example, after land redistribution or tenancy reform, alternative economic opportunities may emerge that entice the farmer off the field. Agriculture may no longer provide a sufficient incentive to the new beneficiaries while the old owners stand disenfranchised. This might defeat the very purpose of tenancy reform (to increase efficiency of farm output and provide secure incomes to the tenant) as the gainers in the redistribution may have reduced incentives in farming due to alternative income sources. The growth implications are that it might impede adoption of new technology and thereby lower the long-term growth path.

Even if one were to keep issues of institutional change and property-rights structures aside for a moment, asset redistribution in the presence of non-convexities could reduce productivity. If the technology is such that it involves high initial costs, small farmers in the presence of an imperfect credit market may not be able to bear these costs and therefore get trapped in a low productivity cycle—the so-called Olson effect (Baland and Platteau 1997).

It must be noted here that a large part of the above debate is in the context of privately owned resources—redistribution of land already in the private domain. However, we now join issue with the second question that drives this study, what happens when common property is privatized?

9.2.1. *Privatization and the commons*

The property rights school has argued that when commons have associated externalities, privatization would be the best solution because it would enable the resource owner to internalize all the costs and benefits (Demstez 1967). This obviously is an efficiency-enhancing argument because public (and resource) economics has struggled to suggest policy instruments to achieve this without privatization. The external costs which are not accounted for under community ownership are expected to be internalized under private ownership—especially individual ownership. And, of course, it does not matter who owns the resource because it would not affect the equilibrium outcome (Coase 1960).

The literature, however, is aware that there are numerous situations where privatization would not lead to efficiency gains. If contracts are incomplete, it could loosen cooperative bonds and thereby reduce the extent of efficiency gains (Seabright 1993). This could happen in two ways. Firstly, it could reduce the mutual social interdependence that creates cooperation (Ostrom 1990). Secondly, since property subsequent to privatization becomes tradeable, it makes agents less interested in long-term cooperative behaviour, and people put in less effort to build up cooperation (Grossman 2001). Under such conditions, a self-governing local community with commons might have a more efficient production locus than if private property was established.

This of course brings us to the question that when we are targeting homogeneity, and it is done through privatizing the commons, what would be the likely outcome especially in the context of ecological sustainability (Baland and Platteau 2003; Dasgupta and Maler 1995; de Janvry *et al.* 2001; Knox and Meinzen-Dick 2001)?

The neutrality theorem suggests that a change in asset distribution should not affect the provision of public goods. This is however dependent on two crucial assumptions—the public good is pure such that all have equal access to the good and all agents contribute irrespective of asset changes. If the redistribution actually increases the number of contributors then the supply of public goods will increase and on the other hand if number of contributors decline then supply will decline (Bergstrom, Blume, and Varian 1986).

The importance of this for CPR management is crucial for two reasons. We need to understand whether asset distribution increases the number of contributors to the public good or whether it leads to its reduction. If the distribution leads to greater homogeneity in asset ownership but leads to a reduction of contributors (increase in number of free-riders) then the resultant situation though socially desirable in terms of the homogeneity goal would not be ecologically sustainable. This is a possible outcome when there is a decline in 'institutional supply' simultaneous with the redistribution (Ostrom 1990; Becker and Gibson 1998).

We address these questions in the context of the agrarian institutional transition in Goa, a small state in western India, which was one of the earliest (and last) European colonies in India (1510–1961). The issues that we focus on relate to the impact of inequality on cooperation and of privatization on efficiency and sustainability. In the following sections, we describe the history of agrarian institutions, their transition through the post-colonial phase and examine the impact of tenancy legislation on the land management system. The historical material is collated from existing secondary literature on Goa's history.

9.3. Agrarian organization in Goa

Goa has a long-established tradition of community land ownership and management. A large part of the state's 'recovered' lands (*khazans*) and hill tracts were owned by a community institution called the *communidade* (or *Gaunkarias*). The original settlers of the village were called *Gaunkars* and male descendants were given that title on reaching adulthood in the system. They jointly laid claim to the ownership of village lands and cultivated them by renting lands through periodic auction. Auction rents were used

Table 9.1. Distribution of land under private and *communidade* ownership (prior to land reforms)

Taluka	Total area under paddy cultivation (in hectares)	Paddy area under *communidades*	Per cent under *communidades*
Goa	44698	14765	33.0
North Goa	23553	8624	36.6
Ilhas	6398	3569	55.8
Bardez	6664	3764	56.5
Pernem	3504	0	0.0
Bicholim	2599	548	21.1
Satari	1609	1	0.1
Ponda	2779	742	26.7
South Goa	21145	6141	29.0
Sanguem	2422	90	3.7
Canacona	2682	42	1.6
Quepem	4838	195	4.0
Salcete	10184	5207	51.1
Mormugao	1019	607	59.6

Source: GoG 1964a: 16.

for maintenance of the embankments and sluice gates (soil-protection public works) among other things like dividends to the *Gaunkars* (Pereira 1981).

Soon after the liberation of Goa in 1961, the government appointed a land reforms commission (28 February 1963), which submitted its report in 1964. It recorded that a large proportion of the agricultural land in Goa continued to be held under the *communidade*—approximately 33 per cent of the area (129,009 hectares) under paddy cultivation (Table 9.1 and Figure 9.1). This amounted to 65 per cent of the net sown area in Goa and in coastal areas it was nearly 92 per cent. In the *talukas* (*concelhos*) of Salcette, Bardez, Mormugao, and Goa (now known as Tiswadi *taluka*), where lies the largest concentration of the area under paddy, the *communidade* owned more than 50 per cent of the cropped area (Table 9.1 (GoG 1964a)).

This is also the area of the 'old conquest', where the Portuguese colonization lasted the longest and the rules and regulations regarding the *communidades* got codified.[2] The 'new conquest' areas which became part of the Portuguese colonial territory after a gap of almost two centuries (in the eighteenth century) did not see a similar preservation of *communidades*' functionality. There were historical distortions to natural evolution. Pernem *taluka*, for example, was handed over to the *Ranes* to defend Goa from the aggression of *Marathas* (a neighbouring rival kingdom) (de Souza 1987).

[2] The Portuguese colonization which began in 1510 was in two distinct phases in Goa. The 'old conquests' (*Velhas Conquistas*) included the conquest of the areas of Tiswadi, Mormugao, Bardez, and Salcete. The 'new conquests' (*Nuovas Conquistas*) was separated by two centuries (late 18th century—between 1763 and 1788) when Ponda Quepem, Canacona, Pernem, Sattari, and Bicholim came under the Portuguese rule (Xavier 1993).

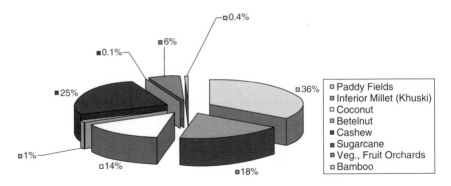

Figure 9.1. Type of cultivation in area (hectares and percentage)
Source: GoG 1964*a*: 12.

9.3.1. *History of land management*

Documentation on the *communidades* for the colonial period indicates that these village-level institutions played a very important role in the agrarian economy of Goa. Some argue that till not so long ago, the entire agricultural area was owned by the *communidades*. The process of creation of private cultivable lands happened mainly during the Portuguese period when land grants were made by the colonial state to expand its support base and in later decades (1540 onwards) when the Portuguese crown undertook inquisition in all its colonies to encourage religious conversion (D'Costa, undated).[3] The financial buoyancy of the *communidade* depended on the productivity of its lands, their main source of revenue and its outgoings. Table 9.2 summarizes the incomes and expenditures for the period 1954–63 under different heads undertaken by the *communidades*.

9.3.2. *Institutional transition*

In 1964 the government enacted the Goa Tenancy Act, which took the powers of land auction out of the hands of the *communidades* and transferred the responsibility for embankment maintenance to tenants. It provided for security of tenure for the tenants and through subsequent notifications and the

[3] Afonso de Albuquerque who established the Portuguese colony in Goa (1510) encouraged intermarriages between Portuguese soldiers and widows of slain Muslim and Hindu soldiers. Villages which made land grants to these couples were allowed to forgo their *coxi vordo* (voluntary contribution to the king). Prior to this, private ownership of land was limited to the house plot (Xavier 1993). The second big boost to private property in Goa was at the time of the Inquisition (1541). The state confiscated all lands of temples, and those who refused to convert or conform to the edicts of the Inquisitorial authority. The confiscated lands were distributed among Christian missionary institutions for economic support and new converts to seek their cooperation.

Table 9.2. Main sources of income and expenditures of the *communidades*

Main income categories	Period 1954–63	Main expenditure categories	Period 1954–63
Rent from lessees of agricultural lands	86%	Land tax	18.5%
Foro (form of rent) and income from auction or lease of fishing rights, salt pans, etc.	11% approx.	Administrative expenses	20–7%
		Expenses on ordinary and extra-ordinary works—construction and maintenance of bunds, sluice gates	16%
		Contribution to Juntas de Fregusia (Village Associations)	5%
		Contribution of charity, churches and temples	6%
		Jonos (dividends) to members	16%

Source: GoG 1964*a*: 39.
   GoG 1967*a*: 59–63.

issue of rules and regulations (1975) gave the tenants the right to buy land at a low fixed price.[4]

Importantly, simultaneous with the tenancy reform there was an institutional transition from one form of local self-governance—the *Gaunkaris* (or *communidades*), to another form—the *panchayats* which created incentive-incompatibilities (Mukhopadhyay 2002*a*). The much-talked-about effectiveness of local self-government (in the form of *panchayats*) to undertake ecological sustenance has been put to test in Goa. Since the *panchayats* in all rural areas in Goa issue licenses for construction, there has been large-scale land conversion in the coastal zones with active help from panchayats (Alvares 2002). Construction fees and licenses contribute to the bulk of their finances, and therefore the institutional imperative is to encourage construction which is mainly non-agricultural in nature.[5]

The government presumably realized that with the reduced financial capability, the soil conservation and productivity-enhancing activities of the *communidades* including maintenance of embankments, de-silting of rivulets, etc., had to be undertaken by a different agency. The *communidades* used to undertake these activities out of the profits earned from the public auctions of cultivation rights.[6] Now that there were little or no revenues accruing to

---

[4] It also reduced the rent to one-sixth of the last-auctioned value prior to the Tenancy Act. Currently, tenants are reportedly not paying even this rent to the *communidades* since they cannot be evicted.

[5] The following *talukas* cover the coastal zone of Goa—Bardez, Tiswadi, Salcete, Mormugao, Canacona, and Pernem.

[6] The *taluka*-wise expenditure and income statement of *communidades* (in rupees for the period 1954–63) is provided in Table 9.11 (in Appendix 9.1) to give a measure of their financial buoyancy. Table 9.2 earlier shows the main heads of incomes and expenditures.

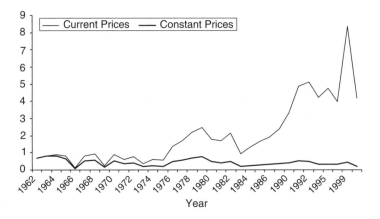

Figure 9.2. Government expenditure incurred in embankment maintenance (in Rs million)

Source: GoG (various years).

the *communidades* they would be financially incapable of undertaking these activities.

In 1958 the Portuguese government had constituted a Bunds Committee to supervise the maintenance of embankments which oversaw the expenditure of an estimated Rs 8,34,400 in the two years prior to liberation to bring back into cultivation about 959 hectares of land. Even after liberation, this committee spent considerable sums in the first few years (GoG 1967a). It was replaced by the Soil Conservation Division in 1969 which was given responsibility for undertaking maintenance of embankments (GoG 1992). It was created with the purpose of assisting tenants who may not have the financial strength to execute large repairs. The total expenditure (in current prices) on embankments has gone up from Rs 0.69 million (in 1962) to Rs 4.16 million (in 2000) while the area protected by bunds has remained the same on a point-to-point basis though there are interyear variations, (see Figure 9.2). However, in real terms, the actual expenditure on embankments has declined. This is a further indicator that physical maintenance is getting worse.

Section 9 of the Agricultural Tenancy Rules (1975) details the process of execution of repairs. The managing committee of the tenants' association was empowered to undertake any immediate repairs without calling for auction of works as long as the amount did not exceed Rs 500 and the *Mamlatdar* (who is the executive and quasi-judicial authority at the subdistrict—*taluka* level) and Soil Conservation Division were informed of the same within twenty-four hours. If the expected expenses exceeded Rs 500, then all the work had to be routed through the Soil Conservation Division up to an amount

Rs 5,000. If the expenses were beyond Rs 5,000 but less than Rs 10,000 then prior sanction had to be obtained from the development commissioner. The *Mamlatdar*, on execution of the work, is expected to recover a portion of the expenses from the beneficiary farmers through the managing committee of the tenants' associations. In case the tenants do not agree then the Soil Conservation Division/*Mamlatdar* were the deciding authority. The designated public authority for overseeing public works on the embankments is the *Mamlatdar* (GoG 1964b).

It has been pointed out by some that the discovery of iron ore deposits in Goa's hinterland (in early 1950s) had a direct impact on embankment maintenance. The decline in tree cover in the upstream areas led to increased topsoil run-off in the mining areas and this was deposited at the river mouth (called sand barring) causing increased tidal movements. Secondly, the barges carrying ore from the mines to the Mormugao port increased wear and tear of the embankments abetting saline inundation (Alvares 2002). This being a new development in the 1950s, the government gave concessional loans (at the rate of 2 per cent payable in 10–15 instalments) for repair of embankments (GoG 1967a).[7]

Section 42A of the Goa, Daman, and Diu Agricultural, Land Tenancy Act (1964) outlines the procedure for discharge of joint responsibility of tenants wherever any 'conservancy, maintenance or repair of any bund, embankment' work involved more than one tenant and states that the government would frame appropriate rules for regulating the same. However, it is only the Agricultural Tenancy Rules (1975) that made it mandatory to form tenants' associations by all tenants cultivating in the vicinity of bund (embankment) and who have benefited jointly from the bund. Anticipating that the tenants may not have sufficient finances to undertake large public works, the government promised to reimburse the expenses undertaken by the tenants association to maintain the embankments (Section 35 of the Tenancy Act 1964 and Section 12A Tenancy Rules 1965). In a review of the functioning of the tenants association, the Agricultural Land Development Panel report (ALDP) found that a total of 138 tenants' associations were created (GoG 1992) and 87 per cent of these associations were in the five *talukas* of Pernem, Bardez, Bicholim, Ponda, and Tiswadi. These five *talukas* also accounted for a similar fraction of *bunds* with sluice gates, 91 per cent

---

[7] The official agricultural efforts and concerns prior to liberation in 1961 can be perceived from some of the reports of the Agricultural Missions that came from Portugal to Goa. Their primary concern was with methods of increasing agricultural production, deciding on appropriate agricultural crops, soil mapping, fertilizer composition, etc. See for example H. Lains e Silva (1961) *Relatario da Activade da Missao de Estudos Agrinomicos do Ultramar deide 17 de Junho ate 31 de Dezembro de 1960*, Lisboa; and J. Sacadura Garcia (1961) *'Communicacoes' Missao de estudos agronomicos do Ultramar*, Lisboa; Hernani Cidade Mourao (1961) *Missao de estudos Agronomicos do Ultramar—'Outline of the Rice Varieties Experiments to be carried out in India'*, Lisboa.

of the land, and 92 per cent of the membership of the associations. However, by 1992 most of these tenants associations were in financial distress (GoG 1992).[8]

The current situation is that even minor repairs are left to the state machinery to execute (GoG 2000). The process involved in activating the state system is cumbersome and lacks local participation. It is evident that in the new regime the tenants associations were unable to sustain collective action due to non-contribution by a critical number of members. In fact, it would be rational for them to anticipate that the state would intervene if there was a decline in embankment maintenance for the very reasons that led to redistributive measures in the first place.

This expectation, however, has not been entirely realized as the incentives for the state to undertake soil conservation are different from those of the tenants. As discussed above, even though there was an increase in expenditures for soil conservation at current prices, there has been a substantial decline in real terms. With reduced local contribution, participation, and a decline in real expenditures, it is but to be expected that embankment maintenance would decline.

9.3.3. Impact of transition

The above discussion indicates that an endogenous self-sustaining institution (the *communidade*) which owned and maintained the village cultivable lands and was responsible for the administration was replaced in the post-1961 (independence) period by two local-level bodies—the *panchayats* and the tenants' association. The *panchayats* neither have the mandate, the incentive, nor the financial strength to maintain such large agrarian public works. The tenants' association, which was given the responsibility for land maintenance and was supposed to bring together the beneficiary tenants failed to sustain itself as an institution.

The Tenancy Act (1964) began the process of creating private rights of tenants on *communidade* (or *Gaunkari*) lands to ensure distributive justice to individual tenants but did not address the question of the ecological impact of this transition. There is a fair amount of reported evidence indicating decline in embankment maintenance (Alvares 2002). In 1999, the embankments in parts of Divar Island gave way which led to setting up of the multidisciplinary committee (de Souza undated; GoG 2000). Smaller breaches have been reported on a regular basis (GoG 1992; TERI 2000).

[8] The main sources of income of the tenants' associations were membership fees (fixed at Rs 10 for enrolment and an annual membership fee of Rs 10), earnings from fishing leases of the sluice gate, and trees (Tenancy Rules 1975, Section 7 (2 & 3)).

9.4. Field survey: a note

In order to understand the current state of the agrarian economy in Goa, 360 households from four villages were interviewed in the years 2002–3. Of the two districts which constitute the administrative division of Goa, three villages were chosen from North Goa (Goltim, Malar, and Calangute) and one from South Goa (Curtorim). The villages of Goltim and Malar are located on two sides of Diwar, an island on the Mandovi estuary, and have one of the oldest and most intricately laid systems of embankments and are rural agricultural systems. Calangute is a seafront village in Bardez *taluka* which has seen rapid urbanization impacts and has the highest visitations of tourists in Goa (GoG, various years). It is a coastal village on the Arabian Sea which still retains a fair amount of agricultural land and activity. Curtorim on the other hand is a village on the Zuari River and is regarded as one of the villages with highly fertile soils and is primarily agricultural as far as economic activity is concerned. These villages were selected to represent different agro-economic zones. The island villages were representative of an economy still largely dependent on agricultural or economic incomes being generated outside the village. Calangute has a fair degree of tourism services, therefore incomes in the village are diversified and offers exit options. Curtorim, Malar, and Goltim on the other hand are river front villages but also have direct road links with the rest of the state. The village selection was done on the basis of peer discussion and the villages were chosen for their particular characteristics which could be representative of similar coastal villages of the state. In each village ninety households were randomly selected from three categories of agents—*Gaunkars* (the male descendants of original village settlers), the tenants who rented *communidade* lands on auction, and the *Mundkars* who were employed on private agricultural lands.[9]

The survey was meant to provide information on: (*a*) The current landholding structure to address the equity and redistribution question, (*b*) the extent of fallow lands due to salinity which relates to sustainability and conservation, and (*c*) the exit options of agents from the agrarian economy.

Secondary data on fallows due to salinity was not available to us either for the current period or the pre-1964 period. However, the interviewees felt that maintenance of the embankments and therefore the protection of the *khazan*

---

[9] According to the Royal Decree of 1901 (24 August) the *Mundkar* is defined as 'an individual residing in a dwelling settled in another's rural property mainly with the aim of cultivating or for looking after the property' (GoG 1967*a*: 283). The *Munddcarato* system prevailed largely as a verbal agreement between the landlord and *Mundkars* and sometimes as unwritten conventions followed over generations. Properly drawn-up contracts were rare (GoG 1967*a*).

lands under the *communidades* was more effective than under the current institutional arrangement. This is also borne out by the field results which seem to report losses of agricultural area in the post-tenancy reform period. We are aware that salinity ingress has been a concern even for the state administration since it appointed a multidisciplinary committee in 1999–2000 to study and find a solution for the protection of embankments (GoG 2000). Almost a decade earlier the Agricultural Land Development Panel (ALDP) too reviewed the functioning of the new institutions (tenants associations) (GoG 1992).

9.4.1. *Heterogeneity in land ownership*

Some basic findings that would be of interest in the current chapter are the changes in landholding pattern, extent of damage due to non-maintenance of public works in contemporary Goa, and the exit of agents from the agrarian system. We begin by briefly discussing the current landholding structure.

To understand changes in heterogeneity we must have a comparative baseline figure. However, there is no secondary data available for the landholding pattern especially for private lands by socio-economic category of owners.[10] We could, however, from our survey findings attempt to reconstruct the pre-tenancy land ownership scenario. We assume that all private lands were under the ownership of the *Gaunkars* and that they continue to hold their private lands within the group. On the other hand, lands claimed by the tenants and *Mundkars* were earlier *communidade* lands.

In our survey we find that the *Gaunkars* claimed to own an average of 0.2788 hectares (ha) of private lands and a total of 0.4877 ha. This implies by our assumption above that tenants and *Mundkars* did not own any private lands in the pre-tenancy period and the *Gaunkars* alone had private lands of 0.2788 ha each. The tenants during the survey claimed to own an average of 0.6291 ha (of which only 0.1111 ha is private or non-*communidade* land). The *Mundkars* claimed 0.2920 ha (of which 0.0407 ha is private land and 0.2513 ha is *communidade* land) (Table 9.3).[11]

So while the *communidades* lost their control over its common lands, the tenants on average gained 0.6291 ha and *Mundkars* gained 0.2920 ha. The post-tenancy legislation scenario therefore is more equitable than the pre-tenancy situation.

---

[10] There is secondary data available from various sources on landholding by size but this is not classified according to socio-economic categories.

[11] There is a possibility of the different categories of respondents overstating or understating claims over land ownership for various reasons. In some cases, the tenants and Mundkars have not transferred the ownership titles to their names and in some cases there are legal disputes over ownership.

Table 9.3. Average landholding by category in hectares (survey results 2002–3)

Category	Average private area	Average *communidade* area	Average total area
Gaunkars	0.2788	0.2089	0.4877
Tenants	0.1111	0.5180	0.6291
Mundkars	0.0407	0.2513	0.2920
All Categories	0.1435	0.3260	0.4696

9.4.2. *Landholding size*

In the eleven *talukas* of Goa, prior to the tenancy legislation, there were 31,259 plots under the *communidades'* control and 30,551 tenants cultivated these fields before the tenancy act came into force (GoG 1967*b*; Table 9.4). Among these plots the maximum number 17,719 (over 56 per cent) were of the size 0.4 ha or more, which is the highest category of plot.

In our primary survey we found that the highest frequency of ownership was in the category 0.4–0.5 ha which is similar to the frequency of plot size prior to land reform (Figure 9.3).

We examine next the issue of migration as the survey data indicates that there has been significant out-migration. A total of seventy-seven households reported as having at least one member abroad, and fifty-three were from the category of *Gaunkars*. An employment opportunity outside the system is described as an exit option. In an agrarian economy this could be off-farm employment, or in the extreme case a physical departure or displacement from the agrarian region implying migration.

9.4.3. *Exit options and the commons*

The impact of exit options on commons in the presence of heterogeneity is a complex phenomenon and is said to depend on the relationship between wealth inequality and exit options. Two possibilities are cited: (*a*) when exit has a 'concave' relationship with wealth inequality—the value of outside option rises with wealth but at a decreasing rate as wealth rises. In this case conservation would decrease with increase in inequality, and (*b*) when it has a convex relationship with wealth—the value of outside option rises with wealth at an increasing rate. In this case, increase in inequality has an ambiguous effect on conservation (Dayton-Johnson and Bardhan 2002). Numerous case studies are available wherein the rich as well as poor are seen to exercise the exit option so it is inconclusive to argue whether it is the rich or the poor who break the cooperation (Baland and Platteau 1999).

We find evidence that securitization of tenure created greater homogeneity, but on the other hand might have been responsible for the exit of the

Table 9.4. *Taluka*-wise distribution of *communidade* plots (in hectares) (prior to tenancy reforms)[1]

Talukas	0–0.0999	0.1–0.1999	0.2–0.2999	0.3–0.3999	0.4–above	Total plots (lotes)	Number of tenants in 1963	Resident Gaunkars & shareholders	Total no. of registered Gaunkars & shareholders
Tiswadi	207	257	541	758	5057	6820	6025	3457	8870
Salcete	206	217	769	1998	7112	10302	11017	4956	12473
Bardez	314	890	2729	2478	3459	9870	9494	14128	25003
Mormugao	21	44	185	281	791	1322	1601	790	2090
Ponda	93	194	315	349	767	1718	1350	1357	2321
Bicholim	19	83	136	145	417	800	641	1022	1290
Pernem	–	–	–	–	–	–	41	0	0
Quepem	6	6	6	3	63	84	165	85	107
Sanguem	230	–	–	–	–	230	146	80	106
Canacona	16	11	18	12	52	109	67	63	133
Satari	1	1	1	1	1	4	4	29	38
Total	1113	1703	4700	6025	17719	31259	30551	25967	52431

Source: GoG (1967b) Annexure No: 6: 18–19.

[1] Pernem is a peculiar case because all the *communidades* of Pernem forfeited their lands and there is no inscription of *Gaunkars* in this *taluka*. During the Portuguese colonial rule, Pernem was a territory bordering the *Maratha* lands and the charge of the entire *taluka* was given to the *Ranes* to protect, thereby disenfranchising the *communidades*.

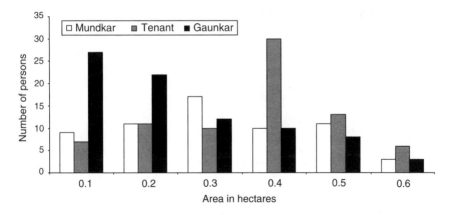

Figure 9.3. Land ownership distribution

disenfranchised *Gaunkars* from the agrarian system.[12] The change in tenancy laws caused loss of control of the *communidade* lands and possibly increased the search for exit options.[13]

The frequency of exit by the three categories in the surveyed villages is shown in Table 9.5 and Figure 9.4. The first migration of this generation in these villages is reported in 1958 from among the *Gaunkars*. The migration from among the *Gaunkars* has been consistently higher than that of the other two categories.

The subsequent migration by tenants and *Mundkars* can be attributed to two factors: (*a*) the declining productivity of land, and (*b*) old social networks wherein the early migrants (*Gaunkars*) passed on information about job opportunities abroad.

9.4.4. *Determinants of exit*

In order to test for determinants of exit (here interpreted as immigration abroad) we used the decline in land productivity due to salinity ingress as a determining factor. The length of the fallow period (in years) is used as a proxy for decline in land productivity. We also wanted to test if any particular category (*Gaunkars*, tenants, or *Mundkars*) exhibited differential behaviour.

[12] Tourism was another exit option that opened up in a big way in the early 1980s (see Mukhopadhyay and Desouza 1997).

[13] It is pertinent here to mention that out-migration is not new to Goa. For over two centuries there has been a significant diaspora of Goans living in different parts of Africa (Portuguese and non-Portuguese colonies at that time) (de Souza 1994). What makes this phase of migration significantly different is its impact on the local economy because of the development of international financial markets which permit easy transfer of remittances from abroad even to remote villages. This has had deep impacts on the local economy which we presume was not the case in the earlier phase.

Table 9.5. Persons with family abroad and receiving foreign remittances (current survey data)

Category (90 persons interviewed in each category)	Households with family abroad	Probability of having a family member abroad	Households receiving foreign income	Proportion of members abroad and remitting money
Gaunkar	53	0.44	25	0.47
Tenant	17	0.14	9	0.52
Mundkar	7	0.05	6	0.86
Total	77	0.213	40	0.38

A Logit model is set up with a dependent dummy variable indicating whether the household has a member abroad or not (Frn_D = 1 for yes, and = 0 for no). This was assumed to be a function of:

- Category to which an agent belonged—we use the *Mundkars* as the reference category and dummies for *Gaunkars* (Gaunk) and tenants (Tenant), as independent variables to test which of these categories showed greater inclination to exit (Gaunk = 1 if *gaunkar*, Gaunk = 0 if non-*gaunkar*, similarly Tenant = 1 if tenant, Tenant = 0, otherwise).

Expected sign of coefficient for Gaunkar is positive (as *Gaunkars* being disenfranchised by the land distribution system are expected to have a higher propensity to exit). The expected sign of coefficient for tenants is uncertain. As beneficiaries of tenancy legislation they should have little incentive to exit, but on the other hand, with increased fallow, search for other income would have a positive impact on exit. However, we include a variable (discussed below) for the number of years land has lain fallow and therefore the negative impact should not show up.

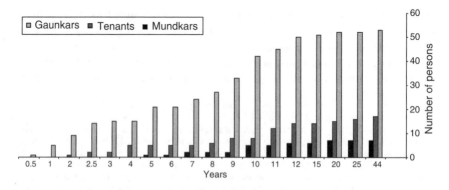

Figure 9.4. Cumulative migration abroad (survey data). Year 1958–2001

Table 9.6. Description of variables and expected signs

Variable	Expected Sign	Description
Gaunk	+	*Gaunkar* dummy (If *Gaunkar* = 1, Otherwise = 0)
Tenant	?	Tenant dummy (If Tenant = 1, Otherwise = 0)
Fal_Yrs	+	Number of years land is fallow
Other_Y	?	Non-agricultural incomes (per month), Categories: less than Rs 500 = 0; Rs 501–1000 = 1; Rs 1001–2500 = 2; Rs 2501–5000 = 4; Rs 5001–above = 5
FSA	+	Family size (adults)

- The number of years land lies fallow (Fal_Yrs) should increase the propensity to search for exit options. Expected sign of coefficient is positive.

- We tested to see if 'Other Incomes' (Other_Y—Non-Agricultural incomes excluding foreign remittances) have any impact on the exit of persons from the agrarian system. Expected sign of coefficient is uncertain. It is possible that the less privileged would have a higher propensity to exit. But it may also be anticipated that the opportunities for exit may be much higher for the better endowed.

- Finally we also wanted to check if the size of the family (adults) was influencing the desire to exit as a push factor in migration. Expected sign of coefficient is positive (See Table 9.6).

Table 9.7 provides the summary statistics of the independent variables in the Logit function.

The logit function tested for is:

$$Frn\_D = f(Fal\_Yrs, Gaunk, Tenant, Other\_Y, FSA)$$

The results of the regression are reproduced in Table 9.8.

Among the variables presented in Table 9.8, the coefficients of family size (adults) and the category tenants (Tenant) are not significant even at the 90 per cent level. The number of years for which land lies fallow is significant at the 95 per cent level. The category of *Gaunkars* and 'Other Incomes' have

Table 9.7. Summary of statistics

	Gaunk (Dummy)	Tenant (Dummy)	FAL_YRS	Other_Y	FSA
N of cases	360	360	360	360	360
Minimum	0	0	0	0	1
Maximum	1	1	25	4	14
Range	1	1	25	4	13
Sum	120	120	754	256	1549
Mean	0.333	0.333	2.094	0.711	4.303
Standard Dev.	0.472	0.472	4.889	1.253	1.906
Variance	0.223	0.223	23.902	1.571	3.632

Table 9.8. Summary regression results
Dependent Variable: Frn_D
Number of Observations: 360

	Coefficient	Standard error	t-ratio	p-values	Odds ratio	Slope (at mean)
Constant	−4.192	0.647	−6.481	0.000	—	—
Gaunk	1.668***	0.491	3.397	0.001	5.304	0.1372
Tenant	0.343	0.552	0.662	0.534	1.409	0.0282
Fal_Yrs	0.070**	0.031	2.273	0.023	1.072	0.0057
Other_Y	0.883***	0.122	7.208	0.000	2.418	0.0726
FSA	0.102	0.094	0.102	0.278	1.107	0.0084

** and *** in the coefficient column represent 95% and 99% level of significance respectively.
Log likelihood: −107.643
Log likelihood of constants-only model = LL(0) = −158.943
2*[LL(N)−LL(0)] = 102.600 with 5 df Chi-sq p-value = 0.000
McFadden's Rho-Squared = 0.323

coefficients which are significant at the 99 per cent level. This confirms the expectation that an agent is more likely to exit if his/her land is fallow and is more likely to exit if the household belongs to the *Gaunkars* category. The Likelihood Ratio (LR test) result indicates that the model is significantly different from the 'constants only' model and the McFadden's Rho-Squared suggests a reasonably acceptable fit. The last column of Table 9.8 provides the slope at mean which measures the Marginal Effect (at mean) that each variable has on the dependent variable (in a Logit function). Expectedly 'Gaunk' has the highest slope.

We next turn our attention to the current status of public works which has direct implications on sustainability of agrarian lands. The embankments which are public goods in nature need to be maintained in order to prevent salinity ingress.

9.4.5. Impact of public works decline

Seventy-three households reported having fallow lands due to salinity ingress. This probably added to the incentive to exit the agricultural sector even in the case of the tenants who were beneficiaries of the tenancy reform. Of the three categories it is noteworthy that it is the tenants who have reported larger fallow lands in terms of total area (Table 9.9). The growth in numbers reporting fallow is shown below as a cumulative frequency graph (Figure 9.5).

The *Mundkars* however reported the highest proportion of fallow lands while *Gaunkars* reported the lowest proportion of fallow lands (Table 9.10 in Appendix 9.1).

Table 9.9. Persons with fallow lands and having family abroad (current survey data)

Category (120 persons interviewed in each category)	Persons with fallow area	Proportion of person owning fallow area in each category	Number of persons abroad among those with fallow land	Proportion of foreign residents among fallow land holders
Gaunkars	21	0.17	8	0.38
Tenants	30	0.26	5	0.16
Mundkars	22	0.18	3	0.13
Total	73	0.21	16	0.21

The *Gaunkars* showed the highest frequency of exit from among those families that reported fallow lands. The (conditional) probability of exit (migration) by each category was *Gaunkars* 38 per cent, tenants 16 per cent, and *Mundkars* 13 per cent (see Table 9.9).

9.5. Discussion

The above results provide interesting pointers. *Communidades* lost their monopoly over agricultural land management in the wake of post-independence tenancy legislation and this led to their decline and the reduced maintenance of public works as there was no financial support for the *communidades*. This appears to have brought about two things: (*a*) increased fallowing due to salinity ingress (*b*) exit of agents from the agrarian economy, mainly *Gaunkars*.

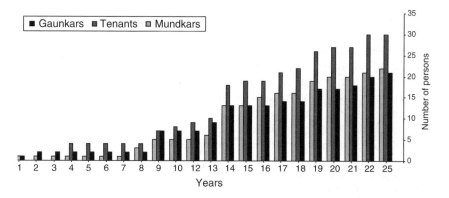

Figure 9.5. Cumulative number of persons reporting fallow area. Year 1977–2001

The major gainers in the land redistribution, the tenants and *Mundkars*, showed willingness to pay for adoption of individual increases in production by investing in mechanization (Mukhopadhyay 2005). However, there is incidence of increasing fallows which is a direct outcome of reduced local public expenditures to undertake productivity sustenance activities. This is typical myopic behaviour and indicative of institutional failure. Some of these outcomes have been anticipated in the evolutionary game-theory literature which suggests that in the absence of punishment, cooperation would break down (Sethi and Somanathan 2004). This punishment must be cheap and feasible otherwise agents may refrain from punishing thereby leading to breakdown in cooperation. In Goa, when the *communidades* had the right to auction their lands prior to tenancy legislation, non-cooperation led to eviction and cancellation of tenures. So punishment was both feasible and inexpensive for the institution.

This brings us back to the issues of property rights regimes, redistribution, and ecological sustainability. In the literature, it is commonly argued that security of tenure is a precondition for agents to undertake conservation measures (Holden and Shiferaw 2002). So expectedly, the security of tenure should have induced better conservation in Goa. Our finding is contrary to this. In the new regime homogeneity and security of tenure increased but cooperation to maintain embankments did not.

The critical question is why did cooperation not emerge? A theoretical explanation of how and when cooperation will emerge is dealt with exhaustively by Dasgupta (this volume). Here it will suffice to state just a few instances relevant to this study. Clear punishment rules (and the willingness to impose them) which are important for ensuring cooperation were missing in the post-tenancy institutional arrangement in Goa. If the beneficiary agents did not cooperate there was very little chance of any punishment (eviction) in the post-tenancy period. Secondly, there was a withdrawal of the previous managers of the agrarian system (*Gaunkars*) from village affairs as they had a reduced role in the new scenario.[14] But all of these possibilities point to one certainty—that replacement of an organic local institution with an inorganic one can at best have unanticipated (or at worst undesirable) consequences. A number of other contributions to this volume have pointed to similar outcomes. In Pakistan's Dir-Kohistan region the contestation between the traditional *jirga* and other organs of the modern state, is leading to conflict and undesirable outcomes for resource management in the region (Khan, this volume). Similarly, in Bhutan, the norms that governed *sokshings* are

---

[14] It is possible to blame the usual suspect of an inefficient credit market which did not permit the tenants from making the financial commitments necessary to maintain public works and simultaneously undertake private investments. Except in this case as we have discussed above, the government offered to reimburse (up to a ceiling of 50%) the expenses incurred on embankment maintenance.

now in conflict with new forest rules and institutions that are being framed compromising the sustainability of forest management there (Webb and Dorji, this volume).

So what are the lessons to be drawn here? In the euphoria of asset distribution, factors of institutional incentives were not examined, as cooperation was expected to automatically emerge among beneficiary farmers. We find that this did not occur. Without a prior history of cooperation (supply of public goods—embankments), the tenants failed to create new self-sustaining institutions even though there were state incentives to do so. This, however, is contrary to Mishra's findings (this volume) in Orissa, India, where despite state neglect, forest users managed to form federating structures for conservation as well as marketing of produce.

The other question that this leaves us with is the impact of homogeneity in the sustainable management of the commons by cooperation. The literature in this area suggests that there could be a threshold-effect with regard to heterogeneity and cooperation (Dayton-Johnson and Bardhan 2002).[15] In the current context, is the reduced state of cooperation indicative of a level of homogeneity beyond this threshold or is the relationship non-convex?[16] This would need further investigation.

Appendix 9.1

Table 9.10. Distribution of fallow land among different categories (current survey data 2002–3)

Category	Persons with fallow area	Total of land area owned (ha)	Amount of land affected (ha)	Proportion of land in entire category
Gaunkars	21	58.524	5.7	9.7
Tenants	30	75.49	15.3	20.2
Mundkars	22	35.04	7.99	22.8
Total	73	169.054	28.99	17.1

[15] It has been suggested that there could be an inverted-U relationship between heterogeneity and cooperation. This implies that initially cooperation increases as the degree of homogeneity increases but decreases after a certain point which is indicative of threshold effect.

[16] However, if there are non-convexities, which are not unlikely, alternative policy solutions could emerge. Non-convexity in such a situation would imply that there could be multiple thresholds in the homogeneity-cooperation relationship. So while there would seem to be a reduction in cooperation at this level of homogeneity, a further increase in homogeneity instead of further reducing cooperation may increase it beyond a certain point. Alternatively, if the other turning points are relatively lower as far as cooperation levels are concerned, then a further increase in homogeneity even in the presence of non-convexities would not lead to greater cooperation.

Table 9.11. *Taluka*-wise total income, expenditures, and balances of *communidades* (in Rupees for the period 1954–63)

Talukas 1	1954 2	1955 3	1956 4	1957 5	1958 6	1959 7	1960 8	1961 9	1962 10	1963 11
Total Income										
Goa (Tiswadi)	1940673	1840549	1541616	1610773	1449316	1213370	1748734	1488528	1131975	1106023
Salcete	1880449	1905106	1685374	1804307	1798689	1683383	1682072	1689024	1338928	1332017
Bardez	1567738	1576528	1436776	1397237	1380224	1341962	1393936	1367613	1183629	1156186
Mormugao	212757	206906	196523	201754	199774	199635	209211	215554	177571	172404
Ponda	450103	450071	410804	391446	354102	337082	354092	344734	306380	286198
Bicholim	173642	209157	137415	158412	128400	132248	145817	199809	124828	140210
Pernem	3774	9656	7905	6323	9906	6674	7165	6957	5032	4858
Quepem	28710	28473	26087	30544	31604	32776	28182	32140	28096	27200
Sanguem	21859	19915	20134	20748	21504	21654	21844	22273	22086	18582
Canacona	21469	19923	14495	15398	14703	14967	14564	15158	24224	17756
Satari	2182	2077	1902	1880	2036	2030	1841	2452	1536	2203
Total	6303336	6268361	5479031	5638822	5390258	4985781	5607458	5384242	4344285	4263637
Total Expenditure										
Goa (Tiswadi)	989382	939454	926487	952380	866668	1062103	1348830	1274212	1009164	1046470
Salcete	762267	844704	738343	820405	870103	769655	934203	965108	892750	941670
Bardez	871676	944606	803095	866308	917372	954128	1032872	1053122	1049748	1053174
Mormugao	161084	114773	112912	107781	108317	117064	136843	150778	151396	145027
Ponda	215348	213216	212953	184163	206217	217014	296930	266356	247818	225603

Bicholim	103474	147168	93039	103407	102512	100817	120111	155666	102279	125525
Pernem	4614	6378	6216	4290	4648	3725	6802	3949	7035	5381
Quepem	25893	29607	29243	29135	30225	31096	30903	29073	26022	25876
Sanguem	23223	22654	20352	20748	21904	23382	23186	26062	19597	20183
Canacona	18915	13463	12344	12328	13056	13940	13876	14010	24224	16631
Satari	1746	1610	1816	1865	1817	1808	1719	2113	1371	1991
Total	3177622	3277633	2956800	3102810	3142839	3294732	3946275	3940449	3531404	3607531
Balance										
Goa (Tiswadi)	951291	901095	615129	658393	582648	151267	399904	214316	122811	59553
Salcete	1118182	1060402	947031	983902	928586	913728	747869	723916	446178	390347
Bardez	696062	631922	633681	530929	462852	387834	361064	314491	133881	103012
Mormugao	51673	92133	83681	93973	91457	82571	72368	64776	26175	27377
Ponda	234755	236855	197851	207283	147885	120068	57162	78378	58562	60595
Bicholim	70168	61989	44376	55005	25888	31431	25706	44143	22549	14685
Pernem	-840	3278	1689	2033	5258	2949	363	3008	-2003	-523
Quepem	2817	-1134	-3156	1409	1379	1680	-2721	3067	2074	1324
Sanguem	-1364	-2739	-218	0	-400	-1728	-1342	-3789	2489	-1601
Canacona	2554	6460	2151	3070	1647	1027	688	1148	0	1125
Satari	436	467	86	15	219	222	122	339	165	212
Total	3125,734	2990,728	2522,231	2536,012	2247,419	1691,049	1661,183	1443,793	812,881	656,106

Source: GoG (1967b) Annexure no: 8: 22–3.

References

Alvares, C. (2002). *Fish, Curry and Rice*. Report. Mapusa, India: Goa Foundation.

Baland, J.-M., and Platteau, J.-P. (1997). 'Wealth Inequality and Efficiency in the Commons I: The Unregulated Case'. *Oxford Economic Papers*, 49: 451–82.

—— —— (1999). 'Inequality and Collective Action in the Commons'. *World Development*, 27/5: 773–88.

—— —— (2003). 'Economics of Common Property Management Regimes', in K.G. Maler and J. Vincent (eds.), *Handbook of Environmental Economics*. Amsterdam: North Holland, 127–90.

Becker, C. D., and Gibson, C. C. (1998). 'The Lack of Institutional Supply: Why a Strong Local Community in Western Ecuador Fails to Protect its Forest', in C. Gibson, M. A. McKean, and E. Ostrom (eds.), *Forests Resources and Institutions*. New York: Forest and Agricultural Organization. Web version: <http://www.fao.org/DOCREP/005/AC694E/AC694E10.htm#P0.0>.

Bergstrom, T., Blume, L., and Varian, H. (1986). 'On the Private Provision of Public Goods'. *Journal of Public Economics*, 29: 25–49.

Coase, R. (1960). 'The Problem of Social Cost'. *Journal of Law and Economics*, 3: 1–44.

D'Costa, A. (undated). *Social Change in Goa*. Margao: Timblo Printers.

Dasgupta, P., and Maler, K. G. (1995). 'Poverty, Institutions and the Environmental Resource Base,' in J. Behrman and T. N. Srinivasan (eds.), *Handbook of Development Economics*, Vol. 3. Amsterdam: North Holland, 2371–463.

Dayton-Johnson, J., and Bardhan, P. K. (2002). 'Inequality and Conservation on the Local Commons: A Theoretical Exercise'. *Economic Journal*, 112/481: 577–602.

de Janvry, A., Dutilly, C., Muñoz-Piña, C., and Sadoulet, E. (2001). 'Liberal Reforms and Community Responses in Mexico', in M. Aoki and Y. Hayami (eds.), *Communities and Markets in Economic Development*. New York: Oxford University Press, 318–43.

Demsetz, H. (1967). 'Towards a Theory of Property Rights.' *American Economic Review*, Papers and Proceedings, 62: 347–59.

de Souza, L. (undated). 'Breached Bunds a Threat to Farming and Water Security in Divar.' Firday Balcao, 3/6, Goa Desc, last accessed on 12 October 2005 at <http://www.goadesc.org/balcao/topic_environment.htm>.

de Souza, T. R. (1994). Goa to Me. New Delhi, India: Concept Publishing Co.

—— (1997). 'The Ranes of Sanquelim: Feudal Lords Unmasked', *GOA TODAY*, March, 28–33.

GoG (various years). *Statistical Handbook of Goa*. Report. Panaji, India: Directorate of Planning, Statistics, and Evaluation, Government of Goa.

—— (1964*a*). *Report of the Goa Land Reforms Commission*. Report. Panaji, India: Government of Goa, Daman and Diu, Government Printing Press.

—— (1964*b*). *Goa, Daman and Diu Agricultural Tenancy Act*. Report. Panaji, India: Government of Goa.

—— (1967*a*). *Aspects of Agricultural Activity in Goa*, Vol. 1. Report. Panaji, India: Government Printing Press.

—— (1967*b*). *Aspects of Agricultural Activity in Goa*, Vol. 2. Report. Panaji, India: Government Printing Press.

—— (1992). 'Report of the Agricultural Land Development Panel'. Report. Revenue Department, Government of Goa, Panaji, India.

—— (2000). 'Report of the Multi-Disciplinary Committee'. Report. Revenue Department, Government of Goa, Panaji, India.

Grossman, H. I. (2001). 'The Creation of Effective Property Rights'. *American Economic Review*, 91/2: 347–52.

Holden, S. T., and Shiferaw, B. (2002). 'Poverty and Land Degradation: Peasants' Willingness to Pay to Sustain Land Productivity', in C. Barrett, F. Place, and A. A. Aboud (eds.), *The Adoption of Natural Resource Management Practices: Improving Sustainable Agricultural Production in Sub-Saharan Africa*. New York: CAB International Publishing, 91–102.

—— —— and Wik, M. (1998). 'Poverty, Market Imperfections, and Time Preferences: Of Relevance for Environmental Policy?'. *Environment and Development Economics*, 3: 105–30.

Jodha, N. S. (1980). 'The Process of Desertification and the Choice of Interventions'. *Economic and Political Weekly*, 21: 1169–81.

Knox, A., and Meinzen-Dick, R. (2001). 'Collective Action, Property Rights, and Devolution of Natural Resource Management'. CAPRi Working Paper No. 11, IFPRI, Washington, DC.

Mukhopadhyay, P. (2002*a*). 'Democratic Representation and Property Rights: Understanding Transition in Local Institutions'. Paper presented at the Beijer Research Seminar, Luxor, March.

—— (2002*b*). 'Institutional Change and Resource Use'. Paper presented at the conference on 'Environmental History of Asia,' Jawaharlal Nehru University, New Delhi, December.

—— (2005). 'Now that Your Land is Mine, Does it Matter?'. *Environment and Development Economics*, 10/1: 87–96.

—— and Desouza, S. (1997). 'Development, Malaria, and Public Health Policy'. *Economic and Political Weekly*, 32/49: 3159–63.

Ostrom, E. (1990). *Governing the Commons: The Evolution of Institutions for Collective Action*. New York: Cambridge University Press.

Periera, R.-G. (1981). *Gaunkari, the Old Village Associations,* Vol. 1. Panjim, India: Printwell Publishers.

Seabright, P. (1993). 'Managing Local Commons: Theoretical Issues in Incentive Design'. *Journal of Economic Perspectives*, 7: 13–34.

Sethi, R., and Somanathan, E. (2004). 'Collective Action in the Commons: A Theoretical Framework for Empirical Research'. Discussion Paper. Indian Statistical Institute, New Delhi, India.

TERI (Tata Energy Research Institute) (2000). 'Population, Consumption and Environment Interrelations: A Tourist Spot Scenario'. TERI Project Report No. 97EM50.Tata Energy Research Institute, New Delhi, India, <http://static.teriin.org/reports/rep16/rep16.pdf>.

Xavier, P. D. (1993). *Goa: A Social History (1510–1640)*. Panaji, India: Rajhauns Vitaran.

10

Is Cooperation Costly with Diverse Economic Agents?

Bhim Adhikari[1]

10.1. Introduction

Institutions and institutional arrangements have become central in the study of the success or failure of environmental resource management in recent years. Scholars often distinguish between four main underlying factors causing environment and resource degradation and the 'tragedy of the commons' situation: market failures, policy failures, population growth, and property rights failure (Pearce and Turner 1990). Property rights failure is considered to be a crucial area of resource degradation as the individuals do not have to consider the social costs of their activities with respect to resource use in the absence of well-defined property rights. Insecure property rights over common pool resources (CPRs) may lead to short planning horizons, which may prevent poorer households from investing in environmental conservation (Holden, Shiferaw, and Wik 1998). On the other hand, tenure security over natural resources encourages resource users to invest in resource conservation activities and to enhance the quality of the environmental resource base and its sustainable utilization. An appropriate form of property rights structure over CPRs is, therefore, considered to be an important part of resource management policy, including land reform, conservation of forest, grazing and wildlife resources, fisheries, and water management (Heltberg 2002).

[1] I would like to thank Ingela Ternström for her constructive comments which were instrumental in improving this paper. Thanks are also due to N. S. Jodha, Rucha Ghate, Pranab Mukhopadhyay, and Nadeem Samnakay for their feedback on the earlier version of this paper. Jon Lovett deserves special thanks for his critical comments throughout the course of this study. This paper was finalized while the author was visiting the Abdus Salam International Center for Theoretical Physics (ICTP), Trieste, Italy. I gratefully acknowledge the South Asian Network for Development and Environmental Economics (SANDEE) for generous financial support.

Recognizing the importance of community-based management of CPRs, transferring the responsibility of resource management into the hands of the local communities has been one of the major policy interventions for management of natural resources in many developing countries in recent years (Agarwal 2001). In Nepal, devolution of authority to groups of resource users to manage forest resources has been the main thrust of the community forestry (CF) programme since the late 1990s when national forests were handed over to forest user groups (FUGs) under a community-based property rights regime. Nepal's community forestry programme is one of the most important attempts to convert the *de facto* open-access forests to common property by devolving ownership and control of forests to their traditional users who are granted usufruct rights to forests through legal enactment. About 25 per cent of potential forest areas had already been handed over to 14,000 FUGs by 2005 in different parts of the country, mainly in the mid-hills, that accounted for about 1.2 million hectares of forested land (see Kanel, this volume).

Although local control over forest resources is now regarded as a win-win solution for environment and local development in the middle hills of Nepal, this has not been a universal result as community forestry does not have the same success everywhere (Nightingale 2002). Along with equity and distributional aspects of community forestry programmes (Adhikari 2005), village-level differences in terms of the socio-economic attributes of households are often considered crucial when it comes to gauging the different levels of success (Baral 1999). Particularly, local levels of inequality among forest users may increase the costs of coordination which in turn influence the likelihood of collective action. There are plenty of case studies on the conditions that are most likely to be conducive for local-level collective action (Wade 1988; Bromley and Cernea 1989; Ostrom 1990; Oakerson 1992; Tang 1991; Bardhan 1993; Nugent 1993). Further, other studies have also emphasized the importance of transaction costs in collective action (Hanna and Munasinghe 1995; Davies and Richards 1999; Adhikari and Lovett 2006a). However, to our knowledge, none of these literatures examines the relationship between group heterogeneity and transaction costs and their impacts on local-level collective action. As Libecap (2002: 2) pointed out, 'only by identifying the transaction costs involved and their impact on the actions taken is it possible to understand the timing and array of institutions adopted and why they are unlikely to coincide with more idealized theoretical remedies'.

In this paper, we first intend to examine how local-level differences and some measures of inequality among resource users are associated with the different levels of transaction costs incurred by households participating in community forestry programmes. We will then compare both start-up and recurrent transaction costs with the degree of collective action. We particularly raise the following two research questions in this paper: (*a*) is there any relationship between group heterogeneity and the level of transaction costs? (*b*) could the costs of transaction be an argument for the different levels of success of FUGs or the degree of collective action?

This study utilized the primary data collected for a study on the distributional implications of community forestry of eight different FUGs in the mid-hills of Nepal. In order to compare transaction costs incurred by households with group heterogeneity, we develop simple measures of inequalities (*gini* of land inequality and caste heterogeneity) and FUG-level differences (for example, distance to forests, representation of women and lower caste households in the decision-making body, exit options available for households outside the commons, etc.). We then derive an index for collective action for each FUG to see whether high costs of transaction inhibit cooperative effort or the degree of collective action. The index of collective action was measured by subjective judgment of a few important variables that capture the performance of FUGs such as forest stock condition, diversity and abundance of vegetation, forest user groups' monitoring and operational rules, incentive structures, and systems of fines and penalties in case of rule violation. Transaction costs were measured by the number of days spent by households in various coordination activities related to the management of their community forests.

The empirical analysis indicates that transaction costs could be higher in communities where the land inequality is greater. Moreover, FUGs with some degree of women's representation in FUG committees reduce the costs of coordination and demonstrate a higher degree of collective action. Though not consistent, large group size is also related to the higher costs of transaction as predicted in the theoretical literature. The analysis also indicates that FUGs with low transaction costs succeed better than groups with higher costs of transaction.

The chapter is structured as follows. The following section contains a theoretical discussion on heterogeneity, transaction costs, and the collective action. Section 10.3 explains methodological issues, survey design, and data collection. Section 10.4 reports on the results obtained from the analysis. It does so by comparing the local-level inequalities with the costs of transaction. We then compare transaction costs with the degree of collective action. Section 10.5 offers concluding remarks and observations.

10.2. Theory and conceptual framework

After Coase's (1937, 1960) seminal work on transaction costs, scholars have initiated debate on this topic arguing that economic growth is dependent on stable political and economic institutions that provide low costs of transaction

(North 1989). Only those societies that succeed in creating institutions that effectively reduce transaction costs will survive in the long run (Wallis and North 1986; North 1990). Transaction costs refer to the costs of defining and measuring resources or claims, plus the costs of utilizing and enforcing the rights specified (Furubotn and Richter 1997). Dahlman (1979) separates transaction costs into three broad categories: (*a*) search and information costs; (*b*) bargaining and decision costs; and (*c*) policing and enforcement costs.

In the context of CF management, search and information costs are incurred as a result of participation in initial community meetings in identifying potential users of CF, negotiating among potential members, forming FUG and forest users' committees (FUC), and gathering information about physical attributes of the resource and attributes of the community. Bargaining and decision costs refer to costs related to the preparation of a specific operational plan of CF including designing management institutions related to resource management and appropriation. The transaction costs of policing and enforcement refer to monitoring costs which are incurred during monitoring and enforcement of agreed rules related to forest use, conflict management, monitoring costs of forest protection, record keeping, and resolution and sanctions for rule violation.

Homogeneity and heterogeneity among resource users are often contested while linking the success of community-based resource management with the level of transaction costs. The degree of heterogeneity within user groups influences the costs of management (Hanna 1998*a*). Received knowledge suggests that collective action is more successful in managing a CPR when the population is relatively homogeneous in social and economic terms as homogeneity might reduce the costs of coordination. Seabright's (1993) model of 'habit-forming' cooperation confirmed that the degree of trust between economic agents participating in some form of collective had a crucial role in the success of common property regimes. Further, the literature on social capital argues that social trust reduces the costs of monitoring and enforcing collaborative agreements (Lubell 2005). In this sense, the level of social capital or trust would be higher in more homogeneous groups, which would in turn enable them to reduce the costs of transaction and make them more likely to succeed in managing the local commons. Pollak (1985 as cited in Lanzona and Evenson 1997) also suggests that transaction costs may be minimized by household extra-economic relationships as the advantages of household cooperation are magnified in more traditional and homogeneous societies.

However, heterogeneity within the group is also thought to be conducive to collective action as better-off members of the community may bear the larger share of costs in initiating the collective action (Olson 1965). In his study of agrarian institutional change in Goa, India, Mukhopadhyay (this volume) argues that although the privatization of common lands (*communidades*) has increased homogeneity and tenure security, it has not increased the level of cooperation in supplying public goods. Moreover, a recent study has suggested that successful communities may be able to craft institutions according to local circumstances that facilitate group success even in more heterogeneous communities (Varughese and Ostrom 2001). In this way, groups with a high degree of inequality may be able to reduce transaction costs through *ex ante* selection of appropriate governance structures.

Along with heterogeneity and transaction costs, the impact of transaction costs on collective action is another area of debate. It is argued that cooperation will be forthcoming when benefits outweigh the transaction costs of negotiating and enforcing collective agreements. Transaction costs could also be an important determinant of cooperative behaviour. High transaction costs may pose significant constraints to participation and prevent many important transactions from being achieved. Since costs of monitoring and sanctioning can be high in any cooperative action, the degree of cooperative success will depend on the mechanisms the group adopts to economize on such costs (Hetcher 1990). In their general equilibrium model of trust and growth, Zak and Knack (2001) demonstrated that homogeneity or heterogeneity among agents often reflects the level of trust. This in turn influences the emergence of institutions through their impact on costs of transactions. In his study of participatory watershed management in the USA, Lubell (2005) argues that the advantage of watershed partnerships over traditional command-and-control institutions lies in their ability to reduce the real or perceived transaction costs of collective choice. He further argues that the decision to cooperate is a function of collective-action beliefs related to the benefits and transaction costs of collective action.

Quite a few studies have examined the transaction costs of collective action (Adhikari and Lovett 2006a; Mburu, Birner, and Zeller 2003; Richards *et al.* 1999; Kuperan *et al.* 1998). For instance, in their study on co-management of fisheries in the Philippines, Kuperan *et al.* (1998) observed that monitoring emerges as the activity accounting for more than 50 per cent of the total costs of all the activities involved in co-management. Aggrawal (2000) observed the high costs of negotiation in the case of the expansion of group-owned wells in southern India, particularly in groups where heterogeneity among members in terms of their endowments and needs is high. Richards *et al.* (1999) undertook a participatory economic analysis of community forestry in Nepal, including transaction costs, and found that the transaction costs of forest management were between 5 to 20 per cent of total resource management costs. Adhikari and Lovett (2006a) observed that transaction costs for CF management as a percentage of resource appropriation costs are higher for poorer households (26 per cent) than for middle-wealth (24 per cent) or rich households (14 per cent) in the same villages. They also noted village differences in the level of transaction costs. However, these studies quantify the transaction costs without examining the implications of group hetero-geneity on the level of transaction costs. Further, empirical literature on the relationship between the extent of transaction costs and success of collective action is still scarce. This study aims at filling these gaps.

Heterogeneity in this work refers to socio-economic inequality such as land and caste inequality and other local-level differences among FUGs. We hypothesize that a high level of heterogeneity among participants may lead to a high level of transaction costs because heterogeneous preferences of actors towards the resource management regime increase the costs of coordination. High transaction costs in turn have negative effects on the likelihood of successful collective action as group coordination would be difficult in a more heterogeneous society. The argument is that cooperative action could be very expensive because of the assurance problem as agents in heterogeneous settings are not confident that every individual will reciprocate by behaving rationally, or that it would be privately optimal in the long run. This kind of tendency poses a great threat to the effective functioning of community institutions and encourages deviant behaviour among economic agents. We will first compare transaction costs with measures of inequality and local-level differences and then with the level of collective action in order to see whether the degree of collective action is associated with the extent of transaction costs.

10.3. Survey methods and data collection

Fieldwork was undertaken in two selected districts, Kavre Palanchok and Sindhu Palchok, located in the mid-hills of central Nepal. The middle hill region comprises more than 30 per cent of the total area of the country (HMGN/MPFS 1988). The forests of the mid-hills can be categorized into three broad groups for purposes of simplification according to species composition, structure, and conditions of the stand. These three categories are: hardwood forest with mixed or pure broadleaf species; conifer forest with little or no broadleaf species understorey; mixed forest with pine species and substantial broadleaf species understorey (Gilmour, King, and Hobley 1989). Subsistence agriculture is the mainstay of rural economic activities for households as the agriculture sector dominates the social and commercial life of these two districts. Table 10.1 compares land-use patterns in the two districts with Nepal as a whole and gives some indication of the range of crops and the size and make-up of the agricultural holdings.

The next task was to select the study villages and FUGs from the two districts under consideration. Four FUGs (Saradadevi FUG, Jyala Chiti FUG,

Table 10.1. Area of holding by land-use pattern (hectares)

Location	Temporary crops	Temporary fallow & meadow	Permanent crops	Permanent meadow & pasture	Wood & forest	All others	Total
All Nepal	2,250,197	372,099	29,154	42,543	14,975	89,549	2,463,717
Sindu Palchowk	1,073	52	1	14	1	1,256	12,117
Kavre Palanchowk	55,575	951	663	2,781	1,346	1,258	62,574

Source: Collett *et al.* 1996.

Mahavedsthan FUG, and Thuli Ban FUG) in Kavre Palanchok districts and four FUGs (Gaurati FUG, Shree Chhap FUG, Janghare FUG, and Karki Tar FUG) in Sindhu Palchok district were selected for intensive study. This implies that only one FUG per village was selected for the study. The villages are different in terms of their accessibility. Of the eight villages (FUG), only three, Thuli Ban, Jyala Chiti, and Janghare, are connected by an all-weather road and, hence, by a bus service. Three villages, Karki Tar, Mahavedsthan, and Shree Chhap, are situated more than 5 km from the nearest market. While all villages have one primary school, health infrastructure is uniformly underdeveloped in all villages.

The primary data on household-level variables, and use and management of community forestry was collected through a structured questionnaire survey designed for a study on the equity and distributional implication of CF initiatives in these villages. It should be noted that this paper relies totally on this data set. Although the number of households surveyed was large enough to quantify the transaction costs incurred by households, an econometric estimation of the relationship between group heterogeneity and transaction costs, and transaction costs with the degree of collective action, was not possible due to the small number of FUGs. Hence, the findings of this study may not be generalized to other FUGs.

In order to collect household data, sample households were divided into three income groups—poor, middle, and rich—based on landholding, livestock ownership, and income from off-farm agricultural activities. About 20 per cent of households from each income group were randomly selected giving a total number of 309 households for the structured questionnaire survey. In addition to demographic information and socio-economic information, data were also collected on forest and forest-resources utilization, and households' participation in different activities of community forest management. Table 10.2 presents the socio-economic characteristics of sample households.

The *tole* (hamlet)-level meetings were held separately for men and women in smaller and homogeneous groups with open-ended questions. The discussion was carried out on various issues such as gender issues, benefit and

Table 10.2. Characteristics of sample respondents

Attributes of respondents	Average value
Age	43.4
Gender	
Male	79.6
Female	20.4
Household size (number of individuals in a family)	6.4
Education (%)	
Illiterate	28
Literate (including primary and high school, and university)	72
Caste (%)	
Lower caste (untouchable)	12
Higher caste (other than untouchable)	88
Landholding (hectares)	
Poor	0.15
Middle	0.51
Rich	1.33

cost-sharing practices, decision-making processes, caste and gender representation in users' committees, nature of existing conflicts, ownership over agreed-upon decisions, and other institutional arrangements of resource use and management.

As discussed earlier, information was collected on three different components of transaction costs using the household questionnaire survey. The search and information costs incurred during the process of FUG formation were collected for time spent in identifying traditional users, settling conflicts, gathering information about forest resources, and establishment of FUG and executive committees. Data on bargaining and decision costs were collected by calculating the time spent in carrying out implementation activities to comply with the management decisions made. These costs are incurred while negotiating about mode of management and preparation of the management plan for the CF, and decisions about obligatory forestry activities such as rules on resource exploitation and punishment in cases of violation. Transaction costs of policing and enforcement-related activities were derived for time spent by user households in monitoring and enforcement of agreed-upon rules.

Monitoring and maintenance are important operational activities of the forest user groups and they are carried out through cash contribution and/or rotation of labour provided by households. Time is also invested in keeping records in the form of minutes and accounts in a register. In order to elicit this, household heads were asked to recall the total number of days they put into various meetings and other transactions related to the CF activities described earlier. The minute books of the executive committees of FUGs and FUG assemblies provided the attendance figures at meetings and levels of participation in these activities. It was possible to refer to the minute book and the files of user groups, detailing the costs and extent of participation, in order to keep track of all labour input into CF activities. We then calculated the average transaction-cost days for each FUG and compared this with the measure of inequalities and local-level differences in these groups.

Gini coefficient of land inequality was calculated for each group to compare it with the transaction costs incurred by user groups and the level of collective action in these villages. Further, caste heterogeneity was computed by an index of ethnic fractionalization, that is, 1– (sum of squares of shares of households of each site). This relationship can be depicted by the following formula:

$$Index\ of\ caste\ heterogeneity = 1 - \sum_{i}^{n} (P_i)^2$$

Where P_i is the proportion of total households in the ith caste group. Caste heterogeneity varies from 0 to 1 indicating a maximum value of unity with extreme inequality and a minimum of zero at pure equality (see Adhikari and Lovett 2006*b*).

We have followed Varughese and Ostrom (2001) in order to develop an index for the degree of collective action. The degree of collective action was assessed through subjective judgment by asking a set of questions during the field survey. The main variables that were considered in order to devise the index of collective action were FUG rules regarding monitoring and operation, the incentive-sharing mechanism, activities undertaken by FUGs with regard to forest restoration, and the effectiveness of the fines and penalties system in case of rule violation.

A low level of collective action (L) towards forest conservation was recorded in those forest user groups where individuals were aware of local forest degradation, but where no formal rules existed to regulate forest product extraction. A moderate level of collection action (M) was noted where there was some kind of formal harvesting and entry rules with a minimal level of forest development activities and not very explicit monitoring rules. Here, local institutions when it came to sanction for rule violations were also not always very clear. A high level of collective action (H) was recorded in situations where a group of users have harvesting and entry rules, effective monitoring by members, and organized forest-related group activities as well as forest restoration. In groups with a high level of collective action, the person who violates the FUG institutions is normally sanctioned through warnings, fines, and, finally, with social exclusion if the case is very severe. For each FUG, an index of collective action was derived using these measures (see Adhikari and Lovett 2006*b* for a detailed discussion). Finally, these indices were compared with the recurrent transaction costs in order to elucidate the relationship between the transaction costs and the degree of collective action.

10.4. Results and discussion

This section first reports on transaction costs incurred by households and compares these with the measures of inequalities and local-level differences among FUGs. This will be followed by the second-level analysis on the relationship between transaction costs and the level of collective action.

10.4.1. *Heterogeneity and transaction costs*

We have discussed three different types of transaction costs earlier. But it should be noted that these costs were incurred in two different stages such as start-up and recurrent costs of transaction. Start-up costs are basically related to organizational efforts to collectively mobilize community members towards the management of community forests. These costs were incurred during the initial stage of CF for the identification of users and forests in question, which is a fixed cost in nature. The recurrent transaction costs, on the other hand, were incurred annually, especially due to monitoring and protection-related activities. It would be important to disaggregate these costs in order to see how big each of these costs is and also to compare them with the measure of inequalities in the following section. Table 10.3 gives a breakdown of the average time spent on the various CF activities by households in each forest user group. While the first column reports on start-up costs (transaction costs incurred at the initial stage of the CF programme), the second column presents the annual recurrent costs of transaction. The start-up cost is almost half of the recurrent annual transaction cost spent in CF initiatives. At this stage, villagers have to spend time identifying the actual users of community forests, and negotiating with groups of varying interests and with forest departmental officials. This is a time-consuming activity which is not always straightforward due to a variety of conflicts related to forest-resource use.

Table 10.3. Breakdown of transaction costs for each FUG assessed (days)

Forest User Groups	Start-up costs	Recurrent costs	Total
Saradadevi	5	18	23
Jayala Chiti	10	18	28
Mahadevsthan	6	16	22
Thuli Ban	4	12	16
Gaurati	5	17	22
Shree Chhap	7	22	29
Janghare	16	23	39
Karki Tar	7	22	29

Table 10.4. Land and caste inequality and transaction costs (days)

Forest User Groups	Recurrent transaction costs	*Gini* of land inequality	Index of caste inequality
Janghare	23	0.57	0.58
Shree Chhap	22	0.33	0.70
Karki Tar	22	0.33	0.24
Saradadevi	18	0.33	0.61
Jayala Chiti	18	0.44	0.62
Gaurati	17	0.32	0.50
Mahadevsthan	16	0.35	0.56
Thuli Ban	12	0.40	0.52

Some local-level arrangements with regard to community meetings such as the meeting venue, procedure, and practice are also worth mentioning here. It appears that both start-up and recurrent costs are higher in Janghare and Jayala Chiti FUGs where there is no fixed venue for community meetings unlike in the case of the other user groups considered in this analysis. The other FUGs have a well-defined procedure for meetings, that is, venue and dates for the meetings as well as community houses where all members can meet at a specified time and location. Coordination costs will be high in communities without a common place for meetings where they can discuss matters related to CF.

When it comes to recurrent annual transaction costs, monitoring is the most important activity (an average of ten days for all FUGs), followed by implementation (six days) and information-related tasks (four days). In most forest user groups, monitoring, information gathering, resource maintenance, and attending community meetings to decide on various implementation activities are the major activities.

Table 10.4 compares measures of inequalities (*gini* of land inequality and index of caste heterogeneity) with recurrent transaction costs. First, we compare the recurrent transaction costs with *gini* of land inequality. Some relationships between *gini* of land inequality and transaction costs were evident. For example, the two FUGs with a higher level of land inequality (0.44 for Jayala Chiti and 0.57 for Janghare) incurred higher transaction costs. Figure 10.1 depicts the relationship between transaction costs and *gini* of land inequality as presented in Table 10.3. It appears that transaction costs are an increasing function of inequality but the transaction costs seemed to be lower at medium-level inequality. Bardhan and Dayton-Johnson (2000) noted a U-shaped relationship between inequality and commons management suggesting that very high and very low levels of inequality are associated with better commons performance. Dayton-Johnson (2000) observed a similar negative effect of increasing the *gini* coefficient for farmer-managed irrigation systems in Mexico. These observations suggest that as in the case of heterogeneity

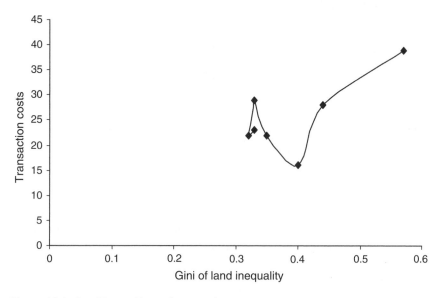

Figure 10.1. Land inequality and transaction costs

and commons performance, recurrent transaction costs could be lower at the moderate level of land inequality and rise sharply with increasing inequality in landholding. Higher inequality may lead to different preferences towards CF management and make coordination costly as the time and effort needed are greater to bring unequal parties together for a common objective. Alesina and La Ferrara (2002) noted negative relationships between *gini* of income and trust in their study on heterogeneity and trust in the USA and concluded that income heterogeneity is associated with a low level of trust. This in turn increases the costs of transaction.

When comparing caste inequality with the recurrent transaction costs, there is no clear-cut evidence to indicate that the more heterogeneous FUGs in terms of caste incurred higher costs of transaction. To substantiate this, we compare two FUGs having an equal amount of transaction costs (that is, Shree Chhap and Karki Tar) but with considerably different caste inequality as Shree Chhap is more heterogeneous than the Karki Tar FUG. But there can be exceptions to this too. So, the transaction cost incurred by Shree Chhap (0.33) and Karki Tar (0.33) is as high as that of Jayala Chiti although the latter is a more homogeneous group in terms of landholding.

The costs of generating local-knowledge information with the participation of stakeholders will depend very much on how well stakeholders are integrated across the geographic area of the resource (Hanna 1998*b*). Table 10.5 presents the recurrent transaction costs incurred for each FUG member in

Table 10.5. Transaction costs and local differences

Forest User Groups	Recurrent transaction costs (days)	Average distance to CF (km)	Exit option (off-farm income in NRs)	% of women in FUG committee	% of lower caste in FUG committee	Group size (no. of households in FUG)
Saradadevi	18	0.55	4098	0	0	133
Jayala Chiti	18	0.63	59501	13.3	13.3	222
Mahadevsthan	16	0.80	33161	23	15.4	147
Thuli Ban	12	0.60	59720	20	0	292
Gaurati	17	0.37	37698	22	0	144
Shree Chhap	22	0.56	120000	18.2	10	216
Janghare	23	1.03	45604	20	0	255
Karki Tar	22	1.06	40296	7.7	38.5	140

relation to some local differences. Of the eight FUGs studied, two FUGs, Janghare and Karki Tar, with a higher average distance to the community forests (with average distance to forest at 1.03 km and 1.06 km respectively) seemed to spend more time in coordinating the group effort. However, there is no systematic association between groups with proximity to community forests and the extent of transaction costs. For instance, forest users in Gaurati FUG live nearest to the forest (0.37 km) but the transaction costs are almost equal to that of Mahadevsthan FUG (0.80) where users are far from the community forest. In fact, distance cannot be a good predictor of transaction costs in these villages as they are not really far from the community forests. Every village in the mid-hills of Nepal has got at least one CF which is in close proximity to the settlement.

During the group discussion it was found that FUGs devise various mechanisms that allow them to overcome the problem created by locational differences. For example, in Karki Tar FUG, those who live further away can pay an extra fee in exchange for reduced monitoring duties. They also do not need to provide voluntary labour for the rotational system of watching as long as they pay cash in lieu of labour. In their study on the contested role of group heterogeneity when it comes to collective action in the mid-hills of Nepal, Varughese and Ostrom (2001) also demonstrated that FUGs are able to design a set of rules and regulations that actually overcome the problem induced by locational differences.

Economic opportunities available to resource users outside the local commons could also increase the coordination costs as resource users with a better exit option may not be interested and it would be time-consuming to bring such users together for cooperative action. They would not be interested in optimal conservation as when wealth declines the gain from conservation falls off more rapidly than their gain from exercising the exit options (Bardhan and Dayton-Johnson 2000). But, in this analysis, we found no strong evidence of the exit option, as measured by differences in outside earning opportunity and the level of transaction costs. Although Shree Chhap FUG shows high costs of transaction (with the highest exit option), Saradadevi FUG, which had the lowest exit option, is not considerably different when it comes to transaction costs from Shree Chhap FUG which had relatively better exit options. In light of this, the relationship between the exit option and the level of transaction costs could not be confirmed.

There is some evidence that representation of women (that is, 20 per cent in the case of the Thuli Ban FUG) can reduce the costs of transaction. Furthermore, two other FUGs, which indicate a high level of women's representation (23 per cent for Mahadevsthan and 17 per cent for Gaurati) show relatively lower transaction costs. Some experimental studies on gender-cooperative behaviour indicate that women contribute more than men due to a greater interdependent utility and altruism (Folbre 1994) and that cooperative outcomes might be more likely to occur in groups with higher female participation (Molians 1998). Rural women play a significant role in collecting environmental goods (fetching water, collecting grass and fodder, gathering firewood, etc.). They are also more knowledgeable about the local resource base. This type of knowledge could make coordination activities easier and reduce the costs of group coordination. However, this analysis could not support the argument that representation of lower-caste households in the FUG committee (that is, the executive body of FUG) reduces the cost of coordination.

Although not consistent, group size is associated with high costs of transaction as three FUGs with a bigger group size incurred relatively higher coordination costs. For instance, Janghare FUG has 255 households and spends twenty-three days annually in transaction-costs-related activities. Moreover, two other FUGs with a large number of households (Shree Chhap 216 and Jayala Chiti 222) incurred higher transaction costs. However, Karki Tar and Thuli Ban are exceptions as the former, with a relatively smaller size, incurred high transaction costs while the latter, with a larger group size, incurred lower costs of transaction. Referring to some earlier studies (for example, Cornes, Mason, and Sandler 1986), Ostrom (2002: 27–8) posits that,

increasing the level of heterogeneity, say size of a group, is likely to be associated with at least the following changes: (1) an increase in the transaction costs of reaching agreements; (2) a reduction of the burden borne by each participant for meeting joint costs such as guarding a system and maintenance; and (3) an increase in the amount of assets held by the group that could be used in times of emergency.

Decision-making procedures become more complicated and costly with increasing group size, since the time and effort required are usually rapidly increasing functions of the size of the group.

Table 10.6. Transaction costs and the degree of collective action

Forest User Groups	Start-up costs	Recurrent transaction costs	Index for the degree of collective action
Saradadevi	5	18	H
Jayala Chiti	10	18	M
Mahadevsthan	6	16	H
Thuli Ban	4	12	H
Gaurati	5	17	H
Shree Chhap	7	22	M
Janghare	16	23	L
Karki Tar	7	22	H

10.4.2. *Transaction costs and the degree of collective action*

In this section, we attempt to see whether a high level of transaction costs inhibits the level of collective action through its impact on the emergence of local management institutions as hypothesized earlier. Higher transaction costs could be associated with low levels of collective action. If the transaction costs of enforcing a contract among the players are sufficiently low, the likelihood of successful collective action would be higher. In Table 10.6, the degree of collective action is compared with the recurrent transaction costs. Transaction costs appear to be higher in groups where the level of collective action is lower. For instance, the FUG recording the highest number of transaction-cost days (Janghare) has the lowest level of collection action. Moreover, two other FUGs (Jayala Chiti and Shree Chhap) with a medium degree of collective action seemed to incur higher transaction costs, the exception being the Karki Tar FUG.

FUGs with lower transaction costs exhibit a high degree of collective action as they use collective-choice rules more effectively to avoid high costs of transaction. As group heterogeneity increases, transaction costs also increase with regard to communicating, information-sharing, monitoring, and reminding people of their commitments—all of which may lead to a low level of collective action. It could be said that economic and social heterogeneity may be linked to the level of collective action through their impacts on the costs of transaction. And their impact on collective action is difficult to avoid unless institutions are strong enough to minimize these costs.

Along with recurrent transaction costs, an attempt was made to compare start-up costs with the degree of collective action. Although start-up costs are sunk costs and, hence, these costs *per se* should not affect individual behaviour in relation to forest management later on, it was indicated that FUGs with high start-up costs also exhibit lower levels of collective action. Similar to the impacts of recurrent transaction costs on collective action, large start-up costs may appear to influence the cooperative effort to some extent at the initial stage of CF management which may have some residual effects on the capacity of the community to organize and sustain local institutions of resource management. High recurrent costs definitely reduce the likelihood of successful collective action and this could be further aggravated if start-up costs in initiating collective action are high. For instance, FUGs recording low- and medium-level collective action incurred higher start-up costs compared with other FUGs considered in this analysis. This is a very consistent observation and perhaps one of the most clear-cut results in our analysis.

To refer back to the discussion on heterogeneity, transaction costs, and collective action, it appears that heterogeneity, to some extent, may inhibit innovation in local management institutions since it creates distrust and suppresses the level of mutual understanding among community members. Although this study could not measure the level of trust directly, trust within the community may also be related to transaction costs and collective action. If people trust others, transaction costs in economic activities are reduced and the likelihood of successful collective action becomes high (Alesina and La Ferrara 2002). Empirical literature again and again has shown that trust does matter (Coleman 1990; Putnam 1993; Alesina and La Ferrara 2002). Alesina and La Ferrara (2002) concluded that interpersonal trust is lower in more racially heterogeneous societies as well as in communities with higher income inequality. They concluded that the observed effect of heterogeneity on trust is due to the fact that people trust those more similar to themselves. Ostrom (1990) has argued that none of the successful CPR situations involves participants who vary greatly with regard to ownership of assets, skills, ethnicity, race, or other variables that could strongly divide a group of individuals.

Although the extent of transaction costs is not the sole predictor of collective action, this analysis indicates that land inequality appears to have a negative effect on collective action through its impact on costs of coordination. Of the eight groups considered, four FUGs (Saradadevi, Mahadevsthan, Gaurati, and Karki Tar) have relatively lower land inequality (mean = 0.33) and show a high degree of collective action. The *gini* coefficient of land inequality is highest for Janghare FUG (0.57), which shows a low level of collective action. The next highest *gini* coefficient is for Jayala Chiti FUG (0.44), which has a medium level of collective action. This study thus reveals that the higher the inequality in landholding and transaction costs, the lower the degree of collective action. Somanathan, Prabhakar, and Mehta (2006) have also demonstrated the relationship between land inequality and the degree of collective action in pine forests in the Himalayan districts of Kumaun and Garhwal in northern India. According to Kant and Berry (2001: 338), the greater the heterogeneity, the less will a shared interest in a given regime help to make it work effectively, either in the positive sense of assuring a positive contribution, as necessary, to effective management, or in the negative sense of assuring that no members of the group will behave in ways that sabotage or lower the payoff from the resource.

In general, it could be said that transaction costs are one of the important factors when it comes to collective action as these costs are a function of group heterogeneity (Libecap 2002).

It is also worth mentioning that a successful group may also be able to avoid local differences through an appropriate governance mechanism for resource management. The transaction costs of collective action are reduced when there is a good match between the structure (rules and practices) of institutions and the characteristics of the resource in question. For example, even though there is a very low percentage of women and no lower caste households in the FUG committee of the Saradadevi FUG, the level of collective action for this group is high. In this group, the informal rules require that there should be enough representation of women in all FUG committee meetings. Moreover, there is a better mechanism for involving a wide range of stakeholders, including low-caste households, in determining community development programmes to be carried out by FUGs based on local aspirations. During the group discussion, most members felt optimistic about reaching their common goals as these kinds of informal arrangements continue. The trust felt by the group's members towards office bearers of the FUG committee was shown clearly at a series of meetings during the field survey. It also appears that the group members strongly believe in the committee chairman and his leadership. In order to address the lack of women's representation on the committee, they invite one or two women members to every meeting on a rotational basis. Hence, women members get an opportunity to raise their concerns at those regular meetings.

Finally, it should be noted that it is not just transaction costs which influence cooperative behaviour as conflicts within the groups too may have some role to play. For instance, two FUGs recording a low level of collective action expressed their concern about the leadership in the FUG committees. About nine FUG committee members in Jyala Chiti and five in Shree Chhap have remained on the executive committee since the establishment of community forestry in the area and there is a lack of trust between the FUG committee and members of the user groups. Moreover, compared with the other groups, Janghare differs in terms of forest-product distribution rules. During the household survey, it was revealed that about 60 per cent of women and lower-caste households in this FUG were not aware of, or familiar with, forest operational plans, or with the rules and regulations, policy, goals, and processes of CF management. Attendance of households in the FUG meetings was low in this group because people believe that even if they attend they would not be able to change the use rights. There is no opportunity for informal discussion other than regular assemblies and committee meetings, and conflicts seem to originate from a lack of clear record keeping. Saradadevi and Madhavsthan FUGs have the highest collective action and are the most innovative FUGs in terms of crafting institutions for resource use and management. Group discussions in these FUGs revealed no conflicts among the members with regard to forest-products harvesting and distribution.

10.5. Conclusions

Most variables considered in this analysis could not confirm the claim that higher inequality leads to high costs of coordination. But the findings from this study indicate that transaction costs could be higher in communities where the land inequality is greater. Higher land inequality may create diverse preferences towards forest management regimes and the negotiation will be costly in terms of arriving at consensus decisions with regard to forest management in such communities. It appears that representation of women in the decision-making body of FUGs (measured by the percentage of women in the executive committee) also had some effect. FUGs committees represented in part by women demonstrated a higher degree of collective action, thus reducing coordination costs. This indicates that adequate representation of women in decision-making positions would reduce the costs of transaction as women are heavily involved in the collection of environmental goods and are knowledgeable about the state of the local resources as well as the types of intervention needed to manage them sustainably. This may be crucial to reduce the time spent in a variety of community meetings in order to reach consensus on management decisions. Though not consistent, large group size is also related to the higher costs of transaction as predicted in theoretical literature. Perhaps the most clear-cut observation in our study is that cooperative behaviour is influenced by high start-up costs as it might reduce the willingness to cooperate in collective action. Large start-up costs are associated with the problem of group coordination and this may continue onto the later stage of CF management giving rise to higher recurrent costs and subsequently leading to problems with regard to collective action.

The analysis shows that FUGs with low transaction costs would succeed better than groups with higher costs of transaction. We consistently observed that those FUGs which incurred lower levels of transaction costs revealed a high degree of collective action. However, it should be noted that information obtained through group discussions revealed that users are capable of crafting institutions of resource management that suit the local conditions and that the problem created by socio-economic differences can be resolved through innovative institutional design. Varughese and Ostrom (2001) also concluded that successful FUGs overcome stressful heterogeneities by crafting innovative institutional arrangements well matched to their local circumstances. Transaction cost is clearly an important determinant of collective action. But such correlation needs to be explored further with a larger number of FUGs under investigation. While case-study work such as this is invaluable in developing the hypothesis on transaction costs, heterogeneity, and collective action, empirical testing of this hypothesis from a comparative perspective requires a larger set of quantitative data that can be generalized across different FUGs. This study provides an avenue for future investigation using a more quantitative approach in order to obtain generalized patterns of such relationships that may exist.

References

Adhikari, B. (2005). 'Poverty, Property Rights and Collective Action: Understanding the Distributive Aspects of Common Property Resource Management'. *Environment and Development Economics*, 10: 1–25.

—— and Lovett, J. C. (2006a). 'Transaction Costs and Community-based Natural Resource Management in Nepal'. *Journal of Environmental Management*, 78: 5–15.

—— —— (2006b). 'Institutions and Collective Action: Does Heterogeneity Matter in Community-based Resource Management?' *Journal of Development Studies*, 42/3: 426–45.

Aggrawal, R. M. (2000). 'Possibilities and Limitations to Cooperation in Small Groups: The Case of Group-owned Wells in Southern India'. *World Development*, 28/8: 1481–97.

Agrawal, A. (2001). 'Commons Property Institutions and Sustainable Governance of Resources'. *World Development*, 29/10: 1649–72.

Alesina, A., and La Ferrara, E. (2002). 'Who Trusts Others?' *Journal of Public Economics*, 85: 207–34.

Baral, J. C. (1999). 'Community Intervention and Local Processes in Community Forestry in the Hills of Nepal'. Ph.D. Dissertation. Australian National University, Canberra.

Bardhan, P. (1993). 'Symposium on Management of Local Commons'. *Journal of Economic Perspectives*, 7/4: 87–92.

—— and Dayton-Johnson, J. (2000). 'Heterogeneity and Commons Management'. Unpublished Manuscript, Department of Economics, University of California, Berkeley, Mimeo.

Bromley, D. W., and Cernea, M. M. (1989). 'The Management of Common Property Resources: Some Conceptual and Operational Fallacies'. World Bank Discussion Paper no. 57. Washington, DC: The World Bank.

Coase, R. (1937). 'The Nature of the Firm'. *Economica*, 16: 386–406.

—— (1960). 'The Problem of Social Cost'. *Journal of Law and Economics*, 3: 1–44.

Coleman, J. S. (1990). *Foundations of Social Theory*. Cambridge, UK: Harvard University Press.

Collett, G., Chhetri, R., Jackson, W. J., and Shepherd, K. R. (1996). 'Nepal Australia Community Forestry Project: Socio-Economic Impact Study'. ANUTECH, Canberra, Australia.

Cornes, R., Mason, C. F., and Sandler, T. (1986). 'The Commons and the Optimal Number of Firms'. *Quarterly Journal of Economics*, 101: 641–6.

Dahlman, C. J. (1979). 'The Problem of Externality'. *Journal of Laws and Economics*, 22: 141–62.

Davies, J., and Richards, M. (1999). 'The Use of Economics to Assess Stakeholders' Incentives in Participatory Forest Management'. European Union Tropical Forestry Paper 5. London: Overseas Development Institute.

Dayton-Johnson, J. (2000). 'Determinants of Collective Action on the Local Commons: A Model with Evidence from Mexico'. *Journal of Development Economics*, 62: 181–208.

Folbre, N. (1994). *Who Pays for the Kids: Gender and the Structures of Constraint*. New York: Routledge.

Furubotn, E. G., and Richter, R. (1997). *Institution and Economic Theory: The Contribution of the New Institutional Economics*. Ann Arbor, MI: University of Michigan Press.

Gilmour, D. A., King, G. C., and Hobley, M. (1989). 'Management of Forests for Local Use in the Hills of Nepal. 1. Changing Forest Management Paradigms'. *World Forest Resource Management*, 4: 93–110.

Hanna, S. (1998a). 'Co-management in Small-scale Fisheries: Creating Effective Links among Stakeholders'. Plenary Presentation, International CBNRM Workshop, Washington DC, 10–14 May.

—— (1998b). 'Managing for Human and Ecological Context in the Maine Soft Shell Clam Fishery', in F. Berkes and C. Folke (eds.), *Linking Social and Ecological Systems: Management Practices and Social Mechanisms for Building Resilience*. Cambridge: Cambridge University Press, 190–211.

—— and Munasinghe, M. (1995). 'An Introduction to Property Rights in a Social and Ecological Context', in S. Hanna and M. Munasinghe (eds.), *Property Rights and the Environment: Social and Ecological Issues*. Washington, DC: The Beijer Institute of Ecological Economics and the World Bank, 3–11.

Heltberg, R. (2002). 'Property Rights and Natural Resource Management in the Developing Countries'. *Journal of Economic Surveys*, 16/2: 189–214.

Hetcher, A. (1990). 'The Attainment of Solidarity in Intentional Communities'. *Rationality and Society*, 2/2: 142–55.

HM Government of Nepal/Master Plan for Forestry Sector (1988). 'Master Plan for Forestry Sector in Nepal: Main Document'. Ministry of Forest and Soil Conservation, Baber Mahal, Kathmandu, Nepal.

Holden, S., Shiferaw, B., and Wik, M. (1998). 'Poverty, Market Imperfections and Time Preferences: Of Relevance for Environmental Policy?'. *Environment and Development Economics*, 3: 105–30.

Kant, S., and Berry, R. A. (2001). 'A Theoretical Model of Optimal Forest Resource Regimes in Developing Economies'. *Journal of Institutional and Theoretical Economics*, 157/2: 331–55.

Kuperan, K., Mustapha, N., Abdullah, R., Pomeroy, R., Genio, E., and Salamanca, A. (1998). 'Measuring Transaction Costs of Fisheries Co-management'. Paper presented at the 7th Biennial Conference of the International Association for the Study of Common Property, Vancouver, Canada. <http://www.indiana.edu/~iasap/Drafts/Kuperan.pdf>.

Lanzona, L., and Evenson, R. E. (1997). 'The Effects of Transaction Costs on Labor Market Participation and Earnings: Evidence from Rural Philippine Markets'. Centre Discussion Paper No. 790, Economic Growth Centre, Yale University, New Haven, CT.

Libecap, G. (2002). 'Transaction Costs and Institutional Responses to the Common Pool'. Paper presented at the Coase Institute's Workshop on Institutional Analysis, Cambridge, MA, 22–7 September 2002.

Lubell, M. (2005). 'Do Watershed Partnerships Enhance Beliefs Conducive to Collective Action?' in P. Sabatier, W. Focht, M. Lubell, Z. Trachtenberg, A. Vedlitz, and M. Matlock (eds.), *Swimming Upstream: Collaborative Approaches to Watershed Management* (American and Comparative Environmental Series). Cambridge, MA: MIT Press, 201–32.

Mburu, J., Birner, R., and Zeller, M. (2003). 'Relative Importance and Determinants of Landowner's Transaction Costs in Collaborative Wildlife Management in Kenya: An Empirical Analysis'. *Ecological Economics*, 45: 59–73.

Molians, J. R. (1998). 'The Impact of Inequality, Gender, External Assistance and Social Capital on Local-level Collective Action'. *World Development*, 26/3: 413–31.

Nightingale, A. J. (2002). 'Participating or Just Sitting In? The Dynamics of Gender and Caste in Community Forestry'. *Journal of Forestry and Livelihood*, 2/1: 17–24.

North, D. C. (1989). *Institutions, Institutional Change, and Economic Performance*. New York: Cambridge University Press.

—— (1990). *Institutions, Institutional Change and Economic Performance*. Cambridge: Cambridge University Press.

Nugent, J. B. (1993). 'Between State, Markets and Households: A Neo-institutional Analysis of Local Organizations and Institutions'. *World Development*, 21/4: 623–32.

Oakerson, R. J. (1992). 'Analyzing the Commons: A Framework', in D. W. Bromley (ed.), *Making the Commons Work: Theory, Practice, and Policy*. San Francisco, CA: ICS Press.

Olson, M. (1965). *The Logic of Collective Action: Public Goods and the Theory of Groups*. Cambridge, UK: Harvard University Press.

Ostrom, E. (1990). *Governing the Commons*. Cambridge: Cambridge University Press.

—— (2002). 'Type of Good and Collective Action'. Paper presented at the University of Maryland, Collective Choice Center in Honor of Mancur Olson. Center for the Study of Institutions, Population, and Environmental Change, Indiana University, Bloomington, IN, 22 February 2002, 27–8.

Pearce, D., and Turner, R. K. (1990). *Economics of Natural Resources and the Environment*. Hemel Hempstead: Harvester Wheatsheaf.

Putnam, R. (1993). *Making Democracy Work: Civic Traditions in Modern Italy*. Princeton, NJ: Princeton University Press.

Richards, M., Kanel, K., Maharjan, M., and Davies, J. (1999) 'Towards Participatory Economic Analysis by Forest User Groups in Nepal'. ODI, Portland House, Stag Place, London.

Seabright, P. (1993). 'Managing Local Commons: Theoretical Issues in Incentive Design'. *Journal of Economic Perspective*, 7/4: 113–34.

Somanathan, E., Prabhakar, R., and Mehta, B. S. (2006). 'Collective Action for Forest Conservation: Does Heterogeneity Matter?', in J. Baland, P. Bardhan, and S. Bowles (eds.), *Inequality, Cooperation, and Environmental Sustainability*. Princeton, NJ: Princeton University Press, 234–45.

Tang, S. Y. (1991). 'Institutional Arrangements and the Management of Common-pool Resources'. *Public Administration Review*, 51/1: 42–51.

Varughese, J., and Ostrom, E. (2001). 'The Contested Role of Heterogeneity in Collective Action: Some Evidence from Community Forestry in Nepal'. *World Development*, 29: 747–65.

Wade, R. (1988). *Village Republics: Economic Conditions for Collective Action in South India*. Cambridge: Cambridge University Press.

Wallis, J. J., and North, D. C. (1986). 'Measuring the Transaction Sector in the American Economy 1870–1970', in S. L. Engerman and R. E. Gallman (eds.), *Long-Term Factors in American Economic Growth*. Chicago, IL: University of Chicago Press, 95–161.

Zak, P. J., and Knack, S. (2001). 'Trust and Growth'. *The Economic Journal*, 111/470: 295–321.

11

Who Pays for Conservation: Evidence from Forestry in Nepal

Arun Khatri-Chhetri

11.1. Introduction

The agrarian economy of the rural communities in Nepal is well integrated with forest-resource use. A majority of the rural households are subsistence farmers and rely on forest products for meeting their daily requirements. Fuelwood is used for cooking and heating purposes, fodder and grass for livestock, leaf-litter for manure, and timber for constructing houses and for making agricultural implements. In addition, households seasonally collect other forest products such as wild foods, fruits, vegetables, resins, wax, etc. These products are a critical part of rural consumption strategies.

In recent years, forests have been recognized as rich reservoirs of not just timber but other valuable biological resources. A growing body of scientific study has suggested that, given certain basic conditions, non-timber forest products (NTFPs) can help communities meet their needs without destroying the forest resources (Peter, Gentry, and Mendelsohn 1989; Gunatilake 1998). Furthermore, rights to forest resources are particularly important for poor people in many developing countries because the poor have no capital and few productive assets (Sterner 2003). Access to commons, or even to degraded open-access areas, may constitute a significant, even crucial, contribution to their welfare. Cavendish's (2000) study from Zimbabwe, for example, shows that environmental resources in some rural areas account for more than 40 per cent of the average total household income and that the poorer the household the greater the share of income from these resources. This is partly due to the fact that they are more likely to be dependent on forest resources for their livelihood. Unlike Cavendish's study, Gupta, Urvashi, and van Klaas (2005) argue that poor households are not necessarily more dependent on natural resources than are the rich: dependence may decline at first but then increases with an increase in income, especially in areas where forests are abundant and grasslands are well stocked.

On the other hand, the importance of local institutions[1] in forest-resource management is widely recognized and has become a part of the forest management policy in many countries. In Nepal, as in other developing countries, the development of community-based resource management has led to decentralization of forest management from centralized government control to local forest user groups (FUGs). Within the framework of the community forestry project, implemented by the government with support from several international donor agencies, the acreage of forests officially managed through local institutions is expanding, especially in the hilly areas of Nepal. So far, in Nepal, 1.1 million hectares of forest (about 25 per cent of the national forest area) has been handed over to more than 13,000 community forest user groups involving 1.4 million households (Kanel 2004). This movement towards decentralization of forest-resource control and management promises more efficient, equitable, and sustainable resource use (Hobley and Shah 1996). In terms of governance reform and the coverage of the community forestry project, success has been dramatic. However, there are still many challenges related to equity, livelihoods, and sustainability of forest management (Pokharel 2002; Adhikari 2003). Given the critical role that forests play in Nepalese rural livelihoods, it is becoming increasingly necessary to evaluate the impact of these new management approaches. It is certainly not clear whether the proposed forest reforms would result in improved forest access to low-income people.

Some studies (Arnold and Campbell 1986; Campbell, Shrestha, and Euphrat 1987) have tried to figure out the role of local communities in the protection of forests when there is no government intervention. Fisher *et al.* (1989) and Gilmour and Fisher (1991) have attempted to analyse some of the features of the indigenous systems of forest management and their relevance to forest management policy. Since the launch of the community forestry programme, reforestation work has mostly emphasized timber-oriented tree plantations, which have helped to increase the physical stocks of trees in the forests (Branney, King, and Malla 1994). But some studies in community forestry (Maharjan 1998; Ojha 2000; Bhattrai and Ojha 2001; Adhikari 2003) have argued that restrictions limited the year-round extraction of NTFPs and, moreover, that there is unequal distribution of benefits from community forests. Despite a few studies on indigenous forest management and income distribution due to community forestry, little attention has been paid to the

---

[1] In this paper, 'institutions' refer to rules that individuals use to order interactions affecting themselves and, possibly, others. A forest management institution is basically the set of working rules formally or informally adhered to by individuals and/or a group of users for long-term (managed) procurement of products from a particular forest (Ostrom 1990).

differences in forest management and in benefit distribution under different institutional management systems.

This study seeks to understand the implications of local institutions for forest products extraction and benefit distribution among users. In particular, it examines NTFP extraction in two communities: the first, a government-sponsored formal forest user group and the other a self-initiated informal forest user group. The key questions addressed in this paper are: (*a*) what are the rules and regulations of NTFP extraction in the two types of forest management systems? (*b*) how and to what extent does NTFP use differ among the households? and (*c*) what socio-economic and institutional factors are correlated in the perceived differences with regard to NTFP extraction?

This chapter is clearly interrelated with other chapters in this book. The government intervention in community-based forest-resource management and its outcomes over time in the context of Nepal is discussed by Keshav Kanel. He points out the second-generation reform issues in Nepal's community forestry programme. The theoretical concept related to inequalities in the distribution of benefit from CPR is well discussed by Partha Dasgupta. The inequality in benefit distribution within groups can emerge even in circumstances that are symmetric in private resource distribution. The example of herdsmen and their discount rate of future profits indicate how inequality occurs in CPR use. Rucha Ghate's chapter discusses the evolution of different types of local forest management institutions. The role of the state is important in the long-term sustainability of the self-initiated community forest management system. Ghate discusses in detail what role the state can play and how the state can play a significant role. The present chapter therefore concentrates more on benefit distribution in different types of institutional regimes using two case studies in the same locality as its basis.

The chapter is organized as follows. The following section reviews some of the literature on forest resources and institutional change. Section 11.3 briefly discusses local forest user groups in Nepal. Section 11.4 includes a description of the study site and data extraction methods. Sections 11.5 and 11.6 present the results and discussion. Section 11.8 concludes the chapter and offers recommendations.

11.2. Forest resources and institutional change

Since the publication of Garrett Hardin's influential article 'The Tragedy of Commons' in 1968, there has been an increase in interest in common property resource management. In the absence of property rights, no individual bears the full cost of resource degradation and the result is 'free-riding' and overexploitation (Hardin 1968). Different opinions emerge from the literature on common property in relation to institutional arrangements in order to avoid the tragedy of the commons. Hardin (1968) recommended that 'state control' is a must to prevent the degradation and destruction of natural resources. Other scholars have recommended privatizing the resources to solve the problem of overexploitation and degradation (Johnson 1972; Smith 1981). However, research in the late 1980s showed that local forest management systems, based on indigenous organizations and decentralized collective management by users, could avoid the tragedy of the commons (Arnold and Campbell 1986; Jodha 1986; Fisher 1989; Chopra, Kadekodi, and Murthy 1990) that Hardin had spoken of.

It is becoming increasingly clear that local communities both filter and ignore the central government's rules. More importantly, they also add their own rules, generating local institutions/rules that in use and patterns of activity diverge widely from the legislator's and bureaucrat's expectations (Gibson, McKean, and Ostrom 1998). According to Ostrom (1990), if resource users have the right to devise their own institutions without being challenged by external authorities, they will enforce the rules themselves and will permit the development of their own internal governance mechanisms and formulas so that they are able to allocate costs and benefits to members. On the other hand, local communities living with forests are the primary users of forest products, and create rules that significantly affect forest condition. Hence, their inclusion in forest management schemes is now considered essential by many researchers and policymakers (Arnold 1992).

Recently, there has been growing interest in the decentralization of forest-resource management. The promotion of decentralization can be traced to awareness of the numerous problems associated with state-centric institutions for forest-resource management (Bray *et al.* 2003). The governments of developing countries and international donor agencies are now looking for ways to reduce the cost of delivering services by transferring more management responsibilities to communities. At the same time, communities are demanding greater control over local resources. This 'push' by governments and 'pull' by communities are seen to varying degrees in common resource management throughout the world.

Nepal is a prominent example of institutional change when it comes to forest-resource management in South Asia. The history of forest policy in Nepal can be seen as a shift from privatization to nationalization and then decentralization of forest management responsibility to local communities. With the emergence of nationalization, although new forestry systems were established, they created gaps in relation to pre-existing indigenous forestry (Wakiyama 2004). Consequently, the impact of the policy change appeared negatively, resulting in deteriorating forest conditions and livelihoods of the poor due to the lack of support from local people. Later on, recognizing the effectiveness and benefits of forest management by local communities, community participation in forest management came to be entertained

(Brown *et al.* 2002). The forest management policies in Nepal have gone through a variety of transformations, including the establishment of large protected area networks, and the initiation of community forestry, leasehold forestry, and park buffer-zone management programmes in the mid-1990s (Agrawal, Britt, and Kanel 1999). In 1993, the government of Nepal passed the Forest Act to transfer all accessible forestland from the government to the local communities through the formation of forest user groups. Since the 1990s, community forestry has gained higher priority in forest management policy. This change in policy was the result of the government's realization that forests cannot be managed without the cooperation of local communities (Shrestha 1996). Furthermore, the development of community forestry was introduced along with reconsideration of and studies on the effectiveness of the indigenous forest management system (K. Gautam 1991).

The decentralization of forest-resource management helped establish local institutions in areas where either the indigenous forest management system had been dissolved by the impact of nationalization, or where the local people had not formulated any institutional arrangement (Wakiyama 2004). Furthermore, many indigenous forests were transformed to formal community forests due to the government's vested interest in community forestry. In areas where local institutions were absent, community forestry programmes helped to create a new institution and to fill the institutional gap. But there was to also often the danger of destroying indigenous systems where these institutions had been operating for a long time, in the process of creating new institutions (K. Gautam 1991). In order to enhance local management of forest resources, we first need to know what institutional set-up already exists and how they manage and use forest resources (Gilmour and Fisher 1991). The question of whether government-sponsored community forestry is better than indigenous and other types of forest management systems is still open to debate.

There is limited empirical evidence to support the hypothesis that forest resources are more efficiently managed under the government's community forestry schemes relative to other management systems. Several studies have reported that forest cover and biophysical conditions have improved in many places under the protection and care of community forest user groups, thereby providing economic benefits to the local people (Jackson *et al.* 1998; Webb and A. Gautam 2001; A. Gautam, Webb, and Shivakoti 2002; A. Gautam, Shivakoti, and Webb 2004). Few studies have tried to argue the benefit distribution issue in community forestry (Bhattrai and Ojha 2001; Edmonds 2002; Adhikari 2003). Not much attention has been paid to the institutional difference in forest-resource extraction and benefit distribution at the local level also. The present study seeks to bridge this gap in understanding the effects of different community-based institutions when it comes to forest products extraction.

11.3. Forest user groups in local communities

Indigenous and government-sponsored community forest user groups are the main local-level forest management institutions in Nepal. Alternatively these groups are called informal and formal forest user groups based on legal registration at the District Forest Office. The primary distinction between formal community forests and indigenous is that the forest user committee of a formal community forest is recognized and sponsored by the state. Regardless of their legal title, however, indigenous forests are treated by the local people as a common property resource and are referred to as *hamro ban* (our forest). Community-level indigenous forest management institutions have evolved in the course of time without inputs from outside by way of imposition, inducement, or extension (K. Gautam 1991). Under indigenous forestry, local knowledge is fully utilized and villagers formulate new rules and regulations based on past experience as and when necessary (Agrawal 1995). This system combines traditional authority and in order to organize informal institutions. Households cooperate in such a way that individuals manage and minimize damage to the resources they rely on in order to meet their long-term needs (Soussan, Shrestha, and Uprety 1995). These forests are mostly located near the settlements so that control of compliance with community rules becomes relatively easy.

Government-initiated community forests are national forests handed over to the user groups for conservation, development, and utilization for collective benefit. This is a result of the government's recognition that participation in forest management by forest users who customarily hold *de facto* user rights should be prioritized (Timsina 2002). A prerequisite for a formal FUG is an operational plan approved by the District Forest Officer (DFO), which serves as a contract between the Forest Department (FD) and local users. The forest users prepare this plan in collaboration with forest officials. An important feature is the establishment of a village-level forest user committee, which is authorized to implement forest management and to distribute or sell forest products. They are fully legitimized as an autonomous institution within the local community. In the government-initiated community forest, villagers only have access to forest products. The forestland remains state-owned. Thus, the villagers' access to forest resources is not total.

11.4. Study site and data collection

This study was undertaken in the year 2003 in the Pyuthan District of Nepal which is located in the middle mountain region. Of the total land area in the district, 34 per cent is cultivated land, 59 per cent is forestland, while 7 per cent is other land, which includes degraded pastureland. More than

48 percent of the total forest area in the district is under government-initiated community-based forest management. There are some 280 FUGs within the district who manage these forests. Agriculture is the main occupation of households and the forest is an indispensable resource for the farming system. Among the households' main income sources are: crop cultivation, livestock-raising, off-farm income through agriculture, non-agricultural labour within village and district, government service, and seasonal out-migration for labour work. NTFPs found in the study area include a considerable variety of wild foods, medicinal plants, fuelwoods, fodder, grasses, thatch grass, leaf-litter, and so on. The NTFPs are collected from common forests as well as private lands. Caste and ethnic diversity is also high in the study area with people belonging to the upper castes such as *brahmin, chhetri, magar,* and *gurung* and lower caste such as *damai, kami, sarki,* and *sunar.* The dependence on agriculture and forest resources, the presence of community forestry, and the harvesting of domestic and commercially valuable NTFPs from different institutional regimes make Pyuthan District a suitable study area.

This chapter is based on detailed analyses of two types of community-based forest management institutions. The two villages selected were Chuja with government sponsored formal FUG and Gobanpani with self-initiated informal FUG. The communities were identified on the basis of common use rights to a particular patch of forest. Generally, specific *toles* (hamlets) can use specific patches of forest. The first village, Chuja, with the formal FUG is within 5 km of the district headquarters. The second village, Gobanpani with the informal FUG is more remote, located at 18 km from the district headquarters.

Before the questionnaire survey, households were stratified into large, medium, and small based on the landholding size of households. Small, medium, and large households own 5 *ropani,*[2] 5.1–10 *ropani,* and above 10 *ropani* respectively. The income level and incidence of poverty is highly correlated with landholding size in Nepal. The average household income of large landholders is almost double that of smallholders and the incidence of poverty is very much concentrated among the small landholders (NRB 1988; Sharma and Chhetry 1996). Therefore, stratification of households based on the landholding size in rural areas reflects a household's wealth level.

Primary data on the collection and use of forest products were gathered through a questionnaire survey of one hundred households in the two communities. In the total sample, 50 per cent of respondents were from the formal FUG while the remaining 50 per cent were from the informal community forest user group. The small, medium, and large landholders were thirty-five,

---

[2] One hectare = 19.79 *ropani.*

thirty-four, and thirty-one respectively. Households collected NTFPs from both private forest and common forests. During data collection, questionnaires were designed to separate the collection of forest products from the different types of forests within the household.

Before the household survey, a checklist of all potential NTFPs was prepared to avoid underestimation of harvested NTFPs. Standardization of local units (for example, *doko, muri, pathi, mana, dharni*) was also done during the household survey. The NTFPs include tree and grass fodder, roots, stems, bark and leaf of medicinal plants, wild vegetables, fruits, leaf-litter, etc. Household-level data also includes production, income, and consumption expenditure.

To determine the contribution and distribution of NTFP income among the forest users, the households' incomes were calculated according to economic activities. Household income sources were grouped into five major sources, namely, (*a*) income from agriculture; (*b*) income from livestock; (*c*) income from private forest; (*d*) off-farm income; and (*e*) income from common property resource extraction.

- Income from agriculture: To calculate agriculture income, information on different crops cultivated by each household in one year, area, and output was collected. The households for this study were mostly small-scale farmers producing primarily for home consumption. Most of the inputs are self-supplied. Households rarely hire a labour force or purchase other inputs such as seeds, fertilizer, manure, and pesticides for agriculture production. However, labour exchange practices were common. To avoid the miscalculation of partially applied labour force and difficulty in recalling the exact number of labourers used during cropping time, the gross value of agriculture output was calculated based on the output data.

- Income from livestock: The major livestock in the study area were cattle, buffalo, goat, sheep, and poultry. The total income from livestock includes the value of milk, eggs, as well as animals sold and self-consumed. Livestock dung was excluded to avoid double counting because all households used dung in agriculture production. Labour hiring for livestock rearing was not a practice in this area. Inputs for livestock were self-supplied and were collected from the forests.

- Income from private forest: Households use most of the outputs derived from the private forest in livestock and agricultural production. Income from the private forest includes the sale of highly valuable commercial NTFPs and timber, excluding subsistence use for livestock and agriculture production. Commercially valuable NTFPs such as *timur (Zanthoxylum aramatum), dalchini (Cinnamomum tamala), rittha (Sapindus mukorossi)*, and *chiuri (Bassia butyracea)* were collected from private lands.

- Off-farm income: In this study, income from wage labour, professional work (teaching, government and non-government employment), remittance, and pensions are included as off-farm income. Only a few households were found to be involved in business.

- Income from common property resource extraction: Households in the study areas collect (*a*) dry wood for fuel; (*b*) grass, leaf-fodder, and leaf-litter for livestock; (*c*) thatch grass for roof construction; and (*d*) medicinal herbs and plants. Among these NTFPs, firewood, grass, leaf-fodder, leaf-litter, and thatch grass contribute significantly to the household economy. For the majority of households, the income from NTFP extraction was the sum of the value of these NTFPs.

- Calculation of the gross and net value of NTFPs from the CPR: Gross income from the NTFPs was calculated by multiplying the total quantity of NTFPs collected for twelve months by their respective prices. The potential problem for valuation was that many NTFPs were not traded in formal markets. Instead, they were traded or bartered locally. To value the forest products, different methods of NTFP valuation were used. The valuation of fuelwood and thatch grass was done based on the market prices of these products. Leaf-litter, fodder, and grass were non-marketed NTFPs but it was found that some households barter fodder and grass for food grain. To value the leaf-litter, the willingness-to-pay method was used. A question like how much money or food grain will you pay for a particular amount of leaf-litter was posed to the respondents. All the NTFPs were valued based on the average reported price of particular products. The net income from NTFP was calculated by deducting all cash and labour costs, including the cost of tools and equipment used in the extraction of NTFPs. The net return is the gross value of NTFPs minus all costs except the value of household labour. The total cost includes the labour cost of time directly associated to reach the forest, the extraction and transportation of NTFP from the forest to the house, the cost of tools and equipment, the cost of monitoring and other mandatory activities, mainly tree plantation, and the clearing of unwanted bushes.

11.5. Results and discussion

11.5.1. *Characteristics of households in the two communities*

The households included for this study are mostly small-scale farm households producing all crops and livestock products for home consumption. Maize, rice, wheat, barley, buckwheat, and finger millet are the principal crops in the region. In the first village with the formal FUG, 82 per cent of

Table 11.1. Descriptive statistics

Variables	Formal FUG (mean value)	Informal FUG (mean value)	Mean difference
Education of household members (years of schooling)	5.72	1.58	4.14 (3.51)
Age of household head (years)	41.34	48.75	−7.41 (3.20)
Household size (number)	6.80	6.92	−0.12 (0.21)
Total landholding (*ropani*)	15.88	9.80	6.08 (1.95)
Irrigated landholding (*ropani*)	2.26	1.04	1.22 (1.52)
Non-irrigated landholding (*ropani*)	5.83	5.20	0.63 (0.48)
Land under private forest (*ropani*)	7.87	3.58	4.29 (2.86)
Total livestock holding (cattle equivalent)	4.80	6.43	−1.63 (2.12)
Distance to nearest market (km)	5.08	8.36	−3.28 (7.39)
Distance to community forest (km)	2.35	2.40	−0.05 (0.20)

Note: Figures in parentheses are t-values.

the households are upper caste[3] (*brahmin* and *chhetri*) while only 18 per cent are ethnic groups[4] (*gurung* and *magar*), occupational,[5] or so-called lower castes (*kami, sunar, damai,* and *sarki*). In the case of the second village with the informal FUG, 20 per cent of households are *brahmin* and *chhetri* while 42 per cent are ethnic groups and 38 per cent are occupational castes. In the total sample, 51 per cent of the households are *brahmin* and *chhetri*, 23 per cent *gurung/magar*, and 26 per cent are occupational/lower caste. Sixty-two per cent of household heads are literate in the formal FUG area whereas in the informal FUG only 11 per cent are literate which is fairly low. The average year of schooling of household heads in the formal FUG area is lower secondary level while in the informal FUG this is only primary level. In the total sampled households, only 42 per cent of household heads are literate (Table 11.1).

The average household size is 6.80 and 6.92 in the formal and informal FUG areas respectively. The farmland may be divided into three types: low-land (*khet*), which is irrigated and usually found in valley bottoms, upland (*pakho*), which consists of hillside terraces without irrigation, and private forest (*khoriya*), which is non-cultivated slope and terrace land with fodder-trees, grass, timber, and other NTFPs. The community forestry area with the formal FUG seems to be better off in terms of total landholding, areas under

[3] An integral aspect of the Nepalese society is the existence of the Hindu caste system, modelled after the ancient and orthodox Brahmanism of the Indian plains. Its establishment became the basis of the emergence of the feudalistic economic structure of Nepal with the upper-caste Hindus appropriating lands—particularly lowlands that were more easily accessible, more cultivatable, and more productive.

[4] Ethnic groups share a common origin and are readily distinguishable by outsiders based on traits originating from a common racial, linguistic, or religious source.

[5] The occupational caste—also known as *dalits* or untouchable—is a group of people outside the four castes (*bahun, chhetri, baisya, sudra*), and are considered to be below the latter in status.

irrigation, and private forest. The average total landholding in the formal FUG area is 6.08 *ropani* higher than in the case of the informal FUG area. Similarly, more land is under private forest in the formal FUG area. But the livestock-holding size is higher in the informal FUG area as compared to the formal FUG area.

Most households own some combination of cattle, goat, sheep, buffaloes, and a small number of chickens. For purposes of this study, livestock ownership is computed in terms of livestock units calibrated in cattle equivalents.[6] Households often stall-feed their livestock in the formal FUG area due to restrictions on grazing in the community forest. But, in the case of the informal FUG area, grazing is free throughout the year. The distance to the nearest market from the formal FUG area is less than in the case of the informal FUG area. The distance to the community forest is higher in the informal FUG area. The one-way ANOVA indicates that the four wealth groups (lower 25 per cent, 25–50 per cent, 50–75 per cent, and top 25 per cent) significantly differ in terms of different types of land and livestock holding.

11.5.2. *Institutional arrangement and forest products extraction*

Tables 11.2 and 11.3 present the institutional arrangements in the two types of forest management systems based on the discussion with the villagers. In the informal FUG village, the institution has evolved through the passage of time and due to the self-realization of villagers about the importance of protecting the forest. The customary rights of the users were recognized and identified in the indigenous system, and later legalized with indigenous codes.[7] In the formal FUG, Forest Department officials insisted on formulating and registering the FUG in the District Forest Office. The formal FUG controls and manages the local forests, including independent harvesting and pricing of all forest products while forest management is governed by an executive committee elected in the FUG assembly. In this study, both the informal and formal committees were led by local elites. This suggests that in the formation of local-level forest management institutions, whether formal or informal, local elites play a bigger role than others.

The extraction of forest products differs based on institutional regimes. Before community forestry, state-owned forests were utilized often on the basis of open access to collect NTFPs. In the formal FUG-managed forest, access rules (flow management) and conservation rules (stock management)

---

[6] Buffalo and Cattle = 1 LSU, 1 Sheep and Goat = 0.2 LSU, 1 Poultry = 0.01 LSU according to the Central Bureau of Statistics of Nepal.

[7] The indigenous code refers to the rules and regulations concerning forest-resource management and use, at least in nominated areas, that were developed based on local people's long experience (K. Gautam 1991).

Table 11.2. Institutional arrangements in two types of forest management system

	Informal FUG	Formal FUG
Institution		
Formation	Villagers' initiation and self-organization	Government's intervention and sponsorship
Process	*Self-realization to protect the forest *Control in collection and breakdown of rules took place continuously in the formation of self-organization	*Forest department officials' influence to make formal FUG. *Local elites and forest official developed village-level forest management committee in consultation
Committee	*Unofficial committee, led by village's most influential person, meeting when somebody breaks a rule.	*Officially registered 9 member committee, led by local elite and formal meeting every month.
Rules and regulation		
Characteristics	*Unwritten rules (norms and codes) developed through the passage of time. *Customary law	*Official documents (developed through consultation between villagers and forest officials. *Statute law
Management	*All villagers, as residents in the community.	*All villagers, as members of a formal institution.
Legitimacy	*No legal right to collection and sale of forest products *Informal cooperation between villagers and local forest officials	*Legal right to collection and sale of forest products *Formal cooperation between District Forest Office and FUG

are defined during FUG registration at the district forest office. Management practices mostly consist of control when it comes to the extraction of timber and NTFPs through the definition and control of user rights. In such cases, only the members of a forest user group are allowed to extract NTFPs. Other people living in the area regard these rights as legitimate. The user groups can

Table 11.3. Rules and regulations in forest products extraction and management

Rules and regulations	Formal FUG		Informal FUG	
	NTFPs	Timber	NTFPs	Timber
Quantity restriction	Limited through number and period of entry	FUG have legal right to cut and sell	No restriction	FUG have no legal right to cut and sell
Entry fees	NRs. 5/person/day	No fees	No fee	—
Monitoring	Watchman and villagers		Watchman	
Organizing investment for maintenance and conservation	Low	High	Low	Low
Payment for watchman	By FUG from collected fund		Agricultural products by all users	

decide to close NTFP extraction for a certain period. In such instances, it is the forest user committee that fixes the opening date.

In addition, the FUG can formulate regulations on extraction techniques in order to enhance regeneration and production of NTFPs, for example, by prohibiting branch lopping and uprooting. The extraction time in the FUG-managed forests is short, as the largest quantity is collected on the opening days. Only a limited number of members of each household can obtain admission to the forest after paying a fee to the committee. The user group committee has the right to decide on the punishment for illegal extraction of forest products and the cutting of trees and poles. Watchmen, employed by the FUG, always monitor the forest and receive monthly payments from the FUG. As a result of the harvesting rules and regulations, resource stock management in community forestry is better. But the extraction ban for seasonally regenerated NTFPs from the natural forest is an important issue in community forests managed by the formal FUG.

In the case of forest management with the informal FUG, excepting restrictions on timber and green fuelwood extraction, NTFP extraction is free and open throughout the year. Villagers employ a forest watchman, who is responsible for patrolling the forest and controlling access to the extraction and cutting of timber and green fuelwood, and for excluding outsiders according to the rules set up by the user group committee. He collects seasonal agricultural products from every household as payment. One important difference between the two forest management institutions is that in the formal FUG they have the legal right to cut and sell the timber in the future whereas it is not legal in the case of the informal FUG-managed forest.

11.5.3. *Economic activities and household income*

Table 11.4 shows various income sources in the sample households in the two different forest users and wealth groups. The off-farm income source is the most important activity in both communities that contributes 55 per cent and 62 per cent in the formal and informal FUG areas respectively. This income source includes skilled and unskilled wage labour, services in government and non-government offices, remittances, and small business. Seasonal and year-round out-migration within districts and outside district was common in both areas. In most of the surveyed households, one or two adult men out-migrated to earn money, particularly to India. The second and third important sources are agriculture and livestock farming in the formal FUG area whereas livestock is the second important income source in the informal FUG areas. It is interesting to note that the livestock income in both villages follows an inverted-U curve relative to wealth. In other words, as wealth increases livestock income increases for the middle two wealth categories but then decreases for the highest wealth category.

Table 11.4. Annual average income by economic activity and wealth group (Nepalese rupees)

Variables	Average total income	Wealth groups			
		Lowest 25%	25–50%	50–75%	Top 25%
Community forest (Formal FUG)					
Average income from agriculture	16,138 (23.80)	6,750 (17.81)	13,825 (33.04)	13,133 (20.89)	30,434 (24.05)
Average income from livestock	7,667 (11.30)	3,732 (9.85)	6,835 (16.33)	8,002 (12.72)	12,062 (9.53)
Average off-farm income	42,066 (62.04)	25,912 (68.40)	19,992 (47.78)	39,280 (62.48)	81,170 (64.14)
Commercial NTFP income[1] (private land)	1,927 (2.84)	1,487 (3.92)	1,183 (2.82)	2,445 (3.88)	2,878 (2.27)
Community forest (Informal FUG)					
Average income from agriculture	5,908 (17.34)	2,533 (15.88)	5,498 (16.14)	6,821 (14.44)	8,817 (17.71)
Average income from livestock	7,228 (21.26)	2,497 (15.65)	7,624 (22.38)	10,975 (23.24)	8,136 (16.35)
Average off-farm income	17,830 (52.46)	8,769 (54.98)	17,417 (51.14)	27,350 (54.93)	18,487 (57.24)
Commercial NTFP income (private land)	3,020 (8.88)	2,148 (13.48)	3,513 (10.31)	2,063 (4.36)	4,320 (8.64)

[1] Income derived from selling forest products from private forest (excluding subsistence use). Percentage income from each activity to total income in parenthesis. 1US$ = 75.00 Nepalese Rupees

In the study areas, some commercially valuable NTFPs were found in abundance in common forests a few years ago. However, as marketing agents started visiting villages to collect more NTFPs and paying a high price, these valuable NTFPs more or less disappeared from the forests because local people were encouraged to extract more NTFPs from the common forest. During this process, a gradual transition from extraction of NTFPs from common forests to purposeful cultivation of NTFPs in private lands took place. Significant amounts of commercially valuable NTFPs are now collected and sold from private lands. A large proportion of the income is derived from selling commercial NTFPs such as *timur* (*Zanthoxylum aramatum*), *dalchini* (*Cinnamomum tamala*), *rittha* (*Sapindus mukorossi*), and *chiuri* (*Bassia butyracea*).

11.6. Value of NTFPs collected from the forest

Among all NTFPs, fodder, grass, leaf-litter, and fuelwood extraction from the common forest are significant. Fodder, grass, and leaf-litter do not provide direct cash income but have a crucial role to play in the farming system. Fuelwood is mostly used for cooking and heating purposes and some households generate cash by selling fuelwood to the nearby market. Other NTFPs such as wild fruits and vegetables are collected in small amounts in the different seasons for home consumption.

Table 11.5 shows the average annual value of NTFP extraction from the two types of forest. As the table demonstrates, all wealth groups commonly rely on the local forest for fuelwood needs but blacksmiths and local alcohol distillers are more dependent on fuelwood and forest yeast (*marcha*) for their traditional businesses. Generally, poor households collect more wild fruits, vegetables, and other consumable NTFPs for their own consumption and sale on a small scale. The average NTFPs' extracted value is fairly high in the case of forests managed by the informal FUG. In the formal FUG area, the extraction

Table 11.5. Average value of NTFPs collected by households (NRs)

NTFPs	Formal FUG			Informal FUG		
	% of households collecting NTFPs	Mean value (Rs)	Std. Dev.	% of households collecting NTFPs	Mean value (Rs)	Std. Dev.
Leaf-litter	80	140	198	88	1,743	2,069
Grass	86	248	309	82	796	451
Fodder	—	—	—	98	3,689	1,874
Fuelwood	92	688	415	100	8,759	5,950
Thatch Grass	82	438	307	—	—	—
Total		1367	719		14,987	8,310

Table 11.6. Distribution of net income from NTFP extraction based on wealth group (NRs)

Forest type	Average net income	Wealth groups and net value of NTFP			
		Lowest 25%	25–50%	50–75%	Top 25%
Formal FUG	1,175	964	1,103	1,005	1,621
Informal FUG	9,554	6,218	9,168	10,830	12,000

of fodder was restricted while in the informal FUG area thatch grass was not extracted during the survey time.

11.6.1. NTFPs income distribution among the households

Distribution of net income and net return to households from NTFPs in the two villages are illustrated in Table 11.6. This is the average value of NTFPs extracted from the community forest in a harvesting period (twelve months). The average extracted value of NTFPs between the two sites differs significantly. This value increases from the less wealthy to the wealthier households. Less wealthy households have a small landholding size and fewer livestock so that they cannot use intermediate forest products such as grass, fodder, and leaf-litter, which is a major contribution of NTFPs from the community forest. The one-way ANOVA analysis indicates that NTFP income distribution differs significantly between the lowest 25 per cent and the other upper-wealth groups in the two villages.

Table 11.7 shows the average share of NTFPs from the community forests to the total income of the households. The forest-resource dependence decreases with the increase in wealth. Tables 11.6 and 11.7 indicate that the rich households are not all that dependent on common property resources but that they use more of the natural resources.

Table 11.8 presents the regression result of the effect of income level on total NTFP extraction and dependence on NTFPs. The regression of NTFP income to total income and income squared shows that within a certain level of household income NTFP extraction increases and then falls with an increase in

Table 11.7. Contribution of NTFPs extracted from common property to total household gross income based on wealth group

Community	Wealth groups and % contribution of NTFPs			
	Lowest 25%	25–50%	50–75%	Top 25%
Formal FUG	2.10	1.74	1.30	1.13
Informal FUG	19.52	18.49	12.34	13.90
Total	12.56	11.67	6.63	5.69

Table 11.8. Effect of income level on total NTFP extraction and dependence on NTFPs

Variables	Dependent variable: NTFPs income		Dependent variable: ratio of NTFPs income to non-NTFP income	
	Coefficients	t-Value	Coefficients	t-Value
Constant	1411.606	0.855	0.397	8.741
tot-income	0.239	4.135***	−4.389E−06	−4.180***
tot-income-sq	−8.743E−07	−2.337**	1.017E−11	2.971***

$R^2 = 0.46$, Adj.$R^2 = 0.44$ and $R^2 = 0.19$, Adj.$R^2 = 0.18$ **, *** imply significance at 5% and 1% probability levels, respectively.

total income. The second regression of ratio of NTFP income to total income indicates that a household's dependence decreases gradually with a higher income level. But the positive sign with income squared indicates that NTFP dependence on the forest decreases at an increasing rate. This means that very rich households seldom go to the forest for NTFP extraction. These results confirm the Gupta, Urvashi, and van Klaas (2005) hypothesis of forest use.

11.7. Socio-economic characteristics of households and NTFP extraction

Knowledge about socio-economic determinants of forest dependency and the nature of their impacts are important in forest management policy (Gunatilake 1998). Moreover, the effectiveness in utilization of community forests appears to be linked with a number of socio-economic factors that have affected decision-making in the FUGs in Nepal (Rejal and Petheram 2001). Besides socio-economic factors, rules and regulations imposed by a particular institution may influence the value of NTFP extraction from the forest. To find out the impact of socio-economic factors on NTFP extraction in the two different types of institutional management systems, socio-economic variables were regressed with total NTFP income. The following equation shows NTFP extraction from the forest as a function of socio-economic variables. Hence,

$$Y_i = \beta_{i1} + \sum_{j=1}^{n} \beta_{ij} X_{ij} + e_i \dots \tag{1}$$

The corresponding regression equation (1) is defined as a linear model to explain the determinants of income from the community forest. Output refers to NTFPs collected by households from the forests. In this model, socio-economic and community attributes are considered as input variables that can affect the amount of NTFP extraction. The gross value of output is

Table 11.9. Definition of explanatory variables

Variables	Description
HAGE	Age of household head (years)
EDUCATION	Average education of household (no. of schooling years)
LANDPF	Area under private forest (in hectares)
LIVESTOCK	Number of livestock owned by a household
GENDER	Gender of household head (Dummy, 1 = female-headed households, 0 = otherwise)
CASTEL	Lower caste (Dummy, 1 = if lower caste, 0 = otherwise
FORMALFUG	Forest type (Dummy, 1 = if with formal forest user group, 0 = otherwise)
FAMSIZE	Number of people in household
dFAMSIZE	Number of people in household × Formal dummy
LANDT	Land area under household management excluding private forest (in hectares)
dLANDT	Land area under household management excluding private forest × Formal dummy
DISTANCE	Distance to forest from households (km)
dDISTANCE	Distance to forest from household (km) × Formal dummy

preferred here because this is an alternative method to measure forest dependency. The dependent variable, Y_i, measures household-level returns from the forest (the gross value of outputs). The independent variables, X_{ij}, refer to household and community attributes. Table 11.9 defines the explanatory variables incorporated in the econometric analysis.

Y on X variables and FROMALFUG × X variables were regressed to test first if the slope coefficients in the two villages were the same. This hypothesis was rejected at the 1 per cent level (F = 21.00). However, another test indicated the hypothesis that all variables except FAMSIZE, LANDT, and DISTANCE had the same coefficient in the two villages. Accordingly, Table 11.10 presents the regression, which allows only the coefficient on these three variables to differ between villages. In the model, regression with total NTFP income collected from the forest shows that the R-square and adjusted R-square for the estimation are 0.83 and 0.80 respectively. The F-statistics for overall goodness of fit of the model is 32.65, which is significant at $\mu = 0.000$. Among all the variables, the family size and landholding size have a significant effect on NTFP extraction in the informal FUG area. With the increase in family size and landholding size, extraction of NTFPs increases. However, the coefficient differences of family size, landholding, and distance to forest between the two villages are not significant, that is, t-value is 0.09, 0.09, and 0.51 respectively. This indicates that, due to the limited number and period of entry in the extraction of NTFPs, the value does not differ according to family size and landholding in the formal FUG.

Likewise, the distance to forest has no significant effect on NTFP extraction in the formal FUG area whereas it has a significant effect in the informal FUG area. In the formal FUG area, all households collect NTFPs during the period when the forest is open whether they are near or far from the community forest. However, in the case of the informal FUG area, households

Table 11.10. Determinants of NTFPs income from the forest

Variable	Coefficient	
	Forest NTFPs	Forest + Private NTFPs
HAGE	−13.74 (37.81)	−15.78 (44.55)
EDUCATION	−43.47 (204.96)	−192.62 (241.51)
LANDPF	−35.35 (102.26)	−160.79 (120.50)
LIVESTOCK	164.83 (159.06)	360.93 (187.42)
GENDER	−106.05 (1081.70)	−645.17 (1274.58)
CASTEL	1017.07 (1120.61)	2367.6 (1320.42)
FORTYPE	−7994.21** (3997.77)	−18334.77* (4710.60)
FAMSIZE	1048.06*** (253.05)	1127.77*** (298.17)
dFAMSIZE	−1078.36*** (413.86)	−933.27** (487.66)
LANDT	647.22*** (128.19)	721.94*** (151.05)
dLANDT	−637.94*** (141.25)	−727.07*** (166.44)
DISTANCE	−3130.78*** (746.33)	−4078.08*** (879.40)
dDISTANCE	2960.45*** (812.74)	4013.08*** (957.66)
CONSTANT	9468.44*** (3310.37)	14356.66*** (3900.63)

R^2 = 83% and Adj.R^2 = 80% (Forest NTFP), and R^2 = 78% and Adj. R^2 = 75% (Forest + Private NTFP) *, ** and *** imply significance at 10%, 5% and 1% probability levels respectively. (F = 32.65, N = 100 and μ = 0.000 in Forest NTFP, and F = 24.47, N = 100 and μ = 0.000 in Forest + Private NTFP.)

near the forest visit it more frequently than those residing far from the forest. The dummy variable for forest type shows that NTFP income decreases in community forestry with the formal FUG more than with the informal FUG. This finding is similar to that of Edmonds (2002) who observes that the presence of a forest user group reduces fuelwood extraction from community forests. This suggests that, along with socio-economic characteristics, rules and regulations in relation to NTFP extraction have a significant impact.

Similarly, in the second model, the total value of NTFPs (Forest plus Private NTFPs) used by households was regressed with all the socio-economic variables. The findings are similar to the previous model. The total value of NTFPs is also significantly lower in the FUG area. In this analysis, other independent variables (age of household head, education, land under private forest, livestock, and gender and caste) are insignificant in the case of NTFP value extracted from the forest. Therefore, a strong conclusion regarding the effect of insignificant variables on NTFP extraction cannot be drawn. Further analysis, along with a large sample size, is necessary to find out the effect of these insignificant variables.

11.8. Conclusions

The primary objective of this study was to understand the effect of local institutions on the extraction of forest resources for their daily livelihood purposes and for distribution of income among the households. This study found that NTFP extraction from the common property resource is an important economic activity because local people rely on NTFPs, particularly grass, fodder, and leaf-litter for subsistence agriculture and livestock farming, and fuelwood for household energy demands. The rules and regulations in the two institutions are different for NTFPs and for timber extraction. It was found that the total value of NTFPs collected from the forest is significantly lower in the formal FUG area as compared to the informal area. The lower NTFP income in the FUG-managed forests is due to the new rules and regulations for NTFP extraction after community forestry intervention.

According to this study, the distribution of income from the forest is unequal among the forest users in both the management systems. As in the case of previous studies, extraction of NTFPs from the forest increases with the income level: poorer households use fewer forest resources than do rich households. But household dependence on NTFPs decreases gradually with higher income and this dependence decreases at an increasing rate after a certain level of income. In these study villages, rich households own large private forests. Hence, they are able to substitute privately grown resources for NTFPs collected from the common forest. In a comparison between the two institutions, the poorer households pay a higher cost for reducing forest-resource extraction than do the rich due to the ban on seasonal NTFP extraction in the formal FUG-managed village.

The econometric analysis shows that a household's family size and land-holding size have a positive impact on NTFP extraction in the informal FUG-managed forest whereas these variables have an insignificant impact on the formal FUG-managed forest. Due to the limited number and period of entry to collect NTFPs, family size and landholding size have less effect on total NTFP extraction. On the other hand, the total value of NTFP consumption is significantly lower in the formal FUG area. This suggests that the institutional set-up at the local level has a direct impact on forest-product extraction and benefit distribution among the beneficiaries. Therefore, interventions seeking to manage forest resources must consider local institutions and the immediate need of local people rather than long-term benefits.

In the formal FUG-management system, emphasis has been placed on reforestation by timber-oriented trees rather than NTFPs, which are valuable for commercial purposes. The regeneration of commercial NTFPs in the community forests may be an alternative strategy to increase benefits for poorer households that are unable to use more agriculture- and livestock-related NTFPs. With fewer harvesting rules and regulations, disadvantaged groups among forest users might receive more benefits from the extraction of commercial NTFPs within the existing system of management.

References

Adhikari, B. (2003). 'Property Rights and Natural Resource: Socio-Economic Hetero-geneity and Distributional Implication of Common Property Resource Management'. Working Paper 1-03. South Asian Network for Development and Environmental Economics (SANDEE), Kathmandu, Nepal.

Agrawal, A. (1995). 'Dismantling the Divide between Indigenous and Scientific Knowledge'. *Journal of Development and Change*, 26/2: 413–34.

—— Britt, C., and Kanel, K. (1999). *Decentralization in Nepal: A Comparative Analysis Participatory District Development Program*. Oakland, CA: ICS Press.

Arnold, M. (1992). 'Assessing the Multiple Values of Forests'. Network Paper 13e. Overseas Development Institute, Rural Development Forestry Network, London, 13–18.

Arnold, J. E., and Campbell, J. G. (1986). 'Collective Management of Hill Forests in Nepal: The Community Forestry Development Project', in *Proceedings of the Conference on Common Property Resource Management*, Washington, DC: National Academic Press, 425–54.

Bhattrai, B., and Ojha, H. R. (2001). *Distributional Impacts of Community Forestry: Who is Benefiting from Nepal's Community Forests?* Forest Action Research Series 00/01. Kathmandu, Nepal: Forest Action Nepal.

Branney, P., King, G. C., and Malla, Y. B. (1994). *Mid-Term Review of Nepal's Hill Community Forestry Project*. Report. Washington, DC: The World Bank.

Bray, D. B., Merino-Pérez, L., Negreros-Castillo, P., Segura-Warnholtz, G., Torres-Rojo, J. M., and Vester, H. F. M. (2003). 'Mexico's Community Managed Forests as a Global Model for Sustainable Landscapes'. *Journal of Conservation Biology*, 17: 672–77.

Brown, D., Malla, Y. B., Schreckenberg, K., and Baginski, O. S. (2002). *From Supervising 'Subjects' to Supporting 'Citizens': Recent Developments in Community Forestry in Asia and Africa*. Natural Resource Perspective Series No. 75. London: ODI.

Campbell, J. G., Shrestha, R. P., and Euphrat, F. (1987). 'Socio-Economic Actors in Traditional Forest Use and Management: Preliminary Results from a Study of Community Forest Management in Nepal'. *Banko Janakari*, 1/4: 45–54.

Cavendish, W. (2000). 'Empirical Regularities in the Poverty-Environment Relationship of African Rural Household'. Working Paper Series 99–21. Center for the Study of African Economies, London.

Chopra, K., Kadekodi, G., and Murty, M. (1990). *Participatory Development: People and Common Property Resources*. Delhi, India: Institute of Economic Growth and Sage Publication.

Edmonds, E. V. (2002). 'Government Initiated Community Resource Management and Local Resource Extraction from Nepal's Forests'. *Journal of Development Economics*, 68: 89–115.

Fisher, R. J. (1989). 'Indigenous Systems of Common Property Forest Management in Nepal'. Working Paper 18. Environment and Policy Institute, East-West Center, Honolulu, USA.

—— Singh, H. K., Pandey, D., and Lang, H. (1989). 'The Management of Forest Resources in Rural Development: A Case Study of Sindhu Palchok and Kavre Palanchok District of Nepal'. Research Paper. ICIMOD, Kathmandu, Nepal.

Gautam, A. P., Shivakoti, G. P., and Webb, E. L. (2004). 'A Review of Forest Policies, Institutions, and Change in the Resource Condition in Nepal'. *International Forestry Review*, 6/2: 136–48.

—— Webb, E. L., and Shivakoti, G. P. (2002). 'Local Participants' Perceptions about Socio-Economic and Environmental Impacts of Community Forestry in the Middle Hills of Nepal'. *Asia Pacific Journal of Rural Development*, 12/2: 60–81.

Gautam, K. H. (1991). 'Indigenous Forest Management Systems in the Hills of Nepal'. Thesis for Degree of Master of Science, Department of Forestry, Australian National University. Available online at <http://thesis.anu.edu.au>.

Gibson, C., McKean, M. A., and Ostrom, E. (1998). 'Explaining Deforestation: The Role of Local Institutions', in C. Gibson, M. A. McKean, and E. Ostrom (eds.), *Forest Resources and Institutions*. Rome, Italy: FAO. Available online at<http://www.fao.org/DOCREP/005/AC694E/AC694E00.HTM>.

Gilmour, D. A., and Fisher, R. J. (1991). *Villagers, Forests and Foresters—The Philosophy, Process and Practice of Community Forestry in Nepal*. Kathmandu, Nepal: Sahayogi Press.

Gunatilake, H. (1998), 'The Role of Rural Development in Protecting Tropical Rainforests: Evidence from Sri Lanka'. *Journal of Environment Management*, 53: 273–93.

Gupta, S., Urvashi, N., and Klaas, V. van (2005), 'Poverty and the Environment: Exploring the Relationship between Household Incomes, Private Assets, and Natural Assets'. Discussion Paper 05–18. Resource for the Future, Washington, DC.

Hardin, G. (1968). 'The Tragedy of Commons'. *Science*, 162: 1243–8.

Hobley, M., and Shah, K. (1996). *What Makes a Local Organization Robust? Evidence from India and Nepal*. London: ODI.

Jackson, W. J., Tamrakar, R. M., Hunt, S., and Shepherd, K. R. (1998). 'Land-Use Changes in Two Middle Hill Districts of Nepal'. *Mountain Research and Development*, 18/3: 193–212.

Jodha, N. S. (1986). 'Common Property Resources and the Rural Poor in Dry Regions of India'. *Economic and Political Weekly*, 21/27: 169–81.

Johnson, O. E. G. (1972). 'Economic Analysis, the Legal Framework and Land Tenure System'. *Journal of Law and Economics*, 15: 259–76.

Kanel, K. R. (2004). 'Twenty-five Years of Community Forestry: Contribution to Millennium Development Goals', in K. R. Kanel, P. Mathema, B. Kandel, D. R. Niraula, A. R. Sharma, and M. Gautam (eds.), 'Proceeding of the Fourth National Workshop on Community Forestry'. Community Forestry Division, Nepal, 4–18.

Maharjan, M. R. (1998). 'The Flow and Distribution of Costs and Benefits in the Chuliban Community Forest, Dhankuta District, Nepal'. Network Paper 23. ODI, London.

NRB (Nepal Rastra Bank) (1988). *Multipurpose Household Budget Survey*. Report. Kathmandu, Nepal: NRB.

Ojha, H. R. (2000). 'Current Policy Issues in NTFP Development in Nepal'. Asia Network for Small-scale Bio-resources, Kathmandu, Nepal. Available online at <http://www.mtnforum.org/mtnforum/archives/reportspubs/library/ojhah00a.htm>.

Ostrom, E. (1990). *Governing the Commons: The Evolution of Institutions for Collective Action*. Cambridge: Cambridge University Press.

Peter, C., Gentry, A., and Mendelsohn, R. (1989). 'Valuation of an Amazonia Rainforest'. *Nature*, 339: 655–6.

Pokharel, B. K. (2002). 'Contribution of Community Forestry to People's Livelihoods and Forest Sustainability: Experience from Nepal', World Rainforest Movement. Available online at <http://www.wrm.org.uy/countries/Asia/Nepal.html>.

Rejal, B., and Petheram, R. J. (2001). 'Extension for Community Forestry Development in the Mid-Hill Zone of Nepal'. Proceedings of the Extension Working Party (S6-06-03) Symposium 2001. International Union of Forestry Study Organizations, Australia. Available online at <http://www.regional.org.au/au/iufro/2001/index.htm>.

Sharma, S., and Chhetry, D. (1996). *MIMAP Research on Poverty in Nepal: A Synthesis.* Report. Kathmandu, Nepal: APROSC and International Development Center.

Shrestha, K. B. (1996). 'Community Forestry in Nepal: An Overview of Conflicts'. Discussion Paper Series No. MNR 96/2. ICIMOD, Kathmandu, Nepal.

Smith, R. J. (1981). 'Resolving the Tragedy of the Commons by Creating Private Property Rights in Wildlife'. *The Cato Journal,* 1: 439–68.

Soussan, J., Shrestha, B. K., and Uprety, L. P. (1995). *The Social Dynamics of Deforestation: A Case Study from Nepal.* New York: Parthenon.

Sterner, T. (2003). *Policy Instruments for Environmental and Natural Resource Management.* Washington, DC: Resource for the Future.

Timsina, N. (2002). 'Empowerment or Marginalization: A Debate in Community Forestry in Nepal'. *Journal of Forest and Livelihood,* 2/1: 27–33.

Wakiyama, T. (2004). 'Community Forestry in Nepal: A Comparison of Management Systems between Indigenous Forestry and Modern Community Forestry'. Policy Report. Institute for Global Environmental Strategies, Japan.

Webb, E. L., and Gautam, A. P. (2001). 'Effects of Community Forest Management on the Structure and Diversity of a Successional Broadleaf Forest in Nepal'. *International Forestry Review,* 3/2: 146–57.

12

Community Tanks vs Private Wells: Coping Strategies and Sustainability Issues in South India

R. Balasubramanian[1]

12.1. Introduction

One of the most important common property resources (CPRs) in the relatively resource-poor regions of South India is irrigation tanks. Until recently, irrigation tanks accounted for more than one-third of the area irrigated in the South Indian states of Tamil Nadu, Karnataka, and Andhra Pradesh. The tanks are ancient, and serve the needs of the poor. Their conservation and proper management is crucial for sustainable water use, soil conservation, and agricultural production in many arid and semi-arid areas. Tank maintenance is also important from an ecological point of view. Unfortunately, tank irrigation has been in a process of rapid decline over the last several decades. Much of this decline can be attributed to macroeconomic changes and institutional failures. Traditional communitarian institutions have come under tremendous pressure because of state and market interventions, person-oriented political patronage, and political encouragement for encroachment

[1] I am grateful to the South Asian Network for Development and Environmental Economics (SANDEE), Kathmandu, Nepal, for funding the research project which led to this study. I thank all the members of the technical advisory committee of SANDEE, including Partha Dasgupta, Narpat Jodha, and Thomas Sterner, and the participants in various SANDEE research workshops held at Kathmandu, New Delhi, Bangkok, Dhaka, and at workshops on this book held at Goa, Bangalore, and Trieste for their critical comments and suggestions to improve the focus and methodology of the study. I am deeply indebted to Herath Gunatilake and Priya Shyamsundar who offered incisive comments that greatly helped to improve the quality of this chapter in many dimensions. E. Somanathan offered critical comments on several aspects of this study which helped me to improve the quality of this research. I would like to extend my thanks to all of them. However, I remain solely responsible for any remaining errors and omissions.

(Nadkarni 2000). As noted by Dasgupta (2005), several external factors such as population growth (causing encroachments), state intervention, and increased uncertainties over property rights (due to the emergence of private wells in tank commands) are some of the important reasons for the neglect of tanks. Further, economic development and government subsidies for alternative forms of irrigation have gradually eroded the importance of tanks in agriculture. In response to resource degradation, people often develop both collective and individual coping mechanisms (Scherr 2000). These individual and collective coping strategies, together with group, resource, and household characteristics, determine the level of collective action to conserve and manage the tanks. The extent of collective action affects resource condition and water availability and, hence, has a direct bearing on agricultural productivity and household income. Thus, it is useful, for policy purposes, to investigate the nature of tank degradation in terms of its linkages to collective action and coping strategies. This chapter is based on a study undertaken in the South Indian state of Tamil Nadu in which the nexus between poverty, private coping mechanisms, and collective action when it comes to tank management was analysed.

12.2. The problem of dwindling tank irrigation

Tanks are one of the oldest sources of irrigation in India, and are particularly important in South India, where they account for about one-third of the area irrigated under rice. There are many benefits associated with tank irrigation. For example, tank irrigation systems are less capital-intensive, have a wider geographic distribution than large irrigation projects, and are smaller in size, thus enabling decentralized management. Tanks are eco-friendly; they serve as flood moderators in times of heavy rainfall, and as drought-mitigating mechanisms during long dry spells. They recharge groundwater, which is a major source of drinking water for numerous rural and urban communities. Tank beds provide a place for forestry activities, which provide timber, fruits, fuel, and habitat for wildlife, particularly birds. Furthermore, fish grown in the tank water provides nutritious and affordable food for rural people besides being a source of income to fishermen. Thus, prosperity levels and size of villages in many semi-arid regions are directly proportional to the size and performance of irrigation tanks (Someshwar 1999).

In spite of these economic and ecological benefits, Tamil Nadu has witnessed over the years a diminishing role for tanks in its rural economy. The share of area irrigated by tanks to total irrigated area in Tamil Nadu has declined from about 40 per cent in 1955 to less than 25 per cent in 2000 reflecting many problems besetting tank irrigation. The conditions and performance of thousands of tanks are poor due to inadequate operation and maintenance investments, disintegration of traditional irrigation institutions responsible for managing tanks, heavy siltation, and private encroachments into tank foreshore and water-spread areas. Large-scale development of private irrigation wells has also led to the neglect of tanks. Furthermore, most of the tanks in Tamil Nadu are located in a chain of hydrological networks called tank chains or tank cascades where water from upstream tanks flows to downstream tanks and so on for a large number of tanks, which are interconnected with one another through a feeder channel. The number of tanks in a chain may be as high as a few hundred thus complicating the process of sharing water from a single feeder channel among a group of tanks, and often leading to inter-tank conflicts among farmers.

Tank management problems tend to fall into two distinct categories: the problem of provision and the problem of appropriation. The provision problem relates to problems associated with bringing adequate water to the tank and making it available for use at the outlet. It involves multiple tasks such as conservation of the catchments, maintenance of supply channels, removal and prevention of encroachment into tank water-spread areas, de-silting, and maintenance and repair of the bunds, surplus weir, and sluices. Appropriation problems, on the other hand, relate to sharing of various benefits from tanks such as water for agriculture and non-agricultural purposes, fishes and trees grown in tanks, silt collected from the tank bed, and grasses and other minor benefits from tanks.

12.3. Cooperative behaviour and private action: an overview

Though there are several studies addressing the issue of the interrelationship among the extent of dependence on CPRs, the social and economic heterogeneity of rural communities, and migration and collective action for managing the commons, there are no systematic attempts to understand these relationships in the context of irrigation tanks in South India. Most of the previous studies that have focused on problems confronting tank irrigation address below outlet issues, that is, the appropriation problem. They are: water allocation and distribution (Palanisami and Flinn 1989); modernization of tanks (Balasubramanian and Govindasamy 1991); and the interaction between private wells and tanks (Palanisami and Easter 1991; Janakarajan 1993; Sakurai and Palanisami 2001). A recent study (Palanisami and Balasubramanian 1998) addresses the issue of the impact of private wells on the performance of tanks (measured as the ratio of area irrigated by tanks to the total registered command area of tank) using data collected from a cross-section of 690 tanks spread over four districts in Tamil Nadu. This study, however, suffers from two major shortcomings as far as tank-well interactions and their implications for collective action are concerned. Firstly, it does not directly address the issue of the interrelationship between the entire set of private coping mechanisms available to the village community and its impact on collective action. Secondly, the measurement of tank performance (used as a dependent variable in the study) is plagued with serious problems in the presence of wells.

A more recent study on collective action and property rights when it comes to the irrigation tanks of Tamil Nadu (Palanisami *et al.* 2001) attempts to investigate the relationship between property rights arrangements and the extent of collective action. Though this study has made important contributions to the measurement of tank performance by including non-agricultural uses of tanks, there is no systematic effort to understand the link between private coping mechanisms and common property resource management. No theoretical or conceptual model is being tested and the empirical relationship between property rights and collective action is not clearly addressed. On the whole, a careful review of past studies on tanks reveals a significant gap in the literature when it comes to the issues concerning collective action in tank management. Most studies focus on the appropriation problem (the sharing of tank water below the outlet) rather than the provision problem (bringing more water to tanks through collective effort) even though they recognize the chronic problem of the decline in tank irrigation together with a decline in the community's participation in tank maintenance. The studies that addressed the issue of interaction between private wells and tanks have not focused on private coping strategies such as non-farm income and migration *vis-à-vis* the level of poverty and collective action for tank management. Overall, the complex nexus between poverty, private coping mechanisms, and collective action towards tank management has not been systematically addressed by any of the previous researchers. This study is an attempt to bridge this gap in tank irrigation literature by analysing the factors responsible for tank degradation at the macro level and to more systematically address the issue of the factors affecting collective action for tank management at the micro level. We also address the issue of the relationship between exit options and collective action.

The hypothesis and methodology for the study were developed based on the conceptual and empirical works on cooperation and collective action by Baland and Platteau (1996), White and Runge (1994), Ostrom (1990, 2000), and Wade (1988). A careful review of these studies reveals that the important variables affecting collective action are: (*a*) resource characteristics such as size and boundary; (*b*) characteristics of the beneficiary group such as size (number of users), inequality in wealth (land, etc.), and the level of dependence of group members on the resource in question; (*c*) institutional arrangements, such as the procedures to devise rules, simplicity of rules, ease in enforcing rules, and monitoring adherence to rules; and (*d*) the external environment, for instance, technology and state intervention in resource management.

White and Runge (1994) address the issue of collective action in common property watersheds by conducting a set of statistical analysis to test the correlation between various socio-economic parameters and the extent of cooperation. They find that the physical distribution of land parcels in the watershed, percentage of landholders who have adopted soil conservation techniques, and the manner in which both landholders and non-watershed participants acquire labour are the important factors explaining levels of collective action. Similarly, Lise (2000) investigates the question of peoples' participation in joint forest management and finds that there is an increase in the participation of resource management and conservation when the condition of the resource is good and/or when the people's dependence on the resource is higher. Chopra and Gulati's study (1998) on the nature of linkage between deforestation, land degradation, and migration reveals that the household's decision to migrate and/or to participate in common property resource management are interrelated since it is a part of a household's labour allocation decision. Though this study highlights the interconnectedness of the decisions made with regard to migration and participation in the commons, it does not clearly bring out the direction of influence of migration on participation in the management of the commons.

Ostrom (2000) suggests that out-migration, changes in technology and factor availability, frequent dependence on external sources, international aid that does not take into account indigenous knowledge and institutions, and an increase in corruption and other forms of opportunistic behaviour are the major threats to the survival and sustainability of local institutions responsible for resource management. When it comes to sustainable collective action *vis-à-vis* irrigation tanks in Tamil Nadu, too, these factors pose the real threat. For example, the technological factor impinges on tank management in the form of modern well-drilling and water-extraction technologies that promote and sustain private wells for groundwater extraction. This reduces the dependence on tanks for some farmers. Remittance income from migrants in a similar manner act as a private coping strategy that reduces the dependence on tanks while international aid that helps improve the physical structures of tanks has been misconceived as a solution for collective action problems[2]. Recent empirical work by Bardhan (2000) on forty-eight irrigation communities in Tamil Nadu is of special significance to the analysis offered in this chapter. Bardhan (2000) investigates the factors affecting cooperation among households in maintaining irrigation systems using data collected from forty-eight irrigation communities in Tamil Nadu. The main shortcoming of this

---

[2] The European Community has funded a major tank modernization project in Tamil Nadu, under which emphasis is placed on improvements to physical structures of the tanks rather than reviving and sustaining the institutional mechanisms for tank management. Little attention is paid to traditional knowledge about and traditional institutions for the conservation and management of tanks.

study is that it attempts to capture the extent of cooperation through proxy variables such as the index of the quality of maintenance of distributaries and field channels, the absence of conflicts over water within a village in the last five years, and the frequency of violation of water allocation rules. These are, on the one hand, poor indicators of cooperation. On the other, they are hard to measure. For example, it is difficult to define what constitutes 'conflict', or what is meant by better or poor quality of irrigation channels. This is especially so when one collects data *across tanks* characterized by different sets of people facing different *quality attributes* of tank structures. Moreover, when alternative measures of cooperation, such as the actual amount of labour and money contributed for tank management, are available, the use of such vague proxies for cooperation becomes questionable. Further, Bardhan's is a pooled analysis of irrigation communities in traditional tank and modern canal irrigation systems. Hence, the results from his analysis are not specifically applicable to tank management.

Given this background, the rest of the chapter is divided as follows. Section 12.4 describes the study region and data collection methods. Section 12.5 presents the econometric models used to analyse tank degradation in Tamil Nadu and the district of Ramanathapuram and to understand collective action and its effectiveness. The results of the tank degradation analysis are presented in Section 12.6. This is followed by a discussion on poverty, dependence on tanks, and private coping mechanisms in Section 12.7, and the role of village communities in the conservation and management of tanks in Section 12.8. Section 12.9 of the chapter presents the conclusions and policy recommendations.

12.4. Description of the study region and data collection

In attempting to understand tank degradation at the macro level, the chapter first focuses on the state of Tamil Nadu and then on the district of Ramanathapuram in Tamil Nadu. The district of old Ramanathapuram (comprising present Ramanathapuram, Sivagangai, and Virudhunagar districts) was selected because of the predominance of tank irrigation in the district as compared to other districts in Tamil Nadu. Further, underdeveloped agriculture, a poor resource base, and low commercialization and industrial development make it a typical poor district that fits in with the objectives of the study.

An analysis of decadal trends in the area irrigated by irrigation tanks and private wells in Tamil Nadu and Ramanathapuram reveals that there has been a sharp decline in the area under tank irrigation in the state as well as in Ramanathapuram. The share of tanks in the total area irrigated by all sources in Ramanathapuram declined from about 88 per cent during the 1960s to 75 per cent during the 1990s while the corresponding figures for Tamil Nadu show a decline from 37 per cent to 22 per cent. While both the area irrigated by tanks and the total area irrigated by all sources declined over the last four decades in Ramanathapuram, the total area irrigated by all sources in Tamil Nadu increased in spite of the decline in area under tanks. This is due to the fact that the decline in area irrigated by tanks in Tamil Nadu has been more than offset by the increase in the area irrigated by wells in the state. However, the emergence of private wells in the district of Ramanathapuram could not catch up with the rest of Tamil Nadu, primarily because of the prevalence of saline aquifers in many parts of the district. The presence of a very loose soil structure that prevents the establishment of wells in several other parts of the district is another reason for the inadequate expansion of wells. The dwindling tank performance and concomitant decline in irrigated acreage in the district may have adverse impacts on the rural communities. Hence, revival of tanks in the district may play a vital role in stabilizing irrigated acreage and rural income.

Ramanathapuram is an agricultural district with about 830 mm of average annual rainfall, a net sown area of about 35 per cent, and forests accounting for only 4 per cent of the geographical area. Tanks account for more than 70 per cent of the total area irrigated by all sources in the district while there is no land under canal irrigation. Rice is the major crop under tank irrigation in this district with an average yield of about 2500 kg/ha as compared to about 3500 kg/ha in Tamil Nadu. Even though the district has a very high density of tanks, their dependability is very poor. For example, an analysis of forty-five years of rainfall data for the district of Ramanathapuram shows that in a ten-year period, the tanks received an above-normal supply of water for two years, a full supply of water for four years, an inadequate supply for two years, and a very poor supply for two years. Within the district of Ramanathapuram, the study focuses on two blocks, each representing two diverse agro-economic situations—Paramakudi and Rajapalayam. The former represents a very poor region with the agricultural sector serving as the major source of livelihood while the latter represents a comparatively well-developed non-agricultural sector. From each of these two blocks, fifteen tanks were selected for detailed study. A household survey was then undertaken by select-ing ten farm households and five non-farm households associated with each tank. Two rounds of detailed interviews were undertaken. In the first round, information was collected on the general characteristics of the village commu-nity, village infrastructure, community efforts in tank management, institu-tional arrangements, income from tank usufructs, community coping mech-anisms to overcome problems of poor water supply, and the presence and resolution of conflicts. In the second round of the survey, detailed household information on socio-economic factors, landownership, agricultural practices, perceptions on the problems of tank degradation, private coping mechanisms, participation in tank management activities, etc., were collected.

The demographic profile of the two study sites (Paramakudi and Rajapalayam) shows that both the percentage of rural population and the share of agricultural workers to total workers are higher in the Paramakudi block than in the Rajapalayam block, which is relatively more industrialized. There are a number of cotton textile industries which serve as a major source of non-farm employment opportunity in Rajapalayam, whereas Paramakudi is industrially backward and hence the major coping mechanism for rural people during periods of drought is temporary or permanent migration. The duration of water supply from tanks, the availability of supplemental sources of water, namely wells, and the extent of crop diversification and cropping intensity are the major factors affecting agricultural profitability in the study region. Tanks supply water normally for a period of three to five months immediately after the northeast monsoon season. A few large tanks supply water for two seasons thus facilitating two crops—mainly rice in both seasons, or a long-duration crop like sugar cane or banana. In general, the cropping pattern in tank-irrigated areas is dominated by rice during the tank season, followed by crops such as vegetables, cotton, or sugar cane depending on the availability of alternative sources of water and soil type. Rajapalayam, where there are more private wells, has a higher degree of crop diversity as well as cropping intensity.

12.5. Degradation, poverty, and collective action: an analytical framework

This paper seeks to undertake three types of analysis. The first is a macro analysis of the determinants of tank degradation. In order to do this, attention will be focused on degradation at the state and district levels and an econometric model developed to identify the determinants of degradation. The second part of the analysis focuses on the linkages between poverty, private coping mechanisms, and collective action at the village and household levels. The last part of the analysis will attempt to understand the determinants of collective action. This section will discuss the analytical framework in detail.

12.5.1. Econometric analysis of tank degradation

In order to study the factors affecting tank degradation, a careful econometric analysis of tank degradation in the state of Tamil Nadu and the district of Ramanathapuram was undertaken using time-series data. In the econometric model, the dependent variable is defined as an index of tank degradation—the ratio of the gap between the *potential* area and *actual* area irrigated by tanks each year to the *potential* area that could be irrigated by the tanks. The designed command area of all tanks has been used as *potential* irrigable area.

It is hypothesized that development of well irrigation was a critical factor that affected how communal tanks were viewed and used. The rush for private wells was encouraged by the reality that tanks were becoming an unreliable source of irrigation while the advent of green revolution crops made it a requirement to have assured water deliveries to match increased fertilizer usage. As a result, the national and state governments launched a major initiative to promote the use of wells through subsidized credit for investment in wells and government financing of rural electrification. Previous research has shown that the growth of private wells and the extensive development of water markets in tank commands have had a negative effect on the performance of tanks (Palanisami and Balasubramanian 1998). In this model, the impact of private wells on tank degradation is captured by the well density (WELLDEN) defined as the number of wells per ha of geographical area. A quadratic term is also used for well density (WELLDSQ) so as to identify whether there is a non-linear relationship between growth in wells and tank degradation. Population pressure, leading to increasing encroachment into the tank water-spread areas, supply channels, and catchments, is a serious problem threatening the survival of most tanks. In the absence of reliable macro-level information on the extent of encroachment, population density (POPDEN) is used as a proxy for encroachment. It is hypothesized that this variable will have a positive impact on tank degradation. In spite of the declining role of the community in managing tanks, there is one possible factor, that is, the profitability of rice production, which could revive or sustain the community's interest in tank management. Therefore, it is hypothesized that technical progress in rice[3] production could have a positive impact on tank performance or that it could halt the process of tank degradation over a period of time. Hence, a one-year lagged rice yield (LRICEYD) is used as one of the independent variables to capture the impact of technical progress in rice production on tank degradation. Tank performance is critically dependent on rainfall (RAIN) and it is hypothesized that the effect of rainfall on tank performance will be positive. Finally, a trend variable (TREND) has been added to the regression equation to represent the left-out variables. Data used to estimate this equation come from the Season and Crop Reports for Tamil Nadu published by the Government of Tamil Nadu for a period of forty years from 1960 to 2000. The summary statistics and definition of variables used in the analysis are provided in Table 12.1. The econometric model is specified as a multiple linear regression equation of the following form:

$$\text{TANKDEG} = \beta_0 + \beta_1 \text{ WELLDEN} + \beta_2 \text{ WELLDSQ} + \beta_3 \text{ POPDEN}$$
$$+ \beta_4 \text{ TREND} + \beta_5 \text{ LRICEYD} + \beta_6 \text{ RAIN} \qquad (1)$$

---

[3] Rice is the single most important crop in most of the tank-irrigated areas. Rice accounts for more than 90 per cent of the tank-irrigated areas in the regular tank-season cultivation.

Table 12.1. Definition of variables used, descriptive statistics, and hypothesis

Variable	Description	Tamil Nadu		Ramanathapuram	
		Mean	Standard deviation	Mean	Standard deviation
TANKDEG	Index of tank degradation	0.21	0.17	0.17	0.14
WELLDEN	Well density defined as number of wells per ha of geographical area	0.117	0.0225	0.05	0.01533
WELLDSQ	Square of well density	0.0142	0.00487	0.0027	0.00131
POPDEN	Population density	369.10	73.6	262.67	38.2
LRICEYD	Lagged rice yield (kg/ha)	2206.25	679.25	1256.57	501.04
RAIN	Annual rainfall (mm)	909.26	134.31	830.17	183.58

12.5.2. Factors affecting the persistence of traditional tank institutions and contribution towards collective action: an econometric analysis

A detailed descriptive analysis of the extent of dependence of poor and non-poor households on tanks has been carried out so as to have a broad understanding of the nexus between poverty, private property (access to land and private wells under the tank command), and the nature and extent of dependence on tanks for various agricultural and non-agricultural purposes of the households. The dependence on tanks have been quantified in terms of agricultural income from tank-irrigated lands and the amount of non-agricultural revenue mobilized from tank usufructs such as trees, fishes, silt, and crops raised on tank bunds. The descriptive statistical analysis is followed by an econometric analysis of factors affecting the persistence of traditional institutions and the extent of collective effort for tank maintenance with these two variables serving as dependent variables. The persistence of traditional tank management institutions is captured through the presence of a common irrigator for water distribution (WATMAN) in the tank command area. The extent of contribution to collective action (COLLEFF) is quantified by summing up the monetary value of labour and money contributed for collective work. While the variable WATMAN is an indicator of overall village-level cooperation, the dependent variable in equation (3) COLLEFF is a household's contribution to the collective effort for tank maintenance. While the former (WATMAN) is a discrete choice—a village can either have it or not—and requires the cooperation from all households to have it, the amount of collective effort (COLLEFF) is a continuous choice variable which can be provided at any quantity and does not require unanimous cooperation from all villagers, that is, there could be free-riders. Hence, we resort to estimating these two equations individually using the probit model for equation (2) and tobit model for equation (3). Further, the estimation of equation (2) is based on tank-level variables while equation (3) is based on both tank-level and household-level data collected from 300 farm households spread over thirty villages (tanks).

$$\text{WATMAN} = \beta + \beta_1 \text{REGION} + \beta_2 \text{CASTE} + \beta_3 \text{NWELLS} + \beta_4 \text{TKSIZE}$$
$$+ \beta_5 \text{GINI} + \beta_6 \text{GINISQ} \tag{2}$$

$$\text{COLLEFF} = \beta_0 + \beta_1 \text{REGION} + \beta_2 \text{CASTE} + \beta_3 \text{FSIZE} + \beta_4 \text{FSIZESQ} + \beta_5 \text{NWELLS}$$
$$+ \beta_6 \text{TKSIZE} + \beta_7 \text{REACH} + \beta_8 \text{GINI} + \beta_9 \text{GINISQ} + \beta_{10} \text{NFISHARE} \tag{3}$$

The independent variables for the analysis were selected after a careful review of the literature on factors affecting collective action. Firstly, group size is an important factor determining the extent of cooperation in the commons. Small groups are considered to be conducive for the emergence and stability of cooperative behaviour in view of the lower heterogeneity and transaction costs associated with organizing group action (Wade 1988). As data is not available on the exact number of farmers in each of the sample tanks, tank size (command area) is used as a proxy for group size (TKSIZE). Given the fact that the average landholding size under tanks does not show much variation across tanks, tank size provides a good proxy for group size.

The literature on common property resources is replete with analysis of the impact of income inequality among users as one factor affecting cooperation among village communities. A review of both theoretical and empirical work (Olson 1965; Baland and Platteau 1997 and 1999; Dayton-Johnson and Bardhan 1998; Bardhan 2000) on the relationship between inequality and collective action reveals no definite clues about the direction of its impact. We use the *Gini* ratio for land owned under tank commands (GINI) as a measure of inequality in power and wealth as well as a quadratic term for the *Gini* ratio (GINISQ) in order to verify whether the inverted-U-shaped relationship between wealth inequality and participation in collective action holds good in the context of tanks. People in tank-irrigated villages have three types of private coping strategies, that is, private wells, and non-agricultural options such as migration and non-farm employment. All of these private coping strategies reduce the dependence on CPR tanks. The shift to non-farm employment and migration also reduces the labour availability at household level for CPR maintenance work. We attempt to capture the impact of these private coping strategies on the cooperative behaviour of the people using two variables—the number of private wells (NWELLS) per hectare of command area owned by the households and the percentage of households having non-farm income and remittance income (NFISHARE). It is hypothesized that both NWELLS and NFISHARE would have negative effects on the institutions for tank maintenance and management and, hence, the extent of contribution towards collective effort for tank maintenance. The definition, summary statistics, and the hypothesis on all the variables used in this econometric analysis are provided in Table 12.2.

Table 12.2. Summary of statistics, definitions, and hypothesis for the variables used

Variable	Description	Mean	Standard deviation	Hypothesis
COLLEFF	Collective effort defined as the amount of money and value of labour contributed for tank maintenance works	195.96	313.52	Dependent variable
REGION	Dummy for region, which takes a value of 1 for poorer region and zero for relatively non-poor region	0.50	0.50	Positive
CASTE	Dummy for caste homogeneity, which takes a value of one if more than 75 per cent of agricultural households in the village belong to the same caste, and zero otherwise.	0.27	0.44	Positive
FSIZE	Farm size in ha	2.09	10.23	Positive
FSIZESQ	Square of farm size	13.34	16.47	Negative
NWELLS	No. of wells owned per ha of land	0.21	0.54	Negative
TKSIZE	Command area of the tank in ha	44.59	63.47	Negative
REACH	Location of the sample farm in the tank command which takes a value of one for tail reach and zero for head reach	0.5	0.5	Positive
GINI	*Gini* ratio of inequality in land operated under sample tanks	0.71	1.67	Negative
GINISQ	Square of *Gini* ratio	0.51	2.36	Positive
NFISHARE	Share of non-farm income in the total household income	0.41	0.74	Negative

12.6. Results and discussion

12.6.1. *Factors affecting tank degradation—an econometric analysis*

The results of the econometric analysis presented in Table 12.3 reveal that both in the state of Tamil Nadu and in Ramanathapuram district the variables included in the regression analysis could explain more than two-thirds of the variation in the dependent variable, that is, tank degradation. The results show that in Tamil Nadu all the independent variables except lagged rice yield were found to be statistically significant with expected signs for the regression coefficients while in Ramanathapuram only three of the six variables were statistically significant. An interesting result is the negative relationship between well density and tank degradation both in the state of Tamil Nadu and the district of Ramanathapuram. This result has an interesting policy implication in that the number of private wells has a positive (negative) impact on tank degradation (tank performance). When the number of private wells is sufficiently large, not only do the well-owners reduce their participation in tank management, but they also promote the emergence of competitive groundwater markets in tank commands, which further contributes to reduced dependence on tanks for even non-well-owners (since they become water buyers). Therefore, emergence of private wells in

Table 12.3. Factors affecting tank degradation in Tamil Nadu state and Ramanathapuram district

Variable	Tamil Nadu			Ramanathapuram		
	Coefficient	t-ratio	Prob. of significance	Coefficient	t-ratio	Prob. of significance
Constant	−4.78009	−1.997	0.0544	−0.58844	−0.682	0.5003
TIME	−0.1032*	−2.004	0.0536	−1.05E-02	−0.668	0.509
RAIN	−4.92E-04**	−4.8	0.00	−3.80E-04**	−7.014	0.00
WELLDEN	−6.8030*	−1.735	0.0424	−18.0712**	−3.969	0.0004
WELLDSQ	694.3159*	2.032	0.0505	1806.524**	3.101	0.004
POPDEN	2.02336*	2.176	0.0371	0.502029	1.129	0.2673
LRICEYD	3.72E-05	0.993	0.328	1.62E-05	0.686	0.4977
Adj. R-squared			0.8287			0.8219
F-statistic			33.03			13.88
DW statistic			1.29			1.8544

Note: ** and * indicate significance at 1 % level and 5% level, respectively.

large numbers in tank commands contributes to the declining performance of tanks. As expected, rainfall reduces the pace of tank degradation in both Ramanathapuram and in Tamil Nadu. Even though population density was not significant in Ramanathapuram, it is highly significant with a positive impact on tank degradation in Tamil Nadu. This implies that population pressure is an important factor hastening the process of tank degradation, perhaps through increased pressure on the resource, mainly in the form of encroachments into catchments and water-spread areas.

12.6.2. *Poverty, distribution of tank benefits, and private coping strategies*

Given the broad array of factors affecting tank degradation at a macro scale, the chapter, in this and subsequent sections, discusses crucial issues such as poverty, private coping strategies, and dependence on tanks and their implications for collective action at the micro level. The analysis is based on village and household-level data associated with thirty tanks in two administrative blocks of the district of Ramanathapuram. To understand the nature and extent of the dependence of poor and non-poor households on tanks, sample households were classified into two income categories, that is, households below the poverty line (which are called poor households) and households above poverty line (called non-poor households). This difference helps in understanding their contribution to collective tank-management work. This classification is based on the Government of India's norm for the poverty line, which is currently fixed at an annual per capita income of Rs 18,000.

Table 12.4 shows the link between poverty and dependence on tanks. It is obvious from the table that the poor are much more dependent on

Table 12.4. Poverty and dependence on tanks

Household category	Land owned (ha)		Extent of dependence on tanks (% households reporting complete dependence)		
	Tank command	Non-tank command	Agriculture	Collection of fuel wood and grasses	Watering livestock
Poor	0.48	0.23	92	49	87
Non-poor	2.19	0.92	67	21	24

tanks relative to the non-poor both for agricultural crop production and for non-crop activities such as livestock husbandry and fuelwood collection. More than 90 per cent of poor households depend solely on tanks for agricultural water while only two-thirds of the non-poor households depend solely on tanks for water. Further, over 85 per cent of poor households are completely dependent on tank water for rearing livestock while only less than 25 per cent of the non-poor said that they used only tank water for livestock needs. It is also interesting to note that approximately 50 per cent of poor households are dependent on tanks to meet their fuelwood and grazing needs.

12.6.3. *Revenue from tank usufructs and tank maintenance*

In addition to crop production, tanks support a host of other related activities such as provision of water for drinking by humans and livestock, washing, bathing, etc. Tanks are useful for provision of water and fodder to livestock, tree cultivation, fish culture, and duck rearing. Tank silt is used for brick-making. Though there is a vast potential for growing fish and trees in view of their non-consumptive use of tank water, the current levels of such use is low.[4] Data presented in Table 12.5 shows the importance of trees and

[4] Non-agricultural uses of tanks are beset with problems related to lack of clear rules and rights. When the state took over tank management, it made significant intrusion into community rights over non-agricultural uses of tanks. Yet, the state does not have a clear and uniform policy related to the sharing of non-agricultural revenues. This has led to a system of perverse incentives resulting in unauthorized use of tank usufructs by politically powerful groups and the use of the revenue from tank usufructs for purposes other than tank maintenance. In cases where income from tank usufructs accrues to the government, it is invariably added to the general financial accounts and not spent on tanks. The income from tank-bed tree plantations was generally shared among the local *panchayats* (under the jurisdiction of which the particular tank falls) and the state government. However, neither of these organizations spends the revenue realized from trees exclusively on tanks. The rules for sharing income from tank fishery are more complicated. Though, historically, the rights to fishery benefits were vested with the respective village *panchayats*, there are no systematic and/or uniform rules governing the exploitation of fishery resources. In some places, fishery rights are held by individual farmers, while in some other tanks the *panchayats* or the state government has the right to sell the fishery rights through auctioning. In view of the absence

Table 12.5. Revenue obtained from tank usufructs and its utilization (Rs/ha of command area)

Sources of revenue	Poor	Non-poor
I. Revenue mobilized		
a) Fishery	69.50 (59.41)	38.30* (16.42)
b) Trees	91.00 (62.65)	57.00* (55.74)
c) Sale of silt	0	0
d) Crops on tank bunds	14.50 (18.45)	4.10* (15.61)
Total	175.00 (47.5)	99.40* (28.3)
II. Utilization of revenue from tanks (% of total revenue spent)		
a) Added to village common funds	58.8	77
b) Spent for tank maintenance	41.2	23
Total	100	100

Note: Figures in parentheses are standard deviations.

*denotes significant difference between poor and non-poor households.

fishery as sources of non-agricultural income from tanks. Further, poorer households obtain higher non-agricultural revenues relative to the non-poor. This reinforces our earlier finding that the poor are much more dependent on tanks than the relatively better-off households. Both poor and non-poor households spend a high proportion of the income generated from tanks on non-tank-related activities such as renovation of temples or other common purposes. However, poorer households spend a relatively higher percentage of tank income on tank maintenance activities compared to the non-poor. Thus, poor people, whose dependence on tanks is higher, are also the major contributors to tank maintenance.

12.6.4. *Private wells in tank command and market for water*

Private wells are emerging as a major supplementary source of irrigation in many of the tank-irrigated areas. Emergence of wells is influenced by many factors such as the advent of green revolution technology, which created the need for assured irrigation, commercialization of the village economy, and the increasing uncertainty and instability in water availability from common-pool irrigation tanks. The perverse incentives created by state policies such as provision of electricity for agriculture at full subsidy served as a major external impetus for the emergence of wells. These wells are mainly recharged through the seepage flow from tanks and, hence, there is a close hydrological

of uniform/systematic rules governing tank fishery, unauthorized (open-access) fishing is a common practice in many tanks. In spite of state intervention and the absence of well-defined property rights over tank usufructs, some village communities are successful in realizing non-agricultural revenues from tanks. The extent to which the village communities are successful in mobilizing revenues from non-agricultural uses of tanks is an important indicator of the effectiveness of tank-management institutions.

Table 12.6. Private wells in the tank command and the extent of dependence on community tanks

Particulars	Poor	Non-poor
No. of private wells per ha of land owned	0.11 (0.54)	0.32 (1.20)
Total no. of irrigation done for rice crop using		
a) Tank water	28.6 (34.89)	30.81 (29.63)
b) Own well water	3.62 (26.14)	13.36 (8.08)
c) Well water purchased from others	9.57 (12.33)	3.70 (7.37)
Percentage of water sellers to total number of farmers	14.21 (22.50)	43.20 (26.8)

Note: Figures in parentheses are standard deviations.

linkage between tanks and wells. The hydro-economic interaction between the performance of tanks and the number of wells per unit of tank command area is a complex issue. Though wells complement tank performance through reducing the uncertainties in tank water supply in the short run, a closer look at the role of private wells in common-pool tank command areas suggest that wells negatively affect, or act as a potential challenge to, tank performance through reduced dependence of well-owners on tanks and their vested interest in increasing their income through sale of well water. Quite often the well-owners act as local monopolists in view of the strategic location of their wells in relation to lands belonging to non-well-owners.

The data on private wells and the extent of dependence on tank well water for crop production presented in Table 12.6 reveal that the number of wells per ha of land area was 0.32 for non-poor households while it was only 0.11 for poor households. Consequently, dependence on others—both in terms of the number of households purchasing well water and the average number of irrigations done using purchased well water—was higher for the category of poor households.

12.6.5. The role of village communities in tank conservation and management

Though the tanks in Tamil Nadu have been taken over by the government, the village communities still play a crucial role in the maintenance of tanks. Farmers contribute both physical labour and money for various tank management works. The *modus operandi* of mobilizing the required labour/money generally take the form of an informal meeting of farmers (not all the villagers) at the beginning of the season in order to decide what kind of maintenance work should be taken up and how to mobilize funds/labour. In most cases, the exact contributions are decided on the basis of the nature and urgency of the work to be taken up and the physical condition of different tank structures. Activities of significance that are taken up very frequently and recurrently are

Table 12.7. Extent of participation of households in tank maintenance work (average for the years 1999–2000 and 2000–1)

Collective contribution for tank maintenance	Poor	Non-poor
I. Labour spent on (in man days/ha of command area)		
a) Supply channel maintenance	4.72 (6.16)	2.48* (8.27)
b) Diversion of water for the tank	0.61 (1.20)	0.17 (4.3)
c) Field channel maintenance	1.82 (0.68)	0.94 (1.34)
Total labour spent	7.15 (2.68)	3.59 (2.71)*
Total value of labour spent on all the activities (Rs/ha of command area)	228.8 (23.71)	125.65 (37.15)*
II. Cash contributed for tank maintenance (Rs/ha of command area)	18.45 (21.66)	11.70 (19.42)
III. Total monetary value of contribution for tank maintenance (Rs/ha of command area)	247.26	137.34

Note: i) Figures in parentheses are standard deviations.

ii) * denotes significant difference between poor and non-poor households.

the cleaning up of supply channels and diverting water from the upstream, and minor repairs to sluices, surplus weirs, and tank bunds. Labour-intensive activities such as cleaning supply channels are done by the farmers themselves, the labour of which is equally shared among all farmers irrespective of the extent of land owned under the tank command. Minor activities such as repairs to sluices, surplus weirs, and bunds, which do not require labour from all farmers, are done by hired labour and the expenditure towards such works is met from the funds mobilized for the purpose. The amount of money mobilized for such special work is typically based on the extent of land owned by the individual farmers in the tank command (which is called acre-levy because it is based on the number of acres of land owned under the tank command). Labour- and capital-intensive activities such as removal of encroachments and silt in tank water-spread areas are very rarely done.

The data on collective contributions to tank maintenance and management by the two income categories presented in Table 12.7 indicate that supply-channel maintenance is an important activity to which both categories of households contribute. The extent of participation in tank management is significantly higher among poor households as compared to non-poor households. Labour was the major form of contribution to the collective effort towards tank maintenance. The total amount of labour expended by poorer households was almost 100 per cent more than that by the non-poor households. The field channels serving individual parcels of land belonging to different farmers have to be maintained by the respective farmers. Households were requested to report time spent on this activity too as a component of the extent of participation since the researchers were concerned with all activities related to tank maintenance.

12.6.6. *Determinants of persistence of traditional tank institutions and the extent of collective action for tank maintenance*

12.6.6.1. FACTORS AFFECTING PERSISTENCE OF TRADITIONAL TANK-MANAGEMENT INSTITUTIONS

The results of the probit regression analysis of variables affecting the persistence of traditional tank-management institutions are presented in Table 12.8. All the variables except caste homogeneity are found to be statistically significant in determining the persistence of traditional tank-management institutions. As expected, both private wells and group size (tank size) are found to have a negative impact on traditional institutions while inequality has a U-shaped relationship with institutional set-up, which is in conformity with the results obtained by Bardhan (2000). The poorer region shows a significant probability of persistence of traditional tank institutions as compared to the non-poor region.

Table 12.8. Factors affecting persistence of traditional irrigation institutions—results of probit regression analysis

S. No.	Independent variables	Coefficients	Marginal effects	t-value	Level of significance
1.	Constant	32.65819	12.38099	2.387	0.017
2.	CASTE	0.389669	0.147727	1.51	0.1312
3.	WELDEN	−1.78303	−0.67596	−2.24	0.0251
4.	TKSIZE	−1.35E-03	−5.13E-04	−1.884	0.0595
5.	GINI	−90.1624	−34.1813	−2.315	0.0206
6.	GINISQ	60.65915	22.99638	2.196	0.0281
7.	REGION	1.156892	0.438587	4.671	0.00

12.6.6.2. FACTORS AFFECTING THE EXTENT OF COLLECTIVE ACTION FOR TANK MAINTENANCE

The results of the tobit regression analysis of factors affecting the contribution to collective action towards tank maintenance are presented in Table 12.9. The results are, in general, consistent with the economic theory and empirical literature on the factors affecting collective action in local commons. The regression coefficients indicate that one of the important local private coping mechanisms, that is, the number of private wells owned by a household in the tank command area, was found to be statistically significant in negatively affecting the extent of collective action for tank maintenance. This result provides stronger evidence to the argument that private coping strategies operate against community interests when it comes to sustaining collective action for tank management. Since wells in tank commands are used to privatize common-pool tank water because of the physical interdependence between tank storage and well-water recharge, those who have private wells

Table 12.9. Factors affecting collective action in tank maintenance

S. No.	Variables	Coefficients	Marginal effects	t-value	Level of significance
1.	Constant	−992.421	−399.398	−0.324	0.7462
2.	REACH	22.55	9.076587	0.494	0.621
3.	FSIZE	99.69**	40.12154	2.423	0.0154
4.	FSIZE_SQ	−11.11*	−4.4708	−2.003	0.0452
5.	REGION	−180.10**	−72.4826	−2.426	0.0153
6.	CASTE	1030.97**	414.9107	12.312	0.00
7.	WELLDEN	−590.47**	−237.636	−3.205	0.0013
8.	NF_SHARE	−261.66**	−105.303	−3.44	0.0006
9.	TKSIZE	−1.13**	−0.45671	−5.837	0.00
10.	GINI	2694.38	1084.346	0.303	0.762
11.	GINISQ	−1761.38	−708.865	−0.274	0.7839

Note: * and ** indicate the statistical significance of the variable at 5% and 1% levels respectively.

are less motivated to participate in tank maintenance (Sakurai and Palanisami 2001). However, poor people who cannot afford to invest in wells and hence are directly and solely dependent on tank water contribute more towards tank maintenance. Therefore, the tank management policy should aim at promoting community wells for poor people. Another avenue for safeguarding the poor is to promote policies that encourage diversification of cropping patterns away from rice. Crop diversification may increase incomes and reduce the demand for water, which may enable poor farmers to purchase water from the emerging competitive water markets.

The tank size, which is a proxy for group size, has a negative influence on the extent of collective action probably due to the fact that the larger tanks involve a higher number of beneficiaries. In many cases, these tanks serve more than one village thus increasing socio-economic and cultural heterogeneity that discourages cooperative action among farmers. The negative impact of group size is in contrast to results obtained by Heltberg (2001) in the context of forest conservation in Rajasthan, India. However, our results are congruent with the theoretical literature on the relationship between group size and the extent of collective action. Surprisingly, inequality in landownership has not been found to have a significant impact on the extent of contribution for collective effort towards tank maintenance.

12.7. Conclusions and policy implications

The dependence of poor people on tanks is found to be an important driving force behind their active participation in tank maintenance. More than 80 per cent of the poor households depend on tanks for crop and livestock husbandry while approximately 50 per cent of that number depend on tanks for grazing and fuelwood. Consequently, these poor households generate significant amounts of revenue from various tank usufructs such as fishery and trees and spend significant portions of this income on tank maintenance. Poorer households spend 100 per cent more labour than their non-poor counterparts on tank maintenance activities. An econometric analysis of tank degradation provides strong evidence that there has been a secular decline in the performance of tanks. This decline is mostly due to the decline in the local institutional set-up responsible for tank maintenance as well as changes in the overall socio-economic environment in which the tanks are managed. The negative relationship between the number of private wells and tank degradation has important policy implications. Given the hydrological dependence of wells on tanks as a major recharge mechanism,[5] it could be argued that the wells are partly a mechanism to 'privatize' common-pool tank water. However, given the heavy investment and uneconomical size of their landholdings, the poor are unable to go for this private option.

The above results are reinforced by the micro-level econometric model of collective action, which indicates that the increase in the number of private wells has a negative impact on both the persistence of traditional irrigation institutions and collective action for tank management. However, even though the wells pose a threat to collective action in conserving tanks, supplemental well irrigation has a strong positive influence on rice yield. Hence, farmers have a strong private interest in digging wells, which is in conflict with the collective interest in tank management. The importance of both collective action and private wells in increasing agricultural productivity and the negative relationship between collective action and private wells throws up an important policy issue—the question of the optimal number of wells and the need for an institutional mechanism to regulate the number of wells. Given the increasing risk with regard to tank-water availability, wells have become indispensable for successful crop production in tank command, though the excessive dependence on private wells threatens sustainable tank management. Therefore, promoting community wells instead of private wells is a win-win strategy in the sense that any cooperative effort to manage tanks will complement the cooperative effort needed to provide and operate community wells (and vice versa), which would in turn reduce the dependence on private wells. Proportionate reduction in cropping area depending on tank-water availability together with emphasis on intensive, commercial fish culture and tree cultivation in tanks would not only mitigate risks of crop failure in low rainfall years but also help supplement household incomes during years of water scarcity.

---

[5] A detailed discussion with the farmers in the tank commands indicates that the wells are highly dependent on tanks for recharging. The water table in most wells goes down dramatically within a few weeks of tanks going dry.

Inequality among tank users has been found to have a U-shaped relationship with traditional tank institutions while it does not have a significant impact on contribution towards collective action. As the persistence of traditional governance structures is an important factor affecting the success of sharing scarce tank water and user management of tanks, strengthening the governance structure in areas where the system is in operation and reviving the system in areas where it has become defunct will enhance collective action. Turning over tank management to village communities together with rights over tank usufructs, and empowering local government to remove and prevent encroachments in the tank commons are important steps towards strengthening the governance structure that will promote a sustainable tank management regime.

References

Baland, J.-M., and Platteau, J.-P. (1996). *Halting Degradation of Natural Resources: Is there a Role for Rural Communities?* Oxford: Clarendon Press.

—— —— (1997). 'Wealth Inequality and Efficiency in the Commons. Part I: The Unregulated Case'. *Oxford Economics Paper,* 49: 451–82.

—— —— (1999). 'The Ambiguous Impact of Inequality on Local Resource Management'. *World Development,* 27/5: 773–88.

Balasubramanian, R., and Govindasamy, R. (1991). 'Ranking Irrigation Tanks for Modernisation'. *Agricultural Water Management,* 20: 155–62.

Bardhan, P. (2000). 'Irrigation and Cooperation: An Empirical Analysis of 48 Irrigation Communities in South India'. *Economic Development and Cultural Change,* 48/4: 847–65.

Chopra, K., and Gulati, S. C. (1998). 'Environmental Degradation, Property Rights and Population Movements: Hypotheses and Evidence form Rajasthan (India)'. *Environment and Development Economics,* 3/1: 35–57.

Dasgupta, P. (2005). 'Common Property Resources: Economic Analytics'. *Economic and Political Weekly,* 40/16: 1610–22.

Dayton-Johnson, J., and Bardhan, P. (1998). 'Inequality and Conservation on the Local Commons: A Theoretical Exercise'. CIDER Working Paper No. 096-071. Department of Economics, University of California, Berkeley, CA.

Heltberg, R. (2001). 'Determinants and Impact of Local Institutions for Common Resource Management'. *Environment and Development Economics,* 6: 183–208.

Janakarajan, S. (1993). 'Economic and Social Implications of Groundwater Irrigation: Some Evidences from South India'. *Indian Journal of Agricultural Economics,* 48/1: 65–75.

Lise, W. (2000). 'Factors Influencing People's Participation in Forest Management in India'. *Ecological Economics,* 34: 379–92.

Nadkarni, M. V. (2000). 'Poverty, Environment, Development: A Many-Patterned Nexus'. *Economic and Political Weekly,* 35/14: 1184–90.

Olson, M. (1965). *The Logic of Collective Action.* Cambridge, MA: Harvard University Press.

Ostrom, E. (1990). *Governing the Commons: The Evolution of Institutions for Common Action*. New York: Cambridge University Press.

—— (2000). 'Collective Action and the Evolution of Social Norms'. *Journal of Economic Perspectives,* 14/3: 137–58.

Palanisami, K., and Balasubramanian, R. (1998). 'Common Property and Private Prosperity: Tanks v Private Wells in Tamil Nadu'. *Indian Journal of Agricultural Economics,* 53/4: 600–13.

—— and Easter, K.W. (1991). 'Hydro-Economic Interaction between Tank Storage and Groundwater Recharge'. *Indian Journal of Agricultural Research,* 46/2: 174–9.

—— and Flinn, J. C. (1989). 'Impact of Varying Water Supply on Input Use and Yield of Tank-Irrigated Rice'. *Agricultural Water Management,* 15: 347–59.

—— Paramasivam, P., Karthikeyan, D., and Rajagopal, A. (2001). *Sustainability of Tank Irrigation Systems in South India*. TNAU Monograph. Coimbatore, India: Tamil Agricultural University Press.

Sakurai, T., and Palanisami, K. (2001). 'Tank Irrigation Management as a Local Common Property: The Case of Tamil Nadu, India'. *Agricultural Economics,* 25: 273–83.

Scherr, S. J. (2000). 'A Downward Spiral? Research Evidence on the Relationship between Poverty and Natural Resource Degradation'. *Food Policy,* 25: 479–98.

Someshwar, K. (1999). 'Panchayat Raj Tanks—A Potential for Future Expansion for Irrigated Agriculture in Andhra Pradesh'. *Journal of Indian Water Resources Society,* 19/5: 1–14.

Wade, R. (1988). *Village Republics: Economic Conditions for Collective Action in South India*. Oakland: ICS Press.

White, T. A., and Runge, C. F. (1994). 'Common Property and Collective Action: Lessons from Cooperative Watershed Management in Haiti'. *Economic Development and Cultural Change,* 43/1: 1–41.

Part IV

Statutory and Customary Law

13

Tradition and Sovereignty: Conflicts over the Forests of Dir-Kohistan

Shaheen Rafi Khan

13.1. Introduction

This chapter addresses the links between resource rights, local livelihoods, insecurity and conflict in the Dir-Kohistan Valley (referred to henceforth as Dir-Kohistan) within an institutional framework.[1] It has some of the best-endowed forest resources in the country. Over the past three decades, these resources have degraded severely due to a combination of rapid population growth, increasing market forces, and an institutional set-up favouring resource extraction rather than sustainable use where natural resource ownership and management by communities has gradually been displaced by the state.

The community-based rights and management of resources has its roots in customary law, which is historically known as *garzinda wesh*, or moveable distribution (Sultan-e-Rome 2002). It ensured equitable distribution of land, water, pastures, and forests. State ownership and management of forest resources on the other hand fall within the ambit of statutory law and are defined by two sets of legislation. The 1927 Forest Act was a territorial law with a strong enforcement orientation. It divided forests into three categories: reserve forests, protected forests, and village forests. Dir-Kohistan's forests were declared protected forests in 1975. Under this act, the Forest Department (FD) had the power to close forests and forbid communities from extracting timber, fuelwood, fodder, and other forest products. Where permission to do so was granted, as in Dir-Kohistan's protected forests, it was curtailed by a system of permits and fines. The 2002 North Western Frontier Province (NWFP) Forest Ordinance retained these clauses but also introduced

---

[1] The institutional context refers in this case to resource rights and systems of management and adjudication through which these rights are exercised.

provisions relating to joint forest management (JFM). The ordinance was the outcome of a broader institutional reform process, involving forest-dependent communities in management and monitoring.

Both state and community-based institutions have a say in the mediation of conflicts over the use of natural resources and the distribution of commercial benefits arising from them. The *jirga*, a body of nominated village elders, adjudicates criminal and common-property issues. It is not a permanently constituted body but a flexible one where nominated elders come together over specific issues and in specific places to mediate conflicts and resolve issues. Once a decision is taken, the *jirga* disbands until the next issue arises. Concurrently, communities also have recourse to civil and Islamic courts on adjudication of these issues.

We find an increasing dominance of statutory law, which has subsumed customary entitlements to natural resources. Firstly, institutional inability to enforce these laws has transformed communities from guardians to predators of the commons. Secondly, it has induced ingress by commercial loggers who collude with the Forest Department and local notables to extract timber well in excess of sanctioned limits. Thirdly, the lack of transparency in distributing royalties to communities with entitlements has twice led to conflicts between communities and the state. In one such case, a *jirga* was constituted to mediate the conflict.

A key factor in the disintegration of the state governance system has been the rapid increase in the prices of timber, fuelwood, and non-timber forest products (NTFP) over the past three decades, which has brought about incompatibility between the need for conservation, the commercial interests of loggers, and the financial benefits derived by the Forest Department and civil-administration functionaries. Dasgupta (this volume) refers to the need to study markets 'in order to understand the institutions that govern CPRs'. Agrawal (2001: 1659) provides the local context for this by pointing to 'the gradual change in articulation with reference to external markets'. Available evidence indicates that prices driven by external markets have provided perverse incentives to and engendered uncontrolled logging by what is commonly called the 'timber mafia'.

The rules of the game, which define our frame of analysis, are resource rights (North 1990).[2] The organizational forms, which determine the efficacy of these rights and shape them over time, have two functions: systems of natural resource management and systems of adjudication or conflict resolution. As indicated, two resource rights regimes coexist in the case-study area. Vani (2002) defines these as two distinct frameworks of governance. Customary law invests ownership and user rights in the same collective, namely the local communities. In contrast, statutory law separates ownership

---

[2] The institutional approach of this chapter draws heavily upon North (1990).

and user rights. The management and conflict resolution systems through which these rights are exercised are, respectively, community-centric and state-centric.[3] A factor in such deterioration is the growing incompatibility between the state's conservation mandate and the emerging structure of incentives.

Section 13.2 sets the context for the study. Section 13.3 describes customary and statutory law and the governance systems (for natural resource management (NRM) and conflict resolution) associated with them. It examines the interface between the two systems of law and governance in an evolving context, in other words, how they contradict and complement each other. Local government institutions and their potential for resource management are briefly touched upon. Section 13.4 provides documented and anecdotal evidence of degradation that has occurred concurrently with the emerging dominance of state management institutions. Section 13.5 analyses the emerging structure of perverse incentives and assesses their impacts on relations between the state and communities. Section 13.6 concludes with discussions and policy recommendations.

13.2. The context

Dir-Kohistan has a population of 112,695 with a male-female ratio of 51:49 (Government of Pakistan 1998). The three main ethnic groups are the *kohistanis* (40 per cent), the *pathans* (50 per cent), and the *gujjars* (10 per cent).

Dir-Kohistan is situated in the extreme north of the upper Dir District in the NWFP.[4] It is part of the region, which lies at the confluence of the three highest mountain ranges of the world, the Karakorum, the Hindu Kush, and the Himalayas. It borders the Chitral district to the north and the Swat district to the east. The total area of Dir-Kohistan is 12,000 km^2 (412,570 acres) with land-use classes given in Table 13.1.

The land-use classifications fall within three distinct ecosystems (oak forests, coniferous forests, and alpine pastures) and transitional zones. The oak (*Quercus ilex*) forests radiate upwards from the valley bottom and terminate laterally in the mid-valley section. The mixed coniferous forests are found near the upper ridges of the mid-valley section, converging on the valley floor and up the valley slopes in the northern uplands. The alpine pastures extend beyond the tree line to permanent snowfields with fairly large freshwater lakes.

---

[3] The evolution of resource rights, their impacts on forest management and the communities, and the deterioration of state institutions are well recorded by Guha in his seminal work on ecological history (Guha 1983).

[4] Geographically, it lies between 35.9° to 35.47° north latitude and 71.52° to 72.22° east longitude.

Table 13.1. Dir-Kohistan land-use classification

Land use	Type	Acres	%
Forest	Coniferous	137,000	33.3
	Broad-leaved	11,917	2.9
Agriculture	Rain-fed	17,365	4.2
	Irrigated	16,555	4.0
	Pasture and rangeland	229,338	55.6
Total land		412,570	100

Source: Ghazi Marjan Work Plan, 1973–93.
Note: The data excludes snowfields.

The valley elevation ranges from 4,000 to 12,000 feet above mean sea level. The climate is dry temperate with an annual rainfall of approximately 1075 mm. Precipitation occurs mainly in the winter and the spring. The valley's three micro-ecological zones correspond with specific agricultural practices. Agricultural land cuts across ecosystems. It comprises silt and sediment deposits along the valley bottom, alluvial fans, terraced encroachments into oak forests, and land converted for potato cultivation in coniferous forest and pastures. Although Dir-Kohistan is rich in floral and faunal biodiversity, the wildlife population in the valley is decreasing due to relentless hunting.

The region, historically, has great strategic value. Originally, in the late nineteenth century, British colonial rulers regarded it as a bulwark against Russian expansionism. While stability in the region continues to be vital to Pakistan's political and strategic interests, the imperatives of good governance associated with such stability are lacking. Dir-Kohistan's administrative integration with Pakistan in 1969 triggered divisive forces, which culminated in open conflict on a number of occasions, the most notable being the aerial bombing of the valley by the Pakistan Air Force in 1976.

The genesis of the problem lies in the failure to provide development and justice to the local communities. Dir-Kohistan's social and economic indicators are far below that of the national average. The Pakistan Human Development Report, 2003, has compiled economic and social statistics for all of Pakistan's districts. In Table 13.2, we present indicators (in terms of rank ordering) for the seven poorest districts in the NWFP, which has a total of twenty-four districts. Dir-Kohistan falls in the low to mid-level in these rankings. It does poorly on the income indicators and relatively better on the indicators for health and education. But that is little consolation when, on average, twenty districts in the NWFP perform better.

Literacy levels are well below the national average at 45 per cent. In Dir-Kohistan, the literacy rate is 21 per cent for men and not more than 6 per cent for women. The distressingly low average for women reflects both social and cultural inhibitions and the dearth of educational facilities. Water

Table 13.2. Human development indicators (HDI) in the NWFP

	Literacy	Enrolment	Immunization	Real GDP/PC	Education	Health	Income	HDI
Battgram	3	3	3	5	2	3	3	3
Hangu	7	7	6	1	7	5	1	7
Indus-Kohistan	1	1	1	7	1	2	5	1
Lower Dir	6	6	7	3	6	7	2	5
Shangla	2	2	2	6	3	1	4	1
Tank	5	5	4	4	5	6	6	6
Upper Dir	4	4	5	2	4	4	1	4

Source: Pakistan, National Human Development Report, 2003.
Note: Number 1 represents the most impoverished district.

supply and sanitation, health services, road infrastructure, and energy supply are both deficient and of poor quality.

The social organization in Dir-Kohistan is based on segmentary lineage. Anthropologists classify these societies as a subtype of 'acephalous' or headless societies. In other words, these societies have no internal hierarchies (Barth 1956). Genealogical distances determine kinship loyalties. While male relationships within the community are egalitarian, a strict hierarchy defines male-female relations. More precisely, women are an excluded group, disempowered and marginalized, with no social or economic rights. As indicated later, during the pre-invasion era, the local leaders (khans) did not enjoy hereditary title but were nominated for service to the community and the ability to entertain.

The economy is based on subsistence agriculture, with income from agriculture, forest royalties, livestock, and labour services, both down-country and abroad. Landholdings are small and climatic conditions limit crops to a maximum of two per year. Subsistence involves making use of different ecological spaces, namely agricultural land, pastures, and forests. Sustainable livelihoods depend on a careful husbanding of these resources.

13.3. Resource rights and systems of governance in Dir-Kohistan

13.3.1. Customary law[5] (Riwaj)

A brief foray into Dir-Kohistan's history sets the context for the discourse on resource rights. Dir-Kohistan's history can be traced back more than 350 years. Originally the valley residents were non-Muslim, primarily kohistanis, who presently constitute 40 per cent of the population and lay hereditary claim to the valley's communal resources (coniferous and oak forests, rangelands, and

---

[5] See Sultan-e-Rome (2002). Additional information was gathered through focus-group discussions and interviews with valley residents and notables.

alpine pastures). In 1640, the *Akhund Khel*, a clan of the *Yusufzai pathans*,[6] invaded the valley. The local *kohistanis* residing in the main valleys, Ganshal, Dhogdara, Gawaldai,and the main Dir-Kohistan valley beyond Patrak, fled to the higher and inaccessible mountain areas. In time, partly driven by the need to survive, they converted and returned to their homelands. As the *pathans* settled in the valleys and took up sedentary occupations and multiplied, a two-tiered, centralized leadership emerged in a relatively short time. The *mashers* and *maliks* (elders and chiefs), representing the second leadership tier, began to pay homage to the *Akhund khel khans* of the *Yusufzai* tribe whose progeny became the ruling family of Dir. Ghazan Khan was the most powerful *khan* of Dir before the British invasion in 1895. He died in 1884 and was succeeded by his son, Sharif Khan. In 1895, the British conferred upon him the title of *nawab* as a reward for his loyalty.

Customary law governing rights to natural resources (forests, agricultural land, rangeland, pastures, and wasteland) is rooted in a system known as *garzinda wesh*, defined literally as 'moveable distribution'. The invading *Yusufzai pathans* introduced this system in the mid-seventeenth century and over time the *kohistanis* adopted it too. The guiding rationale was that as land differed in composition, location/accessibility, fertility, and availability of water, it was necessary to ensure equal sharing of its best and worst features. The permanent aspect of this system was the allotment of all categories of land among the main tribes. Each allotment included a mix of agricultural land, forest (*zangal*), pasture (*warshoo*), and wasteland. The sub-tribes within each tribe reallotted the land and houses every five, seven, or ten years, depending on what was agreed upon mutually. The local term for the segments subject to reallotment was *dawtar*. The shareholders in this arrangement were referred to as *dawtaris*.

In addition to the fixed land boundaries separating major tribes, occupations and tribal status also led to the creation of permanent entitlements known as *serai* while the owners of such lands were called *stanadars*. These were community land grants that were turned over to holy families/persons to construct mosques as well as for self-sustenance.[7] A more important type of land grant, which subsequently had significant political ramifications, was to the tribal elders, which was referred to as *khan serai*. Originally, these grants had a functional purpose in providing resources to entertain, a critical requisite for leadership: the categories were *daday serai* (maize-serving area), *mela serai* (guest area), and *telu serai* (oil-burning area in the *hujra*). *Serai* holdings were *mundai* (with defined borders) and did not preclude *dawtar* shares.

---

[6] *Yusufzai* is the tribal generic for various clans, such as *painda khel, akhund khel, and sultan khel.*

[7] Arguably, these grants can be viewed as the first manifestation of private property. A similar reference is made in Mukhopadhyay (this volume) to land grants in Goa, India, given by the Portuguese colonial rulers to European settlers.

In effect, the distribution among sub-tribes was more actively enforced with respect to agricultural lands, villages, and oak forests. In the more remote coniferous forests and alpine pastures, the main tribal partitions determined access rights. The sub-tribes had common access within these partitions reflecting their limited subsistence needs in relation to the vast forest resources. Grazing was a more wide-ranging activity with potential for intertribal discord. But this was resolved through the payment of *qalang* (grazing tax) between sub-tribes in the oak forests and between main tribes in the alpine pastures.

Surprising similarities can be found between this system and the rotational fishing quotas in the study by Gunawardena and Steele (this volume). These similarities span diverse ecological and spatial boundaries. The differences relate to environmental impacts rooted in the respectively fixed and moveable aspects of the two systems.

While the *garzinda wesh* system ensured equitable access to CPRs, the environmental consequences of such a system can only be presumed since they have not been documented. In the absence of a sense of rootedness in a particular area, one could infer communities did not have an interest in resource conservation. However, it is difficult to disentangle the *wesh*-induced effects on degradation from those generated by natural processes, such as population growth and commercial inroads.

13.3.1.1. EVOLUTION OF CUSTOMARY RIGHTS

During the *nawabi daur* (tenure), the *garzinda wesh-serai* system evolved into more formal arrangements. To start with, the *serai* grants were tenure/lifetime entitlements. However, they acquired hereditary status as the leaders acquired more power. In time, the *nawabs* (local rulers) also laid claim to communal resources. Rahmat Ullah Khan who reigned in the last quarter of the seventeenth century was the first *nawab* to impose fiscal burdens on the communities. In return for user rights, he levied various taxes such as *begar* (co-opted labour) and *ushr* (land tax) for the use of agricultural land and forests, and *qalang* (grazing tax) for grazing pastures.[8] The *nawab* claimed control over the forests and forced the communities to provide him with timber and, later, to allow his designated contractors to cut the trees. Initially, the internal customary distributions *(garzinda wesh)* remained intact as long as communities paid the price.

The *quid pro quo* arrangements following the British colonial invasion increased the *nawabs'* hold on community resources. In return for ensuring stability, the British gave the ruling *nawabs* (Muhammad Sharif Khan and his grandson Shah Jehan Khan) a free hand to rule. The period from 1895

---

[8] The communities paid *ushr* directly and performed *begar* on the *nawab's* behest. They collected *qalang* from the *gujjars* and paid a portion to the *nawab*.

up to 1969, when the government of Pakistan formally annexed Dir State, was the most autocratic. It also saw changes in traditional property relations. The *nawabs* gave land grants to favoured courtiers and servants, not to all valley residents. In particular, they allotted residential land to landless *gujjars* in return for *begar* (services in the form of labour). This created a potential conflict situation; especially as later the grantees also claimed forest royalty rights by virtue of their permanent holdings. An important contribution of the *nawab* was to give permanent rights to existing owners of agricultural land. These rights were codified in law.[9]

The Constitution also barred extraction of minerals and medicinal plants from forests except for medical treatment. Similarly, fishing and hunting were banned. However, no formal land settlements took place as in neighbouring *Swat* and *Chitral*. The moveable distribution aspects of the *garzinda wesh* system have virtually disappeared by now. Towards the end of the *nawab's* reign, the sub-tribes and clans began to lay permanent claim to oak-forest tracts. In more recent years, a portion of these tracts has been carved up into private/family holdings. Commercial land transactions are now common. The only feature of customary law, which continues to prevail, is the main tribal partitions in coniferous forests and the alpine pastures. While the *nawab's* fiat restricted extraction of some forest products, customary law continued to govern subsistence activities in these forests.

The accession to and subsequent administrative merger with Pakistan freed communities from the *nawabi daur*, and they stopped paying taxes. To all intents and purposes, the rights-related clauses of the *nawab's* constitution became null and void with the merger. The communities also instituted cases against the *nawab* for illegal appropriation of agricultural lands and urban property, most of which are still in process. The combination of a growing human and livestock population, the interweaving of private and communal property, and the rising price of timber have created an unstable environment with regard to property and access rights. Neither customary nor statutory law has been able to grapple satisfactorily with the emerging claims and conflicts.

Customary law in Dir-Kohistan contains ethnic biases. The *kohistanis* invoke this law to claim forest access rights and the bulk of forest royalties, denying the *pathans* and *gujjars*. In the valleys (Dhok Dara, Gwaldai, Bela) with dominant *pathan* and *gujjar* populations, access and royalty rights are not contested. The problems arise in the predominantly *kohistani* valleys, where minorities have either been granted land by the *nawab*, or have purchased it. The *kohistanis* claim the *nawab's* grants are illegal and have contested them in court. They claim rights to the valley's resources by virtue of lineage.

[9] According to section 25, if a person has a continuous possession of land, residence, and tree for fifteen years then s/he is the actual owner of that property and others have no claims over the property. All the property-related issues/conflicts will be decided according to Islamic law (Constitution of Dir State, 1963).

Customary law also excludes women from a share in forest royalties. The government has deferred to this by excluding women from the list of those entitled to such royalties.

13.3.1.2. NATURAL RESOURCE MANAGEMENT UNDER CUSTOMARY LAW[10]

Subsistence is based upon the simultaneous exploitation of a number of ecological spaces and characteristically involves the coordination of activities. Communities had to ensure an intricate balance between agriculture and herding, supplementing these activities with extraction of wood and non-wood products from the forests. To meet the irrigation requirements for their crops, communities jointly build and maintain a system of head-works and water channels. Head-works diverted river and stream water into irrigation ditches that brought water down to the valley floor. Wooden viaducts were made to span chasms and cliffs. Keeping this intricate system in repair was a substantial challenge for the community and demanded continual joint action. The farmers who benefited from a particular channel worked collectively to maintain it. Water from these channels was also used to power watermills and, presently, power generators.

With climatic conditions limiting agricultural activity to one to two crops a year, livestock herding is an important economic activity both as a source of meat and dairy products. Herding follows the cycle of water and pasture availability. The highland pastures are most productive during spring and summer and the herds migrate up so as not to interfere in agricultural activities. They move back down to the villages after harvesting and graze in the oak forests and fields, with supplements of dry fodder.

The description above serves to illustrate the fact that communities tend to harmonize agricultural activities with what the resource base can support. Sustainable use of natural resources is critical to their survival. By the same token, establishing clear rights with regard to the timber forests offers the promise of lifting them out of their poverty and also ensuring sustainable management of these forests. However, as we note later, the institutional climate encourages predatory practices and communities tend to go along with them for their own survival.

This study finds communal ownership to be a precondition for equity. The conservation benefits are less clear. While there is a presumption that the moveable distribution aspect of the *garzinda wesh* system might be at odds with resource conservation, more recently, the allocations have become permanent, which might lead to sustainable use. But neither aspect has been quantified and attempts to do so would be difficult. This compliments the

---

[10] This subsection is based upon information provided by local community elders and personal observation.

findings of Mukhopadhyay (this volume) wherein equity-conservation links do not evolve as is expected by a section of the literature in this area. He too finds that the increase in equity does not necessarily lead to greater sustainability.

13.3.1.3. ADJUDICATION UNDER CUSTOMARY LAW: THE JIRGA[11]

Despite the historical evolution of customary law and CPR management, differences within and across communities over resource rights and use are bound to be inevitable and require mediation. The traditional *jirga* dates back to pre-Islamic times and in its original, pure form, was shaped by two opposing tendencies. First, it included leaders drawn from patrilineal descent groups. These descent groups were exogamous, meaning that men within each descent group married women from different descent groups, an act which both cemented relations and crystallized identities between these groups. The emphasis was on maintaining peace and was dictated by external threats from other tribes/ethnic groups. Thus, *jirga* decisions had a tempering influence on disputes involving women/wives, property or violence, and factional discord and political disintegration. These decisions favoured conciliation although penalties for murderers and other criminals were harsh with either exile or confiscation of property. Even today *lamo aman* (village peace) is a respected value and to be called *aman pasand* (peace lover) is a compliment, more surprising in the prevailing culture of guns, drugs, and violence.

The *jirga* is a consultative assembly of respected elders nominated by the communities and is entrusted with the authority to take decisions, which are binding upon individuals, feuding groups, or the community as a whole. Communal resource rights give rise to intercommunity differences at many levels, but these tend not to escalate into open violence and are resolved by the *jirga*. The various forms in which these tensions manifest themselves are:

- Within communities: over arable land and private family holdings in oak forests. These are settled within the community.

- Between ethnic groups: primarily over timber. As discussed earlier, the minorities (*pathans and gujjars*) claim rights in terms of forest royalties. While the government has conceded these in principle, it is only a recent *jirga* decision, which has created a precedent for the actual transfer of royalties to them. However, their claims continue to be contested by the *kohistanis*, especially in valleys where they have little representation.

- Between villages: over agrarian land, community oak forests, and boundaries between coniferous forests.

[11] This section draws upon Keiser (2002).

In many ways, the *jirga* is the only hope of redress and it is beginning to both supplant and support formal legal institutions. The local communities often find themselves frustrated by the lengthy, biased, and expensive judicial processes. The *jirga* system is popular because it dispenses speedy justice—albeit within its male-dominated parameters—and is relatively unbiased and inexpensive. The institution has survived political vicissitudes, partly because the judicial and departmental processes have failed to deliver. In fact, on key occasions, the state relied on *jirga* mediation to diffuse potential crises. As we show later, the state empowered it to implement judicial decisions on forest royalties, which it was unable to do itself. By and large, the *jirga* is not prone to be coerced or its decisions subverted because of the inherently democratic manner in which it is constituted and its accountability to the communities. In the few cases where its members have been manipulated by vested interests, such as the forestry department and timber contractors, they have been removed swiftly and have faced social ostracism.

13.3.2. *Statutory law* (qanoon)

Statutory law governing resource rights in Dir-Kohistan has historically been defined by two key pieces of legislation:

- The Forest Act, 1927;
- The NWFP Forest Ordinance, 2002.

The Forest Act, 1927, divided public forests into three classes: reserved forests, village forests, and protected forests. This act also empowered the provincial government to regulate private forests or wasteland (*guzara*). Under this act, the government declared the forests of Dir-Kohistan state forests in 1972 and protected forests in 1975. The NWFP Forest Ordinance, 2002, which supplanted the earlier Act, retains these forest categories. Further, it provides the legal framework for the NWFP Protected Forest Management Rules, 2001. In effect, the legal clauses governing resource rights and access in the two acts are almost identical, empowering the NWFP Forest Department to: (*a*) declare forest categories; (*b*) reserve trees; (*c*) close forests and specify acts prohibited in protected forests; (*d*) make rules for protected forests; and (*e*) impose penalties. The penalties, both financial and custodial, for infractions have been made more stringent under the Forest Ordinance, 2002.

The new Forest Ordinance also represents the culmination of an extended forestry reform process, which began with the National Conservation Strategy (NCS) in 1991. The NCS recognized the importance of social forestry in future development of the forestry sector and recommended the establishment of participatory, community-based management systems, based on cost sharing and with the active involvement of women. The draft NWFP Forest Ordinance includes key social forestry concepts such as participatory forest management plans (FMPs), assigning management rights to village communities, JFM, community participation in regeneration schemes, and leasing out government forests for social forestry and other purposes. However, the emerging consensus is that the Forest Ordinance, 2002, and the Protected Areas Management Rules, 2001, are no different from the anticommunity thrust of the laws and regulations that they have supplanted. Thus:

The existing laws are punitive in nature and do not provide any incentives for compliance with their provisions. Indeed, they are based on the gamekeeper-poacher approach and are considered unduly harsh, not so much in the matter of punishments (which till recently were on the low side) but in the uncompromising application of its provisions, particularly those relating to restrictions on use of timber and other forest produce. Critics have pointed out that the laws make no distinctions between subsistence-oriented violations and violations based on commercial interests. (Hamid 2002: 34)

If anything, the new Ordinance has introduced more stringent fines and penalties, which underscores its enforcement mindset. Moreover, the discretionary power of the divisional forest officer to appoint village forest officers and issue management orders to them, originally applicable to trees and brushwood in wastelands in *Hazara* only, has been extended to cover all forest produce in all types of forests.[12]

Statutory law in Pakistan separates ownership and user rights. It invests ownership of forest resources in the government and curtails user rights for the forest-dependent communities by both subsuming and diluting their customary rights. Implicit in this is a conservation mandate, which is at odds with socio-economic justice. Further, the state agencies do not possess adequate means for enforcement. In a defensive reaction, they tighten statutory law/regulatory controls which, in turn, call for stricter enforcement. Ultimately, forest-dependent communities are alienated from their resource base and other players, as well as members of the community, and begin to exploit the hiatus between the law and its enforcement. This gives rise to conflicts in the mediation of which official courts are either lax or are incapable.

13.3.2.1. NATURAL RESOURCE MANAGEMENT UNDER STATUTORY LAW

Resource management under statutory law has an impact on two types of resource use: subsistence and commercial. Subsistence use (extraction of fuelwood, fodder, other NTFP, timber for house construction, etc.) is governed by a system of permits, fines, and penalties. The prior open access to these resources under customary law is now subsumed under statutory regulations.

---

[12] For a critique of the Forest Ordinance, see Hamid 2002.

These regulations have become instruments for both rent seeking and violations and have brought communities into open conflict with the Forest Department. Notwithstanding recent reform efforts to include communities in forest management, the Forest Department continues to view them as intruders and the forests as a valuable source of timber. The enforcement bent of the line departments is more prone to encourage resource overextraction than sustainable use. When communities are denied or have limited access to resources to meet subsistence needs, they are forced to circumvent the forest laws and engage in predatory acts.

The duality evident in the Forest Department's enforcement make-up and the use of rules and regulations to extract rent also characterizes the commercial exploitation of forest resources. Various timber-contracting systems have been in force after Partition in 1947. In fact, even before Partition, the *nawab* had designated contractors who carried out logging activities and sold the timber down-country.[13] The first system after Partition was one of departmental harvesting. The Forest Department hired the labour crew or work contractors and sold the timber through sealed tenders or open auction. The contractor system eventually replaced this arrangement and the Forest Department began to auction standing forests to timber contractors. Timber prices were fixed and revenues were distributed between the Forest Department, the contractors, and the concessionists.[14] Standing volumes were marked and their cutting time defined. However, as timber prices continued to rise, the fixed prices had to be renegotiated which made the system cumbersome. Moreover, the contractors manipulated the system by cutting well in excess of marked trees and understating sales.

After open conflict between communities and the government in 1976 over forest royalties, the government abolished the contractor system and replaced it with the Forest Development Corporation (FDC), on the understanding that it would promote mechanization and scientific management. Forest cooperatives with the intent of involving local communities were also established. The change was aimed at a more efficient, flexible, and transparent management. In 1987, the net-sale system replaced the fixed-price system. The net-sale system linked revenue distribution to the prevailing price of timber and labour costs. In effect, however, nothing changed. The FDC inflated its costs and delayed sales and royalty payments to the communities. Such

---

[13] Forests were an important source of revenue during the colonial era. Between 1902 and 1927, the *Dir nawabs* sold thousands of trees to outside contractors. To be exact, 39,000 *deodar* (cedar) trees were sold in 1918 and 71,500 trees were targeted for felling during 1921–3. Worried about the downstream impacts, particularly on the *Swat* Canal system (*Panjkora* valley formed the main catchment area), the British initially negotiated with the *nawabs* to stop the cutting. Unsuccessful in their efforts, they sealed off the downstream movement of timber (Mumtaz 1989).

[14] The term concessionists, which is inserted in statutory law, is resented by the communities because it gives a discretionary context to their resource rights.

deferred payments allowed the original contractors to slip back in. Indigent communities needed immediate payments and they sold their concessions to the contractors for a pittance, signing over their rights through collective powers of attorney. The covert practice of harvesting well in excess of the marked trees continued too. The so-called forest cooperatives were subverted into arrangements for perpetuating contractor interests.

13.3.3. *The scope for local government*

The military government established the National Reconstruction Bureau (NRB) in the year 2000. The NRB is a think tank entrusted 'with the mission to formulate policy for national reconstruction to generate fundamental thoughts on promoting good governance to strengthen democracy through the reconstruction of state institutions' (PINs 2006). The NRB prepared a national devolution plan and after extensive stakeholder consultations presented it to the nation in August 2000. Its basic principles are defined as 'people-centred, rights- and responsibility-based, and service-oriented.'

The devolution plan has two crucial implications for forestry:

- It allows the creation of citizen community boards (CRBs) around the issue of forest resources. In other words, the devolution concept would allow the formation of community groups dealing with forestry matters outside the structure (and control) of the Forest Department. Such boards could, in principle, enter into an agreement with the FD for joint forest management and in a much more substantive way than in the present arrangements specified in the NWFP Forest Ordinance, 2002.

- The plan subordinates the district level FD staff to the district coordination officer (DCO) and, through him, to the chief mayor. District-level FD staff would thus lose their importance in the FD hierarchy.

This could be seen as one possible path to institutional remediation, suggested by Vani (2002), which dovetails the micro with the macro. Vani, who argues in favour of a decentralized governance framework on the grounds that it ensures the sustainable management of natural resources better, however suggests a balanced approach that promotes 'harmony between macro-legal (statutory) and micro-legal (customary) frameworks' (Vani 2002).

Shyamsundar (this volume) cites evidence based on a global survey to demonstrate that devolution leads to better interactions between state agencies and communities and enhanced environmental outcomes. However, several caveats, documented by Mishra (2005), are in order, which cast doubt on the viability of decentralized governance frameworks. The underlying premise for his scepticism is the relationship between state-sponsored management institutions and local user communities which he describes as 'one of distrust and confrontation rather than one based on mutual cooperation.' He cites case histories on collaborative management also known as JFM initiatives in Orissa to illustrate their failure. He also demonstrates that pure community-led initiatives in the same state (the *Sulia Paribesh Parishad* in the Sulia forest in the district of Nayagarh) were more successful than the other.

13.4. Perverse incentives in the forestry sector

Perverse incentives arise as a result of a misalignment of incentives and responsibilities. The Forest Department, for instance, which has a conservation mandate, confronts an emerging complex of perverse incentives inimical to conservation. A key contributing factor has been the rapidly rising prices of timber products over the past three decades which has led to ingress into the valley by the 'timber mafia'—that is, contractors who are organized and operate on a large scale. Their excesses are evident in logging well beyond sanctioned limits. Such groups collude with the Forest Department and civil administration functionaries for mutual gain (Khattak *et al.* 1997 and Hamid 2002). The FD staff have seen an erosion in their standards of living, which has made them vulnerable to financial inducements. The risks associated with trying to curb an increasingly lucrative business coupled with the prospect of illegal gratuities makes it difficult for FD staff to resist these inducements. Other factors contributing to the decline in professional integrity and competence are the politicization of appointments, inadequate training, and the lack of non-monetary incentives that might offset the lure of illegal gratuities (Hamid 2002).

There is increasing divergence between forest fines and penalties and timber prices.[15] This, coupled with discretionary punishments, the scarcity premia attached to forest permits, and the lack of transparency in the interpretation of rules and regulations, has created a perverse structure of incentives for unsustainable levels of timber extraction. There is no discernible increase in the real incomes of the staff in the long run. When compared with other sectors (private organizations, donor agencies, semi-corporate bodies, etc.), the trends become even more unfavourable.

Absolution is not possible for the other key player, the communities, either. Forests meet the subsistence needs of communities and have agricultural potential via conversion to cropland. *A priori*, this ought to create nurturing mindsets. But the reality is that weak property rights create uncertainty about future subsistence and income streams, especially in an inflationary environment. The concern is that forests will disappear no matter what the

---

[15] Sustainable Development Policy Institute (SDPI) in-house unpublished calculations (1998).

community might do (Inayatullah 1996). Even in privately owned forests (*guzaras*) 'right holders may see in regeneration a reintroduction of state property rights, which may stifle even natural regeneration' (Azhar 1993). Somanathan (1991) finds that 'the fundamental reason for deforestation is the system of property rights which denies the local people certainty about future benefits from forestry. This has destroyed the incentive to use forests sustainably.'

13.4.1. *Subsistence needs: the trigger for human insecurity*

The Forest Department tends to choose the path of least resistance, coming down heavy-handedly on the disempowered communities, who rely on the forests to meet their subsistence needs, while colluding for personal gain and profit with vested interests. As noted, the rising prices of timber, fuelwood and forest products, an erosion in the standard of living of the forest custodians, fines and penalties that are selectively applied and fail to match the nature of the transgression, and royalties that are appropriated by the rich and powerful have all combined to create a structure of perverse incentives antithetical to conservation. The irony is that the key inroads into forest resources are being made by commercial and development groups which the management is not in a position to oppose and, in fact, cooperates with.

13.4.2. *Forest royalties: the trigger for conflict*

The excesses committed by the timber contractors overshadow community inroads into forests. The timber trade also has a distinct anticommunity bias: while communities are entitled to a substantial share (60 per cent) of royalties from the logging in 'protected' forests, active collusion between the timber contractors, village elders (*masheran*) and the Forest Department have deprived them of the bulk of these royalties.[16] Although the organizational (direct contracts, FDC) and financial (fixed-price, net-sale system) arrangements have been diverse, without exception they have limited the community share in revenues to a minimum.

There have been two episodes of open conflict in Dir-Kohistan over this issue. The first episode occurred in 1976 when the government declared Dir-Kohistan's forests as protected. In an attempt to secure higher royalties and curb the progressively greater inroads into the forests by the contractors who have been engaged in logging activities since the *nawabs* were in power, the local people staged a march against the government at Sheringal, the capital of Dir Kohistan. The government initially deployed the Frontier Constabulary to control them but as the conflict escalated and became more extended, it

---

[16] Information provided by local elders. Also see Khattak *et al.* (1997).

called in the army and, eventually, had to use the air-force to subdue the communities. All three ethnic groups took part in the conflict. Subsequently, the Bhutto government negotiated with the communities and increased their share in royalties from 25 per cent to 60 per cent. The *Sultan Khel* and *Painda Khel* tribes, who took the brunt of the casualties, received a larger share (80 per cent).[17]

The second episode occurred in the 1994–2000 period, and was spurred by a market-driven collapse in governance systems. The main timber species of commercial value are deodar (cedar), blue pine, fir and spruce. Their prices currently range between Rs 1–1.25 lakhs (US$1,500–2,000) per tree.[18] While creating an enormous potential for enriching the communities, wealth of such magnitude also acted as a magnet for the timber contractors. They colluded with the Forest Development Corporation (FDC), local notables (*maasheran*), and the Forestry Department to work the system to their advantage. Through the use of unauthorized powers of attorneys and manipulation of the net-sale system, the contractors appropriated the bulk of the royalties leaving the communities with a pittance. In a weak legal and institutional environment, rising prices have acted as perverse incentives. They underscore the paradigm shift in which resource extraction has begun to take precedence over sustainable use.

Thus, we have a classic case where communities have rights on paper but are without the legal, institutional or political means to avail themselves of these rights–in other words, a growing divergence between *de jure* and *de facto* rights. Ideally, well-defined rights and entitlements, and mechanisms to implement them provide a cushion against external shocks. When this is not the case, external shocks can make weak governance systems even more fragile. In the Dir-Kohistan case, these shocks generate two opposing, conflict-generating trends:

- A direct correlation between rising prices and financial entitlements of communities (royalties);
- An inverse correlation where deteriorating governance denies them these entitlements while contractors take the slice.

The causes for the two episodes of conflict differ. Specifically, in the first case, the disagreement is over royalty rates; in the second, the cause of conflict is manipulation of an ostensibly improved system. Or, to put it differently, where communities were ripped off in the first case, their pockets were picked in the second.

---

[17] *Ibid.*

[18] Personal communication. Compare this with Pakistan's current per capita income of US$730.

13.5. Evidence of degradation[19]

Dir-Kohistan's rich forests and watersheds are important as a source of liveli-hood. Their neglect leads to biodiversity loss, soil erosion, dam sedimen-tation, and down-country floods. Baseline and trend data on degradation have been difficult to obtain, forcing us to draw on descriptive and visual evidence.[20] The descriptive evidence of degradation is presented in various project documents.[21] The causes, symptoms, and visible signs of degradations are indicated in three areas.

13.5.1. *Land-use changes*

Agriculture is no longer able to support the population, forcing people to convert forest and grazing lands to agricultural use. Since the land is not ideally suited to agriculture, large tracts are being converted to compensate for low productivity. Further, these are poorly terraced tracts on upland slopes. Hence, there is high erosion and erosivity (8 per cent of the land in the valley is cultivated). The three major land-use changes are conversion of coniferous forests, rangelands and alpine pastures, and oak forests to agricultural use. In the coniferous forests, rangelands and alpine pastures, this practice is known as *karin*.

13.5.2. *Rangeland and pasture degradation*

Rangeland (temperate and alpine) is being overgrazed and degraded as the growing population attempts to meet its nutrition needs through increasing animal numbers (56 per cent of the land comprises rangelands and alpine pastures; in addition, oak forests provide leaf fodder). Livestock also compete with wild ungulates for rangeland resources. More than 50 per cent of the grazing herds now consists of goats that are voracious feeders. Overgrazing has led to the replacement of grass and scrub with non-palatable seasonal shrubs and forbs. Furthermore, soil erosion due to the loss of vegetative cover is increasingly evident. Area-wise, too, grazing lands are shrinking due to conversion to agricultural use.

---

[19] The sources of information for this subsection are: (*a*) project reports of the Environ-mental Rehabilitation Project in NWFP and Punjab (ENRP); (*b*) EEC Evaluation/Preparation Mission Report, 1992; (*c*) Revised PC-1 of the GoNWFP, Dir-Kohistan Upland Rehabilitation and Development Project, 1995; and (*d*) field observations and consultations with communi-ties.

[20] The IUCN and the European Commission launched a 7-year project in 1996 to address the problem of degradation.

[21] EC Evaluation/Preparation Mission Report, August 1992.

13.5.3. *Wildlife loss*

The area under pristine forest is reducing fast as deforestation and erosion take their toll. This reflects the activities of the 'timber mafia', as well as of local communities striving to make ends meet in a hostile ecological and non-transparent institutional environment. Consequently, although the status of wildlife in Dir-Kohistan is not well documented, there are reports that some species such as markhor (*Capra falconeri*), snow leopard, musk deer, and pheasant have become endangered due to habitat destruction. Illegal hunting also contributes to the problem. A survey carried out by the NWFP Wildlife Department referred to various illegal hunting methods adopted by the locals and out-of-season hunting (Shakeel 2002).

13.6. Discussion and conclusions

13.6.1. *Resource rights*

Two related issues are addressed in this chapter:

- What changes to the existing resource rights regimes need to be made to resolve the problems described and analysed?
- Are existing mechanisms and processes adequate to implement the recommended changes in the existing resource rights regimes and, if not, what is required?

Resource rights in Dir-Kohistan are multifaceted. As indicated, both statutory and customary laws govern resource rights. These can be defined in terms of private property and communal access to resources. Further, they relate to both subsistence and commercial (royalty) aspects.

13.6.2. *Private property*

Customary law governs private property rights. Their historical precedents can be traced back to the *serai* grants which became hereditary entitlements under the *nawabs*. Over time, the *nawabs* forcibly acquired both agricultural land and urban property. They also granted agricultural lands in return for *begar* (labour services) performed by the ethnic minorities *(gujjars)* and migrants who settled in the valley.[22] The expanding scope of private property also reflects land-use changes in the oak forests. The process of converting large forest tracts into private family holdings, and of the lower slopes into terraced fields, has been ongoing for some time. Private property transactions have become a common feature.

[22] The communities are presently contesting these grants in the civil courts.

Tensions over private property tend to occur within and between communities but are resolved by the *jirga*. Such tensions can be diffused further if the existing demarcations and land-use changes were brought within the ambit of the existing land settlement policy as is the case in *Swat* and *Chitral,* especially when they are being entered in the *wajab-ul-arz* (record of rights). However, this should be attempted on a pilot scale and with the concurrence and active participation of the *jirga.* While land terracing may be environmentally unsound, it is driven by demographic realities and needs to be combined with plantation.

13.6.3. *Subsistence rights*

Subsistence rights in coniferous forests reflect the interplay of statutory and customary law. Communities' original subsistence rights were determined under customary law (*garzinda wesh*). These rights have been conceded under statutory law but are heavily restricted, originally under the Forest Act, 1927, and now under the Forest Ordinance, 2002. While the laws restrict and complicate community access to forest resources, they are also ineffective in view of the Forest Department's limited enforcement capabilities. Moreover, statutory restrictions are both resented and ignored. The process of degradation and conversion of forests to arable land and pastures (*karin*) continues apace, fuelled largely by demographic compulsions.

The proposed intervention in this case is the introduction of community forest management (CFM). Nepal's success stories in CFM are well documented (Kanel, this volume). Among other things, a key factor in this success is the socialization of the FD to the potential role of the communities in all aspects of NRM. As a result, the FD has become a facilitator (gatekeeper) rather than co-manager—an arrangement which has proved to be tangibly successful in terms of benefits accruing to the communities and revenues to the FD.

Ghate (this volume) proposes a more inclusive role for the FD. Her contention is that communities are hierarchically structured which distorts participation as well as distribution of benefits. Also, forests generate global ecological benefits which the community may not factor into its activities. Finally, community initiatives need to be supported by the state in the form of technical and financial inputs which communities lack. In particular, Ghate refers to the need to ensure community property rights. It may be mentioned that JFM as defined and practised in Pakistan is a donor-driven idea, which the FD has manipulated to its advantage without relinquishing any of its existing powers. In contrast, Kanel and Ghate see the state's (FD) role differently—as adviser, facilitator, financier, and monitor. In other words, the FD needs to transform its autocratic mindset into a more enabling one.

13.6.4. *Rights to forest royalties*

Rights to forest royalties are determined by customary law and are contentious in that they discriminate across ethnic groups and against women. However, two constituted commissions have weighed in on these issues, recommending a more just and gender-inclusive distribution. Also, *pathans* and *gujjars* have full royalty entitlements in the valleys in which they are in a majority. Basically, the existing lacunae need to be resolved through a process of negotiation between the government and the *jirga* (which remains the most representative and effective institution), and by invoking the provisions of Islamic law governing property rights and entitlements. However, as we noted, inequity in distribution is a source of intercommunity tension but not conflict.

Conflict has had more to do with governance lapses. In the first place, the communities resent being described as concessionists when they feel the forests have historically been theirs to use. But the crux of the problem lies in the manner in which their royalties are flagrantly appropriated. Community forest management (CFM), adapted to emerging market realities, would be an inclusive solution (Jodha 2005).

Clearly, the FD has failed on two counts: first, it has circumscribed community rights to subsistence resources; second, it colludes with the 'timber mafia' to deprive communities of commercial benefits from the forest. Jodha (2005) points to remediation as having two interlinked aspects. First, there is a need to restore community-based management of common property resources (CPR). Second, such management needs to factor in market incentives.

For CPR-revival or rehabilitation, almost exclusive dependence on nature (for biophysical regeneration, flows, etc.), needs to be supplemented by new possibilities provided by modern technologies, market, and management systems, including new change agents and mobilizers. This calls for realization that CPRs are not merely means of resource conservation but productive assets of the communities. Enhanced productivity and incomes through CPR offer better incentive for improved management of CPRs than subsidies, etc. (Jodha 2005: 15)

13.6.5. *Grazing rights*

Grazing rights in the alpine pastures and in the oak forests also come within the frame of customary law. The tribal and sub-tribal divisions remain intact. Use of these pastures across tribes and by itinerant *gujjars* is still subject to payment of *qalang*. Shrinking pastures and increasing livestock numbers are the key threats. These threats should be addressed through technical and environmental interventions, such as increasing animal productivity via nutrition improvements and undertaking environmental conservation/rehabilitation of these pastures. They do not call for fundamental changes in grazing practices, which have survived through centuries, or in the communal ownership and tenure systems in which these practices are embedded.

To sum up, the reach of statutory law should not be extended further given that it is both punitive and ineffective. The first task should be to address this weakness rather than extend its scope. CFM offers the prospects of more efficient management, improved access, and just distribution, both with respect to subsistence and royalty rights. Resource ownership and access rights in pastures, oak forests, and arable land should remain within the domain of customary law. This law and the *jirga*, which mediates tensions arising from the practice of this law, have popular roots and are more enduring. In contrast, state systems, which supplanted the autocratic rule of the *nawab*, have proven to be inept. In fact, as in the case of forest royalties, the *jirga* succeeded where the courts failed to provide redress.

In conclusion, the key resource rights and related system interventions proposed are in the areas of:

- Private property;
- Subsistence;
- Forest royalties; and
- Grazing.

References

Agrawal, A. (2001). 'Common Property Institutions and Sustainable Governance of Resources'. *World Development*, 29/10: 1649–72.

Azhar, A. R. (1993). 'Commons, Regulation, and Rent-seeking Behaviour: The Dilemma of Pakistan's *Guzara* Forests'. *Economic Development and Cultural Change*, 42/1: 115–28.

Barth, F. (1956). *Indus and Swat Kohistan: An Ethnographic Survey*. Oslo, Norway: Forenede Trykerrier.

EEC (European Economic Community) (1992). *Evaluation/Preparation Mission Report, 1992*. Report. Islamabad, Pakistan: EEC Resident Office.

GoNWFP (Government of NWFP) (1995). *Revised PC-1: Dir-Kohistan Upland Rehabilitation and Development Project*. Report. Peshawer, Pakistan: GoNWFP.

—— (2004). *Environmental Rehabilitation Project in NWFP and Punjab (ENRP)*. Project Report. Islamabad, Pakistan: GoNWFP.

Government of Pakistan (1998). *District Census Report of Upper Dir*. Population Census Organization, Statistics Division, Government of Pakistan, Islamabad, May 2000.

Guha, R. (1983). 'Forestry in British and Post-British India—A Historical Analysis'. *Economic and Political Weekly*, 28/44: 1882–96.

Hamid, Z. (2002). *Regional Study on Forest Policy and Institutional Reforms: Review of Laws and Policies Governing Participatory Social Forestry in Pakistan*. Report. Islamabad, Pakistan: Asian Development Bank.

Inayatullah, C. (1996). 'Improvement of Governance in Forestry Sector'. Policy Brief Series. Sustainable Development Policy Institute, Islamabad, Pakistan.

Jodha, N. S. (2005). 'Restricted "Revisit" to Common Property Resources in Dry Regions of India'. Research Paper. ICIMOD, Kathmandu, Nepal.

Keiser, R. L. (2002). 'The Cultural Construction of Violence', in R. B. Morrison and C. R. Wilson (eds.), *Ethnographic Essays in Cultural Anthropology: A Problem-based Approach*. Itasca, IL: F. E. Peacock Publishers.

Khattak, Z., Iqbal, M., Khan, J., and Yusuf, M. (1997). *Report of the Enquiry Committee on the Determination of the Right of Forest Royalty of the Inhabitants of Gawaldai, Kalkot and Lamotai of District Upper Dir*. Report. Peshawar, Pakistan: GoNWFP.

Mishra, A. (2005). 'Conflict over Commons: Competing Paradigms for Managing Forests in the Indian State of Orissa'. Paper. TERI School of Advanced Studies, New Delhi (India).

Mumtaz, K. (1989). *Pakistan's Environment: A Historical Perspective*. Report. Lahore, Pakistan: IPEC-JRC-IUCN.

North, D. C. (1990). *Institutions, Institutional Change and Economic Performance*. Cambridge: Cambridge University Press.

PINs (Pakistan Information Networks) (2006). <http://pin.net.pk/home/portfolio/showcase/nrb/website.aspx>.

Shakeel, M. (2002). *Report on Wildlife Survey in Dir-Kohistan*. Report. Pakistan: Environmental Rehabilitation Project in the NWFP and Punjab (ERNP), European Union-Government of Pakistan.

Somanathan, E. (1991). 'Deforestation, Property Rights and Incentives in Central Himalaya'. *Economic and Political Weekly*, 26: 37–46.

Sultan-e-Rome. (2002). 'Land Tenure and Resource Ownership in Pakistan'. Paper. World Wildlife Fund, Pakistan.

Vani, M. S. (2002). 'Customary Law and Modern Governance of Natural Resources in India—Conflicts, Prospects for Accord and Strategies'. Paper submitted for the Commission on Folk Law and Legal Pluralism, 13th International Congress, Chiang Mai University, Thailand, April.

14

Is the State Passé? Competing Domains in Forestry in Orissa

Arabinda Mishra

14.1. Introduction

The emergence of a state monopoly over forest commons in India during colonial rule, and the simultaneous marginalization of local user communities, are well documented (Gadgil and Guha 1995, 1992). However, beginning with the 1988 National Forest Policy, there has been a significant reversal in the positioning of 'community' in the public policy framework on forest management in the country. This permits, in different ways, a greater exercise of rights and control over forest resources by user communities at the local level. Nevertheless, even then, the relationship between the state and local user communities continues to be, generally speaking, one of distrust and confrontation rather than one based on mutual cooperation (Ghate, this volume; Shackleton *et al.* 2002). The inconsistency between expected and actual outcomes leads to questions about the form of devolution policies, the intent behind them, and the likely implications of differing community reactions to state machinations for the success and endurance of forest management regimes based on collective action. Answers to such questions in different contexts are expected to shed better light on the community-state relationship over the management of forests, which appears to be as yet inadequately explored (Agrawal 2001) but is bound to be of pivotal importance in defining the future of devolution policies.

In India, the attempts of colonial rulers to commercially 'manage' the forests led to a situation where the community-state relationship over the resource became predominantly conflict-based (Pathak 1994). Even after independence in 1947, for nearly four decades, the state continued with con-servationist policies that limited local communities' access to forests. The ineffectiveness of such an approach and a growing community movement in many parts of the country forced the state to revise its policy on forest management in the late Eighties (Ballabh, Balooni, and Dave 2002). New devolutionary policies sought to involve the community in forest management in more meaningful and beneficial arrangements. However, communities by and large remain unconvinced about the benefits to be gained from accepting the state-designed arrangements at considerable loss of autonomy while there are also concerns over what is being perceived as covert attempts by the state to expand its authority over forests (Sarin *et al.* 2003). The consequence has been an intensification of efforts by communities, in many instances, to acquire legitimacy for their self-designed and autonomous institutional systems. Such a process is visible in many parts of India in the way local-level community organizations have united and confronted state agencies over acts of appropriation by the latter.

The present chapter looks at different dimensions of the policy failure relating to forest management and the community response to this in Orissa, a state in eastern India. The focus on Orissa is due to two reasons: first, the size of the forest-dependent population in the state is among the highest in the country and, second, there is a large community movement that has evolved around the issue of forest management. Sections 14.2 and 14.3 discuss, respectively, the literature on the state-community relationship in the context of commons management in general and the evolution of forest management policies in India. Section 14.4 discusses these issues in the context of Orissa and highlights the different forms of public policy failure that may explain the motivation for self-initiated community efforts. The case study discussed in Section 14.5 is illustrative of a local-level community initiative, and provides the basis for the subsequent analysis (in Section 14.6) of its relative strengths over alternative forest management regimes. Section 14.7 concludes the chapter.

14.2. State control, power devolution, and commons management

The mainstream argument in the vast empirical literature on commons management worldwide has been that community-based institutional systems are superior to state-authored systems when it comes to managing natural resources (Baland and Platteau 1996; Ostrom 1990). At the same time, state sanction of community management institutions has been identified as one of the empirical regularities behind successful and enduring community action in commons management (Agrawal 2001). The reasoning is that, with the state legitimizing the rules framed by communities, there is less likelihood of rule violation by the excluded. Similarly, non-communitarian interest groups too will not be entertained either by the judiciary or the executive. On the other hand, the state can also play a disruptive role *vis-à-vis* local community management institutions. Klooster (2000: 2), for instance, cites Monbiot's (1993) fear of a *'real* tragedy of commons' resulting from the intrusive influences of modernizing states in the form of withering community management institutions and the inevitable commons degradation. Few studies explore, at the empirical level, the possibilities of synergistic scenarios in which the state provides an enabling environment for community institutions to manage natural resources with greater effectiveness. However, for community institutions, support from state law is a basic prerequisite for interacting with outsiders, availing themselves of legal protection from external threats, setting limits to state power, preventing abuse of local power, and aligning local decision-making with national interests (Lindsay 1999; Lynch 1998).

State sanction of community institutions for the management of natural resources is usually linked to the broader political process of 'decentralization'. Devolution and decentralization are sometimes used interchangeably because of the common emphasis on empowering local decision makers. However, a distinction between the two may be drawn by associating the former with a transfer of decision-making power and the latter with that of administrative functions (Fisher 1999). In theory, the arguments favouring devolution in natural resource management are usually made in terms of the scope it provides for inclusion of marginalized groups, more accurate needs assessment and prioritization, reduced transaction costs, greater sense of ownership of locally devised management systems and structures, more effective monitoring of resource use, and the exploitation of social capital[1] at the local level (Larson 2002; Sundar 2001). In practice, however, the intent behind devolution in the forestry sector of many countries has been linked to reasons that are quite unrelated to the professed benefits of the process of power transfer. Thus, Li (2002) gives examples from upland South East Asia that link government-supported community-focused forestry programmes to state agendas for intensifying government control over people. Ribot (2003) cites decentralization efforts in many sub-Saharan countries that are aimed at strengthening or creating non-representative agents at the local level. In the Indian context, devolution-based policies for forest management allegedly carry forward the 'territorialization' objectives of the state (Sarin 2005; Sundar 2001).

---

[1] Social capital has many connotations (e.g. World Bank 2000); here, linked up with devolution, it refers to the norms and institutions in a community that act as enabling factors for cooperation among the community members.

Another question might be which type of institutional arrangement needs to be favoured through the devolution process in order to ensure effective community participation in managing forest resources. In the Indian context, the debate revolves around the independent self-governing user-group organizations, local government bodies under the *panchayati raj*[2] system, and the state-structured participatory institutions under the Joint Forest Management (JFM) programme. Democratic participation, downward accountability, and managerial capacity appear to be three key enabling characteristics of a local-level institutional arrangement for its efficient functioning in the forestry sector. From this perspective, state-structured institutions lose out on both participation and accountability while community institutions lack the skills necessary for the 'scientific' management of forest resources. Local government bodies are vulnerable to capture by strong vested interests and may lack the commitment to take and implement strong conservation-oriented decisions. However, equally strong arguments are advanced for entrusting local government bodies with control over natural resources. Ribot (2003, 1999), for instance, points out that such institutions will allow for sustainable arrangements once downward accountability of representation in such bodies is ensured.

All the debates on form, content, and target of devolution/decentralization, etc., need to be examined in the light of empirical evidence of the actual outcome of such processes, wherever they have been affected. So it is necessary to know whether the transfer of power to local level contributes to better resource management; whether local control over the resource results in greater economic empowerment; and how the marginalized sections of the community fare in the regime.

14.3. State's role and the devolution process in India

In India, prior to British rule, the role of the state *vis-à-vis* forests was largely passive in most parts of the country and there seems to have existed sufficient scope for community management regimes to evolve and function successfully (Singh 2001; Gadgil and Guha 1995). The British made systematic attempts to appropriate forests as state property on the grounds that state ownership over forests would lead both to efficient management and augment state revenue but, in the process, severely infringed on the customary rights of the rural community wherever they existed. Thus, state control resulted

---

[2] This refers to the system of decentralized governance in rural areas in independent India. It involves a three-tier structure of local governing bodies at village, block (an administrative unit constituting a group of villages), and district (an administrative unit consisting of a group of blocks) levels.

in significant welfare loss for the people, as evidenced from the many local community-level protests over forest access that erupted against the regime during the colonial period. From an administrative angle, implementing the controls involved high transaction costs, which implies that the efficiency argument did not actually work in practice (Kant and Berry 2001, cited in Singh 2001: 5). State control over the forests, however, continued after independence of the country. In the 1970s and 1980s, the growing conflict between the state and local communities over the use of the forest resources prompted the introduction of the Social Forestry programme. The aim was to involve local people in creating village woodlots in degraded common lands that would serve to cater to the villagers' needs for fuel and fodder. However, this programme is criticized, among other things, for its deleterious impact on food-crop production and demand for seasonal employment in agriculture, thereby contributing to a significant welfare loss for the rural poor (Rangan and Lane 2001; Saxena and Ballabh 1995).

During the 1990s the government came up with the Joint Forest Management (JFM) concept that treats people as co-managers of the forests. It is considered one of the major devolution policies in recent years for the decentralized management of natural resources. The JFM system allows for the involvement of local communities in the management of state-owned forestlands under partnership arrangements with the state Forest Department (FD) and contains specific benefit-sharing provisions with respect to the forest products. At the national level, there has been mixed results in respect of the JFM experiment. The major problem with the JFM appears to be that it is a typical top-down approach of the state with asymmetric power relationships between the state functionaries and the people. Studies have identified the other major constraints of the programme to be related to insecurity of tenure, power imbalances within communities, and inadequate benefit-sharing provisions (Ghate 2003; Sundar 2001; Conroy, Mishra, and Rai 2000).

In December 1996, new legislation called the Provisions of the *Panchayats* (Extension to the Scheduled Areas) Act, 1996 (known in short as PESA) was passed by the central government for designated tribal areas (called Schedule 5 areas) of eight states (that is, Andhra Pradesh, Bihar, Gujarat, Himachal Pradesh, Maharashtra, Madhya Pradesh, Orissa, and Rajasthan). This has led to a major reversal in the hitherto centralizing tendency of the state to acquire and retain control over natural resources. The Act is aimed at empowering local government bodies over a wide range of development-related activities. In the specific case of forest resources, PESA confers ownership rights over minor forest products to the *gram sabha/panchayat*, and not the state government. The Act has been hailed as one that 'creates a space for people's empowerment, genuine popular political participation, convergent community action, sustainable people-oriented development and auto-generated emancipation' (Saxena 2003: 22).

14.4. Managing forests in Orissa: state control, devolution, and policy failures

The state of Orissa is situated on the eastern coast of India. It accounts for almost 5 per cent of the geographical area of the country and has a population that is approximately 4 per cent of India's population (Census of India 2001). According to the latest official estimates, 47.2 per cent of the state's population belongs in the Below Poverty Line (BPL) category, which makes it the poorest state in the country. Paradoxically, the state is endowed with abundant natural resources though much of it is subject to the usual development-related anthropogenic pressures that contribute to the rapid decay and decline of such resources. The forest sector is probably the most exposed to such pressures, considering its linkages with the livelihood systems of the majority of rural households as well as its contribution to their consumptive requirements. Nearly a fourth of the state's population belongs to the indigenous tribal communities, whose lives are intimately linked to forest ecosystems spiritually, culturally, and economically.

The Orissa government continues to manage the forests as if they are state property. This premise of state ownership has remained unaltered even where there have been official attempts to devolve decision-making power to lower units of governance such as the *gram panchayats* (GPs) or to involve local self-governing community-based institutions. Following the 1996 PESA legislation at the central government level, the Orissa government passed a resolution in March 2000 giving licensing and regulatory powers to the GPs for the purchase, procurement, and trade of specified non-timber forest products (NTFPs) so that primary gatherers are not exploited by unscrupulous traders. The other devolution-based strategy is JFM, which the Orissa government adopted in 1988 (with subsequent amendments in 1993 and 1996)[3] to create space for people's participation in forest conservation and management while the state retains its ownership control and commercial interests over the resource. Accordingly, *Van Samrakhyan Samitis* (VSSs, or Forest Protection Committees) have been constituted at the village level to protect adjoining reserve forests.[4] The JFM model allows for certain concessions to be provided to the VSSs so that the villagers' requirements of firewood and small timber are met satisfactorily.

---

[3] The later modifications have essentially aimed at providing representation to marginalized groups (e.g. women and minorities) in the VSSs, and better identification of the usufruct rights granted to participating villagers.

[4] The official website of the Orissa FD informs users that, as of September 2005, there are a total of 9606 VSSs functioning in 8010 villages of the state for protecting and regenerating 8518 sq. km of forest area.

Apart from ownership over forestland, state control is also manifested in the form of public monopoly rights over the commercially valuable NTFPs.[5] The three most economically important NTFP items (that is, *kendu* leaf, bamboo, and *sal* seeds)[6] are nationalized and their trade is directly controlled by state agencies. There is enough evidence from the field (see, for example, Ghate 2005; Saxena 2003) to suggest that state procurement of the nationalized NTFPs has resulted in significant welfare loss for the primary gatherers through, among other things, suboptimal collection, delayed payment of wages, and wasteful storage practices. The loss is aggravated when the government—contrary to the stated priorities—lets its revenue compulsions override the subsistence and livelihood needs of primary users. Saxena (2003) cites the example of bamboo artisans who have suffered due to the government favouring the paper industry, which in practice receives priority and gets bamboo at subsidized prices as well.

With respect to the NTFPs brought under the control of the GPs, too, there are laws that restrict the primary-level value addition to such products, and their storage and transportation for trading purposes. Moreover, GPs have by and large been hesitant in exercising the regulatory powers vested in them under PESA so as not to drive away the traders, even though this has meant continued exploitation of the primary gatherers. As for JFM, it is well established that the model does not go so far as to put the local community and the FD on equal terms: the latter retains its authoritative identity in the arrangement. More importantly, in the Orissa context, the model is strongly opposed by the community management groups who perceive it as a manoeuvre by the state to weaken local-level community initiatives and to allow the Forest Department to regain control over the forests.

14.5. Community forest management in Orissa: a case study

The 1988 JFM resolution of the Orissa government was belated official recognition of a people's movement that had already proved to be successful in forest conservation in the state. As Arora (1994: 694) puts it, both in Orissa and West Bengal, the two states which took the lead in adopting

---

[5] NTFP items are divided into three categories: the first category consists of three nationalized items—*kendu* (*diospyros melanoxylon*) leaves, bamboo, and *sal* (*shorea robusta*) seeds; second category includes all the tree-born oil seeds, barks, resins, etc., on which the state can charge royalties and trading is through registered traders only; all other NTFPs (around 68 items) are under the control of the GPs with no requirement for trade and transit permits, levies, and royalty charges.

[6] *Kendu* leaves are used for making *bidi* (an indigenous cigarette) and are the most valuable NTFP from the state's revenue point of view. Bamboo and *sal* seeds are important raw materials for the paper industry and private oil mills.

the JFM model, 'people's participation and people's power preceded, rather than resulted from, policy change in these areas'. Community management of forests in Orissa has been characterized as a 'spontaneous' response to the failure of the state FD in checking severe degradation of the forest resources in the state (Poffenberger *et al.* 1996). The success stories among such self-initiated community initiatives have been characterized by (*a*) self-realization regarding the livelihood-related consequences of degraded forests; (*b*) leadership coming from social leaders rather than political representatives; (*c*) generally agreed-upon and inclusive systems of rules for access and benefit-sharing; (*d*) social consent to penalties for deviant behaviour; (*e*) mutual understanding and cooperation with neighbouring villages; (*f*) community-based vigilance systems for protecting the forest; and (*g*) informal dispute-settlement mechanisms.

A typical example of self-initiated community management of Orissa's forests comes from Nayagarh, one of thirty districts in the state. The geographic area of the district (4242 sq. km) is 2.5 per cent of the total geographic area of the state and more than a quarter (26.5 per cent) of it is densely[7] forested as compared to the corresponding state average of only 18 per cent (FSI 2001). In terms of the legal categorization of forests uniformly prevalent throughout India, reserve forests constitute 65 per cent of Nayagarh's recorded forest cover of 2003.8 sq. km and most of the rest belongs to the protected forest category.[8]

The practice of organized and self-initiated community-based forest management in Nayagarh can be traced back to the late 1960s and early 1970s. A pioneering effort occurred in the early 1980s in the small village of Kesharpur when villagers used a combination of community participation and moral pressure to stop forest degradation in the region. In 1992, the community movement for forest protection in the district entered a higher stage of collective action when community representatives from over 300 villages met to set up a three-tiered district-level federation, the *Jangal Surakshya Mahasangha* (JSM). Again, five years later, this entity became a founder member of the state-level *Odisha Jungle Mancha* (OJM) or the Orissa Forest Forum with the stated intention of acting as a pressure group for the community organizations in the state.

---

[7] Dense forests have a tree canopy density of over 40 per cent. When open forests (canopy density between 10 to 40 per cent) are included, the district's total forest cover becomes 44 per cent of the geographic area, which is again much above the corresponding state average of 31 per cent.

[8] Both reserved forests and protected forests refer to areas notified under the provisions of the Indian Forest Act or the State Forest Acts; while forests belonging to the reserve category enjoy the full degree of protection (all activities are prohibited unless permitted), the protected forests have a limited degree of protection (all activities are permitted unless prohibited).

14.5.1. *The case of the* Sulia Paribesh Parishad *(SPP)*

One of the village-level constituent units of the JSM is the *Sulia Paribesh Parishad* (SPP, which means Sulia Environment Society). Forest management by the SPP appears to contain many of the key aspects of successful collective action by long-standing community institutions, as cited in the relevant literature. Moreover, both in its evolution and functioning as a self-initiated community institution for forest management, the SPP is representative of similar initiatives in Nayagarh and elsewhere in the state of Orissa. Till the end of the 1990s, the Sulia reserve forest of mixed deciduous type covering 6324 ha was under the control of the state FD and, as people of the area recollect now, was under severe degrading pressures from villagers as well as the timber smugglers. Community involvement in Sulia's management started in 1990 when a few enlightened social leaders realized the disastrous consequences of a fast-vanishing forest and, with the help of a group of village youth, began to mobilize villagers for protecting the resource base. The SPP was formed after numerous village-level meetings and mutual agreements with similar village associations of adjoining areas. In 1994–5, the leaders of the movement got the SPP registered under the Societies Registration Act, which provided the organization with legal recognition and enabled it to enter into a MoU with the FD for the protection of about 1400 ha of the Sulia forest (about 22 per cent of the total Sulia forest area).

14.5.2. *Organizational structure*

In the three-tiered federal structure of the district federation (that is, the JSM), the SPP is a regional committee that forms the bottom of the pyramid. Above the regional committees are the zone-level committees and at the top is the district committee of the federation. There is a clear division of responsibility among the three tiers. While the regional committees are engaged in actual forest protection and management activities, the two major responsibilities vested with the zone- and district-level bodies relate to conflict resolution and community mobilization.

In 1999, members of the federation decided collectively on a uniform organizational structure for all the units working at the village level. Accordingly, the SPP underwent an organizational restructuring the same year, which, as a result, consists of a General Body (GB) and an Executive Committee (EC) now. The GB includes two adults—one male and one female—from each household in the member villages of the SPP. The EC members are however elected by a cluster representative body consisting of five representatives (of which at least two must be women) from each voting ward of each of the member villages. Elections to the EC take place every three years. The President of the society and its Secretary are the chief functionaries. While the GB is expected to meet at least once annually (to approve the annual income-expenditure statement of the organization), the EC meetings take place at least once a month. A core committee is empowered to deal with emergency matters. All office-bearers of the organization render their services on a voluntary basis.

14.5.3. *Membership and usufruct rights*

User-group membership in the case of the SPP is in principle inclusive of all households normally residing in the member villages of the organization. Though the SPP movement started with twenty-three villages, the present membership of the organization consists of eighteen neighbouring villages that are located in four different GPs of the district. The member villages, taken together, are estimated to have a total of about 1600 households, which translates to an approximate total population of 10,000 (as per own estimates of the SPP).

User-group members enjoy equal access and usufruct rights over the forest area protected by the organization. However, actual access to the forest is regulated through a system of entry passes and gate fees. An entry pass is given to a member household who makes a quarterly donation called the *chuli chanda* (explained later in this chapter). It allows the user a one-time access to the forest for extracting specified forest products as per the existing rules of use. Households facing requirements that exceed the permitted quantities have to get special approval from the SPP and, if allowed, are charged with gate fees, that is, predetermined unit rates that vary with product type. The gate-fee system is also applicable to member households who make a living out of selling forest products, particularly fuelwood.

14.5.4. *Forest protection*

Though there is no concrete data[9] to gauge the success of SPP in its conservation efforts, there is universal acknowledgement of the fact[10] by the state FD, the user population, donor agencies, and researchers. There is also plenty of documented anecdotal evidence on Nayagarh's community movement for forest conservation (see, for example, CSE 1999). Forest protection by the SPP in its initial years of formation involved a form of community patrolling system that is unique to the district under study. Locally known as *thenga-pali*, the system involves patrolling by all households of the community in

---

[9] The lack of concrete statistical information relating to forest quality appears to be a general problem for the forests under community protection arrangements that do not allow for any involvement of the state FD. Once the problem of mutual distrust is overcome, one of the promising areas for synergistic action by the FD and community organizations would be the scientific assessment of forest stock and quality using modern methods and technology.

[10] This came out in discussions that the author had with key informants—the district forest officials, community leaders belonging to the region, and NGO functionaries.

rotation. The *thenga* or pole functions as a symbol of responsibility that is passed on from one household to another. The household with the *thenga* accepts the responsibility of sending one of its members to patrol the forest for the day and on completion of the task passes on the responsibility to the neighbouring household by simply placing the *thenga* in front of the house. There is usually[11] no payment for the labour contribution made by households and participation by all is expected to contribute to a sense of ownership among all members of the community over the forest. In the case of the SPP, the *thengapali* system continued for six years before the villagers felt confident enough to replace it with a system that involved paid watchmen to guard the forest.

14.5.5. *Rules of resource use*

In Ostrom's (1999) 'design principles' framework for long-enduring self-governing systems for common pool resources, operational rules are congruent, match local conditions, and are capable of modification by the majority of participants. In the case of the SPP, too, rules relating to the use of forest products are seen to have evolved over time and in such a manner as to balance local requirements with the prevailing state of the forest. The rules clearly display an understanding of factors that contribute to forest degradation in the region and can be seen as the community's self-devised response to the problem. A major strength of the self-devised institutional arrangements by community organizations is the 'control' that it gives to the local resource managers, which thereby enables them to respond effectively to circumstances that warrant quick action (for example, in case of village fires, the affected households need immediate access to forest resources for gathering material that is used for house construction and repair).

In their general design, the rules for resource use are exact and product-specific, seeking to avoid ambiguity in interpretation, but at the same time kept simple to maintain ease in implementation. More specifically, the rules can be categorized as (*a*) complete bans; (*b*) quantity restrictions per member household; and (*c*) associated restrictions relating to (i) the time and frequency of extraction in any given year, (ii) the permitted tree species, and (iii) the permitted areas in the forest in which extractive activities can be carried out at different points of time. Thus, for instance, in the case of fuelwood, the SPP went for a complete ban during the first three years of its management of the Sulia forest (beginning in 1991). A one-time annual collection of one cartload per household was allowed from the fourth year onwards. The collection amount was increased to two cartloads per household

---

[11] There are variants to the system in which the watchers are paid out of a common fund or *kotha* that is created from contributions (often in kind, such as rice) by villagers.

only in the eleventh year of management. There are three approved tree species from which fuelwood can be collected and January is the identified month for annual collection. In the case of grazing, to take another example, a complete ban in the first three years was followed by permission to graze only on hillocks during the next two years. It was only from the sixth year of its management that the SPP has extended grazing permission to all areas of Sulia (except the plantation areas). However, the forest still remains out of bounds for herded goats.

14.5.6. *Rule enforcement*

The penalty system structured by the SPP is based on a mix of monetary fines as well as punitive actions. The latter type of penalties include seizure and auction of the weapons/tools and the collected items, expulsion of the violator from membership of the society and, in extreme cases, expulsion from the community. Offences are well defined and have specific penalties linked to them. Thus, for example, felling a *sal* (*shorea robusta*) tree, which is in the nature of a major offence, carries for a first-time offender a monetary fine of Rs 101 as well as seizure and auction of the tool along with the cut timber. In comparison, a minor offence like the cutting of a non-permitted tree species during the annual fuelwood collection is punished only with a monetary fine of Rs 3 per tree that is damaged. The amount of the fine increases with repetition of the offence and also attracts other kinds of punitive action. A study of the SPP's records for the past five years reveals that there are very few occasions on which the severest penalty for rule violation—that is, expulsion from the community—has been exercised. Discussions with the villagers reveal that rather than the fines, it is the social disapproval attached to rule violations that acts as the dominant disincentive.

14.5.7. *Conflict resolution*

Action against offenders from within the member community as well as outsiders tends to generate conflicts. Villagers generally recognize the disruptive potential of conflicts and rank it as the number one internal threat to community management institutions. The majority of conflicts were between neighbouring conserving communities over the demarcation of forest territory. The conflict resolution process devised by the JSM allows the hierarchical structure of the federation to be used for appeals and counter-appeals by the disputing communities. Thus, for example, if a dispute remains unresolved at the regional level, it comes under discussion at the zonal level and, failing this, at the district level. There is a Judicial Committee at the district level, which, before taking up the task of dispute settlement, asks the involved parties to agree to certain conditions: first, that there will be only a predetermined number of representatives of the parties present during the settlement process; second, that parties will abide by whatever decision the committee reaches; and, third, that costs related to the settlement process will be equally shared by the concerned parties. Once the conditions are accepted by the disputing parties, the Committee sets up a Village Court to settle the dispute. The Courts usually try to reach a compromise solution in the majority of the cases and it is interesting to note that the 'orders' passed by them are almost unfailingly accepted by the disputing parties.

14.5.8. Cost sharing

The main source of income for the SPP is the entry fee charged to member households. Other minor income sources include the fines collected from rule violators and the money recovered through the auctioning of seized items. Sharing of costs among community members is in the form of a *chuli chanda*—a *chanda* (donation) of Rs 1 per quarter of a year per *chuli* (fireplace) in the village.[12] The SPP introduced the system in member villages in the year 2000 following a consensus decision at the district federation level. The sharing arrangement governing the household contributions is such that for each rupee (equal to 100 paisa) collected, 40 paisa goes to the district-level federation, 20 paisa goes to the zone-level organization, 30 paisa is spent at the regional level, and the remaining 10 paisa goes to the source village.

14.5.9. Role of the federation

With many local-level institutions in different districts of Orissa coming together to form regional federations like Nayagarh's JSM, community forest management in Orissa may be said to have reached an advanced stage of collective action. Singh (2001) terms this vertical integration of community institutions a form of 'vertical social capital creation' and links the process to factors, both internal (for example, intercommunity conflicts emerging out of the transboundary nature of the forest resource) and external (for example, threats from the 'timber mafia') to community forest management, as having made the local-level protectors of forest realize the need for suprainstitutions. The federal framework ensures that the community movement has strength in numbers when dealing with the state FD and other external agencies. The federal structure of the JSM is also illustrative of Ostrom's (1990: 90) Design Principle 8, which is about 'nested enterprises' functioning as hierarchically linked multiple layers of cooperative effort. The federations have served to create uniform organizational structures in the local institutions, resolve disputes

---

[12] A common fireplace for a group of people residing together, such as a family, defines the group as a household unit.

among members, and take decisions on issues that go beyond local concerns. The conflict resolution process devised under the federal framework allows the hierarchical structure of the federation to be used for appeals and counter-appeals by the disputing communities.

Since their formation, many of the district-level federations have largely been on a conflict mode in their interactions with the state. In the Nayagarh case, there were instances when the JSM had to mobilize villagers in large numbers to demand action from the government against timber smugglers and to obtain compensation for the families of the village forest guards who lost their lives combating criminal elements. There are also instances in which mass protests have served to challenge specific actions taken by local FD officials, especially when such acts have been construed by the community as attempts by the government to reassert its sovereign right *vis-à-vis* the forest.

14.6. Discussion

The success of the community movement for forest conservation in Nayagarh and in other parts of Orissa is in consonance with the well-accepted empirical finding that self-devised systems for natural resources management tend to function more effectively than those imposed on users from outside (Baland and Platteau 1996; Ostrom 1990). The example of SPP serves to illustrate such a system for forest management in which rule formation and enforcement is by the resource users themselves with minimal monitoring costs. Further, self-initiated community institutions have the advantage over JFM entities in terms of autonomy in decision-making as well as accountability that flows downward rather than upward. By their very design, the unequal distribution of power between the state (FD) and the community in JFM-type institutions ensures that the structured attempts at collective action result in distrust and apprehension. At the same time, one should not overlook the strengths of the JFM model: the legal backing that it enjoys from the state, the participatory approach that it endorses in principle, and the opportunity that it provides for local communities to take advantage of the FD's expertise in modern techniques of forest management. Ghate's (this volume) documentation of different community experiences under JFM clearly brings out the problems as well as the possibilities of this model. Though her case studies come from a different state (that is, Maharashtra), the different nuances of the community-FD relationships that come out from the analysis are applicable to the case of Orissa and are equally policy-relevant. Table 14.1 presents the different institutional paradigms currently acting on Orissa's forests in a comparative framework. It is important to note that it is only in the case of the self-initiated and own-designed community institutions that the primary management objective directly addresses the livelihood-related concerns of the dependent

Table 14.1. A comparison of the institutional aspects of different management paradigms currently acting on Orissa's forests

Institutional aspects	Institutional paradigms			
	State control	PESA	JFM	Self-organized community institutions
Primary motivation	Revenue generation from forests and their conservation by keeping out people	Tribal welfare by checking exploitative practices in NTFP trade	Forest protection & regeneration with people's participation	Maintaining flows from the forest to livelihood- & subsistence-based activities
State recognition	Maximum	Highest with constitutional backing	High and firmly enshrined in the policy framework	Least: Lacking formal recognition in government policy
Nature of collective action	Nil	Mandated by law; *gram panchayats* empowered to establish a multiple buyers system at the village level and penalize unscrupulous traders	Structured by the FD; little space for community leaders to play a positive role; localized and functioning in fragmented manner; thus, always dependent on the FD for resolving transboundary issues	Spontaneous and voluntary; critical role of leadership from within the community; considerably networked with similar institutions and federated up to the state level; well developed mechanisms to resolve transboundary conflicts independent of state interference
Rule enforcement	Generally low; high monitoring costs; dependent on the formal legal system	Constrained in practice on account of limited capacity & institutional constraints	Potentially high, provided the community overcomes its distrust of the FD and the latter, in turn, is supportive	Highest; user involvement leading to least monitoring costs; based on social sanctions
Autonomy in decision-making	Absent	Partial; involvement of district administration in price fixation	Limited; authoritative identity of the FD in the partnership arrangement	Complete

Downward accountability	Nil	High, democratic, but possibly ineffective because of a mixed electorate (i.e., presence of non-interest groups)	Upward accountability: FD has the right to disband JFM organizations if they violate any of the terms but there is little the villagers can do to hold the FD accountable	High, democratic, and effective as long as there is no elite capture
Capacity for resource maintenance	High and based on scientifically structured working plans	No direct link	Potentially high: Partnership with the FD ensures that forests are managed scientifically and modern silvicultural practices can be adopted	Low: largely based on traditional knowledge and practices; shortage of financial resources often act as a major constraint
Equity in benefit-sharing arrangement	No benefit-sharing arrangement	No benefit-sharing arrangement	Potentially maximum but elite capture possible in collusion with FD officials	Potentially high but elite capture possible depending on social composition and dynamics

community. Though PESA is also linked to livelihood, the focus is not so much on the sustainable use of forests as on the control of exploitative practices by private traders of NTFPs through *panchayat* empowerment. Similarly, in the case of JFM, the community interest is implicitly equated with potential long-term revenue gains from timber generation. There is little scope in the design of the system to take into account the diversity of forest usage among communities and across locations.

Successful and long-running collective action has firm social foundations in the form of interdependence within the community, social relationships, prevalent norms and social arrangements, all of which contribute to cohesion and trust among members. Norms-based compliance with agreed-upon rules in commons management overcomes the 'enforcement problem' by lending credibility to socially sanctioned penalties for deviant behaviour (see Dasgupta, this volume). Thus, for example, in the case of the SPP, the threat of expulsion from the community has functioned as a highly credible threat against rule violations, judging by the rarity in its exercise. Elsewhere in the state, in institutional arrangements similar to that of the SPP, offenders have been treated to public humiliation, mock hangings, boycotts, etc. It is the underlying social sanction to all such practices that explains their greater effectiveness in checking violations as compared to the penalties contained in the formal legal framework. The importance of social sanction for the functioning of institutions is also evident in the case of the dispute settlement process. This has evolved outside of the formal legal system and yet has gained acceptance among forest-conserving communities in Orissa. In contrast, there is little space in the JFM design to allow for different village-level VSSs with competing claims over the same forest to come together and use mutually recognized social/institutional arrangements (for example, arbitration by community leaders, village high courts, etc.) to resolve disputes.

An uncritical acceptance of community-based resource management systems tends to ignore the possibility of elite capture and discriminatory practices in such institutions, which would result in the marginalization of underprivileged groups (including women) in the benefit-sharing and decision-making processes. Though the possibility of elite capture and discriminatory practices exists in both JFM-type entities and the self-organized institutions, the involvement of external agencies plus the statutory provisions relating to representation of marginalized groups in the JFM policy make the former, at least in theory, relatively less vulnerable to such undesirable outcomes. An important success factor in the case of the SPP is that the benefits of forest conservation have gone to the deserving sections. Table 14.2 presents some simple estimates based on household-level survey data collected from the member villages of the SPP. The percentage share of the money value of collected forest goods in household incomes are observed to decrease significantly with increase in social status and farm incomes, thereby suggesting

Table 14.2. Distribution of the monetary value of forest goods collected across different income groups under community management of the *Sulia*

Income[a] range	% of sample HHs	Social category[b] (average rank)	Average HH size (in adult equivalent terms[c])	Average income (INC) (in Rupees)	Total land cultivated (in acres)	Average distance to forest (in km)	Money value[d] (MV) of forest goods[e] (in Rupees)	MV as % of INC
< 10000[f]	7	2.2	5.0	2045	0.2	5.1	2284	111.7
10000–15000	15	2.4	5.8	10000	1.1	6.4	1235	12.4
15000–18000	29	2.7	6.1	15000	1.7	5.6	1492	9.9
18000–20000	24	3.0	6.7	18000	2.0	5.9	1092	6.1
20000–22000	19	2.9	6.8	20000	2.7	4.6	1300	6.5
> 22000	6	3.4	6.9	28895	3.9	5.2	1363	4.7
All sample HHs (300)	100	2.8	6.3	15840	1.9	5.5	1374	8.7

Source: Field survey conducted by author (during March–April 2005), covering 300 randomly selected households in 11 sample villages that are members of the SPP.

[a] 'Income' here relates only to the agricultural income and wage earnings of a household's adult male & female members during the year 2004–5 (agriculture i.e. from 1st March 2004 to 31st March 2005).

[b] Ranks given to different social categories are as follows: Scheduled Tribe = 1, Scheduled Caste = 2, Other Backward Caste & Religious Minorities = 3, and General (including the upper caste categories) = 4.

[c] Two children are treated as one adult equivalent.

[d] Many value has been calculated using local market prices of the collected forest goods.

[e] 'Forest goods' collected by the sample households specifically includes fuel wood, bamboo and bamboo twigs, long twigs of finger width (used for house thatching) and small poles.

[f] This includes the landless agricultural labourers and marginal farmers.

the comparatively high dependency of the weaker socio-economic groups on the forest.

So, where does this leave us in terms of devolving authority and control to local user communities with respect to the management of forest resources? Ground realities suggest that the *panchayat* bodies lack the capacity to effectively implement the PESA provisions.[13] Again, in the context of Orissa at least, the JFM model has failed in practice to convince a large number[14] of user communities that the state can be a reliable partner. On the other hand, empowering the self-governing community institutions would require the state to address the contentious issues of legal recognition to the entities and their demand for tenurial rights over the forests. To be effective, the devolution-based policy framework has to be realigned to factor in these ground-level realities. It would be futile to think of a uniform structure that can accommodate all the varied community settings. Instead, it makes sense to think of a devolution policy that concentrates on strengthening the institutions that have emerged from the interplay of social dynamics linked to collective action rather than attempting to engineer the latter through externally imposed institutional systems. While extending legal recognition to the self-initiated institutions is part of the empowerment process, the issue of devolving ownership rights calls for a closer examination, in particular, of the likely distributional impacts. The role of the state, in such a devolution scenario, would be that of a provider of an 'enabling environment', in terms of legal, technical, and resource-based support.

The formation of regional federations (like the Nayagarh JSM) by self-organized local communities in Orissa needs to be understood in the above context. Successful community initiatives like the SPP present an opportunity, however challenging, for the state to build trust and promote synergistic actions. In Orissa, unfortunately, the state FD has done little to allay fears among the village communities engaged in protecting forests that it will not start a reclamation process once the regenerated timber stock goes to the harvesting stage. Alternatives to the JFM-style arrangement, which the communities find unacceptable, are absent. Even now, the official position that communities lack the expertise to manage forests scientifically is seen as part of the attempt by the state to create ground conditions on which the reclaiming process will be anchored. Similarly, devolution policies involving sub-state governance structures are viewed as state machinations to

---

[13] In fact, the Planning Commission's Mid-Term Appraisal of the 10th Five Year Plan (2002–7) mentions (chapter 17) that in Orissa the *panchayats* have been assigned very few powers by the government in order to make PESA effective in the state. (The document is available from the Planning Commission's website <http://www.planning-commission.nic.in/>).

[14] CSE (1999) reports in an unofficial estimate that 400,000 ha of forest area in Orissa is protected under self-governed community management institutions functioning in more than 5000 villages.

undermine the community movement by introducing the divisive force of political power play.

With the increase in clout of federations among local communities—in some cases, their emergence as potent political forces in the region—it is possible that the state may try to co-opt these organizations. This may happen in a variety of ways—for instance, with the state 'involving' the latter in project/programme funding, raising resources from external donor agencies, and so on. It is then quite possible that we have a typical 'principal—agent problem' with divergent incentive structures for the local-level institutions (principal) and the federal organization (agent) at the district/state level. Moreover, there is always the possibility of the potentially divisive issue of fund-sharing raising its head among the member organizations in the event that external aid gets channelled through federal organizations either at the district or at the state level. This will only put further strain on the community movement in the state.

14.7. Conclusion

The uniqueness of the community forest-management movement in Orissa is that it has evolved from the bottom up and is currently considerably networked. And, in both evolution and networking, at least during the formative stages, it can be said to be self-initiated to a significant extent.[15] From the devolution perspective, the movement provides an interesting contrast to the top-down JFM paradigm in terms of the *nature* of people's participation in community-based forest management as well as the way in which such action has evolved *upwards* hierarchically and, in the process, become stronger.

There is little that the state government can do to reverse the community movement on forest management in Orissa. Ignoring its presence would probably mean an opportunity forsaken. The extent of development of collective action in the state, with respect to forest management, requires the devolution protagonists in the public policy-making domain to come out of their traditional mould for thinking about 'community' and 'people's participation'. Given the importance of social dynamics within and across communities for the success of collective action in forest management, it should be obvious that a uniform institutional design will fail in the face of social heterogeneity. It is also vital that the 'trust gap' between the state and the 'community' is bridged. Moreover, since, in the Orissa context at least, the

[15] External donor agencies like SIDA and OXFAM have played a catalyzing role in the creation of grass-roots alliances among local community management institutions in the forest sector.

latter has acquired different dimensions at different levels of collectivization, the state would be required to play a role befitting the state-community relationship at each level.

References

Agrawal, A. (2001). 'Common Property Institutions and Sustainable Governance of Resources'. *World Development*, 29/10: 1649–72.

Arora, D. (1994). 'From State Regulation to People's Participation: Case of Forest Management in India'. *Economic and Political Weekly*, 29/12: 691–8.

Baland, J.-M., and Platteau, J.-P. (1996). *Halting Degradation of Natural Resources: Is there a Role for Rural Communities?* Oxford: Clarendon Press.

Ballabh, V., Balooni, K., and Dave, S. (2002). 'Why Local Resources Management Institutions Decline: A Comparative Analysis of Van (Forest) Panchayats and Forest Protection Committees in India'. *World Development*, 30/12: 2153–67.

Conroy, C., Mishra, A., and Rai, A. (2000). 'Learning from Self-initiated Community Forest Management in Orissa, India'. *Forests, Trees and People Newsletter*, 42: 51–6.

CSE (Center for Science and Environment) (1999).'On the Warpath'. *Down to Earth*, 8/9: 32–42.

Fisher, R. J. (1999). 'Devolution and Decentralization of Forest Management in Asia and the Pacific'. *Unasylva*, 50/4: 3–5.

FSI (Forest Survey of India) (2001). *State of Forest Report 2001*. Dehradun, India: Forest Survey of India, Ministry of Environment and Forest.

Gadgil, M., and Guha, R. (1992). *This Fissured Land: An Ecological History of India*. New Delhi, India: Oxford University Press.

—— —— (1995). *Ecology and Equity. The Use and Abuse of Nature in Contemporary India*. New Delhi, India: Penguin Books.

Ghate, R. (2003). 'Ensuring "Collective Action" in "Participatory" Forest Management'. Working Paper No. 3-03 South Asian Network for Development and Environmental Economics (SANDEE), Kathmandu, Nepal.

—— (2005). 'Need-assessment of Forest-Dependent People from Three States of "Tribal Belt" of Central India'. Report No. 2-05. SHODH: The Institute for Research and Development, Nagpur, India.

Klooster, D. (2000). 'Institutional Choice, Community, and Struggle: A Case Study of Forest Co-management in Mexico'. *World Development*, 28/1: 1–20.

Larson, A. M. (2002). 'Natural Resources and Decentralization in Nicaragua: Are Local Governments up to the Job?' *World Development*, 30/1: 17–31.

Li, T. M. (2002). 'Engaging Simplifications: Community-based Resource Management, Market Processes and State Agendas in Upland Southeast Asia'. *World Development*, 30/2: 265–83.

Lindsay, J. M. (1999). 'Creating a Legal Framework for Community-based Management: Principles and Dilemmas'. *Unasylva*, 50/4: 28–34.

Lynch, O. J. (1998). 'Law, Pluralism and the Promotion of Sustainable Community-based Forest Management'. *Unasylva*, 49/3: 52–6.

Ostrom, E. (1990). *Governing The Commons: The Evolution of Institutions for Collective Action*. Cambridge: Cambridge University Press.

—— (1999). 'Self-governance and Forest Resources'. Occasional Paper No. 20. Center for International Forestry Research (CIFOR), Bogor, Indonesia.

Pathak, A. (1994). *Contested Domains: State, Peasants, and Forests in Contemporary India*. Thousand Oaks, CA: Sage Publications.

Poffenberger, M., Bhattarcharya, P., Khare, A., Rai, A., Roy, S. B., Singh, N., and Singh, K. (1996). *Grassroots Forest Protection: Eastern Indian Experience*. Research Network Report No. 7. Berkeley, CA: Asia Forest Network.

Rangan, H., and Lane, M. B. (2001). 'Indigenous Peoples and Forest Management: Comparative Analysis of Institutional Approaches in Australia and India'. *Society and Natural Resources*, 14: 145–60.

Ribot, J. C. (1999). 'Accountable Representation and Power in Participatory and Decentralized Environmental Management'. *Unasylva,* 50/4: 18–22.

Ribot, J. C. (2003). 'Democratic Decentralization of Natural Resources: Institutional Choice and Discretionary Power Transfers in Sub-Saharan Africa'. *Public Administration and Development*, 23: 53–65.

Sarin, M. (2005). 'Laws, Lore and Logjams: Critical Issues in Indian Forest Conservation'. Gatekeeper Series 116. International Institute for Environment and Development (IIED), London.

Sarin, M., Singh, N. M., Sundar, N., and Bhogal, R. K. (2003). 'Devolution as a Threat to Democratic Decision-making in Forestry? Findings from Three States in India'. Working Paper 197. Overseas Development Institute, London.

Saxena, N. C. (2003). 'Livelihood Diversification and Non-timber Forest Products in Orissa: Wider Lessons on the Scope for Policy Change'. Working Paper 223. Overseas Development Institute, London.

—— and Ballabh, V. (1995). 'Farm Forestry in South Asia', in N. C. Saxena and V. Ballabh (eds.), *Farm Forestry and the Context of Farming Systems in South Asia*. New Delhi, India: Sage Publications, 23–50.

Shackleton, S., Campbell, B., Wollenberg, E., and Edmunds, D. (2002). *Devolution and Community-based Natural Resource Management: Creating Space for Local People to Participate and Benefit?* ODI Natural Resource Perspectives 76. London: Overseas Development Institute.

Singh, N. M. (2001). 'Towards Democratizing Forest Governance: Creation of Vertical Social Capital through Federations in Orissa'. Working Paper, Workshop in Political Theory and Policy Analysis. Bloomington, IN: Indiana University.

Sundar, N. (2001). 'Is Devolution Democratization?' *World Development*, 29/12: 2007–23.

World Bank (2000). *World Development Report 2000/2001: Attacking Poverty*. New Delhi, India: Oxford University Press.

15

Efficiency and Low Costs Under Non-Limiting Supply Conditions in Bhutan

Edward L. Webb and Lam Dorji[1]

15.1. Introduction

Scarcity of a resource is an important environmental constraint that can become a key element in the evolution and maintenance of institutional regimes to manage, protect, and utilize the limited resource (Gibson 2001). Where there is no scarcity of the relevant resource, there may be little or no impetus to incur the transaction costs associated with institution building because long-term costs of open access are perceived to be low. From the perspective of resource appropriators, a seemingly unlimited resource may not require institutions to manage or protect it from degradation until it becomes so limited that the potential costs associated with future procurement of the nearly extinct resource outweigh the costs associated with forming and enforcing new institutions. While it has been argued that there can be literally dozens of facilitating conditions that may lead to institutional development (Agrawal 2003), scarcity is a fundamental facilitating condition that, along with salience, is consistently necessary across CPR systems in order for institutions to be built (Gibson 2001). Indeed, one of the two main features that define a CPR is its extractability, which in turn implies perceptible limitations on the amount of the resource available.

Bhutan represents an exception to the rule governing this theory about institutional development. Forest cover in this small (46,500 km²) Himalayan

[1] Data collection was supported by an AIT-Austrian government scholarship, and by a grant from the MacArthur Foundation through the Workshop in Political Theory and Policy Analysis, Indiana University. Comments on an earlier draft by Clark Gibson, Shaheen R. Khan, and Ingella Ternstrom are gratefully acknowledged.

kingdom is approximately 68 per cent or 31,950 km^2. The present population of Bhutan is currently about 750,000 persons, resulting in a present-day forest-to-person ratio of about 4.3 ha per person. If we consider the fact that this population has grown at a rate of approximately 2 per cent and presently consists of not only Bhutanese but also recent migrants to the country, we will see that the forest-to-person ratio only a century ago was even larger than the current figure. Forests in Bhutan thus have not been a resource in short supply. Hence, scarcity of forest products would be infrequent or non-existent.

Despite the extensive forest resource base in Bhutan, research has shown that there is rich diversity in locally crafted forest institutions in Bhutan that have evolved and have persisted for generations (Dorji, Webb, and Shivakoti 2003). These institutional regimes are in place to manage, utilize, and conserve forests and forest derivatives (for example, swidden agriculture plots) near villages. Rules and regulations exist on land use. There are in addition particular institutions that govern access, appropriation, management, and exclusion of resources in those land-use types. The apparent conundrum represented by Bhutan simply put then is the following: a robust array of forest-related institutions have evolved and persists to this day despite conditions of non-limited supply.

With 'development', and the eventual integration of Bhutan into an international market economy, some level of change in rural livelihoods was inevitable despite policies promoting a 'middle path' strategy, along with a government-promoted development philosophy that argues 'happiness' to be a more sophisticated concept than simply increased income. Development, which is buttressed by policy formulations, can lead at best to the modification of traditional, locally derived institutions, or at worst to a total breakdown of traditional institutions leading to major losses in both social and biological systems. It is therefore crucial to understand not only the present-day institutional regimes of Bhutan, but also to understand (*a*) why those institutions evolved, and (*b*) whether the development process is maintaining the stability of locally crafted institutions, or leading to an unstable situation that may threaten the social and biological systems of rural life.

In this chapter we pose three questions: firstly, in a country with vast resources and an extremely generous forest-to-person ratio, why do ancient, locally crafted forest management institutions exist across Bhutan? We argue that many of these institutions evolved in response to an acute need for agricultural optimization and social efficiency. Second, did those institutions improve agricultural productivity and reduce transaction costs to local people? Third, has the emergence of a modern political state in Bhutan created an unstable context for traditional forestry institutions?

We address these questions via consideration of the history of Bhutan and the linkages between an emerging centralized authority, agricultural livelihoods, and forests. We consider the evolution of the most common forest management institutions and deduce that they are solutions to the problems posed by external changes, namely, the rise and consequences of a centralized authority system requiring efficient agricultural systems. Second, we analyse forest conditions in order to evaluate their contribution to solving a dilemma posed by the emerging state, and also look at institutional regimes over those forests in order to evaluate whether they reduce costs to communities. Third, we consider the impact of contemporary policy initiatives on those long-standing institutional regimes.

15.2. Study sites and methodology

This paper is based on a survey conducted from mid-2001 through mid-2002 in twelve randomly selected villages located in the broadleaf zone of the middle Himalayas of the Kingdom of Bhutan (see Dorji, Webb, and Shivakoti 2003). Elevations of the villages ranged from 1,300 to 2,300 meters above sea level. Six districts were chosen where the majority of forests were broadleaf. Next, villages under each selected district were listed and villages without broadleaf forests were eliminated. From the list, two villages representing a rural and semi-urban area in each of the selected districts were randomly selected. Primary information for this study was generated mainly through the application of the International Forestry Resources and Institution's (IFRI) research strategy and instruments (Ostrom and Wertime 2000).

Our information on Bhutan's rural history was gathered from two principal sources. We conducted interviews with both groups and key informants (particularly elders) in each of the twelve villages. The oral histories provided were supplemented with literature on Bhutan's history. It must be emphasized that our interpretation of how forest institutions probably emerged in Bhutan are deductions based on these two sources of information and hence can be expressed as more hypothesis than historical fact. Because there have been no texts, either historical or contemporary, that have directly raised this question, we consider it our task to piece together the most rational explanation for the emergence of institutions under seemingly 'unlimited' resource supply conditions. For the biological analysis, we used quantitative forest surveys. The methods for that part of the research will be described later. Finally, we use a property rights approach to analyse the possible instabilities created by the rise of the modern Bhutanese state.

15.3. The evolution of *sokshings*

In this section, we argue that locally crafted forest management institutions in Bhutan evolved under non-limiting conditions in response to the rise of an elite class, which imposed heavy taxes that required mechanisms to maximize productivity and efficiency in agricultural production. This in turn required institutions to govern forest resources. Our hypothesis of institutional evolution requires us to first consider the livelihoods of rural Bhutanese farmers and, secondly, the emergence of centralized authority and its effect on livelihoods.

The primary source of livelihoods in rural Bhutan is agriculture.[2] Principal crops in Bhutan are rice and wheat, which are complemented by animal husbandry, especially cattle, which are used for a range of services from the tilling of soil to the production of milk and meat products. Both livestock and farming rely on forests for their productivity. Grazing provides nutrition for draft and milk-producing animals in the case of livestock and is therefore essential for their productivity. In the case of agriculture, forests act as a source of manure and irrigation. The forest cover protects the watershed, and ensures the supply of leaf-litter, that is, dried leaves, which are mixed with cattle manure and used as fertilizer. In Bhutan, leaf-litter of certain oak species (*Quercus* spp.) is preferred. This traditional, organic fertilizer maintains soil fertility and apparently improves crop productivity. Agrarian livelihoods based in traditional, rural Bhutanese society consisted of interdependence between agriculture, animal husbandry, and forestry.

15.3.1. *History*

Very little is known about Bhutan prior to roughly AD 747. Archaeological records indicate that a tribe called the *Monpas* may have inhabited what is now Bhutan from 500 BC until about AD 600 (Savada 1993). It is known that Tibetan Buddhism was introduced to Bhutan with the visit of Guru Padmasambhava in AD 747. By then, some form of government existed with the presence of Sindhu Gyap as the King of Bumthang, and petty rulers or *debs* who ruled over the eastern parts of the country. The influx of Tibetan Lamas (saints) in the ninth to eleventh centuries resulted in the establishment of Tibetan religious and cultural dominance in western and central Bhutan (Hasrat 1980; Sinha 1991). Until the beginning of the seventeenth century, local governance was clan-based and tribal in nature (Sinha 1991).

In 1616, the ascendance into power of the Buddhist leader Zhabdrung Ngawang Namgyel (1594–1651) led to the establishment of centralized religio-political rule in Bhutan (Sinha 1991). Zhabdrung was able to use his religious stature to assume political power and initiate political reforms. He established the dual system of government, which consists of political leadership and religious leadership (a body of monks) commingling and working in the same

---

[2] Although some modern non-farming technology has penetrated into even the most remote villages, farming systems still follow traditional practices.

355

physical structures (*dzongs*). Zhabdrung was successful in consolidating what was previously a dispersed group of clans into a more cohesive society that was governed by a religio-political elite.

Following the death of Zhabdrung, *desids* or temporal rulers exercised full civil, military, judicial, and revenue administration powers over the country (Hasrat 1980). A total of fifty-six *desids* governed Bhutan from 1651 to 1907. This period was marked by internal strife and struggle for power among different factions (Das 1974) until Ugyen Wangchuck installed the hereditary monarchy in 1907.

Besides establishing the first formal proto-national government over what is now Bhutan, Zhabdrung initiated a series of taxes that in some cases began as offerings to the religio-political leaders but which later came to be converted into an obligatory payment of goods and/or services.[3] According to Pain and Pema (2000), taxation emanated from a contract drawn in the seventeenth century between Zhabdrung Ngawang Namgyal and those who provided offerings. *Wangyon, thojab, doepa,* and *wulah* were the different types of taxes imposed. *Wangyon* refers to the taxes levied on households as a legacy of their past one-time offering made to reciprocate the blessings made by Zhabdrung, his reincarnates, and stand-ins. *Thojab* was a form of tax that was based on the agricultural landholdings of a household. In the case of *thojab*, tax rates were commensurate with the area of the land cultivated, that is, households with more agricultural land paid more taxes. In-kind labour taxes such as *dhoepa* for porterage of consignments, and *wulah* for construction work were also frequently imposed. Village elders, interviewed during the study, recollected difficult times when the requirement to serve authorities meant sacrifice of the economic welfare of families. Some reported that local administrations, as in the case of the Paro district, collected fine ash from household stoves as taxes, to be used as detergents (known as *thheykhu*) to wash clothes and as soda for tea. The villagers of Taksha-Sili-Tsara, for example, had to pay a range of in-kind taxes.[4]

Table 15.1 has two items of importance for our hypothesis. First, most of the taxes were in the form of agricultural or livestock output. This meant that total output of agriculture and livestock was an important consideration for farmers. Second, taxes were based on cultivable area and not gross agricultural output. This meant that farmers had an incentive to cultivate the smallest area of land possible so that taxes were minimized while maximizing the efficiency of the farming system.

Two physical outcomes of the historically high taxation rate in Bhutan are the following. Firstly, the amount of forest converted to agricultural land

[3] Although after Zhabdrung's death in 1651 the centralized authority system dissolved into a fragmented array of autonomous local administrations, the local taxation system continued so that local lords could maintain a 'militia-like military force' (Mancall undated).

[4] This taxation system was abolished in the 1950s by the second and third kings of Bhutan.

Table 15.1. Annual household in-kind taxes paid in village Taksha-Sili-Tsara prior to 1950s

Type of tax	Particulars	Amount per year	Collector
Grain tax (*Wangyon*)	Grains (Rice, wheat, etc.)	According to initial offering	*Punakha Dzong*
Grain tax (*Thojab*)	Rice Wheat	According to landholding According to landholding	*Nyerchen* (Chief Steward), *Wangdi Dzong*
Land tax	Bundles of cotton textile (then known as *Keray*)	Applied to only those who owned land at Ngaba and Babche	*Daga Dzong*
Butter tax	Butter Additional for every female calf	2 *sang* (1 kg) per cow 1 *sang* (0.5 kg) per female calf	*Zimpon Nangm* (Chamberlain)
Meat and skin tax	Beef cattle	Information not available	*Gorab* (Gate controller)

has remained small. Local people tilled the land only to subsist under heavy taxation. To cultivate more land was a disincentive as it meant more tax obligations. Secondly, accumulating wealth was nearly impossible as farmers needed to meet local government demands for tax and services with harvest timings and outputs.

Given the environment-livelihood linkages described earlier, agricultural productivity was dependent on organic fertilizer, which consisted partly of leaf-litter. On the other hand, cattle-based products such as butter and meat were dependent on productive pastures. However, the management regimes of these two goods are not spatially compatible, that is, leaf-litter cannot be produced where cattle graze, whereas livestock need large pastures that would reduce the forest cover. Therefore, even though there were abundant total forest resources per household, the combination of high taxation and the necessity for forest resources (leaf-litter and grazing grounds) to maximize both agricultural and livestock outputs created a need for two things. It required, on the one hand, management systems to improve the productivity of agriculture, which could be accomplished through high leaf-litter production. It required, on the other, institutional mechanisms to prevent and resolve land/forest-use conflict.

We hypothesize that villages evolved institutions to simultaneously increase agricultural efficiency while decreasing potential land-use conflicts. The first part of the hypothesis agrees with economic as well as biological research showing that humans seek the most efficient means of obtaining and utilizing resources. The second half of the hypothesis agrees with studies showing that institutions decrease social costs to participants.

In the following sections we examine the management and local institutions that govern *sokshings* to investigate whether locally evolved institutions improved agricultural productivity while reducing transaction costs. A *sokshing* is a small, intensively managed forest plot belonging to an individual household or a community for the purpose of producing leaf-litter and, less frequently, fuelwood. *Sokshings* vary in size, but are on average approximately one hectare. Households may hold proprietary rights over an individual *sokshing*, and traditionally these rights are inherited. Collective *sokshings* are forest areas that are designated for collection of leaf-litter by the community.

15.3.2. *Do* sokshings *improve agricultural productivity?*

Central to our understanding of *sokshing* institutional evolution is the assumption that *sokshings* did not arise simply as a means to improve agricultural output for its own sake. We assume this because *sokshings*, or any variants thereof, are not found in other parts of the Himalayas. While private forestry is becoming an important feature in the landscapes of Nepal, for example, those plots are for fuelwood, timber, or fodder and have been increasing in importance recently probably because of a short-age of available products in forests due to degradation of natural forests or harvesting restrictions brought on through community forestry institutions (Springate-Baginski *et al.* 2003).

A direct test of the impact of *sokshings* on agricultural productivity would be a controlled, replicated experiment where varying levels of leaf-litter enriched fertilizer would be compared with control plots where no leaf-litter fertilizer was applied. We are not aware of the existence of any such published study. However, our respondents were convinced that the leaf-litter enriched fertil-izer maintained soil fertility and, in turn, agricultural productivity. Given their extensive experience, we accept these assertions as accurate.

We can also pursue the question from a different angle by exploring whether *sokshings* are managed in order to provide the necessary resources for improved agricultural practices. If *sokshing* management institutions did evolve in response to a need for high agricultural efficiency, then it would be reflected in the biophysical properties of the forest that produced the leaf-litter. From a forester's perspective, the management techniques used by farmers are well-implemented silvicultural techniques designed to maximize both the quality and quantity of leaf-litter produced per unit of *sokshing* area (Dorji, Webb, and Shivakoti 2003). In terms of quality, management tech-niques are employed to reduce the regeneration of unwanted species, so that the plot would be dominated by species that produced high-quality litter, in particular *Quercus* species. Seedlings and saplings of valuable species would be given special protection by caretakers. The caretakers would occasionally clear the forest floor of unwanted species, tend natural regeneration of desirable species, and prune trees at or above 1.8 m in height, so as to increase the branching. This would result in well-branched trees that produced more leaves than unpruned individuals of the same species.

Table 15.2. Composition, density, and relative abundance of tree species in non-*sokshing* natural forest and *sokshing* forest in the middle Himalayan broadleaf forest of Bhutan

Non-*sokshing* forest (5.64 ha)			*Sokshings* (1.57 ha)		
Species	N per ha	RA %	Species	N per ha	RA %
Castanopsis hystrix	32.6	13.6	*Quercus griffithii*	216.6	65.6
Pieris ovalifolia	16.1	6.7	*Rhododendron arboreum*	33.8	10.2
Quercus griffithii	15.6	6.5	*Pieris ovalifolia*	30.6	9.3
Quercus lanata	14.2	5.9	*Schima wallichii*	17.8	5.4
Rhododendron arboreum	13.5	5.6	*Pinus bhutanica*	8.3	2.5
Schima khasiana	12.8	5.3	*Schima khasiana*	7.6	2.3
Aucuba himalaica	10.6	4.4	*Castanopsis tribuloides*	6.4	1.9
Castanopsis tribuloides	10.6	4.4	*Rhododendron fulgens*	1.9	0.6
Lithocarpus elegans	9.4	3.9	*Syzygium operculatum*	1.9	0.6
Litsea doshia	8.5	3.6	*Pentapanax leschenaultii*	1.3	0.4
Quercus lamellose	6.4	2.7	*Quercus lanata*	1.3	0.4
Persea fructifera	6.0	2.5	*Alnus nepalensis*	0.6	0.2
Castanopsis indica	4.6	1.9	*Castanopsis hystrix*	0.6	0.2
Pentapanax leschenaultii	4.4	1.9	*Cinnamonum bejolghota*	0.6	0.2
Other species (69)	73.8	30.8	*Glochidion acuminatum*	0.6	0.2
Total	239.2	100	Total	329.9	100

Note: N per ha, that is, number per hectare.

RA %, the percentage of all trees belonging to that species.

Biological data was collected using circular forest survey plots in *sokshing* and non-*sokshing* forests of six villages (see Dorji, Webb, and Shivakoti 2003). We studied a total of fifty plots in *sokshing* forest (1.57 ha) and 180 plots in non-*sokshing* forest (5.64 ha). Each plot had a radius of 10 m, within which all trees at least 10 cm in diameter were surveyed for diameter, height, and species name. Concentrically nested within the 10 m radius plots were 3 m and 1 m radius plots, within which all saplings (2.5 cm to 9.9 cm diameter), seedlings, and herbaceous species were surveyed respectively. In this chapter, we will only report on saplings and trees.

Table 15.2 reveals three results relevant to our hypothesis. First, non-*sokshing* natural forest exhibited a much greater number of tree species (eighty-three) than *sokshing* forest (fifteen). Second, tree density was greater in the *sokshing* forest than in the non-*sokshing* natural forest. Third, the dominant species differed greatly between the two forest types. In the case of non-*sokshing* forest, *Castonopsis hystrix* was the dominant species, followed by *Pieris ovalifolia* and *Quercus griffithii*. *C. hystrix* is a typically dominant or co-dominant species in this region of Bhutan and in other parts of the Himalayas. In *sokshing* forest, *Q. griffithii* was by far the most dominant species, accounting for 66 per cent of all tree stems in the *sokshing* plots. Moreover, size class distributions (not shown) revealed that although sapling densities (defined as trees 2–10 cm diameter) were greater in non-*sokshing* forest than in *sokshings,* the difference disappeared in larger-size classes and in fact was the opposite for many of the other size classes (that is, more trees in *sokshing*).

These results indicate that *sokshings* are intensively managed plots of forest, designed to be dominated by *Q. griffithii*, which produces high-quality leaf-litter. The understorey of *sokshings* is open, which facilitates leaf-litter collection (Dorji, Webb, and Shivakoti 2003). Thus, while it may not be possible to prove that the *sokshing* institution evolved in response to the need for agricultural efficiency, it is clear that *sokshings* do enhance agricultural productivity and that this is recorded in the history of Bhutan's villages.

15.3.3. Do sokshings *reduce social conflict and transaction costs?*

Our second line of enquiry examines whether *sokshings* reduce social conflict and transaction costs. In our hypothesis, high costs would most likely be incurred by conflicts over land use because of spatially incompatible needs for leaf-litter (and, hence, agricultural) productivity and livestock productivity. Land-use partitioning would represent an efficient way to achieve both goals. Thus we describe the relevant *sokshing* institutions and discuss whether they prevent conflict through resource partitioning and/or resolve resource-related conflicts when they occur.[5]

As noted above, conflicts over land and resource management, under conditions requiring high production efficiency, are likely to emerge when disagreements arise over land and/or resource appropriation. In the first case (that is, land appropriation), conflicts and their associated costs could be avoided if the resource is clearly bounded in space and all members of the community are aware of that boundary (Ostrom 1990). In the second case (that is, resource appropriation), conflicts could be avoided if there are clear exclusionary rules in the case of individual *sokshings* and equitable resource allocation or appropriation rules in the case of collective *sokshings*.

The physical characteristics of *sokshings* make them unmistakably different from surrounding natural forest. Low densities of seedlings and saplings and an open understorey due to cleaning techniques used by caretakers distinguishes a *soshking*. Its proprietors would use physical markers such as cliffs, rocks, ravines, and footpaths to demarcate boundaries. Thus, each *sokshing* has a well-defined boundary that is known to all members of the community through oral traditions, the structure of the forest, and physical features established by people.

It was evident throughout the study area that rules regarding exclusion in individual *sokshings,* and equitable appropriation in collective *sokshings,*

---

[5] It should be emphasized that we do not argue that *sokshings* increase the economic efficiency of agriculture in the traditional sense of the word. Improving economic efficiency entails reducing direct costs. In the case of *sokshings*, they do reduce collection time, but this cannot be equated with a reduction in opportunity cost because in remote mountain villages, in general, there are few alternative employment opportunities that could replace or, more realistically, complement farming. Therefore it is the reduction in social costs, particularly transaction costs related to conflict resolution that is emphasized here.

exist across rural Bhutan. These institutional arrangements reduced conflict by establishing the rights of a *sokshing* owner to protect the resource and to recover losses due to encroachment.

The rules governing individual *sokshings* were very simple and respected by the community members. Traditionally, the *sokshing* owner would have complete ownership rights over the plot, in particular the leaf-litter and fuelwood. Any attempt by another individual to appropriate material without the consent of the owner would be considered a breach of customary rules.

The conflict resolution mechanism worked informally. Hence, when exclusionary rules were violated, direct negotiation between the two parties would be the first step in resolution. Normally, an appropriate penalty such as the replacement of an equal or greater amount of leaf-litter, as well as a reconciliation gesture, such as a drink, would be expected. During our interviews, there was never a case where a respondent could recall a confrontation escalating beyond the first stage. A possible explanation could be that the resource was not critically scarce. Moreover, any person could enter into the non-*sokshing* forest and retrieve leaf-litter although the quality and efficiency of collection would be lower.[6]

For collective *sokshings,* resource allocation rules differed from village to village. Some villages had collective *sokshings* without any specified rule or norm whereby people simply go and collect leaf-litter from the *sokshings* just as they would from non-*sokshing* natural forests. This form of collective management was absolutely equitable and allowed collection to be based on the need of the household. Since there has never been a market for leaf-litter or fuelwood in remote villages, extraction rates never went beyond self-use.

There are also collective *sokshings* where appropriation rules are well defined and adhered to. In one study village named Khankhu, local people collectively maintained their pine forest as a *sokshing*. Institutions defined a set of rules such as the time and amount of litter to be collected. In Khankhu, no individual could collect leaf-litter before *ri tangni,* which literally means 'releasing or opening the forest'. *Ri tangni* happens every year on a date determined by the villagers. During *ri tangni*, all villagers have unlimited access to the forest. Hence, each household hires as many labourers as possible to maximize the leaf-litter collection.

These informal forest management systems are simply sets of agreed-upon rules and practices regulating the way people use forests, and which are commonly understood, strictly observed, and verbally passed down through generations (Gilmour and Fisher 1991). Proprietors of collective *sokshings* take

---

[6] The availability of abundant, but lower quality, leaf-litter in non-*sokshing* forest supports our hypothesis that *sokshing* institutions evolved in response to efficiency needs rather than resource scarcity.

rule infractions very seriously. If an individual is seen collecting leaf-litter before *ri tangni*, the observer will inform other households in the village who will in turn collectively confront the transgressor, immediately confiscate the contraband, and return it to the forest.

The evidence we present above is historical and based on interview data. However, another form of evidence for our second question comes from contemporary sources. Here we describe how the modern judicial system acknowledges the low costs associated with locally crafted institutions regarding land allocation and resource management.

With the rise of the monarchy in 1907 and the formation of the National Assembly in 1953, new policies arose that defined the new government's claim over forest resources. These policies were buttressed by the establishment of the national court system in 1968. The state, by definition, became the official adjudicator of disputes.

When conflicts within villages occur and cannot be resolved within the village itself, the district-level courts adjudicate in the dispute. However, these courts give importance to local institutional arrangements, internal agreements, and traditions. Thus, the formalized legal system of Bhutan recognizes that the locally crafted institutional regimes in villages lower social costs of adjudication and, therefore, rely on them in part for their deliberations.

From our analysis of both field data and historical literature, it is evident that *sokshings* provide a crucial resource to agriculture and animal husbandry, which supports the hypothesis that the *sokshings* evolved in response to an early taxation system that persisted until the middle of the twentieth century. The *sokshings* reduce transaction costs by providing clear and easily interpretable rules regarding spatial boundaries and withdrawal rights. Moreover, the process of conflict resolution, traditionally done face-to-face, was low-cost and efficient because of the clear rules governing individual and communal *sokshings*. This was supported by contemporary evidence that the modern district-level judicial system recognizes and even defers to local arrangements when faced with decisions over land-use conflicts. In the next section, we evaluate the impact of recent national forest policies on local management systems that have evolved over centuries.

15.4. Contemporary national policy and local costs

Two important forest-related legislations have been enacted in Bhutan in the recent past: the Forest Act of 1969 and the Forest and Nature Conservation Act of 1995. In this section, we ask the third question that motivates this study: has the rise of the modern political state in Bhutan created an unstable context for traditional institutions?

In evaluating institutional stability, it is justifiable to first evaluate the rights of people to the resource. These rights, as outlined by Schlager and Ostrom (1992), consist of rights to access, withdrawal, management, exclusion, and alienation. Here, we examine the property rights regimes over both *sokshing* and non-*sokshing* forest, and consider whether the costs, and therefore the potential stability and sustainability of management, have changed since the imposition of these two policies.

Shortly after the formation of the National Assembly in 1953, households and communities were obliged to register their landholdings, including *sokshings,* in the national register.[7] However, in 1969, the Bhutan Forest Act nationalized forests by designating all forests, including *sokshing,* to be 'government reserve' forest and, hence, under the purview and management authority of the central government. Thus, all *sokshing* and non-*sokshing* forest immediately became *de jure* government forests. The Forest and Nature Conservation Act (1995) further delineated user rights and requirements to government reserve forests. This Act required local people to obtain a permit from the Forest Department to extract designated products (denoted as 'Schedule I' species) from the forest. Schedule I species includes all trees that would be cut for timber. However, in recognition of the dependence of rural communities on forest products, the rules under this act provided a certain leverage to the rural populations in appropriating some non-wood resources for subsistence needs (Ministry of Agriculture 2000). Nevertheless, fuelwood or timber products are strictly regulated by the District Forestry Extension Officer and the territorial divisions of the Forest Department. In addition to requiring a permit to be secured for extraction of some forest products, the national government also levied a fee for the permits. Although this fee began as a nominal amount, it was revised upward according to the Forest and Nature Conservation Rules of 2000.

Communities have had two choices since the passing of the Forest Act in 1969. They could modify their institutional arrangements to comply with the new policy, or they could retain their traditional institutional regimes in the face of policy reform. In terms of costs to the society, an increase in costs would be incurred when the community does not adopt institutional reforms to agree with the new policy. This is not to imply that the policy reforms were ultimately 'correct', but rather that this exercise had the objective of determining whether there was disagreement between the *de jure* property rights and the *de facto* (that is, community-recognized) property rights approximately thirty years after the implementation of the Forest Act.

---

[7] Registered *sokshings*, while not being private property, carry significance in that the government officially recognizes them as being claimed and managed by a household or community. However, the registration process also resulted in an upper limit on the number of *sokshings* in Bhutan; after the registration period ended, new *sokshings* could not be made or claimed.

Table 15.3. *De jure* and *de facto* rights of communities over non-*sokshing* and *sokshing* forests before and after the Bhutan Forest Act of 1969

Rights	Non-*sokshing* forest				*Sokshing* forest			
	de jure		Traditional/*de facto*		*de jure*		Traditional/*de facto*	
	Before 1969	After 1969	Before 1969	After 1969	Before 1969	After 1969	Before 1969	After 1969
Access	N/A	Yes	Yes	Yes	N/A	Yes	Yes	Yes
Withdrawal	N/A	Restricted	Yes	Yes	N/A	Restricted	Yes	Restricted
Management	N/A	Restricted	Yes	No	N/A	Restricted	Yes	Restricted
Exclusion	N/A	Yes	Yes	Yes	N/A	Yes	Yes	Yes
Alienation	N/A	No	N/A	N/A	N/A	Yes	Yes	Yes

How did the two policies change the context for property-rights institutions? We address this question by examining the *de jure* changes to property rights, and whether the contemporary *de facto* institutions expressed by communities agreed with those *de jure* requirements. Table 15.3 shows how *de jure* and *de facto* property rights (Schlager and Ostrom 1992) of the household or village have changed since the legal implementation of the 1969 Forest Act. These rights include access, withdrawal, management, exclusion, or alienation of either *sokshing* forest or non-*sokshing* forest. The Forest Act changed two of the five property rights, namely withdrawal and management, in both *sokshing* and non-*sokshing* forests (Dorji, Webb, and Shivakoti 2006).[8]

Withdrawal rights refer to whether a person has the right to extract resources from the forest. The *de facto* withdrawal rights for community members to harvest products from *sokshing* and non-*sokshing* forests before 1969 were absolute; community members could cut trees, go hunting, and collect other materials from the non-*sokshing* forest in order to fulfil subsistence needs. These activities were regulated by traditional institutions, such as rituals prior to hunting and protection of sacred or spiritual zones in the forest. But, in general, there were few community-crafted restrictions on product withdrawal from non-*sokshing* forest. A *sokshing* owner could extract any product necessary from her/his *sokshing* for the livelihood of the household.

The 1995 Forest and Nature Conservation Act imposed important restrictions on the kinds and amounts of materials that could be withdrawn from forests. Subsistence-oriented products such as dried fuelwood, leaf-litter, grazing, stones, sand for building, and water could be collected without a government permit. Hunting was prohibited except for 'crop protection'. All trees and other Schedule I species were protected and extraction required a permit from the government.

---

[8] Loss of alienation rights will not be discussed here, because communities never practised alienation of non-*sokshing* forests.

The application of *de jure* withdrawal restrictions to *sokshings* would not have imparted a significant cost to communities. Although traditional rights of withdrawal before 1969 were extended to all products, *sokshings* were never managed for products other than leaf-litter and secondary products like fuel-wood. In other words, the withdrawal restrictions contained in the Forest Act were compatible with the traditional objectives of *sokshing* management for leaf-litter. Therefore, communities could modify their institutions to restrict withdrawal rights with little or no cost to the *sokshing* owner. *De facto sokshing* withdrawal rights thus became restricted, in compliance with the *de jure* restrictions of the Acts. It should be noted, however, that this 'adjustment' to the institutional regime was more a recognition of the policy rather than an active institutional adjustment.

On the other hand, a sizeable cost was imposed on rural households who had for generations practised withdrawal from non-*sokshing* forests. This is best demonstrated by describing the process required to actually get a permit for withdrawal of 'protected' species. In order to cut a tree, a person would be required to obtain a permit from the District Forestry Extension Officer (DFEO). After approval from the DFEO, a permit would be obtained from the DFEO's office upon payment of the appropriate royalty. If the product is timber, a field officer of the Forest Department would be entrusted with the task of going to the applicant's village to mark trees for extraction. The ease of acquiring the permits for an individual household therefore would depend on the location of the village. In villages far from the main administrative centres, the process of applying and marking trees for timber and firewood would be costly. As visits by forestry personnel are constrained by lack of manpower in the Department of Forestry Services, the application must be taken by the applicant to the forestry office.

Not surprisingly, then, rural communities have tended to retain the *de facto* rights of product extraction because government enforcement is low in many villages, and no village member dissuades another member from extracting products. Moreover, under the current monitoring efforts of forestry officials in remote villages, the probability of being caught cutting a tree is very low. Therefore, trees are cut illegally for subsistence purposes without applying for a cutting permit. In other words, the contemporary *de facto* withdrawal rights from non-*sokshing* forests by farmers have essentially continued unaltered despite the emergence of contemporary forest policy restricting forest-product extraction. Hence, adopting the *de jure* withdrawal regulations of the 1969 Forest Act is costly to households due to restricted use of non-*sokshing* forest and the cost of potential conflict. Moreover, the economic cost of obtaining a permit reduces the likelihood of compliance.

Management rights can be described as the rights to manipulate the forest to meet particular objectives. An example of transformation is the rapid altering of forest structure and composition by clear-cutting, possibly followed by planting useful species. The management rights prior to 1969 for both *sokshing* and non-*sokshing* forests were absolute for the *sokshing* owner and the community at large respectively. For example, transformation of non-*sokshing* forest into a swidden plot (*tseri*) could be done with the permission of the village, as long as it did not negatively impact other households.

The Forest Act of 1969 substantially narrowed the *de jure* management rights of communities over both forest types. Government endorsement is required to carry out any significant transformation activities in the forest. The Forest Act prohibited any transformation from forest to non-forest, except under circumstances where the person would apply for and receive from His Majesty the King a land *kidu*, or land grant. Similar to the situation of obtaining a withdrawal permit, applying for and obtaining a transformation permit incurs a high cost to the local forest user.[9] The spirit of the policy is that *kidu* land cannot be sold or transferred outside the family although some households have been known to sell *kidu* land.

In contrast to the laborious and expensive task of obtaining a transformation right, lower-intensity activities such as seedling removal and pruning are not expressly forbidden by government policy. In terms of improvement, there is no provision in the 1969 Act that prohibits the planting of species in forested areas to improve production of any product. However, improvement plantings have not been recorded in our study areas. Therefore, although the total array of *de jure* management rights was restricted by the 1969 Act, communities could continue to actively manage *sokshings* in the traditional fashion. In sum, traditional *sokshing* improvement practices are both retained by the communities (*de facto*) and allowed by the contemporary forestry policy (*de jure*).

But despite the high costs of compliance, we found that communities have implemented the *de jure* management restrictions over non-*sokshing* forests. Respondents in our study villages claimed that transformation activities have significantly declined. The reason for this adoption was that forest transformation (for example, conversion to agriculture) could not be undertaken without the knowledge of the Forest Department. Forest transformations, which are

[9] For the land *kidu* process, the household submits an application to the district administration, which reviews the application and requests, among other things, a local Forest Department representative's inspection and determination of whether the forest conversion can be done without serious environmental impacts. After the Forest Department submits a report to the local administration, the applicant takes the application to the Ministry of Agriculture in the capital city Thimphu, securing a letter of clearance endorsing conversion, and returns it to the local administration office. Thereafter, the entire application packet is forwarded to the *zimpon* office in Thimphu, which is an office dedicated to the receipt of *kidu* applications. The *zimpon* office will then take the applicant and the application before His Majesty the King for consideration. Decisions of the King are later transmitted to the applicant through the *zimpon* office, with a copy going to the district administration. Successful applicants then initiate formal registration of the granted land, which provides legal transformation and permanent ownership rights.

both spatially extensive and temporally long term, are easily observable by monitors who may visit a village only once a year. If a Forest Department representative were to visit the village, a transformation activity could earn severe penalties. This is perceived as a high risk (and potentially high-cost activity) that would outweigh potential benefits.

In sum, we found only one case where the contemporary *de facto* property rights do not explicitly comply with the *de jure* rights. This was in the case of non-*sokshing* withdrawal rights. This implies that communities are not willing to undertake costly institutional adjustments (monitoring, enforcement, and behaviour modification) to comply with a provision that restricts their historical right to harvest forest products outside of *sokshings*. Not clearly expressed, but also encountered, was the increased cost to households from the restriction on transformation rights to non-*sokshing* forests. While compliance of people with this *de jure* rule is in agreement with contemporary policies, this is only because the cost of being caught for non-compliance outweighs the costs associated with compliance and the sacrifice of time and/or the ability to immediately transform forest into another form. Thus, contemporary policy has resulted in substantial costs to two important components of farmers' lives: withdrawal in, and transformation of, non-*sokshing* forests.

15.5. Conclusion

The existence of forest-related institutions across rural Bhutan may appear somewhat enigmatic if one considers Wade's (1988) assertion that a small, that is, limited resource base is a 'facilitating condition' for the evolution of collective-action institutions. Moreover, scholars (for example, Ostrom 1990) argue that well-defined resource boundaries (producing spatial limitation) facilitate conditions for institutional development. Indeed, CPRs are by definition extractable and therefore limited. But the question of why rural farmers decided to transform sections of the 'unlimited' natural forest into *sokshings* is not sufficiently explained by the limitation/boundary hypothesis. Since the forest-people ratio was so high in Bhutan, the total area of forest claimed by a village was enormous and never constrained the resource flow (Dorji 2003) although there were boundaries that separated 'village forests'. Moreover, complex forest management systems and institutional regimes for resources will not emerge unless the benefits outweigh the costs of institutional development, enforcement, and monitoring.

The conclusion is that *sokshing* management and its related institutional regimes were the solution to externally applied pressures from the emerging state for efficient agricultural production at the lowest social cost. This conclusion, however, should be considered with caution. Communities are not always able to respond efficiently to externally imposed demands, and these failures may result from an extensive number of conditions including the resource base characteristics, the community characteristics, or the support framework of the governing body. Moreover, the conditions that allowed Bhutanese communities to adapt to the changing contexts may not be present in other locations. Clearly, the application of this particular case study to other systems is limited because of the fact that very few, if any, pastoral environments such as ancient Bhutan exist today, where communities pursue subsistence farming in an environment that offers abundant forest and natural resources, and whose demands for institutional adjustment can be developed over generations rather than months or years.

We see two general paths to solving the problem of institutional instability in rural Bhutan. The first would be through increasing the rights of communities over withdrawal, management, or both. A second path would be to subsidize communities for the costs incurred by the policies. Increased rights over withdrawal would not necessarily require backtracking with regard to the 1969 Forest Act. Rather, the implementation of collaborative management, or community-based forest management, similar to a community forestry programme, is possible. By delineating areas outside of *sokshings* where communities could undertake sustainable extraction activities, commensurate with both Bhutan's overall conservation objective as well as community management objectives, the costs of compliance with harvesting limitations in the majority of forests under national control would be reduced. These types of models are both abundant and diverse throughout Asia, and it would be worthwhile to develop similar programmes in Bhutan.

Subsidization of communities for the costs they incur for compliance with withdrawal and management regulations is also a possibility. Subsidization may be more relevant with regard to defraying costs of transformation. Inability to transform land into temporary agriculture (swiddens) increases livelihood risk. In order to compensate for this, the Bhutanese government should take steps to support agricultural intensification or expansions. Alternatively, the government could consider provisions to allow limited shifting agricultural practices although this is probably the least realistic solution because soil fertility cannot be maintained under short fallows. Ultimately, the challenge to compensate for the costs imposed on communities as a result of compliance with management restrictions may be greater than those associated with reducing costs for withdrawal restriction.

References

Agrawal, A. (2003). 'Sustainable Governance of Common-pool Resources: Context, Methods, Politics'. *Annual Review of Anthropology*, 32: 243–62.

Das, N. (1974). *The Dragon Country: The General History of Bhutan*. New Delhi: Orient Longman.

Dorji, L. (2003). 'Assessing the Evolution, Status, and Future Implications of Forest Resources Management in the Inner Himalayas of the Kingdom of Bhutan'. Ph.D. dissertation. Bangkok: School of Environment, Resources and Development, Asian Institute of Technology.

—— Webb, E. L., and Shivakoti, G. (2003). 'Can a Nationalized Forest Management System Uphold Local Institutions? A Case of Leaf Litter Forest (*Sokshing*) Management in Bhutan'. *Asian Studies Review,* 27: 341–59.

—— —— —— (2006). 'Property Rights, Incentives and Forest Management in Bhutan'. *Environmental Conservation,* 33: 141–7.

Gibson, C. C. (2001), 'Forest Resources: Institutions for Local Governance in Guatemala', in J. Burger, E. Ostrom, R. B. Norgaard, D. Policansky, and B. D. Goldstein (eds.), *Protecting the Commons: A Framework for Resource Management in the Americas.* Washington, DC: Island Press, 71–89.

Gilmour, D. A., and Fisher, R. J. (1991). *Villagers, Forests and Foresters: the Philosophy, Process and Practice of Community Forestry in Nepal.* Kathmandu, Nepal: Sahayogi Press.

Hasrat, B. (1980). *History of Bhutan: Land of the Peaceful Dragon.* Thimphu, Bhutan: Education Department, Royal Government of Bhutan.

Mancall, R. (undated). 'Gross National Happiness and Development: An Essay'. Selected paper on Gross National Happiness, United Nations Development Programme, Thimpu, Bhutan. Available online at <http://www.undp.org.bt/Governance/GNH/GNH.htm> (accessed 23 November 2005).

Ministry of Agriculture (2000). 'Forest and Nature Conservation Rules of Bhutan 2000 (Vol. I & II)'. Internal document. Ministry of Agriculture, Royal Government of Bhutan, Thimphu, Bhutan.

Ostrom, E. (1990). *Governing the Commons: The Evolution of Institutions and Collective Action.* New York: Cambridge University Press.

—— and Wertime, M. B. (2000). 'International Forestry Resources and Institutions (IFRI) Research Strategy', in C. C. Gibson, M. A. McKean, and E. Ostrom (eds.), *People and Forests: Communities, Institutions, and Governance.* London: MIT Press, 243–68.

Pain, A., and Pema, D. (2000). 'Continuing Customs of Negotiation and Contestation in Bhutan'. *Journal of Bhutan Studies,* 2: 219–27.

Savada, A. M. (1993). *Nepal and Bhutan: Country Studies* (3rd edn.). Washington, DC: Federal Research Division, Library of Congress.

Schlager, E., and Ostrom, E. (1992). 'Property-Rights Regimes and Natural Resources: A Conceptual Analysis'. *Land Economics,* 68: 249–62.

Sinha, A. C. (1991). *Bhutan: Ethnic Identity and National Dilemma.* New Delhi, India: Reliance Publishing House.

Springate-Baginski, O., Dev, O. M., Yadav, N. P., and Soussan, J. (2003). 'Community Forest Management in the Middle Hills of Nepal: The Changing Context'. *Journal of Forest and Livelihood,* 3/1: 5–20.

Wade, R. (1988). *Village Republics: Economic Conditions for Collective Action in South India.* San Francisco, CA: ICS Press.

16

So Far So Good: Next Steps in Community Forestry

Keshav Raj Kanel[1]

16.1. Introduction

Community forestry was initially started in Nepal in 1978, and has gradually evolved over time. Learning from practices, refining them over time, and legitimizing these practices have been the hallmarks of community forestry policy development in Nepal. Instead of formulating a policy and implementing it in the field, community forestry policy development has first facilitated good practices in the field and then legitimized them through consultations with different stakeholders. This has originated in and evolved from the indigenous practices that the community used to follow in managing the resources for their own consumption (Gilmour and Fisher 1991).

This programme is an institutional innovation for empowering local communities when it comes to managing forest resources as 'commons' for their benefit in coordination with the government. Presently, the Forest Act of 1993 and the Forest Rules of 1995 describe the process of programme implementation throughout Nepal. The process of handing over part of the national forests to local villagers as community forests, and the advisory and regulatory roles to be played by forest officials and other units are also elaborated in the community forestry guidelines of 1995. The local communities of forest users, as Community Forest User Groups (CFUGs), are registered at the District Forest Office (DFO) with their charter of association/constitution. They are recognized as independent, voluntary, and self-governing institutions by the Forest Act and regulations of Nepal. Under the broad policy framework of the act and regulations, the groups can design their own operational rules, monitor forests, and enforce and sanction rules of forest protection and utilization.

---

[1] I am indebted to Ms Ingela Ternstom from Beuer Institute for her critical review and suggestions in finalizing the paper.

Furthermore, they may set their own prices for the forest products they use within the group although they have to sell the surplus forest products to outsiders at market rates.[2] The groups' funds, generated from the sale of forest products and other sources,[3] can be used for the management of their forests, and for community development and poverty reduction activities. An operational plan of the forest is prepared by the group and approved by the DFO.

Forest users organized into CFUGs can resolve exclusion and extraction difficulties inherent in classical forest management regimes. The constitution, prepared by the CFUG members and registered at the DFO, resolves the exclusion issue. The Operational Plan resolves the extraction issue as the plan (drawn up for five to ten years) includes sustainable harvest schedules and other management activities. The forest legislation and rules have led to a conducive governance environment leading in turn to better forest conditions and livelihoods for local people.

However, although the CFUGs presently have access, extraction, exclusion, and management rights over the community forests (Agrawal and Ostrom 2001), they cannot sell the land nor change the land use. According to some, the structure of the relationship between CFUG and DFO is therefore still asymmetrical (Kanel 2001). The DFO, for example, can withdraw a previously handed-over (community) forest if a CFUG (*a*) is engaged in activities detrimental to the environment; (*b*) is unable to implement the Operational Plan; and (*c*) does not comply with the provisions as specified in the Forest Act and regulations.

Within these policy constraints, the CFUGs have flexibility in forest management and fund utilization. Face-to-face interactions among members of the CFUGs and joint formulation of operational rules, as well as their monitoring and sanctioning by the user groups themselves, have greatly enhanced trust, reciprocity, and reputation of the CFUG committee members among the members of the CFUG. Since the present number of CFUGs exceeds 14,000 over Nepal, their leadership and management capacity also differ across space and time (see Adhikari, and Khatri-Chhetri in this volume). Reoriented foresters have further helped in facilitating the process of institution building at the local level.

About 1.2 million hectares of forested land (25 per cent of the total) have so far[4] been handed over to these CFUGs, the members of which constitute about 35 per cent of the total population of Nepal. Denuded forests have been regenerated and the condition of forests improved mainly because forest users decide and enforce forest extraction on a sustained yield basis. These activities are based on the decisions of the users themselves.

---

[2] Sine 2003, the government collects 15 per cent of the value of surplus timber of two valuable species (*Shorea robusta, Acacia catechu*) sold in the market by the CFUGs in the Terai.

[3] Other sources include donations, fines, entry fees, etc.

[4] That is, up to November 2005.

There are now about 143,000 elected committee members (of which 35,000 are women), who make day-to-day decisions about forests, funds, and other development activities. Their leadership capacity too has substantially increased with the result that many of them have taken leadership positions in district development and village development committees. The Master Plan for the Forestry Sector (MPFS) in 1989 focused on enhancing the participation of local villagers in decision-making and benefit-sharing in community forestry. A quick glance at the national-level CFUG database, which is updated daily at the Community Forestry Division, shows that about 24 per cent of CFUG committee members are women. Moreover, there are more than 600 CFUGs whose committee members are only women. Thus it could be said that community forestry is contributing to the promotion of gender equality and the empowerment of women through social mobilization.

However, although the primary aim of community forestry in expanding the greenery has been achieved (see Section 16.3.1), its contribution to human development as expressed in the Tenth Plan (2002–7) of Nepal and the Millennium Development Goals[5] are yet to be fully achieved. Linking community forestry to these human development issues is the second-generation challenge. Another challenge lies in increasing the productivity of these forests, as they are still passively managed. Enhancing the productivity of the forests would lead to an increased supply of forest products. The poor could use more of these products or sell the surplus. The money thus generated could be used on pro-poor programmes.

The reason for giving priority to community forestry under present forest legislation was to reverse the forest degradation caused by the Forest Nationalization Act of 1957. This act did not recognize indigenous (informal) forest management practiced by the local people. Instead, it took the responsibility of managing them under the state authority. Forest management under a central government that lacks the ability to enforce laws and protect forest resources is similar to land management under an absentee landlord—natural resources are rapidly depleted and the land is not well managed. The inherent problems of principal and agent, as well as the moral hazard and their associated cost of transaction in a centralized system culminated in accelerated deforestation and degradation in Nepal (World Bank 1978). This situation led to an institutional innovation in the management of forests with the result that forest management rights were devolved to local communities (Kanel 2001). The devolution of rights in the Nepali context includes the reconfiguration of property rights in forest resources so that local communities have long-term incentives to conserve and sustainably utilize the forests (Agrawal, Britt,

---

[5] The eight MDGs are the following: eradicate extreme poverty and hunger; achieve universal primary education; promote gender equality and empower women; reduce child mortality; improve maternal health; combat HIV/AIDS, malaria, and other diseases; ensure environmental sustainability; and develop a global partnership for development.

and Kanel 1999). Birner and Wittmer (2000) also suggest that if the state's capacity is low, and the community's capacity to manage local resources is high, community-based management would be the appropriate governance structure for natural resource management.

This chapter argues that community forestry is a dynamic and adaptive programme. Several case studies show that the original objective of restoring and expanding greenery has been more or less achieved at least in the hills of Nepal (see Section 16.3.1). Linking the achievements in forestry with the social and economic development of rural people is the evolutionary challenge in community forestry programmes at present. The next stage of the programme will have to focus on livelihood promotion, good governance, and sustainable forest management. These are also the 'second-generation' issues in community forestry programming. The orientation of the programme towards meeting these goals could also contribute to the attainment of poverty reduction as set out in the tenth five-year plan (2002–7) of Nepal.

The chapter is organized into six sections. Section 16.2 presents the emergence and evolution of community forestry in Nepal. It is followed in Section 16.3 by an analysis of achievements so far made. Section 16.4 presents the second-generation challenges while Section 16.5 discusses the lessons that others may elicit from the community forestry programme of Nepal. The final section (16.6) presents the summary and concluding remarks.

16.2. Evolution of the community forestry agenda

The initial phase of community forestry starting in 1978 was geared towards assigning the responsibilities and rights of local forest management to the village-level political bodies. It was based on protecting and planting trees to meet the forest-product needs of the local people based on the principle of 'gap analysis'. The gap analysis basically assumed that a sustainable supply of forest products would not be enough to meet the growing needs of the population under the prevailing institutional arrangement. Thus the deficit or gap would have to be met from the depletion of the stock of forests, leading in turn to further degradation of the forest areas in Nepal. A World Bank study of 1978 projected that Nepal's forests would be depleted within fifteen years in the hills and within twenty-five years in the plains or the *Terai*. This study rang alarm bells across in the country and led to the recommendation of a massive plantation programme to mitigate the deficit. However, a pilot forestry project implemented in two districts (adjoining Kathmandu) with support from the Australian government (Gilmour and Fisher 1991) had shown that involvement of local people in forestry activities from the inception gives them an incentive to protect adjoining forests.

This led to an amendment in the Forest Act in 1978 with the provision that government forests could be assigned to local political bodies for their management.

After three years of rigorous study and wider consultations in the preparation of the Master Plan for the Forestry Sector, the foundation was laid for handing over forests to groups of traditional forest users. The plan recommended that these groups could meet their basic forest-product needs while conserving the forests at the same time. Reorientation of foresters was also considered essential for the sustainable management of these community forests. The plan further stressed that participation of local communities in both decision-making and benefit-sharing was essential for the conservation of forest management. The endorsement of the plan in 1988 and the political regime change (restoration of democracy) in 1990 were instrumental in the formulation of the new Forest Act in 1993 and the forest regulations in 1995. The focus of the new act and regulations was on institutionalizing CFUG as an independent and self-governing entity. It provided a regulatory mechanism to expand CF not only in the hills but also in the *Terai* by providing utilization and management rights to these CFUGs and making DFOs the 'gatekeepers' of community forests.

There are differences between the hills and the plains region known as the *Terai*. Community forestry originally emerged and evolved in the hills. The intimate linkage between forests and farming; the mosaic pattern of village settlements, agricultural fields, and nearby forests; and the insignificant revenue that the government obtained from forests in the hills prompted the government to hand over national forests to communities in the hills. But the forests in the *Terai* are highly valuable and also a source of revenue to the government. These forests are located in large contiguous blocks extending district boundaries, and lie in the northern portion of the *Terai* (but at the foothills of lower hills known as *Churia*). The original settlers live in the southern portion of the area creating what is called the 'distance-user dilemma'. Since the eradication of malaria in the 1950s, hill people too have been resettled in the *Terai* after clearing forests.

The scant economic opportunities in the hills have also caused hill people to migrate to the *Terai* and to encroach upon the forests. About 70,000 hectares of *Terai* forest have been encroached upon by these migrants. The resettlement in and the encroachment upon the *Terai* forest by hill people have succeeded in creating a buffer between the forests and the original people residing in the *Terai*. Some of the key differences between the hills and the *Terai* with respect to community forestry programmes are shown in Table 16.1.

According to some (Baral and Subedi 2000; Pokharel and Amatya 2000), the handing over of forests to forest-adjacent peoples favour recent settlers at the expense of original user-settlers who now live further away

Table 16.1. Key differences between the hills and the *Terai*

Attributes	Hills	*Terai*
Terrain	Hill and slopes	Plain or flat
Forests and settlements	Mosaic	Forests on the north and settlements on the south
Forests and farming system	Highly integrated	Not much integrated
History of indigenous management system	Very old	Few among *Tharu* communities (indigenous communities)
History of formal CF management	Initially innovated	Replicated from the hills
Donor assistance in CF	Since beginning	Recent
Involvement of distance users	Not an issue	Big issue
Ease of demarcating CF and CF users	Easy	Relatively difficult
Commercial value of forests	Low	High
Revenue to the government	Negligible	High
Access to market	Low	High
Forest Product theft	Very low	High
Forest encroachment	Very low	High
Heterogeneity in HH income and wealth	Low	High
Present in-migration	Negative	Net increase
Consensus on CF (social capital)	High	Contentious
Livelihood potential from CF	Relatively low	High
Need for forest governance reform	Relatively low	Urgent and very important

from the forests. The government also believes that handing over forests to these recent migrants could create both problems of equity as well as a political firestorm. This was what led to the cabinet decision of 2000 to freeze forest handing over (except scattered patches) to communities in the *Terai*. However, based on the experiences of several case studies, Bampton *et al.* (2004) argue that community forestry could effectively be carried out even in the *Terai*. They mention that CF is so much a flexible programme that it can easily be implemented in the *Terai*. Moreover, the present Forest Act and regulations also do not discriminate between the hills and the *Terai*.

The Millennium Development Goals agreed upon by the United Nations including Nepal in the year 2000 specifically aims at reducing the level of global poverty by half by the year 2015. The tenth plan of Nepal also aims at poverty reduction. The last meeting (in 2003) of the Forestry Sector Coordination Committee, a coalition of government, donors, and forestry non-governmental organizations in Nepal stressed that the community forestry programme needs to resolve the second-generation issues of livelihood promotion, good governance, and sustainable forest management if it is to be relevant in the present context. The latest forestry paper presented at the Nepal Development Forum (2004) has also stressed the need to link the community forestry programme with the overall development goal of the tenth plan.

16.3. Analysis of achievements

A review of the community forestry programme shows that substantial progress has been made in devolving forest management rights and responsibilities over a large area of national forests to locally organized CFUGs. Analysis of achievements shows that community forestry in Nepal has been successful in designing and implementing policies because it has been governed by practice and pragmatism. The two-way communication between the CFUGs and the government has helped it to be more adaptive. Multiple stakeholders have collectively assimilated field-level lessons. It is thus now accepted by many that local people's participation through decentralization is essential in the management of natural resources.

The lessons from community forestry are being disseminated into other areas as well. Programme implementation in soil conservation and watershed management, for instance, is now carried out through community development groups. Similarly, the concept and practice of users' group and users' committees is replicated in the management of forests and other resources of buffer zones (that is, impact areas adjoining national parks and reserves) as well. Such devolution of authority to local communities has enabled local communities to coordinate their collective activities resulting in better resource management. The programme has also reduced the principal-agent problem at the central level. The communities can now use the nearby forests the way they like under the framework of the operational plan prepared by them. This has created an incentive to the villagers to use the forest in a sustainable manner. Hence, the impact of CF can be interpreted in terms of better forest conditions, social mobilization, and income generation for rural development and institution building, or social capital formation at the grass-roots level. The achievements in terms of forest condition, income generation, expenditures, and social mobilization and governance are discussed below.

16.3.1. *Improvement in forest condition*

The Community Forest Division (CFD) has maintained a database of the forested area handed over to CFUGs over time. The pattern of handing over in terms of forest area and CFUGs is shown in Figure 16.1.

The figure below shows that forest handing over to CFUGs was slow during the initial period, increased during the 1990s, but has now reached a plateau. This is due to the fact that (*a*) most of the accessible forests of the hills and mountains have already been handed over; (*b*) the government has restricted forest handover in the *Terai* to scattered patches disjointed from large blocks of forest (more on this in the following sections); and (*c*) the Maoist conflict hinders group meetings and field-level visits by the forestry staff. The CFD

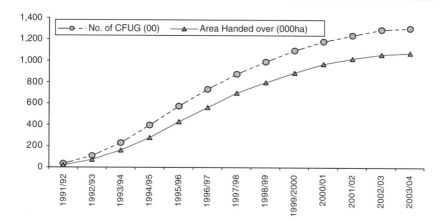

Figure 16.1. Pattern of handing over of community forests
Source: CFD 2005.

database shows that only about 9 per cent of the CFUG and 14 per cent of community forests are located in the *Terai*.[6]

Both ocular observations made during field visits and case studies (summarized below) indicate that the condition of community forests has substantially improved. However, no macro-level in-depth study has yet been undertaken to assess the magnitude of improved forest conditions under the community forest-management regime. Summarized below are some studies that indicate the magnitude of forest condition improvement under CF.

- Branney and Yadav (1998) assessed the changes in forest conditions and management of community forests during 1994–7 in four eastern hill districts. The study shows an overall improvement in CF conditions over the study period. The total number of stems per unit area has increased by 51 per cent. The basal area of forest in poor condition increased significantly by 29 per cent. There is a lower level of grazing in CF (from 94 to 71 per cent) than in the national forests during the study period. Fire incidence and illicit felling are also lower in CF. The proportion of 'active' forest management increased from 3 to 19 per cent and 'no forest management' has decreased from 97 to 43 per cent. When it comes to forest-product utilization, 43 per cent of CFUGs are harvesting more timber while 14 per cent are harvesting less than before the formation of CFUGs. Twenty-seven per cent of CFUGs are harvesting more fuelwood while 47 per cent are harvesting less than before. Similarly, 87 per cent CFUGs are harvesting a lower level of fuelwood while 47 per cent are harvesting a lower level of timber than the productive capacity of the forest.

---

[6] This was the database as of August 2004. However, this figure was 9 and 14 per cent respectively in December 2005.

- Jackson *et al.* (1998) undertook a land-use change study in two central districts (Sindhu and Kavre) using aerial photographs from 1978 and 1992 supplemented by rapid rural appraisal and information from local villagers. Their study covered 15 per cent of the total area of these districts. Community forestry at lower altitudes was shown to have beneficial effects on forest cover. Shrubland and grassland are being converted to more productive categories of forests reflecting the strength of communities in managing and conserving their own forest resources. The area of total forestland increased from 7,677 to 9,679 hectares (by 26 per cent) between 1978 and 1992. This was mainly due to 1,352 hectares of new plantation, but also to an increase in the area of mixed forest.

- Gautam *et al.* (2003) carried out a study of land-use change in a watershed covering an area of 153 km² by comparing satellite images from 1976, 1989, and 2000. The study shows that the number of forest patches decreased substantially between 1976 and 2000 suggesting a merger of patches in the latter periods due to forest regeneration and/or plantation establishment on land previously separating two or more forest patches. For example, the number of forest patches decreased continuously from 395 in 1976 to 323 in 1989 and 175 in 2000 while the average patch area increased continuously during the same period. Among the major land-use groups, around 81 per cent of agricultural and 77 per cent of the forest area in 1976 remained unchanged until 2000. Forest lost 22.5 per cent of its 1976 area to other land uses but gained 37.4 per cent from other land classes, resulting in a net increase of 794 hectares in forest area during the study period.

- Livelihood and Forestry Programme (LFP) carried out a baseline study in 2003 to understand the livelihoods, aspiration, priorities, strategies, and dynamics of households in four eastern and three western hill districts. The study shows that the majority of users feel that forest conditions are improving (93 per cent of respondents in the west, and 72 per cent in the east) and that managing CF is a worthwhile endeavour.

- Rana (2004) using remote-sensed imagery concludes that the conditions of community forests in Saptari district in the *Terai* have improved.

- The Department of Forests (2005) carried out an analysis of forest-cover change from 1991 to 2001 in twenty *Terai* districts. Previously, the rate of deforestation in these districts was 1.3 per cent per year, but it has declined to 0.08 per cent per year within the last ten years. This decline in forest depletion is partly due to the expansion of community forests in the *Terai*. The deforestation rate would have further declined had the government not put a freeze on handing over parts of large blocks of forests to local communities.

Table 16.2. Forest products harvested, used within, and sold outside the CFUG

Forest products	Used/sale	Quantity (in million)	User income (in million Rs)	Stumpage value (in million Rs)	% of total user price
Timber (cubic feet)	Internal use	8.00	286.84	930.27	38.38
	External sale	2.93	356.54	340.46	47.71
	Subtotal	10.94	643.39	1,270.73	86.09
Fuelwood (kg)	Internal use	335.64	30.17	335.64	4.04
	External sale	2.33	9.80	2.33	1.31
	Subtotal	337.97	39.97	337.97	5.35
Grass/fodder/bedding materials (kg)	Internal use	370.64	14.23	185.32	1.90
Khair (kg)	External sale	3.13	37.04	31.31	4.96
Medicinal/herbal products* (kg)	External sale	0.09	1.53	1.53	0.20
Pine resin (kg)	External sale	1.34	7.30	4.04	0.98
Other forest products* (kg)	External sale	0.37	3.88	3.88	0.51
Total	Internal use		331.24	1,451.24	44.32
	External sale		416.10	383.56	55.68
	Total		747.34	1,834.80	100

Source: Kanel and Niraula 2004.

Note: * Price based on CFUG records.

16.3.2. *Income generation*

CFD carried out a rapid appraisal of forest-product utilization, income, and pattern of expenditure of 1,788 CFUGs from twelve districts covering both hills and the *Terai*. The survey data were collected in 2003 although the information is for 2002. The data were extrapolated for all CFUGs in Nepal. The findings are reported in Kanel and Niraula (2004) but some of the salient features of this study are presented in the following paragraph.

A variety of forest products are collected, used, or sold by the CFUGs. The funds are used mainly on forest and community development activities. Table 16.2 presents the type and magnitude of forest products collected and sold within and outside the CFUG. The value of forest products harvested and used is calculated by using both user and stumpage price. User price refers to the actual money CFUGs get by selling forest products within and outside the groups. Stumpage price refers to the economic value (weighted for different products) of these products at the site. Again, these figures are for all community forests and CFUGs extrapolated from the samples as mentioned above.

Table 16.3 shows that the groups generate income from diverse products. The total annual income from the sale of forest products from community forests is about Nepali Rupees (Rs) 747 million[7] (about US$10 million). However, if the value of forest products used within the CFUGs at the market

---

[7] One US $ equals 74 Nepal Rupees (Rs) in December 2005.

Table 16.3. Distribution of annual income (Rs in millions) of CFUGs

Income source	% of total *Terai*	% of total hills	Total income	% of total income
Forest product sale	59.15	92.85	747.34	83.72
GO/NGO grants	1.67	1.13	11.42	1.28
Fine/punishment	0.79	0.46	4.90	0.55
Membership fees	2.09	1.03	11.75	1.32
Entrance fees	0.97	0.37	4.78	0.53
Other income	35.30	4.16	112.53	12.60
Total income	242.18	650.58	892.76	100

rate is calculated, the annual value of these forest products increases to about Rs 1.8 billion. Among the forest products, timber generates the highest percentage (86 per cent), followed by *Khair* (wood product used as paste in preparing betel chewed in northern India and the *Terai*) and fuelwood (10 per cent), grass/fodder and bedding materials (2 per cent), and other NTFPs (2 per cent). Forest users sell a major proportion of forest products outside the group. Medicinal and herbal products, pine resin, and other unidentified forest products are also collected from community forests but their share is very low in terms of monetary value.

In both *Terai* and hill regions, CFUG members use the bulk of timber and fuelwood internally. *Khair*, medicinal and herbal products, and pine resin are entirely sold outside the group.

Apart from the income earned from the forest products, CFUGs also earn from other sources such as grants, membership and entrance fees, fines, and punishments, etc. The breakdown of total CFUG income is given in Table 16.3. The annual income of CFUGs is Rs 893 million. Forest products are the major source of CFUG income, which constitutes around 84 per cent of total income. It is even higher in the hills (93 per cent), but not so high in the *Terai* (59 per cent). The second largest source of CFUG income is from 'other sources',[8] not well explained by the users during the survey. However, it is substantially higher for the *Terai* than for the hills. Although only about 12 per cent of community forests lie in the *Terai,* more than one-fourth of CFUG income (27 per cent) is generated from the *Terai* region indicating that *Terai* forests are financially more valuable than those of the hills.

16.3.3. *Expenditure*

Details of annual expenditure incurred by the CFUGs are given in Table 16.4. Community development comprises the highest proportion of CFUG expenses (36 per cent), which includes school support, road construction, and other community infrastructure development. The analysis shows that

---

[8] Other sources include interest on loans provided by CFUGs to their members.

Table 16.4. Distribution of annual expenditure (Rs in million) of CFUGs

Items	% of *Terai*	% of hills	Total expenditure	% of total
Forest watcher	14.99	6.83	46.16	10.10
Silvicultural operations[1]	16.97	19.29	83.88	18.36
Training, study tour, W/S	1.59	2.13	8.75	1.91
Stationery	2.06	9.71	30.34	6.64
Building construction	6.60	6.53	29.97	6.56
Rent/equipment	1.09	0.70	3.91	0.86
Salary/allowance	7.58	2.01	19.39	4.24
Meeting/assembly	4.10	0.51	8.91	1.95
Other group operational	0	0.08	0.23	0.05
School support	6.07	8.73	34.99	7.66
Road construction	0.54	8.17	23.36	5.11
Other infrastructure	10.10	21.01	76.01	16.63
Pro-poor programme	0.88	4.04	12.65	2.77
Miscellaneous	27.44	10.27	78.40	17.16
Total expenditure	183.35	273.60	456.95	100

Source: Kanel and Niraula 2004.

[1] Forest-related cultural activities such as pruning of trees, weeding, thinning, and other harvesting of plants and trees in the area are called silvicultural activities.

CFUG are spending 28.5 per cent of their income on forest protection and management. This is higher than the mandatory level (of 25 per cent) mentioned in the Forest Act and regulations. The operational cost is the third biggest area of CFUG expenditure. Stationery, equipment, rent, allowances, etc., are included under this heading. CFUGs also spend a high proportion of money (17 per cent) under miscellaneous headings, which is an unidentified area of expenditure. Although it is very low (3 per cent), CFUGs also spend their money directly on pro-poor programmes. However, the hill CFUGs appear to spend more on pro-poor programmes than their *Terai* counterparts. The CFUG expense on training and extension, which is a basic activity to develop human capital of the CFUG members, is only a small fraction (2 per cent). A high level of government and NGO support may motivate them to spend less on this component. This support might also have shown up under other sources of income.

A comparison of expenditure between the hills and the *Terai* shows that *Terai* CFUGs tend to spend more on hiring watchers to protect their forests and on paying salary and allowances to the CFUG committee members. This suggests that *Terai* CF are more commercially managed and CFUGs' social capital is more diluted in comparison to that of the hills. Investment in infrastructure is higher in the hills than in the *Terai*, partly because the cost of building roads, schools, and drinking water supplies is higher in the hills than in the *Terai*. They also spend more on miscellaneous items, an item which is not well-defined in their expenditure category. They also spend more on pro-poor programmes than their *Terai* counterparts.

The total annual budget of the Department of Forests was about Rs 680 million, and the annual income of the Department was about Rs 550 million in the year 2002. The income comes mainly from the sale of timber and fuelwood. Other sources of revenue are from the sale of NTFPs such as resin, medicinal and aromatic plants, and stones and sand. Community forests cover only about 25 per cent of the total national forests, but generate more than Rs 740 million per year, proving that this programme is highly effective in forest management and in resource generation.

The data presented above provides information on the amount and pattern of forest products and financial resource utilization by the CFUGs. However, the question of how these investments contribute to poverty alleviation at the individual level has yet to be analysed in detail. It is mentioned that at least 3 per cent of the total expenditure (Rs 12.6 million) is spent on direct pro-poor programmes. This has directly contributed to poverty reduction as well as helped contribute towards the first millennium development goal of eradicating extreme poverty and hunger in the rural areas of Nepal. Users are also spending their income on receiving education and receiving assistance in conducting non-formal education at the CFUG level. The literacy level of women and other disadvantaged groups is also increasing with these pro-grammes. A community forestry project implemented (from February 1998 to July 2005) in thirty-eight hill districts showed that 163,879 CFUG members participated in 4,621 events of various types of trainings, workshops, and study tours (DANIDA and HMG 2004). The participation of women in these events was 39.5 per cent. Therefore, the CF programme has contributed to meeting the second MDG, that is, achieving universal primary education in the rural areas. Obviously, more needs to be done in attaining these goals.

16.3.4. Social mobilization and governance

CFUGs contribute voluntary labour with respect to forest protection and management. It accounts for a higher fraction of their contribution than stipulated in forest legislation. Users are involved in forest protection, silvicul-tural operations, and in CFUG meetings. People generally spend whole days on forest protection and silvicultural operations, whereas only a few hours are spent on meetings and assemblies. If eight hours a day is considered as a one-person day and the opportunity cost of labour as Rs 65 per day,[9] the amount of CFUG voluntary contribution in monetary terms is about NRs 165 million (see Table 16.5). On average, more than 40 per cent (42 per cent) of

[9] People are engaged in agricultural activities during two thirds of a year. About one third of a year is the off-peak agricultural season. The agriculture season represents full-time employment, whereas the opportunity cost of the off-peak season is about half this wage rate. An estimate of a day's wage rate is about Rs 80. Thus, the weighted average wage rate or the opportunity cost of labour is about Rs 65 per day.

Table 16.5. Participation of CFUG members in community forestry activities

Area of participation	*Terai* person days (No.)	% of *Terai*	Hills person days (No.)	% of hills	Total person days (No.)	Total Value (in million Rs)	Total %
Participation in forest protection	105,861	20.59	962,958	47.59	1,068,819	69.47	42.12
Participation in silvicultural operations	50,339	9.79	303,764	15.01	354,113	23.02	13.95
Participation in forest-product harvesting	211,358	41.10	272,495	13.47	483,853	31.45	19.07
Participation training, study-tours, W/S	2,319	0.45	9,527	0.47	11,846	0.77	0.47
Participation in CFUG meeting and assembly	97,515	18.96	395,550	19.55	493,065	32.05	19.43
Participation in community development	46,810	9.10	79,133	3.91	125,953	8.19	4.96
Total participation	514,202	100	2,023,427	100	2,537,629	164.95	100

their contribution is for the protection of CF. It is even higher in the hills (48 per cent) than in the *Terai*. This is followed by participation in meetings and assemblies (19 per cent) and in forest products harvests (19 per cent). There appears to be a substitution between labour and capital in forest protection. In the *Terai*, proportionately more money is spent on forest watchers, and forest-product harvesting, while the labour proportion seems to be low. It is just the opposite in the hills. And similar to the trend observed above when it comes to CFUG expenses, participation in training, study-tours and workshops is also very low (less than 1 per cent) in both the *Terai* and the hills. This could indicate the lower priority placed on human capital development. Moreover, their participation in community development activities is only 5 per cent. Hence, it could be concluded that they appear to be willing to spend money but contribute less in terms of labour for infrastructure development.

Regular interactions and meetings between forest users and forest officials, and facilitation of the process by other civil society members, have empowered CFUGs to devise operational rules, which are more democratic and relevant. Although decision-making and benefit-sharing mechanisms are yet to be fully equitable, community forestry has helped in the promotion of local-level institutions (social capital) and better governance at the field level. The challenges lie in further improving the accountability, transparency, and equity of CFUG governance, and the relationship with government units and other stakeholders so that the rules crafted at the operational and policy levels are more responsive and predictable.

16.4. Challenges

Although it is evident that the CF programme generates substantial income, concerns about the distributional effects of this programme are being raised. For example, a case study of four CFUGs (Richard *et al.* 1999) shows that poor users do not derive as much benefit from community forests as others. In other words, rich and middle-income groups receive more benefits than the poorer households (Kanel, Karmacharya, and Karna 2003). A recent study by Bandopadhyay, Shyamsunder, and Kanel (2005) has shown that the presence of a CFUG in a village increases household consumption by about 6 per cent. However, the programme provides little benefit to the asset-poor and land-poor households. Similarly, Adhikari (2003) shows that the transaction cost of managing community forests is borne more by the poorer subgroups than the richer and middle-income subgroups of a CFUG. Of course, right now there is no large-scale or macro-level data to support these case studies, but the government is considering how to redesign CF programme activities in order that the poor, the disadvantaged, and women benefit more.

It has also been observed that these grass-roots organizations such as CFUGs also face principal-agent problems at the local level. This has resulted in the capture of decision-making fora and benefits by the local elites.

Misappropriation of CFUG funds by committee members is also on the increase (Shrestha 2005). Therefore, how to make these institutions more accountable and responsive to the poor, the disadvantaged, and women is a challenge. How to strengthen more inclusive processes of representation in the CFUG committees so that they are more accountable and responsive to forest users is yet another challenge in community forestry as we enter the twenty-first century. Similarly, the other challenge lies in building a relationship and synergy between and among communities, government, and forest management so that sustainable benefits from better forest management are directed towards poverty reduction.

Many of the community forests are not productively managed. Better manipulation of trees and shrubs over the same space at different time intervals (silviculture) can increase the productivity of the forests. However, up to now their managements can only be called passive. The challenge lies in managing the forests intensively so that a higher level of forest products can be annually harvested in order to meet the needs of the poor by selling the surplus and reinvesting the money on programmes benefiting the poor. Allocating a part of community forests to a subgroup of poor and marginalized households, and offering them micro-credit and other services through local service providers, are also possible ways by which to intensify forest management and to reduce poverty at the same time.

The cabinet decision of 2000 on not handing over part of a large block of national forest to communities has created a controversy over the handing over of *Terai* forests to local communities. As a result, there are roughly 380 legally constituted CFUGs to which the forests (about 48,500 hectares) have not been handed over formally. However, the groups manage the forests 'informally'. Moreover, there are the 'informal' CFUGs, which are not registered at the DFO, but still protect 'their' forests. A national level workshop on *Terai* forestry was proposed during February 2006, but it could not be held due to disagreement between the government and other stakeholders. The challenge when it comes to the *Terai* lies more in resolving the so-called 'distance-user' dilemma. It could be resolved through a benefit-sharing mechanism between the CFUG and the distance users. In fact, some of the CFUGs in eastern *Terai* (Morang district) are already experimenting with the benefit-sharing mechanism. It may be too costly to directly involve the 'distance users' in the day-to-day forest management activities, but their assistance in controlling forest theft and encroachment can be very useful. They could be compensated for this role as well. Once the tensions between CFUG members and 'distance users' are resolved, community forestry in the *Terai* could proceed in a normal manner.

It has been observed that as the income from forests increases, decision-making systems of CFUGs also become more complicated (Shrestha 2005). The committee becomes more powerful than the CFUG as the income from the forest increases. The issue of transparency in the sale of forest products and the allocation of funds then becomes very important. Contractors, CFUG committees, and the DFO staff may form a coalition and attempt to grab the rents from the community forests. Public auditing and the facilitating role of the NGO become very important during this stage. Creation of district- and village-level fora for deliberation and negotiation can enhance transparency and accountability at the CFUG level.

These challenges could be resolved via consultations so that the cost of transaction or reform is minimized both at the individual as well as at the societal levels. Many reforms have been guided by either deductive or inductive methods of logic. But since community forestry reforms have mostly been led first by experience and then by legislation, the programme aims to continue to follow this pragmatic approach of reform or transformation.

16.5. Lessons for others to learn

Social or, more narrowly speaking, forestry reform, is not a linear but an iterative and 'muddling through' process. There is a unanimous and converging view that community forestry has brought about a fundamental shift in the forest management paradigm. This shift in mindset could be put the following way: that institutional innovation or reform should precede technical innovation in forestry development. Since rural people are so dependent on forests for their livelihood (Khatri-Chhetri, this volume) and other ecological services, they need to be involved in forest management and utilization. The process of participation involves creating institutional arrangements so that the local people have a say in both decision-making and benefit-sharing. That way people will have incentives to better manage and sustainably utilize the forest.

Starting negotiation and building consensus among forest stakeholders are key to changing or reinventing forestry organizations. Nepal's community forestry was initially led by working forest officers. Internalization of this concept by a critical mass of foresters, as well as the training provided to them, also helped to move community forestry beyond the domain of government organization.

Forests in developing countries face exclusion and extraction problems. The Forest Act and regulations of Nepal have tried to resolve these twin problems first by allowing locals to constitute themselves into CFUGs. The group of nearby households then has both rights and obligations in using and protecting the forests handed over to them. They have the right of access to the forests while others who are not members of the group have no such rights. The CFUG is legalized as they are registered at the DFO. Secondly, the CFUGs have to prepare an operational plan of the forest as well as obtain approval for it by the DFO. The plan provides schedules of extraction activities from the forest so that it is managed in a sustainable manner. Crafting rules of forest access, withdrawal, and management are described in the forest plan. The monitoring and sanctioning of rule breakers is also performed by the CFUGs. How the forests will be managed at the local level is devolved to the CFUGs within the constraints of the operational forest plan. In sum, user and management rights when it comes to forests are transferred to the users. However, they cannot sell the land; nor can they change the existing forest land-use type to another. One could call it a change of property right from the state to the local communities.

A unique characteristic of community forestry in Nepal is that all forest-product benefits from the community forest belong to CFUG members. The CFUG members may use the forest products for themselves or sell them to outsiders. The money thus generated has to be used for forest development or for other community development activities. The users elect their committee (about eleven members) from among themselves to implement decisions made by the CFUGs. In other words, the committee members are accountable to the CFUG. Thus, community forestry is also an institution-building process at the lowest level. It has helped to build social capital (Dasgupta, this volume) at the village level. It is also a unique process of devolution to democratically elected institutions at the local level.

Another characteristic of community forestry in Nepal is that the communities have legal rights over forest management and utilization. The process of forest handover and the rights and duties of CFUGs are clearly stated in the Forest Act, forest regulations and guidelines. The joint forest management in India, on the other hand, is still governed by the executive order of the state government (Arabinda, this volume). In India, people may have a privilege when it comes to forest use whereas in Nepal, the communities have legal rights. They can sue the government if it makes decisions contrary to the ones specified in the Forest Act and regulations. In fact, the federation of CFUGs filed a case in 2001 against the cabinet decision to levy a 40 per cent tax on the sale of surplus timber from community forests in the *Terai*. The Supreme Court gave a verdict (on 28 March 2003) against the cabinet decision stating that imposing a tax on the sale of forest products from community forests is against the provisions of the Forest Act. The government later inserted a provision in the Finance Act to levy a 15 per cent tax on the sale of surplus timber (of *Sal* and *Khair*) of *Terai* CFUGs.

The other lessons from the community forests of Nepal is that the classical mode of forest management needs to be disaggregated to at least three functions to be performed by different institutions. Firstly, the regulatory and policy formulation (enabling environment) function should be performed by the government. Secondly, the forest management function should be performed by the devolved community organizations. Their capacity needs to be strengthened while government forestry staff should be reoriented and retrained to execute their new functions. Thirdly, forestry associations and the federations of CFUGs or NGOs should play the role of advisor to these forest management organizations. One may depict this disaggregation of forestry functions as the key reform in forestry governance. This way, forests can be better managed and communities can resolve the *de facto* open-access problem inherent in classical forest management.

Some of the accessible community forests are commercially important. Experience from agriculture suggests that micro enterprise based on food processing and marketing has helped in generating employment and reducing poverty (Scherr, White, and Kaimowitz 2004). Similar experiments are underway and will continue to be initiated so that forest products can be processed locally and sold in competitive markets, thus generating employment and entrepreneurship (value addition) at the local level.

As forests become commercially important, selling forest products and utilization of funds become contentious. The state may also attempt to intervene and try to tax the proceeds from the sale of forest products. The government could also impose a freeze on handing over commercially important forests to the users although the Act and regulations do not differentiate between different types of forests. Hence, the communities and their organizations at federation level should be aware of such potential interference.

16.6. Conclusions

Community forestry was legalized in Nepal initially in 1978. Since then, it has evolved from protection forestry to institutional innovation with a strong focus on the devolution of management authority to local communities organized and legitimized as self-governing units. There are now more than 14,000 CFUGs scattered throughout the country. They manage more than 25 per cent of national forests and generated more than Rs 740 million or US$10 million in 2002 from the sale of forest products within and outside the groups. Micro-level studies carried out in different locations show that forest conditions have improved with the devolution of forest management authority to CFUGs. This information however is still very preliminary and in-depth information and knowledge gaps at macro level still exist. Exactly how the poor and disadvantaged groups obtain benefits from the community forestry interventions is also not known in-depth. Projects and programmes related to community forestry should compile project- or programme-level information on the impacts of community forestry on poverty reduction and forest condition in close consultation with the DFO and local units of community forest-users' federations.

There is no doubt that the community forestry programme of Nepal is an institutional innovation in managing forests for local and national benefits. Nepal has formulated a unique legislation to resolve the *de facto* open-access problem through a 'muddling through' approach. The approach basically relates to the gradual devolution of forest management and user rights to locally organized groups of forest users. The programme has led to the deepening and expansion of greenery, and to the building of democratically elected local institutions mainly responsible for forest and fund management. However, social issues are yet to be fully linked to the CF programme and action.

The strategies for reforms are related to channelling benefits from the community forestry programme to poor and disadvantaged groups. In the *Terai*, resolving the so-called 'distance-users' dilemma may help to better manage the forests by providing some of the financial or forest product benefits to the 'distance users'. The interventions needed to promote pro-poor CF include provision of package programmes to these groups in an integrated manner, promotion of pro-poor enterprises with marketing facilities, and intercropping of NTFPs in the forests. It is also necessary to carry out adaptive and collaborative research on sustainable forest management and to monitor the impacts of CF projects and programmes at macro level in order to feed the information to policy makers. Service provision to CFUGs will also have to be liberalized so that civil society and private sectors can provide technical and social services to CFUGs. Moreover, forestry coordination committees will need to be established at district and village levels so that community forestry programmes become transparent and relevant at the field level.

References

Adhikari, B. (2003). 'Property Rights and Natural Resources: Socio-economic Hetero-geneity and Distributional Implications of Common Property Resource Management'. Working Paper No 1.03, South Asian Network for Development and Environmental Economics (SANDEE), Kathmandu, Nepal.

Agrawal, A., and Ostrom, E. (2001). 'Collective Action, Property Rights, and Decentralization in Resource Use in India and Nepal'. *Politics and Society*, 29: 485–514.

—— Britt, C., and Kanel, K. (1999). *Decentralization in Nepal: A Comparative Analysis*. Oakland, CA: Institute for Contemporary Studies Press.

Bampton, J., Vickers, B., Rana, B., and Statz, J. (2004). 'Community Forestry in the *Terai*', in K. R. Kanel, P. Mathema, B. R. Kandel, D. R. Niraula, A. R. Sharma, and M. Gautam (eds.), *Twenty Five Years of Community Forestry: Contributing to Millennium Development Goals*. Kathmandu, Nepal: Community Forestry Division, Department of Forests, 317–32.

Bandyopadhyay, S., Shyamsunder, P., and Kanel, K. (2005). 'Forestry User Groups in Nepal: Can Institutional Change Lead to Economic Development?' Paper presented at Nepal Poverty Assessment Seminar organized by National Planning Commission Secretariat, His Majesty's Government of Nepal (HMG), Asian Development Bank, the World Bank, and Department For International Development in Kathmandu, Kathmandu, Nepal, 12 May.

Baral, J. C., and Subedi, B. R. (2000). 'Some Community Forest Issues in the Terai, Nepal: Where do We Go from Here?'. *Forest, Trees and People Newsletter*, 42: 20–5.

Birner, R. and Wittmer, H. (2000). 'Co-management of Natural Resources: A Transaction Cost Economic Approach to Determine the 'Efficient Boundary of the State'. Paper presented at the Annual International Conference of the International Society of the New Institutional Economics (ISNIE) in Tuebingen, Germany.

Branney, P., and Yadav, K. P. (1998). *Changes in Community Forest Condition and Management 1994–1998: Analysis of Information from the Forest Resources Assessment Study and Socio-economic Study in the Koshi Hills*. Project report G/NUKCFP/32. Kathmandu, Nepal: Nepal-UK Community Forestry Project.

DANIDA (Danish Ministry of Foreign Affairs) and HMG (His Majesty's Government of Nepal) (2004). 'Programme Completion Report'. Natural Resource Management Sector Assistance Programme (NARMSAP)—February 1998–July 2005, DANIDA and HMG, Nepal.

Department of Forests (2005). *Forest Cover Change Analysis of the Terai Districts (1990/91–2000/01)*. Report. Kathmandu, Nepal: His Majesty's Government, Ministry of Forest and Soil Conservation, Department of Forests.

Gautam, A. P., Webb, E. L., Shivakoti, G. P., and Zoebisch, M. A. (2003). 'Land Use Dynamics and Landscape Change Pattern in a Mountain Watershed in Nepal'. *Agriculture Ecosystems and Environment*, 99: 83–96.

Gilmour, D. A., and Fisher, R. J. (1991). *Villagers, Forests and Foresters*. Kathmandu, Nepal: Sahayogi Press.

Jackson, W. J., Tamrakar, R. M., Hunt, S., and Shepherd, K. R. (1998). 'Land Use Changes in Two Middle Hills Districts of Nepal'. *Mountain Research and Development*, 18/3: 193–212.

Kanel, K. R. (2001). 'Forests, Collective Action, and Policy Instruments in Nepal: Aligning Decentralization with Fiscal Responsibility', in K. Suryanata, G. Dolcemascolo, R. Fisher, and J. Fox (eds.), *Enabling Policy Frameworks for Successful Community-Based Resource Management*. Proceedings from the Ninth Workshop on Community-Based Management of Forestlands (5 February—2 March 2001). Honolulu, Hawaii: East-West Centre, 70–82.

—— and Niraula, D. R. (2004). 'Can Rural Livelihood be Improved in Nepal through Community Forestry?' *Banko Janakari* 14/1: 19–26.

—— Karmacharya, M. B., and Karna, B. K. (2003). 'Who Benefits from Institutional Reforms: Case Studies from Four Community Forests', in Keshav R. Kanel, Mukunda B. Karmacharya, and Birendra K. Karna (eds.), *Human—Institutional Natural Resources Interactions: Understanding the Interface between Social and Natural Resource Systems*. Proceedings of a Seminar held in Pokhara, Nepal, Kathmandu: Rising Son Printers, 66–82.

Livelihood and Forestry Programme (LFP) (2003). *Hill Livelihoods Baseline Study, Part 1: Main Report of Quantitative Findings with Supplementary Qualitative Information, Part II: Report of Qualitative Findings*. Report. Nepal: Livelihoods and Forestry Programme (LFP) in collaboration with TANGO International, Inc., USA, and Development Vision.

Pokharel, B. K., and Amatya, D. (2000). *Community Forest Management Issues in the Terai*. Issue Paper 9. Kathmandu, Nepal: Joint Technical Review Committee on Community Forestry, Ministry of Forests and Soil Conservation.

Rana, B. (2004). 'Understanding Conflicts between Government Resource Users: A Multi-criteria Analysis of Community Forestry Performance in *Saptari* District, Nepal'. M. Sc. thesis. International Institute for Geo-information Science and Earth Observation, Enschede, the Netherlands.

Richards, M., Kanel, K., Maharjan, M., and Davis, J. (1999). *Towards Participatory Economic Analysis by Forest User Groups in Nepal*. London: ODI, Portland House, Stag Place.

Scherr, S. J., White, A., and Kaimowitz, D. (2004). *A New Agenda for Forest Conservation and Poverty Reduction: Making Markets Work for Low-Income Producers*. Washington, DC: Forest Trends.

Shrestha, K. (2005). 'Evaluation of Ongoing Performance of Strengthening the Role of Civil Society and Women in Democracy and Governance (SAMARPAN) Project'. Report. Submitted to *CARE*, Nepal.

World Bank (1978). *Nepal Staff Project Report and Appraisal of the Community Forestry Development and Training Project Document*. Report. Washington, DC: World Bank.

Index

Index